Neoliberal Citizenship

Neoliberal Citizenship

Sacred Markets, Sacrificial Lives

LUCA MAVELLI

OXFORD
UNIVERSITY PRESS

OXFORD
UNIVERSITY PRESS

Great Clarendon Street, Oxford, OX2 6DP,
United Kingdom

Oxford University Press is a department of the University of Oxford.
It furthers the University's objective of excellence in research, scholarship,
and education by publishing worldwide. Oxford is a registered trade mark of
Oxford University Press in the UK and in certain other countries

Impression: 1

Published in the United States of America by Oxford University Press
198 Madison Avenue, New York, NY 10016, United States of America

British Library Cataloguing in Publication Data
Data available

Library of Congress Control Number: 2021944880

ISBN 978–0–19–285758–3

DOI: 10.1093/oso/9780192857583.001.0001

Printed and bound by
CPI Group (UK) Ltd, Croydon, CR0 4YY
Photo by Joel Sharpe/Getty Images

Per chi lo immaginò

Acknowledgements

Initially sparked by the dramatic events of the refugee crisis, the original idea for this book took a more concrete shape in 2016 when the personal experience of the Brexit referendum pushed me to forcefully confront the transformations of citizenship. In 2017, I realized that to fully appreciate the meanings and implications of neoliberal citizenship I had to explore its 'sacred' foundations and thus reflect on my previous research on religion and secularism from a different angle. In 2018, this prompted me to engage with the concepts of resilience and sacrifice and to think of them in relation to the events that had begun to unfold ten years earlier with the Global Financial Crisis and the Eurozone crisis. It was not until 2019 though that, on a rainy summer day in Innsbruck, eventually armed with a structure and a sense of urgency, I began to write this book in a systematic fashion. When the pandemic erupted in 2020, it was immediately clear that its causes and effects would be crucially relevant for the argument I was making. Most of the book was written during the lockdowns of 2020 and 2021.

Over these years, I have benefited from the invaluable ideas, support, and encouragement of many colleagues and friends. Erin K. Wilson has been pivotal in developing a challenging joint research programme on religion and the refugee crisis on which many ideas of this book build; Jonathan Joseph has been a source of inspiration and encouragement for thinking about neoliberal resilience and its role in the governmentality of crisis; Antonio Cerella has provided crucial insights for approaching the question of scarcity and was always there to discuss the crisis of modernity; David Chandler has pushed me to reflect on the possibility of post-neoliberal alternatives and sharpen my understanding of the other side; Nick Vaughan-Williams has prompted me to critically examine the biopolitics of the refugee crisis from a different angle and offered essential advice in the final stages of the book.

I also owe a particular debt of gratitude to Jeff Haynes, Mariano Barbato, Scott Thomas, Wolfgang Palaver, Francesco Capello, Elena Fiddian-Qasmiyeh, Fabio Bravo, Jemima Repo, Rich King, Mustapha Pasha, Dario Lolli, Richard Amesbury, Yvonne Sherwood, and David Herd for informative and inspiring conversations on many of the topics explored in this project.

Some of the arguments advanced in this book draw on, substantially rework, and significantly expand ideas that I originally explored in four articles. Specifically: Chapter 3 draws on 'Citizenship for Sale and the Neoliberal Political Economy of Belonging', *International Studies Quarterly* 62, no. 3 (2018): 482–493; Chapter 4 builds on 'Governing Populations through the Humanitarian Government of Refugees: Biopolitical Care and Racism in the European Refugee Crisis', *Review of International Studies* 43, no. 5 (2017): 809–832; section 1 of Chapters 6 and 7 present discussions advanced in 'Neoliberalism as Religion: Sacralization of the Market and Post-Truth Politics', *International Political Sociology* 14, no. 1 (2020): 57–76; finally, passages from 'Governing the Resilience of Neoliberalism through Biopolitics', *European Journal of International Relations* 23, no. 3 (2017): 489–512, are scattered throughout the book. I am grateful to the Editors of these journals and the eleven anonymous reviewers for their feedback and suggestions, which have contributed to remarkably improving the original submissions. Permission to reuse this material from Oxford University Press, Cambridge University Press, and Sage is gratefully acknowledged.

Other ideas explored in this book have been presented at conferences, workshops, and seminars at Leiden University, the University of Groningen, the University of Nottingham, the University of Duisburg-Essen, the University of Innsbruck (2019 Colloquium on Religion and Violence), the University of Notre Dame, the Vatican, the University of Kent, the 2017 ECPR Joint Session, and the 2018 BISA and ISA Annual Conferences. Many thanks to Atalia Omer, Ed Frettingham, Mariano Barbato, Erin K. Wilson, Jonathan Joseph, Michaela Neulinger, and Marie-Luisa Frick for inviting me to these events and for their wonderful hospitality. I have greatly benefited from their feedback and that of those in attendance.

A special thanks goes to the Delegates of Oxford University Press for their warm support and suggestions and to the editorial and production teams for their meticulous work. Dominic Byatt has been a remarkable commissioning editor. His prompt, precise, and reassuring guidance has made navigating through the submission, review, and production process a pleasant and steady journey. I am very grateful for his advice and encouragement.

Many friends have indirectly and mostly unwittingly supported my work over these years by providing the necessary distance and distraction (and the occasional remarkable intuitions that only lay persons can have): Fabio, Rodolfo, Giovanni, and Francesco in Santa Maria; Carlo, Roberta, Giuliana, Carlone, and 'Il Davia' in Leuca; Ciro and Massimo in Milan; Khaled in

Berlin; Stefano in Canterbury; and Maurizio, whose unmatched creative spirit continues to churn beautiful songs from somewhere we cannot see.

My final thank you is to my family: to my parents Ignazio and Adele, who have taught me that stones at the bottom of the sea can be brought back to the surface; to my brother Riccardo, whose understated kayaking spirit is always a source of reassurance; to my daughters Anaïs and Elisa, the only ones really capable of restoring meaning and sense; and to my partner and colleague Harmonie Toros who, while reading my work and providing invaluable comments, has taught me how to love the wind.

Contents

List of Abbreviations

ABCP	Asset-backed commercial paper
AIDS	Acquired immune deficiency syndrome
CDOs	Collateralized debt obligations
CDS	Credit default swaps
CV	Curriculum vitae
DFID	Department for International Development
EU	European Union
Frontex	European Border and Coast Guard Agency
GDP	Gross domestic product
HIV	Human immunodeficiency virus
HNWIs	High-net-worth individuals (whose individual assets exceed US$1 million)
IMF	International Monetary Fund
IOM	International Organization for Migration
MERS	Middle East respiratory syndrome
MP	Member of Parliament
NGOs	Non-governmental organizations
NHS	National Health Service (UK)
NZ	New Zealand
OECD	Organisation for Economic Co-operation and Development
PIIGS (derogatory)	Portugal, Ireland, Italy, Greece, and Spain
PPE	Personal protective equipment
SAR	Search and Rescue
SARS	Severe acute respiratory syndrome
UHNWIs	Ultra high-net-worth individuals (whose individual assets exceed US$30 million)
UK	United Kingdom
UKIP	United Kingdom Independence Party
UN	United Nations
UNHCR	United Nations High Commissioner for Refugees
UNICEF	United Nations Children's Emergency Fund
US/USA	United States of America
WHO	World Health Organization
WREDA	Wellington Regional Economic Development Agency

1

Introduction: The neoliberal value of citizenship

1. Neoliberal citizenship

On 10 September 2019, the newly elected President of the European Commission, Ursula von der Leyen, appointed the Greek Margaritis Schinas as vice-president 'for protecting our European way of life'. According to the Mission Letter, Schinas' task would be to ensure a 'well-managed legal migration' which serves the needs of 'our evolving labour market', while 'address[ing]' and allay[ing] legitimate fears and concerns about the impact of irregular migration on our economy and society' (Von der Leyen 2019: 4). In March 2020, following Turkey's decision to open its border with Greece to allow migrants to enter the European Union (EU), Greek border guards reportedly fired live ammunition on unarmed civilians. Commenting on these events, von der Leyen publicly thanked 'Greece for being our European *aspida* [shield in Greek]'. She announced that the country would receive €700m in funds to upgrade and improve its border infrastructure and border patrolling capacity. The Greek border, she stated, 'is also a European border' (Rankin 2020).

Just a few years back, the appointment of a Greek as vice-president 'for protecting our European way of life' and the celebration of Greece as a fully fledged member of the EU would have been unthinkable. The Greek debt crisis starting in 2010 had cast a sinister shadow on the country. European leaders openly stated that Greece should have not been allowed into the EU in the first place (see Elliott and Traynor 2010). The Greeks were blamed as irresponsible, fiscally lax, incompetent, and lazy. The Greek debt crisis was compared to a pandemic ('like Ebola') and portrayed as a feral threat to the very survival of Europe (see Tracy 2012). This rhetoric quickly spilled over and the punitive austerity measures imposed upon Greece to purportedly straighten out its finances and boost its economy were embraced by other European countries and deployed against their own citizens. The most outspoken country in this regard was the United Kingdom (UK), which openly declared a war on

Neoliberal Citizenship. Luca Mavelli, Oxford University Press.
 DOI: 10.1093/oso/9780192857583.003.0001

benefits, regarded as a dangerous virus that made people indolent. Welfare recipients were turned into 'scroungers' (see Cooper and Whyte 2017) who lived off the backs of laborious citizens and were responsible for the supposedly dire financial situation of the country. Austerity, with its related grammar of punishment, suffering, and sacrifice, became the new normal.

In 2020, a real virus arrived with the COVID-19 pandemic.[1] Austerity-stricken countries struggled due to a lack of hospital beds, personal protective equipment (PPE), ventilators, doctors and nurses, and many of them chose to let the virus run free, particularly among the weakest. Elderly patients in care homes died in the order of thousands to the point that, between February and July, they accounted for almost half of the total death toll of the pandemic in Europe and North America. The rationale for this sacrifice is captured by the words allegedly uttered by Dominic Cummings, then chief adviser of British Prime Minister Boris Johnson. At a private event taking place at the onset of the coronavirus crisis, he reportedly summarized the government's approach as 'herd immunity, protect the economy, and if that means some pensioners die, too bad' (*The Guardian* 2020b). To different degrees, in the United Kingdom and elsewhere in Europe, governing the pandemic was framed as a trade-off between saving the market and saving lives. This meant that some lives had to be sacrificed to preserve the economy (Barnett 2020).

At first sight, these events may be regarded as instances of different phenomena. Von der Leyen's initiative and statements may be read as attempts to please and co-opt far right-wing populism and mainstream its agenda. The rehabilitation of Greece is aimed at securing Greece's cooperation in managing the migration crisis. The blaming and punishment of Greece was instrumental to cover the responsibilities of the European banking system which was bailed out with public money, with the stigmatization of welfare recipients as a further step in this process of concealment. The war on benefits is yet another manifestation of the dismantlement of the welfare state. Deaths in care homes reveal poor management of the pandemic crisis and arguably a disregard for those perceived as less active and productive members of society.

Taken in isolation, these explanations are perfectly valid. The main thesis advanced by this book, however, is that these events are epiphenomenal of a deeper transformation that connects all of them in a common framework. This is a pervasive neoliberal mutation in the logics of citizenship that increasingly

[1] Throughout the book, the terms COVID-19, COVID, and coronavirus will be used interchangeably.

subordinates the possibility of inclusion, protection, and belonging to rationalities of value. From this perspective, migrants deemed *valuable* for the EU labour market can be included, while those subjects superfluous to economic needs and regarded as unproductive consumers of resources—be they undocumented migrants, debased citizens of austerity, or elderly people in care homes—must be excluded, disposed of, and sacrificed for the well-being of the economy. Similarly, the very 'lazy' Greeks who threatened the stability of the European financial system, for which they were punished with harsh austerity measures, are now a *valuable* resource to fight undocumented migration. Greeks are *valuable* because they are a barrier against *valueless* migrants, hence they can be awarded (at least for the time being) the status of deserving citizens of Europe.

These introductory remarks indicate that I problematize and analyse the category of citizenship beyond its formal status, and therefore as applicable to nominal citizens (debased citizens of austerity, the elderly) and non-citizens alike (undocumented migrants). Indeed, a crucial feature of my argument is that citizenship as the status to which is attached the enjoyment of a set of rights is increasingly disconnected from the nominal fact of being a citizen. Undoubtedly, being a citizen of a country in the Global North guarantees rights and privileges (in terms of mobility, healthcare, welfare provisions, and employment opportunities) that are often denied to non-citizens (and to citizens of countries in the Global South). Yet, it is also the case that the nationally bound universalism that underpins the status of citizenship in the Global North has been increasingly eroded by a plurality of phenomena. These include the 'uneven regression of the welfare state' (Balibar 2004: 163), the introduction of rights that are granted to wealthy residents and denied to citizens, and the commodification of citizenship (as epitomized, for instance, by the exponential growth of citizenship-by-investment schemes).

The investigation of neoliberal citizenship that I advance in this book explores these transformations as part of a perspective that challenges the classic dichotomies inside/outside, inclusion/exclusion, and members/strangers that underpin traditional understandings of citizenship. My approach draws inspiration from critical border studies' insight that 'borders are increasingly fractured throughout society in ways that do not respect traditional understandings of the inside/outside distinction but are often no less violent in their effects' (Vaughan-Williams 2015: 6). The seminal work of Étienne Balibar is crucially relevant here, as it magnifies 'the paradox of the movement of borders from the "edge" to the "center" of public space' and how this has resulted in the internal 'reproduction of "ethnic borders"' (Balibar 2004: 111). In Europe,

Balibar (2004: x) contends, this process has resulted in the emergence of a 'virtual apartheid': a condition of 'reduplication of external borders in the form of "internal borders"' that beyond simplistic topographies of inclusion and exclusion, rests on the 'stigmatization and repression of populations whose presence within European societies is nonetheless increasingly massive and legitimate.' The result, he suggests, is that 'the traditional figure of the external enemy is being replaced by that of the internal enemy' precisely because 'the "insides" and the "outsides" express the same structural dynamics' (Balibar 2004: 172).

Balibar's pioneering remarks enable us to see how the harsh austerity measures imposed upon Greece (which, as I shall discuss, have resulted in neoliberal dynamics of exploitation and dispossession) are expressions of a 'neocolonial' logic that Europe had traditionally reserved for 'outsiders' (Balibar 2015). Their deployment towards 'insiders' has had the effect of turning the Greeks into non-European or 'defective' European citizens while still within the European polity. This is a striking illustration of the internal 'reduplication' of an external border and of how this process underpins a system of citizenship dependent upon logics of value. For the purposes of my analysis, however, Balibar's approach has a major limitation: it relies on a perspective of 'zoning' which primarily sees the reproduction of the outside within the inside along spatial lines (see Balibar 2015). While this approach reveals crucial insights about the Greek case, it struggles to cope with and analyse under a single framework some of the instances of disarticulation and rearticulation of citizenship mentioned at the beginning of this chapter that mostly transcend strictly geographical demarcations. These include the stigmatization of debased citizens of austerity and the sacrifice of the elderly in care homes during the early stages of the COVID-19 pandemic.

Recent research in critical border studies has acknowledged the 'elusiveness of spatial formations' and how the increasingly deterritorialized 'geographies of globalization' may be 'marked as much by differentiation as by connection' (Mezzadra and Neilson 2012: 59). In particular, Sandro Mezzadra and Brett Neilson have theorized a more radical process of 'disarticulation of citizenship' in which the transfigurations of inside/outside formations become a regime of 'differential inclusion' that partially transcends spatial determinations. At the heart of their argument is the idea that 'the specific connection between labour and citizenship that culminated in social citizenship' has been progressively disarticulated by 'the proliferation of borders and the multiplication of labour' (Mezzadra and Neilson 2012: 62, see also 2013). This has resulted in 'the proliferation of subject positions that are neither fully included nor fully excluded from the space of citizenship and from labour markets, of subjectivities that are neither fully insiders nor fully outsiders' (Mezzadra and Neilson 2012: 62). Mezzadra and Neilson's concept of 'differential inclusion' crucially highlights the 'substitution of the binary distinction between inclusion and exclusion with continuous parametric modulations—that is, processes of filtering and selecting that refer to multiple and shifting scales, ratings and evaluations' (Mezzadra and Neilson 2012: 68).

This approach has the merit of opening the conceptual space required to analyse the transformations of citizenship across a plurality of deterritorialized phenomena and beyond static, formal models as it incorporates a sense of constant mutability. However, the understanding of value that underpins the notion of 'differential inclusion' and related practices of filtering, selecting, rating, and evaluating is mostly a function of the neoliberal political economy of labour—that is, of the capacity of labouring bodies to be inscribed in and contribute to neoliberal mechanisms of production, accumulation, and dispossession. This view makes it impossible to conceptualize value independently from the requirements of the global labour market. Hence, while this perspective reveals key aspects of the political economy behind von der Leyen's call for 'protecting our European way of life', it struggles to incorporate and account for the 'rehabilitation' and 'reintegration' of Greece into the European family as expressions of a mutating neoliberal citizenship that subordinates protection and inclusion to value. The reason is that the value in question is not linked to labour.

Albeit scant and fragmented, the existing research on neoliberal citizenship offers a more encompassing understanding of value than one confined to the political economy of labour. This can be broadly described as the capacity of an individual or a population to contribute to 'economic growth'. Existing accounts have emphasized how states have increasingly adopted a 'market-mediated citizenship regime' (Sparke 2006: 155) characterized by the 'contractualization of citizenship' in which 'market value is the chief criterion for membership' (Somers 2008: 22, 5; see also Ong 1999, 2006a, 2006b; Brown 2015; Feher 2020). The implication is that, as Aihwa Ong (2006a: 499) observes, in the existing neoliberal order 'strict discriminations between the citizens and foreigners are dropped in favor of the pursuit of human capital. Such modes of governing engender a checkerboard patterning of the national terrain, thus producing an effect of graduated or variegated sovereignty.'

More specifically, neoliberal citizenship scholarship has explored how citizenship has been increasingly emptied from within by four decades of neoliberal 'market-driven governance' (Somers 2008: 2) characterized by privatization, deregulation, and dismantlement of the welfare state. Shortly before the onset of the 2008 financial crisis, Margaret Somers (2008: 2) had already denounced how 'growing numbers of once rights-bearing citizens' have been turned 'into socially excluded internally rightless and stateless persons'. This process, I will show, has been further aggravated by the adoption of austerity in the aftermath of the crisis. In relation to non-citizens, scholars have focused on how neoliberal entrepreneurial states have endeavoured to attract 'elite migrant subjects' and 'wealth-bearing and talented foreigners' which may advance their economic growth and international competitiveness (Ong 2006a: 501; see also Brown 2015). Likewise, entrepreneurial states have placed particular effort on attempting to exclude all those 'strangers'—refugees, undocumented migrants, and 'low value' economic migrants—perceived as an economic burden or unable to positively contribute to economic growth.

While this understanding of value offers a powerful framework to analyse some of the cases at the beginning of this introduction, it still struggles to account for the Greek 'rehabilitation' and a whole series of regimes of inclusion and practices of protection that seemingly question the reduction of value to the capacity of contributing to economic growth. The response to the death of Alan Kurdi—whose rationalities and implications will be explored at length in this book—is a paradigmatic case. Alan Kurdi was the sadly famous three-year-old Syrian boy who, in September 2015, drowned off the coast of Turkey during his family's attempt to reach Europe. His dead body lying on the shore was immortalized in a picture which has become an iconic image of the refugee crisis. His death sparked a massive outcry and temporarily amplified calls for more compassionate policies towards Syrian refugees, thus placing pressure on governments all over the world. Following Alan's death, several countries which had taken a hardline stance on refugees not only committed to increase their quotas by privileging Syrian refugees, but also pledged to prioritize Syrian refugees with physical and mental disabilities.

Why did governments from the UK to New Zealand choose to include individuals who would inevitably be a 'burden' on the health system? Is not this case at odds with the logic of neoliberal citizenship, which subordinates membership and protection to the capacity of individuals and populations to contribute to economic growth? Aihwa Ong (2006a: 504) argues that '[i]n recent decades, health-based claims have become an important part of citizenship rights in the West.' For Ong (2006a: 499), this means that modern citizenship is increasingly shaped by 'universalizing [and contending] criteria of neoliberalism and human rights.' This struggle between contending systems of value—economic value versus the intrinsic value of being human—is part and parcel of the hollowing out of state sovereignty, she claims. Hence, 'instead of all citizens enjoying a unified bundle of citizenship rights, we have a shifting political landscape in which heterogeneous populations claim diverse rights and benefits associated with citizenship, as well as universalizing criteria of neoliberal norms or human rights' (Ong 2006a: 500). From this perspective, the response to the death of Alan Kurdi should be understood as a victory of the human rights camp that ascribes value to the simple fact of being human against the neoliberal economic logic of value.

In this book, I challenge this analysis and advance a different reading. Following the global emotional wave triggered by Alan's death, governments were under heavy pressure from public opinion to open their borders to those in greater need on the grounds that they were failing the test of compassion and acting selfishly and callously. To reverse this perception, some countries decided to 'invest' in a small number of refugees with physical and mental disabilities who could be undeniably recognized as 'victims' and thus contribute to boost the pride, moral worth, and sense of self-esteem of the country. Despite being a prospective economic burden on the health system, these refugees were considered *emotionally valuable* for the host population and therefore deserving of protection. From this perspective, the decision to include economically 'burdensome' refugees (along with other similar instances of inclusion that will be explored later in the book) does not indicate the demise of the neoliberal logic of value but its victory. This logic extends *beyond* the mere economic sphere. It co-opts and colonizes other domains of human existence, including that of emotions, and rewrites them in economic terms, even in the absence of a distinctive monetary transaction (Brown 2015: 37) or with the latter being negative.

To better understand this argument, which represents a central theme of the analysis that will unfold in the following chapters, it is necessary to introduce some initial qualifications of the specific understanding of neoliberalism that guides my analysis. Neoliberalism has been variously described as an economic theory, political philosophy, ideology, and governmental rationality characterized by a heterogeneous set of ideas, practices, and regimes of power. Neoliberal ideas include: a belief in the superior capacity of markets over states to create and allocate wealth; the view that states should be scaled back in order to free up markets; the notion that growth can be promoted through competition, privatization, deregulation, and financialization; a belief in the individual as a source of human capital, and in inequality as a reflection of one's own endowment of human capital and as necessary to foster entrepreneurship; and the view that all relations can be analysed and measured in economic cost/benefit terms. These ideas have translated in a varied set of practices, such as fiscal discipline, austerity, debt conditionality, structural adjustments, removal of trade barriers, commodification of goods and services, privatization of profits and socialization of losses, retrenchment of the welfare state and privatization of welfare provisions, financialization of the economy and everyday life, labour flexibility, and the race to the bottom in labour standards.

For those scholars—including myself—writing in the wake of Michel Foucault's seminal work on neoliberalism, these ideas and practices are derivative of a more foundational dimension which sees neoliberalism as process of *economization* or *marketization* that disseminates the model of the market to all spheres of human activity. With neoliberalism, the traditional separation between politics, the economy, and society that characterized liberal forms of capitalism *à la* Adam Smith has been eroded (Foucault 2008: 242, 273–6). The discrete logic of the liberal market has been progressively replaced by the totalizing logic of the neoliberal market which has become the overarching framework that through rationalities of competition, commodification, and inequality governs all spheres of human activity—from education, to work, leisure, and health, up to the whole social and political domain (Foucault 2008: 242; Dardot and Laval 2013: 17; Brown 2015: 31).

This book argues that the market value of non-citizens—be they wealthy foreigners, undocumented migrants, or refugees—and citizens alike is not confined to their capacity to boost economic growth but also the *emotional* welfare of a country and its population. Hence, my goal is to widen the meaning and implications of the concept of economization as currently theorized by the critical scholarship on neoliberalism and explore its implications for neoliberal citizenship. To this end, I will pursue a 'deepening' of the rationalities of value that underpin the neoliberal order. Specifically, the argument I advance is that neoliberal citizenship is sustained and substantiated by a three-dimensional regime of governance whose axes are constituted by *biopolitics*, *scarcity*, and *the sacred*. These dimensions will be briefly introduced in the next section.

2. Biopolitics, scarcity, and the sacred

The first relation to consider is that between neoliberalism and biopolitics. This connection has been seminally suggested by Foucault—although he never properly developed and theorized it—and has become the object of an extensive literature. This literature, however, has hardly explored the neoliberal–biopolitical apparatus in connection with citizenship and the problem of value.

For Foucault (1978: 138), biopolitics stands for a substantial transformation in the logic of power: from the traditional sovereign power 'to take life or let live' to the modern biopolitical 'power to foster life or disallow it to the point of death'. Hence, Foucault (1978: 136) contends, modern biopower does not operate as a regime of deduction of wealth, labour, services, and 'ultimately life itself', but as one of production, whose main task is to 'incite, reinforce, control, monitor, optimize, and organize the forces under it: a power bent on generating forces, making them grow, and ordering them'. This productive effort is ultimately a rationality of 'care' deployed within a capitalist framework of extraction that invests in the capacity of those 'cared for' to generate value 'for themselves, for a business, and for a national or postnational economic constellation such as the European Union' (Brown 2016: 3).

I argue that in the totalizing logic of economization that characterizes neoliberalism, this value is not confined to the pure monetary domain, but invests social relations, affects, dispositions, and spheres of existence—like humanitarianism—by rewriting them in neoliberal terms. Thus, for instance, the introduction of more restrictive asylum policies (expression of a general process of securitization of migration) has been accompanied by a less noticed neoliberal–biopolitical phenomenon: the growing demand for 'good refugees' regarded as valuable, whose care is a way of caring for the host population. 'Good refugees' are women, children, and suffering bodies which may be unconditionally recognized as victims (Fiddian-Qasmiyeh 2016: 459). 'Good refugees' are Christians (rather than Muslims), Syrians (rather than Afghanis or Somalis), and white (rather than black), as part of a neoliberal logic of value that incorporates—and, as I shall discuss later, occasionally rewrites—traditional racial, religious, and ethnic markers.

The universalism of asylum has been broken down in a scheme of valuation, system of ranking, and practice of commodification that mixes and makes virtually indistinguishable rationalities of value and rationalities of care. This regime is not dissimilar in its underlying logics from the points-based immigration system. Both perform the fundamental task of filtering in order to achieve two main goals: first, 'instituting differential inclusion' through 'the submission of migratory subjects to different and ever more highly calibrated parameters that purport to measure their worthiness and suitability to enter certain political spaces' (Mezzadra and Neilson 2012: 69); second, separating the valuable from the less valuable in order to draw a line between who 'must live' and who 'must die' (Foucault 2003: 254).

In this regime, the biopolitical 'letting die' of the 'less valuable' is not simply a by-product of neoliberal citizenship, but one of its essential components.

The 'less valuable' or 'valueless' are not just lacking in value, but actually have a *negative* value. In the neoliberal–biopolitical order, the poor are welfare recipients that consume rather than produce wealth and are regarded as responsible for their own condition. They are debauched and dissolute individuals, unable to contribute to society. The poor represent an increasingly moral and material problem as they cause unemployment and economic recession, pollute the culture, poison the morals, and deplete the welfare state. Unwanted migrants regarded as lacking in economic or emotional value pose the same problems on a bigger scale. Their status as non-citizens, however, authorizes more radical responses. These include letting them die in borderzones such as the Mediterranean or the US–Mexican border, or including them in conditions of debasement and subjugation, for instance by keeping them in a status of illegality, which has the added benefit of turning them into a valuable source of cheap and exploitable labour.

Neoliberal citizenship is thus crucially linked to the deployment of what Foucault (2003: 255) describes as biopolitical racism: 'a relationship between my life and the death of the other' that frames and justifies the killing or 'letting die' of those belonging to 'the bad ... inferior race' as 'something that will make life in general healthier: healthier and purer.' Yet, the biopolitical racism that I explore in my research transcends the dichotomous boundaries of Foucault's argument—making live or letting die—by considering a whole range of combinations and modulations in which biopower becomes *making live by letting die* or *letting die by making live*. The active institution of illegal immigration—the *letting die by making live* through the reduction of undocumented migrants to exploitable labour in a neoliberal regime of extraction, debasement, and dispossession—is probably the most visible manifestation of these biopolitical formations.

A more concealed manifestation that will be explored at length is that of the EU's decision to suspend search-and-rescue missions in the Mediterranean in 2014. This decision has contributed to turn the Mediterranean into one of the world's largest migrant graveyards, and will be analysed as an instantiation of a biopolitical racism which rules that *if Europeans want to live, refugees must die*. At the same time, the suspension of search-and-rescue missions will be regarded as an expression of a biopolitical rationality of care that I label 'neoliberal humanitarianism'. This is a regime of solidarity enacted through the deployment of market signals: letting migrants die in the Mediterranean in order to deter prospective migrants to undertake the dangerous sea journey, hence as an instantiation of *making live by letting die*. In the regime of neoliberal citizenship, migrants are saved—that is, allegedly prevented from drowning—by letting some of them drown. This policy is based on the over-simplistic and misleading market-based assumption that migrants' decisions are primarily based on whether search-and-rescue missions will be in place. This oversimplification is indicative of the economization of humanitarianism, which becomes a transactional market rationality in which states are boosting the supply of death and suffering to reduce the demand of border crossing through the establishment of a fundamental scarcity of solidarity.

These considerations bring us to the second dimension of the triangular regime of governance that underpins the rationality of value of neoliberal citizenship: scarcity. The problem of scarcity is widely regarded as foundational to the economic domain. Indeed, economics is often defined as the study of the efficient allocation of resources under conditions of scarcity, which in turn tends to be regarded as a natural condition. Although the existing literature on biopolitics has mostly ignored the issue of scarcity, I contend that it is absolutely central to the biopolitical task of separating the valuable from the valueless, particularly if scarcity is interrogated and approached as the other side of a problem of overabundance or surplus.

Von der Leyen's call for a 'well-managed legal migration' which serves the need of 'our evolving labour market' and recognizes 'legitimate fears and concerns about the impact of irregular migration' highlights a problem of scarcity: that of valuable migrants, and therefore a problem of an excess of less valuable and valueless migrants at the gates of Europe. Likewise, the idea that welfare recipients pose a practical and moral problem signals their scarcity of restraints, civic virtue, human capital, and willingness to sacrifice for the economy—all of which translates into the overabundance of unworthy citizens. The imposition of austerity measures has been purposefully designed to correct this deviance: establishing an artificially created scarcity to reduce the surplus of less valuable citizens. The same logic has been at play in the management of the Greek debt crisis, where austerity has had the goal of addressing the alleged behavioural and moral deficiencies of the Greek people—that is, their scarcity of economic virtue—that according to mainstream biopolitically racist readings was responsible for the crisis.

The related bailout of European banks—which had massively speculated on the peripheral sovereign debt of countries such Portugal, Ireland, Italy, Spain, and most of all Greece—and its repackaging as a crisis 'internal to the eurozone and centered on the politics of public debt' (Tooze 2018: 7) can also be read as a response to the problem of scarcity. The bailout addressed the scarcity of liquidity which threatened to devastate the European financial system, with catastrophic consequences for neoliberal financialized life. The socialization of losses following the privatization of profit was instrumental to relieve of responsibility the neoliberal market order by placing the blame on Southern European citizens. The latter's moral deficiencies have been portrayed as indicative of a fundamental scarcity of values which makes these populations less attuned to the requirements of neoliberal citizenship.

These preliminary considerations highlight how scarcity is fundamentally ambivalent: it represents a problem that triggers the very process of separation, evaluation, and ranking performed by neoliberal citizenship and yet, at the same time, it is one of the primary means of addressing and punishing deviance from the requirements of neoliberal citizenship. This means that scarcity, far from being a natural condition, is socially instituted (Xenos 1989; Dumouchel 2014; Tellman 2015, 2017), and not just in order to separate the 'valuable' from the 'less valuable' and allegedly teach the latter the virtues of the former, but also to create value. Once again, the case of Alan Kurdi offers a tragic illustration of this dynamic. The momentary relative abundance of solidarity following Alan's death was not just a product of the fact that Alan was an innocent and vulnerable child and, as such, embodied the figure of the 'ideal refugee' that the Europe of 'solidarity in diversity' (one of the slogans of the EU) could and should have taken care of. The value of Alan's suffering and sacrifice stemmed primarily from the fact that it was packaged, presented, and marketed as a scarce and therefore valuable commodity.

Conversely, the oversupply of suffering carried by overcrowded vessels crossing the Mediterranean crammed with migrants has been met with fear and disgust, to the effect of turning undocumented migrants into threatening 'surplus populations'. Undocumented migrants are a threat because they are regarded as competitors for scarce material resources—jobs, welfare provisions, health services, homes—at a time of prolonged austerity, as well as competitors for scarce ideational resources. The anxieties surrounding the predominantly Muslim identity of the migrants coming to Europe and the related re-awakening of a Christian identity are the product of a reckoning of the latter's scarcity. The perceived overabundance of Muslims increases the value of Christianity and engenders a competition for the scarce resources of identity and belonging.

Although scarcity-driven biopolitical manifestations of racism draw on established categories of otherness, scarcity has the power to create new ones. This is the case of the elderly in care homes during the COVID-19 pandemic. The scarcity of hospital beds, PPE, ventilators, doctors, and nurses in a growing neoliberal framework of privatization and deregulation prompted a series of decisions—the transferring of elderly patients from hospitals to care homes to free beds and the transferring of staff from already shortage-stricken care homes to hospitals—which ultimately turned elderly (and often physically and mentally disabled) patients into sacrificial victims. In the most classic formulation of biopolitics, their death became necessary to cure and care for the healthy part of the population. As Foucault (2003: 255) reminds us, 'the more inferior species die out, the more abnormal individuals are eliminated, the fewer degenerates there will be in the species as a whole, and the more I—as species rather than individual—can live, the stronger I will be, the more vigorous I will be.'

What makes scarcity so foundational to the point of including elderly patients into the categories of 'inferior species' and 'degenerates' together with undocumented migrants, Greek workers, and debased citizens of austerity? My contention is that scarcity is not just the expression of a totalizing process of economization that disseminates the model of the market to all spheres of human activity. Differently said, the rationalities of neoliberalism are no longer entirely captured by the notion of economization. The fact that the 'reduplication of external borders in the form of "internal borders"' exceeds Balibar's idea of the exclusion of the racially, ethnically, and religious 'others' living within the community signals a qualitative shift in the biopolitical and scarcity-driven rationalities of neoliberal citizenship. Beyond economization, I argue, neoliberalism now encompasses a distinctive sacralization of the market, which has turned the latter into a partially unknown domain, system of relations, and epistemic framework that cannot be questioned or challenged, even when it demands the exclusion and sacrifice of 'normal' fellow citizens like the elderly. The sacred is the third dimension of the triangular regime of governance that underpins the rationality of value of neoliberal citizenship.

To introduce the relevance of the sacred for our discussion, we can start from the consideration that, over the last few years and particularly following the 2008 financial crisis, depictions of neoliberalism as 'religion', 'kind of faith', 'theology in disguise', and 'market fundamentalism' have multiplied (see, for instance, Petrella 2008; Stiglitz 2009; Peck, Theodore, and Brenner 2009; Block and Somers 2014; Graeber and Piketty 2014). Scholars and commentators have used these analogies to highlight the seemingly irrational fact that a neoliberal crisis of financialization and deregulation has been addressed through neoliberal policies of austerity and further deregulation. These depictions, however, have remained largely impressionistic and failed to excavate the multiple implications of neoliberalism as a religion that sacralizes the market and establishes a distinctive political economy of sacrifice.

As philosopher Giorgio Agamben (2007) reminds us, the notions of *sacred* and *sacrifice* are intimately connected. They share the same semantic root—*sacer*—and sacrifice literally means 'to make sacred' or 'consecrate', namely, shifting something from the sphere of the secular/profane to that of the gods. Agamben's famous image of 'homo sacer' rests on the alleged disruption of this link in the modern order of sovereignty. We are all virtually 'homines sacri', Agamben (1998) contends, who can be sacrificed on the altar of sovereignty, and yet our sacrifice does not make us 'sacred'.

In this book, I depart from Agamben's argument in three ways. First, I argue that the sacralization of the market, rather than the sacralization of sovereignty, should be regarded as the 'most fateful force in our modern life'—to borrow Max Weber's (2003 [1905]: 17) famous formulation. Second, I question the assumption that we are all 'homines sacri'. Our chances to be sacrificed on the altar of the market are inversely proportional to our perceived value as neoliberal citizens. Third, to claim in philosophical terms that 'homines sacri' cannot be sacrificed (in the sense that they cannot be made sacred) equates to the claim, in economic terms, that they are economically worthless and thus their death will not increase the glory, power, and strength of the market-God. More broadly, the idea that those whom biopolitics lets die are 'valueless' is a misconception that is implicitly shared by most biopolitical accounts, which approach the question of the divide between 'making live' and 'letting die' through the categories of 'worthy' and 'unworthy'.

This binary approach not only neglects that between these two poles there exists a whole range of valuations, modulations, and rankings which translate in complex systems of differential inclusion beyond simple regimes of inclusion and exclusion. Most importantly for the purpose of my argument, this approach is oblivious to the fact that the unwanted migrants who are left drowning in the Mediterranean (to take one of the groups that will be explored at the greatest length in this book) are not worthless, but have a negative value, which is not the same as worthless. If not prevented from reaching the European shores, it is argued, unwanted migrants will contaminate the culture, drain the welfare state, 'steal our jobs', become a burden on the healthcare system, and impoverish us all. In other words, they will have a subtractive effect on resources that are already in scarce supply. Unwanted migrants should therefore be regarded as a by-product of the rationalities of competition, exploitation, and inequality of neoliberal capitalism. They are a negative externality and, therefore, the bearers of a negative value. Their sacrifice—through death or differential inclusion in a condition of subjugation (for instance as exploitable 'irregular' migrants, source of cheap labour)—will strengthen the neoliberal market order, thus enabling 'deserving' neoliberal citizens to grow healthier and stronger in line with the biopolitical predicament.

In outlining a theory of neoliberal citizenship as sacrificial, I build on Wendy Brown's seminal work on the subject (2015, 2016). Yet, whereas Brown (2016: 4) frames sacrificial citizenship as 'a national-theological discourse' that demands nominal citizens to sacrifice themselves for the sake of the market order, I approach sacrificial citizenship as a triangular relation in which self-sacrificing citizens vis-à-vis the market actively engage in a process of transfer of blame and scapegoating. Self-sacrificing citizens identify other groups as responsible for economic and moral failures and actively demand their sacrifice. Poor citizens in receipt of welfare provisions who are blamed as idle consumers of wealth are encouraged to blame undocumented migrants for their condition of scarcity. Northern European countries have blamed Southern European countries for the Eurozone crisis and both have blamed the austerity-stricken Greeks. The latter have turned their anger towards the undocumented migrants, who have become the target of multiple and growing manifestations of violence at the hands of the Greek coastguard, border police, and paramilitary squads (see Vasilaki 2020)—a violence sanctioned and sanitized by the likes of von der Leyen as a noble attempt to 'shield' Europe.

This sacrificial violence that pits increasingly disentitled, scarcity-stricken subjects (nominal citizens and non-citizens alike) against each other is the product of a mimetic fear of sameness, the result of a race-to-the bottom egalitarianism, which is ultimately the product of a remarkable inversion performed by neoliberal citizenship. It is no longer life that is sacred and the market profane and instrumental to sustain the sacredness of life by advancing prosperity and well-being. It is now the neoliberal market that is sacred. It dictates who must live and how and who must be sacrificed for the sake of the market. This inversion, I argue, is the product of a process of sacralization of the market that unfolds along two equally important trajectories.

The first trajectory is that of a totalizing process of commodification that invests every sphere of human existence—including citizenship—and leaves no outside from which the neoliberal market can be questioned or challenged. Building on Agamben's (2007, 2009, 2011) recent reflections on economic theology, I will show how the 'commodification of everything' entails the very sacralization of the market as a transcendent domain that, following Émile Durkheim's (1995 [1912]: 44) classic definition of the sacred, is 'set apart and forbidden'. This trajectory has been compounded by a second one marked by a significant mutation in the 'rationality and technologies' (Dean 2014: 159) of neoliberalism. From an economic system based on the 'supposition of economic equilibrium and its triumphalist narratives of the welfare-generating properties of the omniscient market' (Dean 2014: 161), neoliberalism has progressively turned into a market-based regime of government and God-like institution whose complexity and presuppositions are claimed to greatly exceed human comprehension. The effect is the emergence of the market as a source of truth and revelation that cannot be subjected to rational scrutiny, but only worshipped, even when it delivers suffering, crises, and shocks. Focusing on leading neoliberal thinkers Milton Friedman, Gary Becker, and Friedrich Hayek, these two trajectories will be explored both in their conceptual declensions and practical implications for the construction of neoliberal citizenship's metrics of valuation.

3. Approach and outline

As the above remarks suggest, in this book I will not undertake an open-sea navigation through the waters of theory, but a coast-wise conceptual journey with frequent perusals on the terrain of specific events. The aim is to benefit from a context-based perspective of the theoretical sea and its wavy formations. This approach takes inspiration from Balibar's view that 'political matters cannot be examined from a deductive point of view (be it moral, legal, philosophical, sociological, or some combination of these), but can only be theorized *under the constraints* imposed by the situation and the changes in the situation that one observes or tries to anticipate' (Balibar 2004: viii, emphasis in original). Hence, the theoretical considerations that will be advanced in this book seek to '*incorporate as much as possible a reflection on its immediate conditions*, which determine the understanding and use of concepts' (Balibar 2004: viii, emphasis in original). This means that the three conceptual dimensions that guide my analysis—biopolitics, scarcity, and the sacred—will not be explored in a sequential fashion.

Drawing on Foucault' 'toolbox' and particularly his reflections on genealogy (Foucault 1974, 1984), these dimensions will be investigated as part of a stratified and incremental narrative that, starting from 'a diagnosis of the current situation' (Dreyfus and Rabinow 1982: 119), adds layers of analysis by descending into an excavation of the tensions, fractures, breaks, and discontinuities that have shaped present-day manifestations of neoliberal citizenship. This exploration will be carried out against the background of four ongoing and interconnected crises that have had a crucial impact on neoliberal citizenship: the Eurozone or sovereign debt crisis beginning in 2009, the refugee crisis beginning in 2014, the 2016 decision of the UK to leave the EU (the so-called Brexit crisis), and the 2020 COVID-19 pandemic. As I shall discuss, this crisis constellation and the response to these crises have been crucially shaped by neoliberal rationalities of inequality, competition, deregulation, austerity, and scarcity. My focus is on how this neoliberal regime of crisis governance has been mobilized to accelerate the neoliberal transformation of citizenship.

This transformation is a global phenomenon and neoliberalism's worst excesses are often associated with the United States. However, most of the event-specific discussions that will support my theoretical propositions come from Europe, with some further illustrations from New Zealand. The reason is the following. Contrary to the United States, where neoliberalism has been normalized and embedded in the socio-political discourse to become virtually indistinguishable from it, Europe and New Zealand, while embracing and developing through neoliberal rationalities, have seemingly attempted to resist their totalizing hold. The widely accepted image of New Zealand as a 'social laboratory' evokes the famous notion of the 'European social model', and thus a self-understanding grounded in collective solidarity that allegedly rejects the market as an all-encompassing framework of meaning. However, this effort has ultimately ended in an almost total capitulation to the sacred order of the marked and encouraged neoliberal rationalities to adapt and disguise themselves (as in the strikingly similar 'humanitarian' approach to Syrian refugees adopted by the UK and New Zealand that I shall explore in Chapters 3 and 4). As spaces of contradictions and sites of resistance-capitulation to neoliberalism, Europe and New Zealand represent two remarkable (and tragic) laboratories to investigate how neoliberal citizenship has grown within the folds of welfare-oriented democracies.[2] Two further considerations on the relevance of Europe for my analysis are in order.

[2] My argument acknowledges that under the broad umbrella of the 'European social model' there are significant regional differences (traditional taxonomies identify three main welfare state models—the 'Scandinavian', the 'Continental' or 'Christian Democratic', and the 'Anglo-Saxon'—and occasionally a fourth one—the 'Mediterranean' as different from the 'Continental'; Esping-Andersen 1990; Sabater 2005; Barr 2020). Likewise, following Brown (2015: 48), it also recognizes that neoliberalism is 'neither singular nor constant in its discursive formulations and material practices' and that 'in its differential instantiations and encounters with extant cultures and political traditions, it takes diverse shapes and spawns diverse content and normative details'. My aim, however, is not to investigate difference, but sameness, that is, to explore how the crisis of the European social model (however uneven) and the adoption of neoliberal citizenship (however differentiated) transcends national cultural and institutional differences. In Chapter 3, for instance, I will show how the trend towards 'citizenship for sale' has also been embraced by those countries that do not have a citizenship-by-investment scheme.

First, Europe's attempt to overcome and displace borders has eventually resulted in their reinforcement and multiplication. In the early 2000s, the European Union—the institutional embodiment of Europe[3]—was still praised and perceived as a cosmopolitan polity which had set in place a seemingly unstoppable process of deconstruction of national boundaries and allegiances (see, for instance, Linklater 1998; Habermas 2003; Delanty 2005; Beck and Grande 2007; Rumford 2007). The EU was enlarging through a cosmopolitan model that incorporated and dissolved 'its territorial borders through integration of the external periphery into an internally homogeneous space' (Casanova 2006a: 90). Europe was seen as the cradle of constitutional patriotism, 'a proceduralist view of democracy and deliberative politics' (Habermas 1996: 21) capable of reconciling Kantian universalism and Hegelian communitarianism, allegiance to universally shared principles and emotional attachment to multiple political communities (local, national, and supranational). Less than fifteen years later, the idea of cosmopolitan Europe is a distant and almost meaningless memory. Concerns about Europe being 'invaded' by Africans, Middle Easterners, and, most of all, Muslim migrants, have been at the forefront of social and political debates. The internal reduplication of borders anticipated by Balibar is a reality that transcends the mere geographical domain and calls into question the very European social model.

This is the second instance of resistance-capitulation that warrants a focus on Europe. The notion of 'European social model' describes a type of embedded capitalism that values 'job security, progressive tax rates and large social transfer payments' (Judt 2005: 793). According to late historian Tony Judt (2005: 793), it is the expression of a vision of the world that regards poverty as a product of 'social circumstances and not individual inadequacy' and thus supports a mode of solidarity in which the wealthy are willing to 'pay higher taxes if these were directed to alleviating poverty.' For Judt (2005: 748), the European social model stands in contrast to the so-called American way of life as resting on extreme competition, individualization, and privatization—that is, on the worst excesses of neoliberal capitalism. Writing in 2005, Judt

[3] In this book, while acknowledging that 'the spatial and legal limits of the "European Union" are related to but not coterminous with that of "Europe"' (Vaughan-Williams 2015: 14, note 2), I use these terms as signifiers of the same neoliberal space and expressions of mutually supportive grammars that draw on complementary vocabularies to deploy regimes of neoliberal citizenship. This approach also reflects the fact that clear distinctions between these terms are often not drawn in popular and academic usage. This does not simply indicate analytical shallowness or the belief in a fundamental identity between Europe and the European Union. It is often the expression of a rationality of power that evokes and performs in the same political domain both the institutional (the EU) and the civilizational (Europe), as in the President of the *EU* Commission's appeal 'for protecting our *European* way of life.'

recognized that 'the European model of society' had been weakened since the 1980s, but still regarded it as central to the European project and ultimately as 'what binds Europeans together' (Judt 2005: 748).

In the post-2008 austerity-stricken climate marked by the scapegoating and punishment of Greece and the blaming of the poor for their own condition, the European social model, like cosmopolitan Europe, also appears as a distant memory. Borrowing the title of one of Judt's most famous essays, it could be argued that in Europe 'the past is another country' (Judt 1992). From this perspective, the notion of the European social model is not just a descriptive, but a diagnostic tool: its crisis is a measure of the introjection of neoliberal rationalities. Europe's approach to the Eurozone crisis is a vivid illustration of this introjection. As a 2013 Oxfam report observed, this approach 'bears striking similarities to the structural adjustment policies imposed on Latin America, South-East Asia, and sub-Saharan African in the 1980s and 1990s' (Cavero and Poinasamy 2013: 4). The principle of debt conditionality, which subordinates bailouts to 'public-spending cuts, the nationalization of private debt, reductions in wages, and a debt management model in which repayments to creditors of commercial banks took precedence over measures to ensure social and economic recovery' was brought into the very heart of Europe, despite its catastrophic outcomes elsewhere in the world (Cavero and Poinasamy 2013: 4).

This neoliberal turn in European economic governance has been provocatively labelled 'Berlin-Washington Consensus' (Fitoussi and Saraceno 2013). For economists Jean-Paul Fitoussi and Francesco Saraceno (2013: 1), 'the European Union has gone farther than any other country or institution in internalizing the prescriptions of the Washington Consensus', the set of neoliberal policies that the International Monetary Fund, the World Bank, and the US Treasury (all based in Washington) have enforced upon developing countries experiencing financial crises. The European introjection of neoliberalism has prompted an internal dynamic of domination and exploitation with the effect that the 'reduplication of external borders in the form of "internal borders"' and the related construction of 'internal enemies' exceeds the already bleak diagnosis performed by Balibar (2004: 172) in the early 2000s. Tragically, Europe has become an almost 'ideal-type' for understanding the momentous neoliberal transformation of citizenship. This book is an attempt to investigate the trajectory, impact, and implications of this transformation. The remainder of the book is organized as follows.

Chapter 2, *The creative destruction of citizenship*, argues that neoliberalism is a crisis-driven mode of governance and explores the mutually constitutive nature of neoliberalism and crisis through the prism of Joseph Schumpeter's notion of 'creative destruction'. It introduces the Eurozone, refugee, and Brexit crises and explores how Europe's multiple crises have been seized and exploited to advance the creative destruction of citizenship and its neoliberal reconstruction. It then discusses two crucial features of this process: the 'mystique of complexity'—a fundamental neoliberal technology of crisis management that establishes the market as a transcendent domain partially beyond human understanding and criticism—and the politics of scapegoating—instrumental to deflect responsibility from the market to the most vulnerable groups. Finally, the chapter considers two distinctive requirements of neoliberal citizenship: resilience and sacrifice. The latter is the simultaneous willingness to sacrifice and proactively demand the sacrifice of certain individuals and groups that fail to comply with the requirements of neoliberal citizenship.

Chapter 3, *Citizenship for sale*, focuses on one of the most visible manifestations of the neoliberalization of citizenship: the proliferation of citizenship-by-investment schemes. It contends that these schemes exceed commodification in its narrowest sense (the fact that citizenship is traded for money) and are part of a broader process of economization that, by extending the logics and metrics of the market to all spheres of human activity, rewrites in neoliberal terms the criteria required for the protection and recognition traditionally associated with citizenship. Neoliberal citizenship is thus a regime of differential inclusion based on a logic of valuation that encompasses both economic and emotional attributes regarded as valuable for the host community. This logic is applied to nominal citizens and non-citizens alike. To substantiate this argument, the chapter explores a series of illustrations from New Zealand which are relevant to appreciate the global reach of neoliberal citizenship and how the pervasive penetration of neoliberal rationalities has been particularly pernicious in welfare-oriented democracies. The New Zealand case offers crucial insights to explore the neoliberalization of citizenship in Europe and shows how, under specific circumstances, the decisions to include wealthy billionaires and disabled refugees, while excluding disabled residents, respond to the same neoliberal rationality of value.

Chapter 4, *The emotional value of refugees*, further explores the notion of 'emotional value' introduced in the previous chapter. To this end, it builds on the existing literature on humanitarian government by showing how the growing intermingling of humanitarianism and security is part of a process of filtering aimed at granting protection only to refugees regarded as valuable. The chapter elaborates on how the notion of 'ideal refugee' signals an ultimate commodification of solidarity which subordinates the demand of refugees to their perceived market value. It shows how these neoliberal rationalities of value are mobilized through and overlap with a biopolitical rationality of care of the host population, and thus how neoliberal citizenship crucially rests on the mobilization of biopolitical racism. The exclusion of those lacking in economic and emotional capital becomes mandatory under neoliberal rationalities of value and biopolitical rationalities of care, which therefore become indistinguishable. To illustrate these arguments, the death of Alan Kurdi and several other cases from the UK, Germany, France, Italy, and Spain will be discussed.

Chapter 5, *If European want to live, refugees must die*, delves into the biopolitics of the refugee crisis by exploring the moral and political economy which makes it *necessary* to sacrifice—by killing or letting die—the undocumented migrants coming to Europe in order to enhance the life and well-being of its host populations. It introduces the concept of scarcity as a fundamental and largely neglected component of the neoliberal-biopolitical apparatus and shows how the latter incorporates important elements of Malthusianism, including a concern with surplus populations. This apparatus subverts and rewrites the grammar of solidarity grounded in human rights and protection of life. From this perspective, the 2014 suspension of search-and-rescue missions in the Mediterranean, which has resulted in thousands of preventable deaths, is not just the outcome of the securitization of migration, but part of the very logic of solidarity of neoliberal citizenship. Letting some migrants drown becomes a market signal that indicates to prospective migrants that solidarity is in short supply and therefore they should not attempt the dangerous sea journey. This neoliberal humanitarianism, I will argue, frames solidarity as a 'perverse incentive' that only aggravates the problem it aims to solve.

Chapters 6 and 7, *Sacred market, sacrificial lives (I)* and *(II)* discuss how the ascendancy of neoliberal biopolitics in the logics and practices of citizenship exceeds mere dynamics of economization, to encompass a fully fledged process of sacralization of the market. Building on the thought of Agamben, Chapter 6 explores a first trajectory of sacralization: a process of totalizing commodification that, by leaving no domain or space beyond itself, turns the market into an overarching and unquestionable framework of meanings and significations. The implication of this sacralization is explored with reference to the neoliberal citizenship regimes advocated by economists Milton Friedman and Gary Becker. Whereas the former praises the illegalization of migration as beneficial for both the migrant and the host community, the latter supports the idea that citizenship should be for sale and the fact that those in need (nominal citizens and non-citizens alike) may sell their organs for cash. These accounts are oblivious to issues of inequality and exploitation. They reduce life and its biological components to commodities and subordinate citizenship to its capacity to contribute to the production of other commodities. Both accounts will be shown to be a response to the problem of scarcity, which in turn will emerge as the other side of a problem of overabundance that sees neoliberal capitalism actively engaged in the biopolitical production and elimination of surplus populations.

Chapter 7 analyses a second trajectory of sacralization of the market through an extensive engagement with neoliberal forefather Friedrich Hayek. This trajectory ascribes to the market an unconquerable complexity and capacity of coordination that vastly exceed human comprehension and rests on the absolutization of the 'mystique of complexity' discussed in the second chapter. It entails a distinctive 'leap of faith' in the ultimate goodness of the market, even when the latter delivers suffering, crises, and shocks. The resulting regime of neoliberal citizenship is a rendering of Malthus' theory of overpopulation that celebrates suffering and justifies the sacrifice of the less valuable as necessary for the reproduction of the market order. The chapter shows how the scarcity that underpins this regime is: (a) not natural, but socially instituted and instrumental to preserve and reproduce the neoliberal logic of value; (b) not confined to material resources, but also concerning values, which are seemingly threatened by the overabundance of migrants, the poor, and unwanted others. Neoliberal citizenship produces a race-to-the-bottom egalitarianism based on a mimetic fear of sameness, rather than difference, which ultimately asks us to sacrifice the very ones we could become.

Chapter 8, *The sacrificial citizenship of COVID-19*, focuses on the implications of the ongoing coronavirus pandemic for neoliberal citizenship. It explores how this crisis has been shaped by a neoliberal rationality of scarcity—of intensive care beds, ventilators, PPE, qualified and properly trained staff—which has materialized in years of underfunded public healthcare infrastructure and just-in-time managerial approaches aimed at saving costs at the expense of the capacity of saving lives. Indeed, saving the market or saving lives has been the fundamental neoliberal rationality governing the crisis. This has prompted the further internalization of the categories of 'sacrificial others' to include nominal 'normal' citizens like the elderly in care homes. Their sacrifice has been made imperative by a biopolitical 'calculus of lives' that increasingly subordinates the 'right to have rights' associated with citizenship (Arendt 1973) to one's individual perceived value. The coronavirus pandemic, the chapter discusses, has contributed to further strengthening the hold of neoliberal citizenship by normalizing the idea that lives are sacred only insofar as they can survive scarce health provisions without affecting the functioning of the neoliberal order.

The concluding Chapter 9 brings the different strands of the argument together and evaluates their implications for a post-pandemic world. In particular, it raises the question of whether the rejection of austerity that to date has characterized the response to the crisis signals the possibility of a post-neoliberal shift. I argue that this is a misleading interpretation that neglects the symbiotic relationship between neoliberalism and biopolitics and how rationalities of care, through the modulation of scarcity, are instrumental in preserving the market order at times of acute crises and thus in preserving its sacred status. Neoliberal citizenship, I will contend, emerges as a fundamental category of the post-COVID-19 order, one in which the nominal status of citizenship is weakened and borders between self and other are strengthened. This is an order in which we are all migrants, yet walking different routes. Whether ours involves red carpets, corridors, walls, mazes, or graveyards ultimately depends upon our neoliberal value.

Note on terminology

Before turning to the second chapter, a brief note on terminology is in order. A debate that has accompanied the European migrant/refugee crisis is whether those who try to reach Europe by boat or other irregular means and routes should be defined as 'migrants' or 'refugees' (Malone 2015; Taylor 2015; Sengupta 2015; Marsh 2015; Ruz 2015). The traditional distinction between the two groups revolves around the element of voluntariness. As the International Organization for Migration notes, the term 'migrant' is 'usually understood to cover all cases where the decision to migrate was taken freely by the individual concerned for reasons of "personal convenience" and without intervention of an external compelling factor' (Perruchoud and Redpath-Cross 2011: 61). The 1951 Refugee Convention defines the refugee as someone who has been forced to flee their country 'owing to a well-founded fear of being persecuted for reasons of race, religion, nationality, membership of a particular social group or political opinion.'

In a Europe increasingly described as under 'siege' this distinction has important political implications. It implicitly frames the refugees as the ones who deserve protection and humane treatment and the migrants as the ones who need to be rejected. However, this distinction is problematic for three reasons. First, it is extremely blurred on the ground and often untenable. There are vast numbers of people who do not specifically and individually experience persecution, yet live in daily fear for their lives because of conflict and violence, not to mention the degree to which indirect forces such as poverty, political instability, environmental catastrophe, and other factors affect a person's 'choice' to migrate. As Jørgen Carling observes:

> A Nigerian arriving in Italy might have left Nigeria for reasons other than a fear of persecution, but ended up fleeing extreme danger in Libya. Conversely, a Syrian might have crossed into Jordan and found safety from the war, but been prompted by the bleak prospects of indeterminate camp life to make the onward journey to Europe. Regardless of the legal status that each one obtains in Europe, they are both migrants who have made difficult decisions, who deserve our compassion, and whose rights need to be ensured.
>
> (Carling 2015)

Second, the analytical problem of classification is often compounded by a no less relevant normative consideration. As Carling notes, the migrant/refugee dichotomy 'undermines the humanitarian principles that should guide our response to emergencies. When people drown at sea or suffocate in lorries, our first question should not be, "so, which kind were they, refugees or migrants?"' (Carling 2015).

Third, the inclusion of an individual or a group into the category of migrants or refugees is ultimately a product of rationalities of value. With the persistence of the crisis, the very notion that refugees—as opposed to migrants—should be entitled to protection has been increasingly questioned, either by restricting the criteria for being recognized as a refugee or by discriminating between 'good' and 'bad refugees', hence privileging the former as the embodiment of emotional value. The terms 'migrants', 'immigrants', 'undocumented migrants', and 'refugees' will therefore be used interchangeably and as much as possible with the use of qualifiers ('good', 'bad', 'valuable', 'less valuable', 'worthy', 'unworthy', and occasionally with inverted commas as in relation to 'irregular migrants') to indicate that these are ultimately contingent 'subject positions' (Little and Vaughan-Williams 2017: 554), which are a function of the economies of power, knowledge, and value of neoliberal citizenship.

2
The creative destruction of citizenship

Introduction

The notion of 'creative destruction' is most famously associated with Austrian economist Joseph Schumpeter. In his 1942 *Capitalism, Socialism and Democracy*, Schumpeter (2003: 82) argues that '[ca]pitalism ... is by nature a form or method of economic change and not only never is but never can be stationary.... [It] incessantly revolutionizes the economic structure from within, incessantly destroying the old one, incessantly creating a new one. This process of Creative Destruction is the essential fact about capitalism.' For Marxist scholar David Harvey (2005: 11), capitalism's creative destruction has been accelerated by its late twentieth-century mutation from 'embedded capitalism'—its post-war partial enclosure in a system of political and social frameworks aimed at establishing a compromise between labour and capital—to neoliberal capitalism, with capital achieving growing independence from 'social and political constraints'.

With neoliberalism, the process of creative destruction is no longer confined to economic structures, but encompasses 'divisions of labor, social relations, welfare provisions, technological mixes, ways of life, attachments to the land, habits of the heart, ways of thought, and the like' (Harvey 2006: 145). Neoliberalism knows no boundaries between economic, social, and political domains. It incessantly pursues the creation of new markets in areas traditionally regarded as partially beyond mere economic calculations, such as healthcare, education, social security, and public utilities. These domains are creatively destroyed and reconstituted under a new regime of governance that revolves around logics of competition, profit, and value.

In this chapter, I begin to explore how neoliberalism is contributing to the creative destruction of citizenship by increasingly subjecting this institution to economic rationalities. The transformation of citizenship into a market-mediated regime is a broad and heterogeneous phenomenon that encompasses seemingly disconnected transformations and involves nominal

Neoliberal Citizenship. Luca Mavelli, Oxford University Press.
© Luca Mavelli (2022). DOI: 10.1093/oso/9780192857583.003.0002

citizens and non-citizens alike. In relation to non-citizens, one of the most visible manifestations of the marketization of citizenship is the booming offer of citizenship-by-investment schemes by a growing number of countries around the world. These schemes allow wealthy foreigners regarded as the embodiment of valuable forms of capital to obtain citizenship in exchange for an investment or a fee. The mirror image of this trend is the growing securitization of migration, with the proliferation of borders and the strengthening of deportation regimes, aimed at curbing the arrival of economically 'worthless' asylum seekers and undocumented migrants.

When it comes to existing citizens, a combination of structural features of neoliberal capitalism—the fact that the rate of return on capital exceeds that of economic growth (Piketty 2014) and the financialization of the economy—as well as policy interventions—the introduction of systems of regressive taxation, the scaling down or dismantlement of welfare provisions, the casualization of labour, and the privatization and commodification of public services—have resulted in a growing polarization between rich and poor. This polarization exceeds the 1 per cent made famous by the 2011 *Occupy Wall Street* movement (which denounced how 1 per cent of the world richest own over 50 per cent of the world's wealth), as it encompasses a growing divide between the upper class and the middle class, and the increasing proletarianization of the lower classes. The result is that growing sectors of the population are being pushed into poverty and some are experiencing a shortening of their life expectancy. This is part of a regime of neoliberal citizenship in which inclusion, protection, and recognition have been strengthened for the wealthiest and significantly weakened for the working and lower classes; a regime in which an individual's life chances are increasingly commensurate to their economic value.

Engin F. Isin and Peter Nyers (2014: 8) argue that 'citizenship is fundamentally about political struggles over the capacity to constitute ourselves as a political subject.' In particular, they suggest that citizenship involves the struggle 'for a right to be recognized as a right in the first place, and then the struggle for the breadth and depth of these rights (who gets what and how much)' (Isin and Nyers 2014: 8). These two struggles, however, are derivative of a more fundamental condition that enables the very possibility of undertaking these struggles in the name of citizenship: the recognition of political subjectivity (Isin and Nyers 2014: 8).

Most famously formulated by Hannah Arendt (1973), this is the idea that citizenship is the minimum and fundamental requirement for 'the right to have rights' and thus for the possibility of being recognized and treated as a fellow human being endowed with political subjectivity. Stateless people are, for Arendt, the epitome of those who are denied political subjectivity: their 'nakedness of being nothing but human', she (1973: 300) argues, is 'their greatest danger.... It seems that a man who is nothing but a man has lost the very qualities which make it possible for other people to treat him as a fellow-man.' To lose political status, Arendt (1973: 297) warns, equates to 'expulsion from humanity altogether'. In its most basic formulation, then, citizenship is 'the struggle for political subjectivity' (Isin and Nyers 2014: 8) as the struggle for the attainment of humanity.

From this perspective, citizenship does not automatically derive from the nominal status of being a citizen. Consider a damning image of the global refugee crisis which has made the headlines worldwide: the children in cages in immigration processing centres in Texas (detention facilities designed to warehouse undocumented migrants from Mexico waiting to be deported). Then compare it with the almost daily accounts of British children who 'are rifling through bins to find food' or 'are visibly shaking at their desks' because of hunger (Sommerlad 2020): a graphic manifestation of the surge in child poverty following almost ten years of austerity and welfare cuts. Both groups share the same lack of recognition of their humanity. And while the former *lack* the status of American citizens whereas the latter *are* British citizens, both are denied political subjectivity and the related right to be treated as human beings. The reason is that, irrespective of their nominal status, they are regarded as an economic burden. Their condition is the expression of a regime of neoliberal citizenship which makes the amount of inclusion, protection, and recognition that individuals and groups are granted conditional upon their economic value.

The idea of creative destruction of citizenship does not simply describe a transition in the logics and practices of citizenship, with universal notions of solidarity and shared humanity giving way to dehumanizing rationalities of economic securitization. It also invites us to consider the process of 'destruction' as a crucial moment and trajectory in the genesis and reproduction of neoliberal citizenship. In the history of neoliberalism, 'destruction' has materialized in a series of recurrent crises. Indeed, the idea that there is a 'mutually constitutive relationship between neoliberalization and crisis' (Peck, Theodore, and Brenner 2009: 95) and that crises are 'essential to the reproduction of [neoliberal] capitalism' (Harvey 2014a: ix) is shared by both critics and supporters of neoliberalism. In a neoliberal crisis, Harvey (2014a: ix) maintains, '[m]uch gets torn down and laid waste to make way for the new', for 'a new version of what capitalism is about'. Similarly, economist and

Nobel prize winner Milton Friedman (2002: xiv) famously argued that 'only a crisis—actual or perceived—produces real change.' Hence, the question we need to ask is: what is this 'new', this 'change', this 'new version of capitalism' produced by the current crises of neoliberalism?

For Athena Athanasiou, the change in question is the progressive consolidation of a new 'regime of truth' that requires people who struggle with the 'hardship and humiliation' caused by the crisis to acquiescently accept and cope with its consequences, without protesting, revolting, or resisting (Butler and Athanasiou 2013: 149). It follows that neoliberalism is a rationality of government that naturalizes the principle of necessity and the adoption of exceptional measures; it is a crisis-driven mode of governance that establishes the boundaries of the politically possible and acceptable; and it is ultimately a regime of construction of political subjectivities aimed at the creation of citizens capable and, most of all, willing to cope with, adjust, and adapt to the next crisis to come.

Neoliberalism is thus a regime of production of resilient political subjects, that is, of citizens who understand the neoliberal order as a given that constantly requires their adjustment to its uncertainties, perturbations, and shocks. Neoliberal resilient citizenship reinforces and normalizes the idea that individuals are ultimately responsible for their social and economic security (Joseph 2013) and, accordingly, that debasement, destitution, and poverty are not the collective responsibility of states and political institutions, but the responsibility of deficient subjects unable to adjust to the requirement of modern neoliberal life.

By blaming those who fail to successfully inscribe themselves into the logics and mechanics of the neoliberal order, rather than questioning and contesting this very order, neoliberal resilient citizenship authorizes the condemnation and punishment of the undocumented migrants—the children in cages in Texas—and the poor—the British children experiencing malnutrition. In this convergence, however, an important difference must be noticed. Whereas the failure of the British poor is one of *lack of resilience*—their inability to cope with and thrive under neoliberal crises—that of the undocumented migrants is one of *excess of resilience*—their endeavour to survive and secure for themselves a better life by seeking it in a more prosperous country. Therefore, the resilience shown by undocumented migrants in risking their lives to cross borders and enter a country 'illegally' is not rewarded, but punished, because it transcends the limits of political subjectivity and action established by neoliberalism.

This suggests that neoliberal citizenship is not just *resilient* but also *sacrificial*, namely, it demands sacrifice and self-sacrifice in order to preserve the neoliberal order. The undocumented migrants are expected not to seek a better life and endeavour to improve their condition as they are regarded as economically worthless and socially disruptive for a regime that considers market value as a measure of one's degree of humanity. The undocumented migrants, in sum, are sacrificed and expected to sacrifice themselves to guarantee the reproduction of the neoliberal order. This means that the neoliberal market as a scheme and order of valuation has progressively established itself as a sacred and foundational measure of the value of life and framework for the attribution of the status of humanity.

This chapter begins to explore these questions in four main steps. First, I outline the relationship between neoliberalism and crisis in the European context and its implication for neoliberal citizenship. Second, I discuss some initial connections between the Eurozone, refugee, and Brexit crises and how they have been mobilized to advance neoliberal citizenship. Third, I explore how this mobilization has been made possible by two mutually reinforcing discourses: the representation of the market as a complex and partially unknowable entity and the politics of scapegoating. Fourth, I consider how these discourses have established resilience and sacrifice as two essential components of neoliberal citizenship.

1. The opportunity of crisis

'European crisis', 'Crisis in Europe', 'Crisis of Europe', 'Europe's multiple crises': over the last few years, these expressions have saturated the public debate to the effect that the notion of 'Europe in crisis' is now regarded as an almost ordinary state of affairs. The constellation of Europe's crises is complex and variegated. It encompasses an inequality crisis (a growing gap between rich and poor both within and between European countries), an ageing crisis (with significant implications for the sustainability of European welfare systems), a security crisis (with the string of terrorist attacks carried out by Islamic and right-wing extremists in Belgium, France, Germany, the United Kingdom, and Spain since 2004), an identity crisis vis-à-vis Islam (Is Europe secular or Christian? Does Islam belong to Europe?), a pandemic crisis (the recent and ongoing coronavirus outbreak, which has seen Europe becoming one of the main epicentres), and an identity crisis vis-à-vis the EU project which has translated into a persistent institutional crisis.

The crisis of the EU, 'the institutional embodiment of the creation of a common identity for European states and populations' (Laporte 2012: 4), has most vividly manifested itself in three enduring 'headline' crises: the Eurozone or sovereign debt crisis beginning in 2009, the refugee crisis beginning in 2014, and the so-called Brexit crisis, namely, the 2016 decision of the UK to leave the EU. These overlapping crises have seen the rise of Eurosceptic right-wing populist parties calling for more nationalist, sovereignist, and often nativist policies, thus casting serious shadows on the future of the EU project. Existing research has approached this configuration of crises in two different ways, which in turn reflect contending understandings of the notion of crisis.

Moving from a conceptualization of crisis as the breakdown of traditional regimes of governance, several scholars have looked at the institutional weaknesses and limitations of the EU and the external factors which have led to current predicaments. For the Eurozone crisis, the focus has been on the effects of the 2008 subprime mortgage crisis in the United States (USA), the high level of indebtedness of several European countries, and the moral hazard of the European banking system. In the case of the refugee crisis, much has been said on the role that poverty, climate change, and the geopolitical instability of North and sub-Saharan Africa and the Middle East have played in pushing hundreds of thousands of people to seek refuge in Europe. Britain's history of Euro-scepticism and the country's growing concern for immigration have received significant attention in the copious literature on Brexit. These analyses have often concentrated on the limits of the EU and its institutions to confront these exceptional events, on its capacity to survive these crises, and on the potential 'institutional improvements' which could contribute to restore the authority of European regimes of governance (Hobolt 2016; Dinan, Nugent, and Paterson 2017; Jessop 2017; Caporaso 2018).

A second group of scholars has disputed the notion of crisis as the breakdown of traditional regimes of governance caused by seemingly exceptional events. According to this view, crisis *is* a regime of governance (Brassett and Vaughan-Williams 2012; see also Butler and Athanasiou 2013; Roitman 2013; De Genova and Tazzioli 2016) which has enabled the EU and its Member States to adopt and normalize a series of exceptional measures. These 'particular forms of governmental intervention' (De Genova and Tazzioli 2016: 11) have been predicated on the widespread and systematic neglect of human rights and dignity. They include: the prolonged adoption of harsh austerity policies as a response to the Eurozone crisis, which has impoverished large strata of the European population; the fortification of Europe's external borders, the establishment of 'offshore' immigration detention centres, the enforcement of systems of mandatory detention, and the strengthening of the deportation regime as responses to the refugee crisis, which have had the effect of heightening the death toll across the Mediterranean migratory route; the exceptionally long 'prorogation' (i.e. suspension) of the British parliament in the weeks preceding the originally planned exit of the UK from the EU on 31 October 2019, which has raised concerns of an authoritarian turn in British politics.

This book embraces this second conceptualization of crisis as a regime of governance and takes the refugee crisis as its hermeneutic point of entry and main focus of analysis for understanding the productive power of crises in Europe. It shares the view that 'crisis has become an instrument of rule' which 'serves to legitimize political and economic decisions that in fact dispossess citizens [and non-citizens alike] and deprive them of any possibility of decision' (Giorgio Agamben, cited in De Genova and Tazzioli 2016: 11). Yet, my main preoccupation does not lie with the adoption of exceptional measures and permanent states of exceptions, but with a more subtle and, in a sense, fundamental transformation that concerns the very possibility of membership and belonging in the European political community. One of the arguments advanced by this book is that Europe's multiple crises—in particular Eurozone, refugee, Brexit, and, as I shall discuss in Chapter 8, the ongoing (at the time of writing) COVID-19 pandemic—have contributed to accelerate the progressive transformation of citizenship in Europe along neoliberal lines.

In advancing this argument, I am drawing on an established line of thought concerning the crucial interpenetration of neoliberalism and crisis that emphasizes how neoliberalism was born out of and advances through crises. As Mitchell Dean (2014: 157) reminds us, neoliberalism as an intellectual movement was born out of the political, economic, and social crises of the twentieth-century interwar period and established itself as a 'public political force at the end of the 1970s' with the crisis of Keynesianism, which, according to Harvey (2005), marks the end of 'embedded liberalism'. Subsequently, neoliberalism has evolved, progressed, and mutated through a series of crises of its own making, such as the 'Latin American debt defaults' of the 1980s, the 'Asian financial crisis' of the mid-1990s, the 'dot.com bubble' of the late 1990s (Dean 2014: 157), and the 2008 financial crisis, which, until the 2020 coronavirus outbreak, was widely regarded as the cause of the worst depression since the Great Recession of the 1930s.

Europe's multiple crises are part of this neoliberal trajectory. The Eurozone crisis is one of speculation and moral hazard which together have created the conditions of possibility for the adoption of austerity measures. These, in turn, have 'played an important role in shoring support for the UK Independence Party (UKIP) and Vote Leave' (Fetzer 2019a; 2019b), with the Brexit movement capable of projecting onto the EU the responsibility for auto-imposed austerity cuts which have negatively 'affected the living standards of many working people' (Mazzucato 2016). The possibility of a causal connection between austerity and Vote Leave has also been acknowledged by those who initially questioned it (see Fetzer 2019c; Sobolewska and Ford 2020: 234, note 36), and there is a widespread consensus that fear of immigration was one of the primary reasons people voted to leave the EU (Hobolt 2016; Goodwin and Milazzo 2017). Anti-immigrant sentiment has been fuelled by a refugee crisis which cannot be disentangled from the neoliberal global structures of exploitation and inequality supported by EU Member States, despite the effort of dominant crisis narratives to perpetuate 'the problematic notion that the causes of the "crisis"—and therefore responsibility for "it"—are geographically and historically separate from Europe' (Vaughan-Williams and Pisani 2020: 653).

Of course, the European refugee crisis and Brexit have their roots in colonialism and Euro-scepticism which both precede the rise of neoliberalism in the late 1970s and early 1980s with Margaret Thatcher in the UK and Ronald Reagan in the USA. Yet, my point is not to claim that these crises, together with the COVID-19 pandemic, have an exclusively neoliberal origin, but that their development, unfolding, and aggravation is part of a neoliberal matrix that governs through crises and understands and approaches them as strategic opportunities for creative destruction. Hence, my primary aim is to show how Europe's multiple crises have been mobilized to pursue and advance the creative destruction of citizenship and its reconstruction along neoliberal lines.

Citizenship is traditionally regarded as a status to which is attached the enjoyment of a set of rights. It enables the possibility of membership in a political community which is necessary for participating in 'the collective decisions that regulate social life' (Bellamy 2008: 1) and benefiting from social, economic, and political rights. This is the meaning of citizenship from the perspective of those who have it. For those who have not—stateless persons, first of all—citizenship is a regime of alterity (Isin 2002). It discriminates between 'deserving members' who have the racial, linguistic, cultural, ethnic, sexual, and religious attributes to be recognized as citizens and 'underserving strangers' who lack these qualities and can therefore be excluded from the fundamental protections that citizenship grants (Isin 2002).

From this angle, citizenship is not just a political status, but the basic and fundamental 'right to have rights' and thus the necessary condition of possibility for a person to be recognized, respected, and protected as a fellow human being. This central and often neglected feature of citizenship is, in most instances, the result of one's own birthplace, with the effect that the degree of protection and the level of 'humanity' that a person or a group will be accorded is the result of an ultimate randomness. The neoliberal transformation of citizenship is undermining both this element of randomness and the notion of citizenship as 'the right to have rights' because it is turning the possibility of membership and belonging into a function of the market value of individuals and populations. Accordingly, neoliberal citizenship is also progressively disconnecting the nominal status of being a citizen from the effective enjoyment of citizenship, that is, from the enjoyment of membership, protection, and recognition of one's own humanity. The former does not necessarily imply the latter and the latter does not necessarily require the former.

Consider, for instance, the steady rise of poverty among EU workers since the 2008 financial crisis following the adoption of austerity measures and the concurrent rise of super wealthy foreigners buying residency and citizenship across Europe. Austerity has pushed the lower sections of the middle class into poverty, brought devastation to low income families, and, as the United Nations Special Rapporteur on extreme poverty and human rights observed in a 2018 report on the UK, inflicted 'great misery … on the working poor, on single mothers struggling against mighty odds, on people with disabilities who are already marginalized, and on millions of children who are being locked into a cycle of poverty from which most will have great difficulty escaping' (Alston 2018: 2). Austerity has turned nominally right-bearing citizens into a mass of disenfranchised, marginalized, and often stigmatized subjects.

While bent on depriving their weakest citizens of their rights, several European countries—including Malta, Cyprus, Portugal, Greece, the UK, Italy, and France—have lured wealthy foreigners either through the offer of special fiscal regimes not available to ordinary citizens or through citizenship-by-investment schemes which make it possible to 'purchase' citizenship or residency for a fee and/or an investment, or a combination of both. EU counties have been 'competing for the rich' (Trautvetter and Winkler 2019) by offering them tax cuts, tax breaks, and fiscal 'red carpets' often in conjunction with citizenship. At a time of prolonged austerity, these schemes have been de facto subsidised by an already squeezed and struggling middle class. This does not simply mean that 'rights and entitlements once associated with all citizens are becoming linked to neoliberal criteria, so that entrepreneurial expatriates come to share in the rights and benefits once exclusively claimed by citizens' (Ong 2006a: 499), but that a transfer of wealth, opportunities, and—crucially—*rights* from impoverished citizens to wealthy foreigners has been silently and steadily taking place.

This transfer has created a largely undetected moral aporia in a European Union which prides itself as the land of 'human dignity, freedom, democracy, equality, the rule of law and respect for human rights' (as Article 2 of the Treaty on European Union recites). This aporia is amplified by the fact that, over the last seven years, while thousands of passports have been sold, residencies-by-investment granted, and fiscal red carpets rolled out, in the ongoing political struggle over how, which, and whether European states should carry out search-and-rescue missions in the Mediterranean, more than 20,000 undocumented migrants have drowned in the attempt to reach European shores. With the neoliberal transformation of citizenship, the random injustice of its assignment has been replaced by a less random—though arguably no less unjust—rationality of conferral which prizes economic value as the fundamental criteria for the possibility of membership and belonging, and ultimately for the right to live.

2. Banks, austerity, refugees, and Brexit

As David Harvey (2014a: ix) observes, '[i]t is in the course of crises that the instabilities of capitalism are confronted, reshaped and re-engineered' to establish a new iteration of capitalism. Europe's multiple crises have been instrumental in advancing the penetration of neoliberal capitalism in the idea and practices of citizenship. Specifically, neoliberal capitalism has been able to reinvent itself by claiming ultimate authority over the possibility of protection and the degree of humanity that a person or a group is granted. In this process, the Eurozone crisis figures prominently because of its magnitude and implications.

In 2009, the European banking system found itself on the brink of collapse as a result of reckless overleveraging and lending. German, French, and, to a less extent, British, US, Dutch, and Italian banks were overly exposed for a total of over €200 billion, particularly following extensive purchase of Greek sovereign debt in order to reap the higher yields on bonds compared to that offered by other countries in the Eurozone. Their overexposure turned into a liquidity crisis with the eruption of the subprime mortgage crisis in the United States, itself the product of irresponsible lending through the reckless use of derivatives. This crisis threatened the survival of the European banking system and thus of the Europe Union.

European Member States with the approval of the European Commission embarked on a massive bailout with the effect of transforming, almost overnight, a private sector crisis concerning the banks into a sovereign debt crisis concerning the states. This transformation, however, was not just one—as if this was not enough—of who would be responsible for paying off the debt, but also of who should be deemed responsible for causing the crisis in the first instance. What was a market failure of the private sector—the banking system—was repackaged and sold as a crisis caused by the overspending and profligacy of governments and their citizens which now made 'imperative' the adoption of austerity measures.

Austerity, the idea that reducing the state's budget will contribute to restore growth, has resulted in massive cuts to public expenditures—including healthcare, education, public transport, welfare transfers such as child allowances or disability benefits—which have impacted primarily those 'in the middle or the bottom half of the income and wealth distribution' who rely on government services (Blyth 2013: 14). Austerity has triggered peak levels of unemployment, prompted a sharp rise in the number of European households living in poverty, amplified the level of inequality between rich and poor, reduced the rate of increase of life expectancy for the poorest sectors of the population, and caused deaths which would not otherwise have occurred. In the UK alone, some studies estimate the number of preventable deaths linked to austerity at 120,000 (Helm 2019).

In terms of its devastating social impact, austerity in Europe has been compared to the disastrous structural adjustment policies imposed upon countries of the Global South in the 1980s and 1990s (Cavero and Poinasamy 2013). Austerity has contributed to emptying citizenship from within by creating a mass of 'intensely isolated and unprotected individuals, persistently in peril of deracination and deprivation of basic life support, wholly vulnerable to capital's vicissitudes' (Brown 2016: 3). While nominally retaining their citizenship, the disenfranchised and debased citizens of austerity have seen the regime of protections stemming from their status significantly curtailed, with the dehumanizing aggravation that, as I shall discuss later in the chapter, they have also been blamed for their own condition.

This neoliberal transformation of citizenship has been made possible by the stealth sanctification of the market as a sacred identity which cannot be questioned and made responsible for its failures to the point that its sins have to be amended by those who suffer its consequences. And those who endure the consequences of its failures have been encouraged to look for culprits to blame. The undocumented migrants coming to Europe across the Mediterranean and the Balkan routes have become the ideal scapegoat. From potential refugees and disenfranchised individuals seeking a better life, undocumented migrants have increasingly come to be seen as irresponsible risk-takers, queue jumpers, bogus asylum seekers, potential invaders, and as a 'bunch' of culturally, racially, and ethnically different people intent of robbing Europe of its culture, identity, and wealth. Right-wing populist politicians and their sympathetic media have successfully promoted the narrative of undocumented migrants as bent on depriving the austerity-stricken Europeans of their scarce resources—by forcing them out of the labour market, overcrowding public schools, increasing demand for social housing and health services—as well as on destroying their cultural and religious identity. Austerity has provided fertile ground for the evergreen seeds of racism and xenophobia.

In autumn 2014, in this context of heightened social anxiety, the over 200,000 desperate people that since the beginning of the year had crossed the Mediterranean on precarious and unseaworthy vessels quickly became 'a rising tide' and 'an invasion' that threatens Europe's identity, economic livelihood, cultural, and religious foundations. Concerns were raised on whether those attempting the sea crossing were real refugees or rather economic migrants, hence fraudsters intent on taking advantage of Europe's generosity and plundering the continent's scarce resources. This climate resulted in a momentous decision. In October 2014, the EU halted the search-and-rescue mission *Mare Nostrum*—initiated by Italy a year earlier and widely regarded as extremely successful with the rescue of over 150,000 people—because it was deemed 'an unintended "pull factor" encouraging more migrants to attempt the dangerous sea crossing and thereby leading to more tragic and unnecessary deaths' (then UK Foreign Office Minister Lady Anelay, cited in Travis 2015).

Mare Nostrum was replaced by *Triton*, a border patrolling mission with a downsized budget of €3 million a month, roughly a third of that of its search-and-rescue predecessor. As a result of the termination of *Mare Nostrum*, the number of recorded migrant deaths in the Mediterranean rose from 3,283 in 2014 to 4,054 in 2015 and 5,143 in 2016 (Statista 2020a; see also IOM 2020). These figures are quite eloquent on their own, but to fully understand their tragic relevance it is necessary to compare them to the financial effort made to save the banks and to the (much more limited) financial effort to help the disenfranchised citizens of austerity.

Between 2008 and 2011, to bail out the overleveraged and overexposed banks, the EU committed €4.5 trillion, equivalent to almost 37 per cent of its

GDP. To relieve the poorest strata of the population hit by austerity measures, it committed €200bn, corresponding to 1.5 per cent of its GDP (Cavero and Poinasamy 2013: 6). To save the lives of the undocumented migrants crossing the Mediterranean, the €9 million a month of *Mare Nostrum*—the equivalent of 0.0000065 per cent of EU GDP—was considered too much. In the scheme of valuation of neoliberal citizenship, undocumented migrants are almost worthless, whereas disenfranchised European citizens hit by austerity measures are deemed of such a low economic value that the investment afforded to secure their status has only been a fraction of that made to secure the viability and survival of the European banking system.

While these financial comparisons offer an important illustration of how neoliberal citizenship subordinates the possibility of membership, protection, and recognition of humanity to rationalities and metrics of value, the value in question should not be exclusively understood in economic terms. Differently said, the neoliberal value of citizenship should not be reduced to the capacity of individuals and populations to contribute to the economic growth of the country. The Brexit crisis is particularly revealing in this regard. Before and after the 2016 referendum which sealed the fate of the UK outside the EU, numerous authoritative analyses have pointed out how the 3 million EU citizens living in the UK provide a positive net contribution to the country—that is, they inject into the economy through taxes and consumption more than they take in terms of social and health services—and therefore should be regarded as a valuable form of human capital. However, one of the key pledges of the Brexit campaigners was that net migration to the UK would be reduced from the allegedly unsustainable 'hundreds of thousands to the tens of thousands', and that, therefore, immigration from the EU would be drastically cut.

The highly divisive result of the referendum has contributed to turn the 3 million EU citizens living in the UK into the embodiment of overlapping and conflicting forms of capital. Technically, they are valuable human capital that positively contributes to the economy of the country. However, they are negative emotional capital for many 'Brexiteers', who consider them to be foreigners who should not have the same level of protections and entitlements of native British people as they have a 'subtractive' effect on the 'value' of the country (by reducing its wealth, diluting its culture, and corrupting its language). Nonetheless, they are valuable emotional capital for many 'Remainers', who consider that EU citizens enhance the wealth, culture, international outlook, and 'Europeanness' of the UK. The subsequent decision not to grant EU citizens in the UK permanent residency ahead of the UK exit negotiation with the EU has had the effect of officially turning them into another form of capital, 'negotiating capital', in the official words of the Home Office, which the UK should use to strengthen its bargaining position vis-à-vis the EU (O'Carroll 2017).[1]

In this regime of superimpositions, the overarching rationality concerning whether, how, and what degree of protection EU citizens in the UK should be granted is one of value. Yet, this neoliberal rationality of value transcends mere economic and financial determinations to encompass an emotional dimension. In an era of neoliberal citizenship, the degree of protection and the level of humanity that a person or a group will be accorded is a function of their market value, but this value may also encompass a distinctive emotional dimension, which in some instances may be regarded as more relevant than a negative economic value. The reason is that neoliberalism disseminates the model of the market to all domains of existence, including that of emotions, thus subjecting them to a regime of 'economization'. The British response to the death of Alan Kurdi briefly mentioned in the introduction is a case in point.

The British government was under heavy pressure to open its borders to those in greater need on the grounds that it was failing the test of compassion, and thus betraying the identity of the UK as a moral nation capable of abiding by its obligations. The UK was irredeemably damaging its *humanity* value. To avert and reverse this process, in a logic of neoliberal economization of emotions, then Prime Minister David Cameron, who only weeks before had pledged not to take any more refugees, performed a remarkable U-turn and committed to take 20,000 Syrian refugees over a period of five years directly from camps in Syria's neighbouring countries. He explained that the refugees would be selected on the basis of need: 'We will take the most vulnerable: … disabled children, … women who have been raped, … men who have

[1] The perception and treatment of EU citizens as negative human capital has emerged even more vividly in the aftermath of the end of the transition period (30 December 2020, following the exit of the UK from the EU on 31 January 2020), with increasing reports of EU citizens prevented from entering the UK, held for hours at UK airports or detained for days at immigration removal centres, and eventually expelled. The 'hostile environment' policy—the set of measures introduced in 2012 by then Home Secretary and later Prime Minister Theresa May to encourage the departure and discourage the arrival of 'illegal immigrants'—now applies to EU citizens. This includes many documented instances of unlawful detention and deportation which echo, on a smaller scale, the unlawful detention and deportation of hundreds of British subjects of African-Caribbean origin who had lived in the UK for more than forty years—the so-called Windrush scandal which erupted in 2017. This is an illustration of the race-to-the-bottom egalitarianism produced by neoliberal citizenship: the treatment once reserved for overseas migrants is now extended to EU migrants. It is also an illustration of how the securitization of migration works increasingly in conjunction with a system of market incentives—in this case, as part and parcel of a market of punishment—aimed at instituting regimes of self-governance of migration. These dynamics are a product of the process of neoliberal economization, whose theoretical dimensions will be explored in greater depth in Chapter 3.

suffered torture' (cited in BBC News 2015a). The mentally and physically disabled refugees that the UK would cherry-pick at the source are the bearers of an emotional capital which would boost Britain's pride and self-perceived moral worth. Despite being a prospective economic burden on the health system, these refugees were considered valuable and, therefore, worthy of protection.

3. Mystique of complexity and politics of scapegoating

According to Michel Foucault, in order to study the technologies and manifestations of power, it is necessary to analyse 'the political rationality underpinning them' (Lemke 2002: 50) and how these are deployed through different governmental strategies. This section focuses on the neoliberal rationalities of government or *governmentalities* of the Eurozone, refugee, and Brexit crises. These crises have been turned into key moments for the advancement of neoliberal citizenship through two mutually reinforcing governmental strategies: the representation of the market as a complex and partially unknowable entity and the politics of scapegoating. Let me consider them in turn.

A key innovation introduced by neoliberalism over the last forty years is the idea that 'the natural complexity of market phenomena' is such that 'no centralized authority could hope to predict, much less control, the precise evolution of individual elements in the system' (Walker and Cooper 2011: 149). This means that states and financial institutions do not possess the centralized knowledge required to place them 'outside the logic of risk and speculation' and therefore are not able to prevent market crises (Konings 2016: 278). They can and should nonetheless promptly intervene on the market if a financial crisis erupts not just by acting as 'lenders of last resort', but by embracing the logic of risk and speculation all the way down and purchasing the toxic assets of distressed financial institutions (Konings 2016: 274). Complexity requires states and international institutions—such as the EU or the International Monetary Fund (IMF)—to step in and bail out private actors when necessary. Bailouts have become an ingrained feature of neoliberalism—that is, neoliberalism has acted almost from the onset as a mechanism of transfer of risk from private actors to the public and, accordingly, of transfer of wealth from taxpayers to wealthy financial institutions and investors (Mavelli 2019: 231).

The 2008 financial crisis is no exception to this script. Indeed, 'official accounts ... have explicitly and recurrently referred to "complexity" in the nature of the securities transacted (especially collateralized debt obligations [CDOs] and the credit default swaps [CDS] created around them) as well as in the structure of the financial industry' as the main cause of the crisis (Datz 2013: 459). This complexity, the mainstream narrative goes, has eventually compelled states, supranational, and international institutions to intervene 'after the event' by bailing out and recapitalizing the banks at a cost that, according to different estimates, oscillates 'between 3 and 13 trillion dollars', that is, between 3.75 per cent and 15 per cent of the world gross domestic product (Blyth 2013: 15). This massive bailout has triggered a wave of austerity measures which have materialized in the slashing of social spending, the dismantlement of welfare provisions, precarization, casualization, and privatizations.

Complexity, or more precisely what I would like to describe as the 'mystique of complexity' (Mavelli 2019), is what enables neoliberalism to be simultaneously 'remedy' and 'poison'—to evoke Derrida's (1998) famous reading of Plato's Phaedrus. The mystique of complexity is the idea that the financial market is an almost transcendent and mystical entity which cannot be grasped in its totality. Hence, the instabilities, crises, and shocks created by the market cannot be pre-empted through political interventions aimed at 'embedding' the market into systems of political and social regulations because markets cannot be fully understood in their sheer intricacy, let alone managed, by political institutions. Complexity is a convenient scapegoat which, as critics have observed, intentionally 'blurred the element of agency' in its 'deliberate design and commercialisation' (Datz 2013: 460). In fact, 'complexity was not a "natural" affliction that engulfed financial transactions; it was a profitable business strategy' (Datz 2013: 460).

The official account of the 2008 financial crisis is that of an excess of securitization, fuelled by a bubble in house prices, which prompted an exponential demand for residential mortgages in the United States. Many mortgages thus became subprime, that is, they were offered to individuals with poor credit scores. In order to distribute and reduce the higher risk, these mortgages were pooled, tranched, and resold as CDOs, which by the same mechanism, would often be used to create new CDOs (Christophers 2009; see also Datz 2013). The financial institutions that bought CDOs would also generally purchase CDSs, insurance contracts to protect their investment, for which, however, they often did not have the necessary liquidity. Hence, they would purchase ABCPs (asset-backed commercial papers), loans backed by financial assets such as CDOs (see Christophers 2009; Mavelli 2019: 233). Instead of spreading risk, however, this complex mechanism of securitization made it impossible to assess 'the fundamental values and risk profiles of underlying assets' (Pierre Landau, Deputy Governor of the Bank of France, cited in Datz 2013: 466).

When subprime mortgages started to default, the whole mechanism collapsed like a house of cards.

Critics have argued that the complexity at the heart of this failure was not to reduce risk but to boost profits. As Brett Christophers (2009: 820) observes, the story of the subprime mortgage crisis is one 'of loans (ABCP) being made on loans (CDOs) being made on loans (residential mortgages) … The same capital "triplicated", as Marx would have it' by turning each residential property into 'the instrument of three different loans' (Christophers 2009: 820, quoting Adam Smith). 'Each new instrument', Datz (2013: 382) observes, was an opportunity for financial firms to extract more fees and trading profits'. Complexity, in other words, was actively manufactured 'in both market [and product] structure' to pursue 'higher profit' (Brassett and Holmes 2016: 382). Even supporters of neoliberalism such as the *Financial Times* have acknowledged that: 'when products become simpler and more transparent, the [profit] margins typically fall. Bankers … have a strong motive to retain complexity and opacity—which is why the innovation cycle keeps turning' (cited in Datz 2013: 466).

The 2008 financial crisis has thus seen the consecration of the mystique of complexity as a fundamental neoliberal technology and theology of crisis management (Mavelli 2019: 232). By constructing an idea of the market as a quasi-transcendent, otherworldly, and sacred entity which cannot be fully known and grasped, the mystique of complexity has been able to partially deflect the attention from those financial and political actors responsible for the crisis. It has scaled down the greediness, moral hazard, reckless overleveraging, and irresponsible lending of the former, as well as the connivance and responsibility and failures of a political class that over the years has loosened regulations, thus allowing the risk-taking behaviour of private actors.

However, the mystique of complexity on its own cannot fully justify the fact that the public, rather than the bankers and investors who engaged, played with, and ultimately benefited from complexity, has had to pay for the consequences of the crisis. A further strategy was required to turn 'tax-paying workers' into 'an acceptable revenue source for the bailouts of investment banks managed by billionaires' (Brown 2016: 9). In Europe, this strategy became rewriting the crisis beginning in 2009 as one concerning the 'sovereign debt' of the 'Eurozone'. According to this narrative, what Europe was experiencing was a crisis of public finances caused by negligent governments which had indulged in overspending. This irresponsible overspending had been particularly pronounced in Southern European countries and now required 'tightening their belts'. As James Caporaso reminds us, '[t]he most popular explanation [of the Eurozone crisis], not confined to the tabloids, is a cultural one':

> There are two Europes. First there is northern Europe which is fiscally responsible, works hard, invests wisely and lives within its means. Northern Europe includes Germany, Austria, the Netherlands, and Finland. Then there is southern Europe (Greece, Italy, Portugal and Spain) which is fiscally lax, doesn't work hard, engages in periodic consumption binges, and does not save, invest and grow. It's a story of virtue vs. indulgence, saints and sinners, Calvinists and Catholics.
>
> (Caporaso 2018: 1346)

This widely accepted narrative offers a culturally racist and moralizing tale that conceals how the crisis beginning in 2009 in Europe was first and foremost a banking crisis, that is, a crisis of private debt which was eventually turned into a public debt crisis (Clarke and Newman 2012; Blyth 2013; Tooze 2018). There are two main components to the crisis, both of which have to do with neoliberal greed and moral hazard. First, in order to maximize their profits, European banks overleveraged. They reduced their equity and increased their debt to a level considerably higher than their American counterparts, thus undertaking a process of multiplication of capital that was even riskier than that pursued in the United States through the reckless use of derivatives.

Second, in order to maximize their profits, European banks massively invested in the European peripheral sovereign debt of Portugal, Ireland, Italy, Spain, and most of all Greece in order to reap the higher yields on bonds compared to those offered by other countries in the Eurozone. This investment strategy was based on a fundamental moral hazard: since the overleveraging had resulted in banks' asset footprints that largely exceeded the GDP of their countries, a default of the banks would have catastrophic consequences for the Eurozone, hence European banks implicitly relied on the assumption that European countries would have rescued them should a crisis occur (Blyth 2013).

Eventually, this is precisely what happened. When liquidity froze on global markets as a result of the subprime mortgage crisis in the United States, European banks found themselves unable to fund their debt at the normal low rates they had accessed until then and started to sell large amounts of European peripheral sovereign debt. The result was that, in a market in which everyone was trying to sell, the price of bonds dropped, bringing their yields to the roof. This locked European banks with large amounts of peripheral sovereign debts which the southern European countries increasingly struggled to service. The concrete threat of a failure of the European banking system prompted the European governments, together with the European Bank and the International Monetary Fund to engineer a massive bailout with public money.

The banking debt crisis was transformed into a sovereign debt crisis. This required constructing a narrative of blame and guilt which transferred the responsibility of the crisis from the banks (for their moral hazard) and the political elites (for failing to prevent this moral hazard) to a scapegoat. The often derogatorily described 'PIIGS'—Portugal, Ireland, Italy, Greece, and Spain—were blamed for their reportedly lavish and irresponsible spending which now threatened the very existence of the European Union. Greece, including the Greek government and the Greek people, became the primary scapegoat, due to the massive debt—largely exceeding that of the other most indebted European nations—that it had built and struggled to service. To claim that Greece became the primary scapegoat does not mean that it was not responsible for its unsustainable debt and that Greece's insolvency was not of its own making. It means that what threatened the stability of the Eurozone was not Greece but 'the dangerous fragility of an overleveraged financial system' (Tooze 2018: 14).

According to René Girard (1996: 11), a 'scapegoat effect' is that process whereby a multitude, a group, a community is 'reconciled at the expense of a third party who appears guilty or responsible for whatever ails, disturbs, or frightens the scapegoaters. They feel relieved of their tensions and they coalesce into a more harmonious group. They now have a single purpose, which is to prevent the scapegoat from harming them, by expelling and destroying him' (Girard 1996: 11). The designation of Greece as almost exclusively responsible for threatening the stability of the European banking system and the existence of the EU served a specific purpose: relieving the German, French, and, to a less extent, British, US, Dutch, and Italian banks of their responsibilities and re-establishing the authority, legitimacy, and centrality of the European financial system for the development and well-being of Europe.

Accordingly, depictions of the Greeks as lazy, incompetent, and greedy inundated the public debate. The Greeks, it was argued, had lied about their economic and financial credentials, over-indulged in welfare spending (including 'lavish pensions'), and eventually infected with their toxic debt the 'monetary and financial lifeblood of the [European] economic body' (see Langley 2014: 68). As a result, Greece was considered to pose 'as big a risk to the global economy and financial markets as the collapse of Lehman Brothers did in September 2008' (see Elliot and Traynor 2010). According to then German Chancellor Angela Merkel, Greece should not have been allowed into the EU in the first place (see Elliot and Traynor 2010). For the OECD (Organisation for Economic Co-operation and Development), the Greek debt crisis was spreading 'like Ebola'. It nurtured the fear that the 'contagion' of 'the developed world's most crooked economy' lying 'in the cradle of Western civilization' could trigger a 'domino effect' that would undermine 'the very existence of the world's second biggest currency' (see Tracy 2012).

This powerful process of scapegoating has been instrumental in justifying the adoption of a series of bailouts conditional upon the implementation of harsh austerity measures as a solution to the crisis. In particular, the construction of the Greeks as guilty and therefore deserving of punishment (Engdahl 2015) has contributed to overshadowing the fact that the primary goal of the three bailouts received by Greece has been saving the large European banks that owned most of the Greek sovereign debt, rather than helping the Greek economy recover. Since 2010, European Governments, the European Central Bank, and the International Monetary Fund (the so-called Troika) have loaned Greece €252 billion in order to rescue it from default. However, it is estimated that only 5 per cent of the bailout loan has gone to the Greek government to invest in the country and benefit the Greek people (Rocholl and Stahmer 2016). The majority of the loan has been used to pay off debt with, primarily, German and French banks. At the end of 2014, the exposure of European and US banks towards Greece had shrunk to about €35 billion (Nardelli and Merler 2015; Rocholl and Stahmer 2016), while Greece had plunged into an even deeper recession with 25 per cent unemployment, over 44 per cent of the Greek population with an income below the poverty line, a 35 per cent increase in suicides, and 'the collapse of public health and education' (Hadjimichalis 2014: 505).

The scapegoating of Greece has been accompanied by another important process of scapegoating: that of the European poor. The attribution of the responsibility of the crisis to the people of Europe as a whole (through their governments' careless spending) has been quickly turned into the problem of a disruptive culture of welfare dependency which has encouraged the poorest strata of the population to live above their means and prevented them from taking responsibility for their own lives and become active and productive members of society. The UK has been championing this process of scapegoating. The 2008 'Responsibility Agenda' of the Conservative Party (Conservative Party 2008) stated that 'ending Britain's welfare culture is a moral duty for any progressive government'. Six years later, then Prime Minister David Cameron described scaling down welfare provisions as a 'moral mission' (*The Guardian* 2014).

For Cameron, the causes of the 2008 crash had to do with 'Labour overspending' as part of a culture of 'welfare dependency' which 'for years has paid British people not to work' (cited in Burnett 2017: 218). Hence, shortly after the onset of the crisis, Cameron (2009) declared that 'The age of irresponsibility is giving way to the age of austerity.' This narrative has contributed to the construction of welfare provisions as morally and socially despicable and, accordingly, of welfare recipients as 'benefit scroungers', as a weak and morally debauched lot that lives at the expense of the healthy and laborious part of the population and threatens its existence and well-being (Cooper and Whyte 2017). This narrative mimics the one that describes the undocumented migrants coming to Europe—the ultimate scapegoats of Europe's multiple crises—as 'bogus' refugees and thus 'undeserving'; a swarm of 'scroungers, spongers, fraudsters' intent on 'robbing the system' and placing an unduly onerous burden on its laborious population.

The convergence between these narratives highlights a fundamental feature of the politics of scapegoating and the mystique of complexity: these two governmental strategies have been rewriting the meaning of citizenship in a universal neoliberal fashion that transcends national identities and the nominal condition of having citizenship. In a neoliberal order, citizenship as the 'right to have rights', as the recognition of an individual's or a group's political subjectivity and humanity is a function of their perceived economic value. This value can be strictly economical but also emotional as previously considered in the cases of European citizens in the UK and the response to the tragic death of Alan Kurdi. At the heart of the neoliberal logic of value is the idea of the market as a sacred entity, too complex to grasp and yet demanding unconditional allegiance even when it delivers crises and shocks. These crises are not failures of the market but of those who fail to adapt and adjust to its logics, and who, for this reason, will be scapegoated. It follows that, as I shall discuss in the next section, neoliberalism requires citizens to be resilient—to adapt and adjust to the crises and shocks of the market—as well as sacrificial—willing to sacrifice themselves and accepting/demanding the sacrifice of 'threatening others' in order to preserve the sacred order of the market.

4. Resilient and sacrificial citizenship

Mitchell Dean (2014: 159–60) suggests that the 2008 financial crisis has introduced a fundamental mutation 'of neoliberal rationalities and technologies' that naturalizes 'the inevitability of catastrophe' and the incapacity of politics to address economic and social failures. Neoliberalism increasingly requires individuals and communities to be resilient in the face of the next crisis to come. The idea of resilience therefore encompasses a 'pervading fatalism' (Joseph 2016: 381) that directly draws on the neoliberal characterization of the market as a complex and transcendent domain that exceeds our understanding and capacity of coordination. Resilience is the correlate of complexity. Complexity establishes the market as a sacred and transcendent identity that cannot be questioned or challenged. Resilience as an essential feature of modern citizenship ensures preparedness before the catastrophe and adaptation in its aftermath, that is, the supine acceptance of the neoliberal rationality of the market (Mavelli 2019).

Neoliberal citizens are thus expected to be resilient and therefore to stoically bear the burden of exceptional measures, such as austerity policies, required to guarantee the existence of the neoliberal market. They are expected to be adaptable, flexible, entrepreneurial, and capable of adjusting to and thriving in a context of uncertainties, crises, and shocks (Mavelli 2019: 226-7). Even more importantly, resilient citizenship performs an inversion of responsibilities (Joseph 2013). Since global economic and financial processes are too complex, they are beyond the capacity of states to fully understand and manage them. This means that 'the only role for government is that of facilitation and enablement of more adaptive and capable individual choices' (Chandler and Reid 2016: 4). Governments no longer have a duty to protect their citizens from marginalization, social exclusion, and poverty.

By normalizing the idea that individuals are ultimately responsible for their social and economic security (Joseph: 2013) and for their successes and failures, resilient citizenship champions the view that debasement, destitution, and poverty are not the product of structural conditions of inequality and exploitation, and, therefore, are not social issues which have their origin in collective political responsibilities. Rather, they are considered the responsibility of lazy, debauched, and undeserving citizens, unable to adjust to and comply with the requirements of the neoliberal order (Mavelli 2019: 225). Neoliberal resilient citizenship thus carries with it a largely unacknowledged rationality of condemnation and punishment. As we saw, it rests on a scapegoating process that shifts blame from the market onto those who suffer its consequences.

In Section 3, I discussed how the construction of the Eurozone crisis as a sovereign debt crisis, rather than a banking debt crisis, and the neoliberal regime of austerity that followed have contributed to establishing a remarkable identity and close proximity between the Greeks, the European dispossessed, and the refugees coming to Europe. These groups have all been scapegoated as responsible for threatening the financial stability and the very cultural and civilizational existence of Europe. The stigmatization of the Greeks has focused on their profligacy, on the Greek state's incapacity to comply with the requirements of the European Stability and Growth Pact, and on the country's irresponsibility for falsifying its economic, financial, and fiscal situation in order to join the European Union. The European dispossessed citizens of austerity have been increasingly portrayed 'as if they were responsible for their situation and if social protection was a luxury in times of austerity' (Cavero and Poinasamy 2013: 10). The undocumented migrants have been accused of being 'fake', irresponsible for attempting the dangerous sea crossing, and greedy for expecting support from European countries struggling with scarcity in a time of austerity.

These intertwined processes of scapegoating indicate that neoliberal citizenship collapses the formal distinction between citizens and strangers and incorporates resilience as one of its defining features. The exercise of resilience, however, is not expected to be unconditional, but to be practised within the framework of neoliberalism, that is, within the framework established *by* the market and *for* the market. Hence, whereas the European dispossessed are blamed for their *lack of resilience*, as manifested in their incapacity to cope with austerity, the undocumented migrants are blamed for their *excess of resilience*, that is, their attempt to secure a better life at all costs. This process of blaming is ultimately an act of projection that transfers onto the European dispossessed and the refugees coming to Europe (and other groups such as the Greek workers) the responsibility for economic and social difficulties. At this point, neoliberal citizenship is not just demanding these groups to be resilient within the framework of neoliberalism, but to accept their condition of social displacement, material destitution, and economic disposability. It demands that they sacrifice themselves in order to preserve the higher common good of the neoliberal market and, accordingly, the neoliberal life and well-being of Europe. These considerations bring us to the sacrificial component of neoliberal citizenship.

Wendy Brown (2016) has recently advanced the seminal notion of sacrificial citizenship. Brown (2016: 3) argues that the 'economization of political and social life' has resulted in the 'production of everyone as human capital' and thus in the transformation of active, collective, and participatory citizenship into 'isolated bits of self-investing human capital' who are responsible for their successes and failures *and* for the successes and failures of the firm, nation, and 'postnational constellation' to which they belong. In the conceptual framework advanced in this book, the first type of responsibilization is captured by the notion of resilience: resilient citizens are responsible for their successes and failures, which cannot be ascribed to structural conditions of inequality and exploitation. The second type of responsibilization concerns the establishment of the neoliberal subject as a sacrificial citizen, that is, as an individual willing to accept blame for the economic and, more broadly, social difficulties that the firm or the nation may experience, and willing to sacrifice themselves for the sake of the economic growth of the firm and the nation. As Wendy Brown maintains:

> Such sacrifice may range from suffering the direct effects of job outsourcing, furloughs or pay and benefits cuts, to suffering the indirect effects of stagflation, credit crunches, liquidity or currency crises. It may be shared widely as the curtailed state investment in education; it may be suffered individually as a 'last-hired, first-fired' phenomenon; or, as is most often the case, it may be suffered disproportionately by a weak group or class, as is the case with furloughs or reduced government services. Whatever the case, active citizenship is slimmed to tending oneself as responsibilized human capital, while sacrificial citizenship expands to include anything related to the health of a firm or nation, or again, the health of the nation as firm.
>
> (Brown 2016: 9)

The collective self-blame and willing acceptance of 'self-sacrifice' for the sake of the economy, Brown continues, crucially entails the singling out of particular groups as more responsible than others.

> Not only, then, are Greek workers, French pensioners, Californian and Michigan public employees, American Social Security recipients, British university students, European new immigrants, and public goods as a whole cast as thieving dependents operating in an old world of entitlement rather than self-care, they are blamed for sinking states into debt, thwarting growth, and bringing the global economy to the brink of ruin.
>
> (Brown 2016: 9)

My understanding of sacrificial citizenship as a crucial component of neoliberal citizenship draws and builds on Brown's argument, but also departs from it in two main regards. First, Brown (2016: 11) confines the process of sacrifice to the idea that 'this citizen might be said to be oblatory vis-à-vis the project of economic growth' and that certain groups—such as the ones above—more than others need to self-sacrifice or be actively sacrificed for the sake of the economy. In my account, neoliberal sacrificial citizens do not only accept self-sacrifice, but also actively engage in a process of transfer of blame—a dynamic of scapegoating—whereby they identify other groups as responsible for the nation's economic failures and demand their sacrifice.

From this perspective, 'the Greek workers, French pensioners, Californian and Michigan public employees, American Social Security recipients, British university students, [and] European new immigrants' are sacrificial citizens in the double sense of being blamed and actively engaged in a process of blaming. They are simultaneously victims and perpetrators of neoliberalism. The pensioners and social security recipients who suffer the consequences of welfare cuts are blamed for their entitlement and yet they blame migrants for taking away their resources and wealth and demand the closure of borders and the strengthening of the deportation regime. Northern European countries have blamed the 'PIIGS' for the Eurozone crisis, yet both groups have blamed the austerity-stricken Greeks for their laziness and lavish spending. The Greeks have turned their anger at the undocumented migrants, with surges of violence at multiple levels of society: from local residents preventing them to disembark, to right-wing paramilitary groups and the police rounding them up and placing them in detention centres, to the militarization of the border with Turkey, with the use of tear gas and live ammunition. The undocumented migrants are the weakest group and thus the ultimate manifestation of a neoliberal citizenship that demands their sacrifice.

The second way my approach differs from Brown's concerns the underlying regime of power and knowledge that the notion of sacrificial citizenship alerts us to. For Brown (2016: 3), this is primarily the inversion of freedom 'originally promised by neoliberalism'. By binding the individual 'to the well-being of the whole' and 'demanding its fealty and potential sacrifice' (Brown 2016: 4), neoliberalism acts as a form of false consciousness, as a mirror image of reality that promises freedom, but eventually delivers shackles that the subject willingly embraces. While sharing this analysis, my main focus lies with the biopolitical relationship at the heart of neoliberal sacrificial citizenship that frames the active killing or letting die of certain groups—be they Greek workers, European dispossessed, or undocumented migrants—as instrumental to advancing the well-being of society.

With the idea of the common good completely absorbed and exhausted by the notion of economic growth, preventing the arrival of undocumented migrants to Europe, reducing welfare provisions, and imposing harsh austerity measures is instrumental to free resources and wealth for the richest countries and the wealthiest strata of the population. The dispossessive rationality at the heart of sacrificial citizenship thus rests on a distinctive biopolitical logic. The killing or letting die of the weakest, the poor, and the migrant is an extreme form of dispossession, a sacrificial necessity required to enable the healthy and wealthy to survive and thrive in the market order.

The case of Greece is instructive in this regard. As Nobel prize-winning economist Paul Krugman (cited in Trumbo and Baxton 2016) observed: 'The drive for austerity [imposed upon Greece] was about using the crisis, not solving it.' The sacrifice demanded of the Greeks was not primarily aimed at rescuing Greece from default, but at saving European banks and the related neoliberal life of European market-compliant citizens. This sacrifice was enacted through a process of dispossession. As part of the bailout deal, Greece had to agree to a privatization memorandum which committed it to 'sell off €50 billion in public assets'—from airports to ports, from landscapes to service utilities such as railways and water supply networks—in order to raise cash to repay its debts (Rankin and Smith 2015). Privatization, the European Commission opined, is an effective way of reducing public debt and 'increasing the efficiency of companies' and 'the competitiveness of the economy' (European Commission 2015). This plan reflected the European belief of Greek guilt, which required Greece to renounce its material wealth to amend its sins, as well as the European sense of self-righteousness and entitlement, which required this wealth to be transferred to the 'healthy' core of Europe through a regime of dispossession by privatization.

As a result of the privatization process, Greece sold most of Piraeus (Greece's largest port) to Chinese state-owned company Cosco. Similarly, Greece's fourteen most profitable regional airports have been sold to German airport operator Fraport, majority-owned by the German state. Yet, the most controversial aspect of the memorandum concerns the privatization of water supply networks. Germany strongly pushed Greece to sell its water utilities precisely at a time when many European and in particular German cities, including Berlin, were 'bringing water services back under public control in frustration at rising prices and declining service delivery' (Mathiesen 2015; Trumbo and Baxton 2016).

The sacrifice demanded of the Greeks is even more startling in light of Germany's response to the 2008 financial crisis. In late 2008, Berlin launched 'an emergency bailout package of 480 billion euros for German banks', followed by 115 billion euros to strengthen companies with financial problems, and two stimulus packages worth €80 billion in total to relaunch the economy through investment in infrastructures, tax breaks, and business loans

(Bennhold 2008; *Spiegel* 2010). This 'unprecedented large-scale economic investment', supported by government labour subsidies aimed at avoiding redundancies, was highly successful and resulted in a steady growth (*Spiegel 2010*). Many scholars and public commentators (see, for instance, Mazzucato 2015) have argued that Athens would have required a similar investment strategy, accompanied by a series of structural reforms of the Greek economy. Instead, Germany—whose banks were the most exposed to Greek sovereign debt and were leveraged 32 to 1 (Lehman Brothers was leveraged 31 to 1 just before filing for bankruptcy and ushering a massive global financial crisis)—forced Greece to adopt a completely different and thoroughly neoliberal approach to the crisis based on austerity measures, which has had the effect of creating more debt and social devastation.

This double standard is a telling manifestation of a neoliberal citizenship that demands not just a collective sacrifice for the market but also and most importantly the sacrifice of those who fail to comply with and thrive in the neoliberal market order. This is expected for the sake of the market and those market-successful neoliberal citizens as part of a biopolitical rationality that frames the dispossessed, the indebted, the stateless, the poor, and the undocumented migrants as sacrificial on the altar of the metrics of economic value. The latter is the measure of the degree of humanity and protection that an individual or a group will be accorded. And if this individual or group is burdened by an unpayable and inexpiable debt, as in the case of Greece, their dispossession becomes a necessary sacrifice required for the restoration of the neoliberal order.

Conclusion

This chapter has explored the emergence of neoliberal citizenship as a process of creative destruction carried out by neoliberal capitalism through the skilful use of crises. Neoliberal citizenship is a new rationality of government that makes political subjectivity, the recognition of human dignity, and the degree of protection that an individual or a group are accorded conditional upon their economic value. Accordingly, neoliberal citizenship undermines traditional distinctions between citizens and non-citizens. The nominal status of being a citizen is no longer the necessary and sufficient condition of possibility for 'the right to have rights'. This argument, to be sure, does not mean that there was a golden age in which the nationally bounded universalism of citizenship was able to overcome the inequalities of class, race, and gender.

Rather, it suggests that these inequalities are being rewritten and amplified by a process of economization that has invested all spheres of social and political life. This process of economization is, to its normalized extreme, a process of sacralization of the market. The latter has become the foundational episteme and measure for the endowment of political subjectivity. The sacredness of life is now established by the foundational sacredness of the market.

This new configuration of citizenship transcends traditional national boundaries and brings together 'members' and 'strangers', 'insiders' and 'outsiders', nominal citizens and non-citizens alike by asking them to be resilient in the face of a market too complex to be grasped, and to withstand the hardship of their condition and bounce back. And yet, while bringing together debased European citizens of austerity, undocumented migrants, and impoverished Greeks, it also set these groups apart by pitting them against each other through a process of scapegoating instrumental to save the market from any responsibility. Neoliberal citizenship rests on a logic of sacrifice: we can all be sacrificed on the altar of the market, but those who experience the 'nakedness of being nothing but human' (Arendt 1973: 300) are more sacrificial than others. Indeed, we require the sacrifice of the poor, the weak, the stateless, and more broadly of those who fail to inscribe themselves and thrive in the mechanics of the market. The implicit assumption is that their demise, their annihilation, will make us wealthier and stronger. Neoliberal sacrificial citizenship thus crucially encompasses a biopolitical 'struggle for existence' (Foucault 2003: 80). In this neoliberal biopolitics, it is economic value that determines 'the differentiation of species, natural selection, and the survival of the fittest species' (Foucault 2003: 80).

The themes introduced in this chapter will be explored in greater depth in the remainder of the book. In particular, Chapter 3 looks at how states have been competing for 'valuable' wealthy foreigners through the offer of citizenship-by-investment schemes while at the same time endeavoured to securitize their borders to prevent the arrival of 'worthless' undocumented migrants. Chapter 4 further elaborates on the concept of emotional capital and shows how biopolitical rationalities of care and racism are a crucial component of neoliberal citizenship. Chapter 5 advances this analysis by considering how the biopolitics of the European refugee crisis is ultimately a bioeconomy of scarcity in which regimes of value are shaped by imaginaries of necessity. Chapters 6 and 7 elaborate on the 'mystique of complexity' in conjunction with neoliberalism's biopolitical economy of scarcity by exploring how neoliberal citizenship rests on an ultimate sacralization of the market. Chapter 8 focuses on the ongoing coronavirus crisis and shows how the category of sacrificial citizens has been expanded to include—beyond undocumented migrants, Greek workers, and debased citizens of austerity—elderly patients in care homes. The destruction of these lives, I will argue, is part and parcel of the bioeconomic rationality of neoliberal citizenship: the expression of a voracious neoliberalism that knows no boundaries in its appetite for destruction as a necessary 'creative' condition for rewriting citizenship in the sacred image of the market.

3
Citizenship for sale

Introduction

In October 2013, Malta amended its Citizenship Act to include the possibility of purchasing Maltese citizenship for a €650,000 fee. The goal of the scheme, called 'Individual Investor Programme', was to attract 'ultra-high net worth individuals and families worldwide' (Henley & Partners 2015a) interested in gaining the benefits of EU citizenship, namely, internal mobility (with the possibility to reside, work, and invest in any of the EU countries), consular protection, and 'visa-free travel to more than 160 countries in the world, including the USA' (Zenturo Ltd n.d.). The Maltese Government stated that the scheme would raise more than €30 million a year to be used for the economic development of the country. No longer confined to small Caribbean nations, the possibility of obtaining citizenship by investment (waiving residence, language, and other traditional requirements) has been recently offered by several EU Member States, including Cyprus, Bulgaria, and Romania. Numerous other states, such as Greece, Portugal, Spain, Italy, the United Kingdom, and the United States, have strengthened their offer of investment-based residency programmes. While not waiving all traditional requirements, these schemes constitute privileged and facilitated pathways for obtaining citizenship.

Although Malta is not the first country in Europe to offer citizenship by investment, it has been the first to explicitly introduce a 'fee' instead of the more politically and socially acceptable 'investment in the economy of the country'. This novelty, which is more of form than substance, has nonetheless sparked a heated national and European controversy which has placed citizenship- and residency-by-investment schemes in the spotlight. The main criticism is that by selling citizenship outright or making it easier to trade it for money, states are profaning one of the most sacred and foundational dimensions of a political community. In a strong speech at the European Parliament in January 2014, then Vice-President of the European Commission Viviane Reding (2014) emphatically stated: 'Citizenship must not be up for sale!' These events have

Neoliberal Citizenship. Luca Mavelli, Oxford University Press.
 DOI: 10.1093/oso/9780192857583.003.0003

triggered a lively, although still limited, academic debate (Dzankic 2012, 2015; Carrera 2014; Shachar and Baubock 2014; Shachar and Hirschl 2014; Tanasoca 2016; Parker 2017), which has mostly focused on a set of normative questions: Should citizenship be for sale? Does selling citizenship undermine traditional understandings of community and belonging? Does it weaken social solidarities? Is selling citizenship no less arbitrary than citizenship acquired through birth rights?

In this chapter, I depart from these questions and analyse how the proliferation of citizenship- and residency-by-investment schemes is one of the most brazen manifestations of the neoliberal transformation of citizenship. In particular, I advance three main arguments. First, to fully understand the importance and relevance of these schemes, the opening of 'global mobility corridors for the ultra-rich' (Barbulescu 2014: 15) must be explored in conjunction with the hardening of borders for refugees and undocumented migrants. Hence, the fact that at the end of 2016 Malta had sold 477 passports (Micallef 2017) should be analysed in conjunction with the fact that, in the same period (2014–2016), it granted refugee status to about 600 non-EU citizens (UNHCR 2017), whereas more than 12,000 undocumented migrants died in the attempt to cross the Mediterranean (IOM 2020). The existing literature has for the most part considered the selective openness of borders as a product of either the commodification of citizenship or of a country's labour demands, and the closure of borders as a manifestation of the securitization of migration. The result is that these phenomena have been explored largely independently. On the contrary, I contend that the selective openness and closure of borders is a manifestation of a neoliberal rationality of government that is rewriting the meaning of citizenship and belonging in neoliberal terms.

Second, existing research has failed to appreciate this connection because it rests on an understanding of neoliberalism as a change in the balance of power between states and markets in favour of the latter. This view reduces the neoliberalization of citizenship to commodification in its narrowest sense, that is, the possibility that citizenship may be traded for money. In this book, I build on a contending idea of neoliberalism as a process of *economization* or *marketization* which has been actively fostered by the state. Neoliberal economization disseminates the model of the market to all spheres of human activity, including the political domain, with the effect of turning states and individuals into entrepreneurial actors that attempt to maximize their value in economic and financial terms. This means that neoliberalism is a political rationality that states employ to govern the inclusion, exclusion, differential inclusion, and overall level of protection that citizens and foreigners are granted.

Third, in a regime of neoliberal citizenship the market value of existing citizens and migrants is not confined to their capacity to boost the economic growth and global competitiveness of the country but also the latter's *emotional* welfare. This means that the modes of belonging prompted by the neoliberalization of citizenship are not limited to the inclusion of 'the wealthy and the talented' and the exclusion of disenfranchised aliens, but comprise other phenomena such as the opening of 'humanitarian corridors' for particularly vulnerable refugees like the physically and mentally disabled Syrians in the wake of the death of Alan Kurdi. Neoliberal inclusion can also encompass the granting of citizenship to permanent residents or undocumented migrants who have distinguished themselves for important social merits, particularly when their actions have been the object of extensive media attention. These subjects, under certain circumstances, may be considered a relevant source of emotional capital which can boost the international reputation, moral standing, and self-understanding of the country.

The theoretical underpinning of my argument draws on a critical reading of neoliberalism which has its seminal systematization in the work of Michel Foucault and his notion of neoliberalism as a process of *economization* of state and society (Foucault 2008; see also Dardot and Laval 2013; Brown 2015). As Wendy Brown explains, economization means that 'neoliberal rationality disseminates *the model of the market* to all domains and activities—even where money is not an issue' (Brown 2015: 31, emphasis in original), with the effect that every sphere of life becomes informed by neoliberal logics of competition and inequality. It follows that individuals and states are turned into entrepreneurial actors competing against each in order to maximize their value.

Foucault (2008) and Foucauldian scholarship (particularly Brown 2015; see also Ong 2006b; Feher 2009, 2020; Bröckling 2011, 2015; Dardot and Laval 2013; Mezzadra and Neilson 2013) have mostly conceptualized this maximization of value in economic terms. Hence, state rationalities of inclusion and exclusion would be primarily informed by the goal of maximizing their stock of human, economic, and financial capital, whether embodied by affluent and talented migrants capable of investing and innovating or by skilled and unskilled migrants capable of satisfying labour market needs. Broadening this view, I argue that neoliberalism has not just prompted the construction of citizens as human, financial, or economic capital but also as a relevant source of emotional capital.

Hence, the approach I advance builds on, but also distances itself from, existing research on the neoliberalization of citizenship. As I mentioned in Chapter 1, it challenges the view that modern citizenship is increasingly shaped by 'universalizing [and contending] criteria of neoliberalism and human rights' (Ong 2006a: 499) and maintains that human rights and humanitarianism should not be considered independently from neoliberal rationalities of government. The fact that '[i]n recent decades, health-based claims have become an important part of citizenship rights in the West' (Ong 2006a: 504) does not mean that human rights and humanitarianism have acted as a bulwark (however partial) against neoliberal logics. Rather, the fact that a few thousand refugees have been offered protection whereas tens of thousands have been left to die in the Mediterranean and along other migratory routes or in overcrowded and dehumanizing camps is a function of their endowment of capital value or lack thereof. It is a function of their perceived capacity to enhance not just, and often not primarily, the human, financial, and economic capital of a country but also its emotional capital. Hence, what I am suggesting is that the logics and practices of human rights and humanitarianism have been colonized, at least partially, by neoliberal rationalities of value.

The discussion proceeds in four main steps. First, I introduce the current debate on citizenship-by-investment programmes and consider how it has been dominated by an overly limited focus on commodification in its narrowest sense, namely, the possibility that citizenship may be exchanged for money. Second, I discuss how the neoliberal transformation of citizenship needs to be understood in a broader dynamic of neoliberal economization of individuals and states which turns the former into the embodiment of multiple forms of capital for the latter. Third, I begin to consider how neoliberal economization has partially colonized the domains of human rights and humanitarianism. Fourth, I explore the resulting neoliberal political economy of belonging through a series of illustrations from the progressive and yet neoliberal 'social laboratory' of New Zealand.

1. The commodification of citizenship

In October 2013, Malta's decision to sell 1,800 passports—hence, Maltese and European citizenship—for a €650,000 fee prompted a heated European debate on 'citizenship for sale'. Following the protests of the European Union, Malta introduced a minimum (albeit, extremely loose) residency requirement in order to satisfy the principles of genuine connections and personal ties with the country. It also raised the total amount of the investment needed by requiring the purchase of property worth €350,000 and an investment in government bonds or shares of €150,000. These measures, however, have been generally perceived not to change that fact that Malta is de facto selling its citizenship. Malta is not the first European country to have undertaken this initiative. In May 2013, Cyprus launched its investor citizenship programme with two main goals: boosting the country's business environment and compensating those foreign investors who lost millions as a result of the March 2013 bailout (Dzankic 2015: 8). The latter imposed a bank deposit levy on uninsured deposits over €100,000, most of which were held by foreign citizens (primarily Russians) due to Cyprus' status as a tax haven.

Cyprus' scheme (now temporarily suspended as of November 2020 following reports of abuses) offered citizenship for an individual investment of €5 million—in government bonds, real estate, financial assets of Cypriot companies, bank deposits, purchase, creation or participation in Cypriot businesses or companies employing at least five Cypriot citizens—or for an individual investment of €2.5 million if part of a collective investment of at least €12.5 million (Dzankic 2015). For those foreign investors which had incurred losses of at least €3 million as result of the bailout deal, it was possible to deduct this amount from the total investment needed. Henley & Partners (2015b), a private citizenship planning firm in charge of marketing the scheme, advertised Cyprus' programme as top ranking 'in terms of Quality of Life, Visa Free Access, [and] Processing Time.' As Rainer Bauböck (2014a: 1) observes, 'the primary value of citizenship lies in the mobility rights attached to passports', hence the price of Cypriot and Maltese passports 'reflects the instrumental value of free movement rights attached to EU citizenship for the wealthy and mobile global elites.'

Bulgaria and Romania have also introduced citizenship-by-investment schemes that resemble the Cypriot one. They require an investment, rather than a fee, but differ on the residency requirement. Bulgaria stipulates that in order to be eligible for citizenship by investment, the successful candidate needs to have already been a permanent resident for at least a year (no language and culture requirements), whereas in the case of Romania the permanent residency requirement is at least four years and the applicant needs to be able to show proficiency in language and knowledge of the culture (Dzankic 2015). The residency-by-investment programmes offered by several countries, including Greece, France, Portugal, the UK, Australia, and the United States, grant residency for a financial investment (purchase of government bonds, shares, or loan capitals), purchase of property, transfer of capital, or establishment of a business that results in the creation of new jobs.

Moreover, in several European countries—such as the UK, Malta, Ireland, Italy, Belgium, the Netherlands, Spain, Portugal, France, and Greece—citizenship and/or residency-by-investment schemes are often offered in conjunction with favourable fiscal regimes. This offer has been taking place in a heightened regime of competition which has seen European countries undercutting each other to the effect that, as a recent report of the European Parliament noted, it has produced a 'race to the bottom' with regard to personal income taxes for the rich and mobile' (Trautvetter and Winkler 2019: 30). This competition has been further amplified by the exit of the UK from the European Union. The leading destination in Europe for the world's wealthiest, the UK is now facing harsh competition from its European neighbours which 'are slashing taxes and rolling out incentives to persuade the wealthy to relocate' (Clark 2019).

Overall, citizenship- and residency-by-investment schemes vary greatly in terms of the amounts needed, combination of requirements, and length of the investment, and several countries often offer them in conjunction with privileged fiscal regimes. Nonetheless, the general feature of these programmes is that although they do not waive all traditional citizenship requirements, they generally reduce some of them and allow for more expedited procedures. They thus constitute privileged and facilitated routes for obtaining citizenship.

According to Ayelet Shachar and Ran Hirschl, these developments represent, to varying degrees, a vivid instantiation of an ongoing process of commodification. These 'cash-for-passports' programmes, they argue, are 'the sale and barter of membership goods in exchange for ... a large stack of cash' (Shachar and Hirschl 2014: 234). They are a product of '[r]apid processes of market expansionism' that 'have now reached what for many is the most sacrosanct non-market good: membership in a political community' (Shachar and Hirschl 2014: 234). This view is shared by several scholars. For Peter Spiro (2014: 9), '[t]he emerging market for citizenship literally commodifies the status' and is 'a manifestation of citizenship that is already being hollowed out.' David Owen (2014: 31) argues that these programmes are 'blatant examples of the commodification of citizenship' which, according to Jelena Dzankic (2014: 18), are diluting its value 'to a tradable commodity, voiding it of the sense of rights and duties and undermining citizens' solidarity.' For Rainer Bauböck (2014b: 19), the transformation of citizenship 'into a global commodity' is turning citizens from 'stakeholders' with political, social, moral and affective interests in the political community (Bauböck 2009) into 'stockholders', that is, citizen-investors, whose interest in the polity is purely instrumental and of an economic or financial nature (Magni Berton 2014).

This problem was raised by the Vice-President of the European Commission, Viviane Reding in a 2014 speech at the European Parliament. The Maltese sale of citizenship, she argued, threatens to undermine the very notion of belonging to the EU, which should be based on 'personal ties' rather than 'on the size of someone's wallet or bank account' (Reding 2014). For this reason, Reding concluded, citizenship should not be treated as a 'tradable commodity' with 'a price tag on it'. In a similar vein, US Senator Dianne Feinstein (CIS 2015) stated that the EB-5 Immigrant Investor Program—a residency-by-investment programme that requires an investment of at least US$500,000 and the creation or preservation of '10 permanent full-time jobs for qualified U.S. workers'—is akin to commodifying citizenship as it puts investors 'and their direct family on a special path' that is denied to ordinary migrants. According to Feinstein (CIS 2015), this programme sends the wrong message as '[i]t says that American citizenship is for sale, and that's not what our country stands for.'

Unease with the possibility of 'purchasing citizenship' does not stem from the fact that it violates a fundamental principle of equality and justice—indeed, 'the common rules of ius sanguinis, ius soli or residence-based naturalisation' are no less arbitrary (Bauböck 2014a: 2)—but that it replaces the political criteria of membership with economic ones. Citizenship should be about political relations and participation, equality, commitment and mutual solidarity, shared life, and daily engagement in the public sphere (Bauböck 2014b; Ochoa 2014; Shachar 2014). Conversely, citizenship for sale is about economic calculation, individual management of risk, and the strategization of one's own life opportunities. This economic rationality undermines political and social commitments, 'corrupts democracy' and risks 'tear[ing] down a wall of protection that keeps social class from becoming, once again, a formal marker of inequality of citizenship rights and status' (Bauböck 2014b: 20). For these reasons, it is contended, there is a substantial difference between commodifying citizenship by '[p]lacing a price tag' on it and 'selectively focusing on the extraordinary talent and track record of those entering the country through designated skills-based, talent-for-citizenship exchanges' (Shachar and Hirschl 2014: 234; see also Parker 2017: 345). The latter instance encompasses two possibilities: the immigration point system and discretionary naturalization.

The immigration point system evaluates particularly talented and highly skilled migrants on the basis of a series of parameters aimed at ascertaining their potential contribution to the economic development of the country. This pathway to residency, which stands for an assessment of the immigrant's human capital, is offered by several countries, including Canada, Australia,

New Zealand, the United States, and the United Kingdom. Discretionary naturalization, on the other hand, refers to the prerogative of most nation-states to discretionarily grant citizenship on the basis of national interest to individuals who have provided or may provide an exceptional contribution to the country in the fields of science, arts, sport, economy, culture, media, public service and, more generally, to those who have contributed to advancing its international status. In this case, one's human capital becomes a condition not just for residency, but for citizenship. Shachar and Hirschl (2014) maintain that a fundamental distinction should be drawn between capital and human capital contributions. Whereas the former epitomizes a process of economic commodification of citizenship, the latter concerns a political decision about the meaning, identity, and composition of the community.

This attempt to draw a clear-cut divide between the *political* and *economic* logics of citizenship has received two main criticisms. First, it relies on an idealistic understanding which overstates the extent to which citizenship may be equated to political participation (Kochenov 2014) and neglects how citizenship has already been hollowed out by the forces of globalization (Spiro 2014). Second, it overlooks how schemes designed to attract human capital and those designed to attract capital may be the expression of the same neoliberal citizenship regime which aims to admit 'only those who can make an important [economic] contribution' and 'immobilise the less well-off individuals' (Barbulescu 2014: 15) by trading 'access to citizenship for forms of capital (economic, cultural, political, etc.)' held by 'foreign millionaires ... or skilled workers in medical, finance or IT sectors' (Owen 2014: 31). A third criticism that I wish to raise is that this argument neglects how the blurring of the political and the economic logics of citizenship—which I will explore in Section 2 as a process of *economization* of the political logic of citizenship—is contributing to blurring the boundary between citizenship and residency. Citizenship is becoming increasingly 'disarticulated' (Mezzadra and Neilson 2013) with the effect that, for instance, traditional rights associated with citizenship may be granted to permanent residents and denied to citizens. The UK offers an interesting illustration of this argument.

Despite lacking a citizenship-by-investment programme, the UK has acted as a magnet for the world's wealthiest and continues to outrank countries such as Malta and Cyprus. Currently, there are almost 10,000 UHNWIs in the UK (ultra high-net-worth individuals whose individual assets exceed US$30 million), a significant proportion of whom are Russian, Chinese, and Middle Eastern billionaires (Knight Frank Wealth Report 2017). Worldwide, London is the city with the highest number of UHNWIs (4,750) and the second highest number of HNWIs (370,000; these are individuals with financial assets of at least US$1m) (Knight Frank Wealth Report 2017). According to Knight Frank (2017), a real estate consultancy, the exit of the UK from the EU 'will not result in an outflow of wealthy individuals from the UK; rather, it will mean that existing HNWIs will be more likely to remain and indeed to be joined by a growing list of new arrivals'

What makes the UK the most attractive destination for UHNWIs in Europe and one of the most attractive in the world is a combination of political stability, limited taxation on wealth, and a flexible labour market. Most of the UK's foreign UHNWIs and HNWIs have benefited from the Tier 1 Investor Visa, a residency-by-investment programme which enables individuals who invest '£2,000,000 or more in the UK' to apply for temporary residency first, and then for permanent residency after three years for an investment of £5 million, or after two years for an investment of £10 million (GOV.UK nd). This scheme allows wealthy foreigners to bring their spouse. This possibility is currently denied to British citizens who earn less than £18,600 a year and are married to non-UK citizens.

This norm, which endows wealthy foreigners with more rights than British citizens, is estimated to have affected thousands of families, including 15,000 children who have been denied the opportunity to live with both parents (Travis 2017). It was introduced in 2012 in order to reduce the possibility that social welfare benefits may be claimed and as part of a wider strategy of the Conservative government to 'reduce net migration from the hundreds of thousands to the tens of thousands' a year, as then Home Secretary and later Prime Minister Theresa May stated in 2010 (May 2010). The message is clear and, if anything, has become even clearer in the aftermath of the Brexit referendum: those 'who contribute wealth' to the UK 'are welcome'; those 'who come to the country and consume [its] wealth' are not (Britain International Trade Secretary Liam Fox, cited in Stone 2016), irrespective of whether or not they are British citizens. This case may suggest that what matters in the neoliberal political economy of belonging is the economic value of citizens /residents.

However, the case is more complex. Eleonore Kofman and Helena Wray (2013: 1) have shown that the cost–benefit calculations of the government which prompted the £18,600 minimum income requirement for family reunifications failed to take into account that 'single people are more likely to claim benefits than those living with a partner' and neglected 'the advice of the Migration Advisory Committee' by considering only 'the cost of services to migrants but not their overall economic contribution.' The result, they argue, is that 'the Government overestimated the negative impact of migrants', with the effect that this policy, rather than contribute to the country's wealth, may cost up to £850 million over ten years (Kofman and Wray 2013: 1). This argument suggests that the minimum income requirement for non-UK family members may have been primarily motivated by the desire to bring immigration numbers down even if this entails an economic cost. Hence, this norm indicates an evaluation of non-UK spouses more in terms of their *political/emotional impact* than potential cost–benefit contribution.

The arguments advanced in this section suggest two provisional conclusions. First, citizenship- and residency-by-investment programmes are not just the instantiation of a process of neoliberal commodification, but part of a broader transformation of traditional forms of belonging along neoliberal lines that blurs the line between: (a) political and economic logics of citizenship, and (b) citizens and wealthy/talented foreign residents. Second, neoliberal governmental rationalities increasingly prompt states to evaluate, assess, and include/exclude migrants according to their endowment of economic, financial, cultural, and—crucially—*emotional* capital. The theoretical underpinnings of this latter argument will be considered in the next two sections by exploring how neoliberalism encompasses a process of economization that prompts individuals and states to maximize their capital value even in those areas where money is not directly at stake and even if this may imply an economic cost.

2. The economization of individuals and states

According to Pierre Dardot and Christian Laval (2013: 7), dominant critical readings of neoliberalism have been characterized by a fundamental 'diagnostic error', namely, interpreting it as an ideology and economy policy which rests on an understanding of the market 'as a natural reality'. This 'naturalist ontology' (Dardot and Laval 2013: 7, 11–16) has been reinforced by a Marxist perspective which interprets neoliberalism as a progressive 'retreat' or 'end of politics' and 'domination of the market' (see Lemke 2003: 177) or, as Susan Strange (1996: 4) once put it, as a condition in which '[w]here states were once the masters of markets, now it is the markets which, on many crucial issues, are the masters over the governments of states.' In his 1978–79 lectures at the Collège de France, Michel Foucault seminally questioned this mainstream understanding of neoliberalism as an ideology and economic policy which has prompted a shift in the balance of power between states and markets and engendered 'a process of general commodification of social relations' (Duménil and Lévy, cited in Dardot and Laval 2013: 13).

Building on, advancing, and eventually distancing himself from the work of scholars such as Karl Marx and Karl Polanyi, Foucault (2008: 242, 120–34) argues that neoliberalism is not just a political ideology, an economic policy, and a regime of governance, but a political rationality of government based on the 'economization' of state and society. This is the application of the logic of the market—and, particularly, the principle of competition—to all spheres of human existence. For this reason, Foucault (2008: 120, 142–3) maintains, neoliberalism cannot be reduced to the 'retreat' of the state and commodification of all dimensions of life, but entails a fundamental process of *transformation* of all social units—from the individual, to society, to the state—to make them fit for the competitive neoliberal order.

This means that, as Polanyi (cited in Dardot and Laval 2013: 49) famously argued, the market is 'not a method to achieve a thing', it is 'the thing to be achieved'. Foucault (2008: 120–1) makes this perspective his own and maintains that in neoliberalism the market is not a natural entity that spontaneously emerges from the 'shrinking' of the state: it is a regime to be established that requires an active intervention of the state or, as he describes it, an 'active governmentality'. According to Foucault (2008: 147) then, 'what is sought [in neoliberalism] is not a society subject to the commodity-effect, but a society subject to the dynamic of competition. Not a supermarket society, but an enterprise society. The *homo oeconomicus* sought after is not the man of exchange or man the consumer; he is the man of enterprise and production.'

Foucault's fascination for paradox and the subversion of the terms of the ordinary lead him to an overly narrow understanding of commodification and to dismiss too quickly its relevance and implications for the neoliberal order (as I shall discuss in Chapter 6, commodification plays a crucial role in the neoliberal sacralization of the market). Nonetheless, his intuition that neoliberalism cannot be reduced to commodification but entails a fundamental process of entrepreneurialization remains seminal and relevant. Hence, his view can be re-calibrated by considering that neoliberal commodification needs to be understood in a broader process of economization that encompasses the neoliberal construction of entrepreneurial subjects, societies, and states fit for the market.

To better appreciate this argument, it is useful to briefly consider how Foucault understands the difference between liberalism and neoliberalism.

Classical liberalism was based on the idea that the market obeys 'natural' and 'spontaneous' mechanisms which transcend the capacity of governments to fully comprehend them. These mechanisms contribute to the simultaneous maximization of individual and collective value. Adam Smith's *invisible hand*—the idea that the interests of society are best served by the pursuit of self-interest by rational individual agents in a market free from state intervention—is the paradigmatic illustration of this liberal perspective (Foucault 2008: 278–9). For Foucault, this idea promotes an important transformation in the meaning and scope of sovereign power. Since the market is a self-organizing entity capable of maximizing individual and collective interests, sovereign power should not interfere with its functioning (Foucault 2008: 28–9). Liberalism thus establishes a clear demarcation between the political sphere, inhabited by *homines politici* concerned with rights and the pursuit of the common good, and the economic sphere, inhabited by *homines oeconomici* concerned with the pursuit of their individual interests through 'truck, barter and exchange' in the marketplace (Smith 1957 [1776]: 12).

Foucault argues that neoliberalism undermines the liberal divide between politics and economics through two main avenues. First, it pushes to an extreme the idea that the market is the best mechanism to promote individual and collective growth and the efficient allocation of goods and services. It therefore encourages the application of market mechanisms to all spheres of human activity, including politics, family, and education. Second, neoliberalism advances the idea that the market is not a natural and discrete environment based on the dynamics of exchange but an artificial and fragile system of relations centred on the logics of competition that requires constant political and social intervention to ensure its existence and functioning. For Foucault (2008: 121), in the neoliberal order, 'one must govern for the market, rather than because of the market.'

Foucault develops his argument through a critical reading of the German *ordoliberal* tradition which, in his view, has crucially shaped existing neoliberal forms (Foucault 2008: 110–20, 142, 149; Cerny 2016: 7). This school of thought, Dardot and Laval (2013: ch. 3) explain, ascribes a fundamental role to the state for the establishment and preservation of the neoliberal order. It rests on a critical distinction between 'economic order' and 'order of the economy' in which the latter—the active involvement of the state—is deemed essential for achieving the former—the 'economization' of state and society, namely, the application of the logic of the market, and particularly the principle of competition, to all domains of life (Dardot and Laval 2013: 87).

As Philip Cerny (2016: 5–7) observes, in abstract terms the ordoliberal idea that 'markets do not arise spontaneously but are created and institutionalised by the state'—which is also the institution that preserves their conditions of existence—challenges the more famous 'quasi-laissez faire version of [neoliberalism of] the Chicago School.' The latter, popularized by scholars such as Milton Friedman and politicians like Thatcher in the UK and Reagan in the USA, advocates the 'rolling back' of the state in order to let the 'spontaneous' order of the market emerge. In practical terms, however, *ordoliberal* neoliberalism and *laissez faire* neoliberalism have mutually supported each other (Cerny 2016: 9). Laissez faire neoliberalism has constituted the ideological legitimation of an ordo-neoliberalism which has seen the state crucially establishing, and being transformed by, the neoliberal order (Cerny 2016: 10–11).

This perspective challenges mainstream readings of neoliberalism as deregulation and the 'rolling back of the state'. It highlights how a 'strong', 'interventionist', and 'entrepreneurial' state that promotes competition by attracting investments, dismantling labour protections, scaling down the welfare state, privatizing public goods and services, saving the market from its recurrent failures, and *constructing neoliberal entrepreneurial citizens*—that is, citizens compliant with 'neoliberal reason'—has been essential for ensuring the survival and thriving of neoliberalism (Foucault 2008; Sparke 2006; Peck, Theodore, and Brenner 2009; Brown 2015; Chandler and Reid 2016). A central implication of this neoliberal transformation is that investments, speculation, and risk are no longer confined to the market (as a discreet environment), but become general orientations of individuals and states alike. Neoliberalism can therefore be understood as a 'principle of formalization' that engenders the 'economization' of individuals and states (Foucault 2008: 120, 242): the competitive logic of the market becomes the all-encompassing framework of meanings and significations that reshape their sense and purpose.

This neoliberal process of economization has two main implications. First, *homo oeconomicus*—the entrepreneurial self—is no longer confined to the sphere of the market as in classical liberalism, but occupies all spheres of human existence. Neoliberalism marks the birth of individuals as capital (for themselves and for others) whose lives become speculative enterprises aimed at maximizing their own capital value through the logics of competition, accumulation, and strategic positioning (Brown 2015: 17). Second, the state progressively relinquishes its social and welfare functions to turn into an 'entrepreneurial' or 'competition state', namely, one primarily concerned with 'maintaining and promoting competitiveness in a world marketplace' and 'ensuring that citizens keep up with the multiple pressures and demands of that increasingly integrated and interdependent political, economical and social ecosystem' (Cerny 2010: 6).

These two processes are mutually reinforcing. Neoliberal entrepreneurial citizens increasingly perceive themselves as human capital to be invested in education, training, professional development, networking, partnering, self-promotion, showcasing, travelling, social and personal relationships in order to improve their status, wealth, well-being, strategic opportunities, career options, employability, and marketability. According to Wendy Brown (2016), thinking of and acting over oneself as capital to be invested in order to enhance the capital value of the country is a social imperative and an essential requirement of a citizenship turned 'sacrificial', namely, one in which citizens are expected to sacrifice themselves for the health and wealth of the nation. Yet, as we saw in Chapter 2, the sacrificial nature of citizenship also rests on the fact that citizens are encouraged to demand the sacrifice of the less productive and economically costly members of society. Citizenship as the possibility of inclusion and protection thus becomes 'wholly conditional upon the ability to exchange something of sufficient market value' (Somers 2011: 26). That is, it becomes a function of the neoliberal political economy of belonging: a political rationality of government that enthrones the market as the fundamental and essential measure of the value and worth of citizenship.

It follows that, when it comes to the rationalities of inclusion, exclusion, and protection of citizens and non-citizens, the entrepreneurial state emerging from the process of economization will approach them as 'living resources that may be managed and harnessed' for economic purposes (Ong 2006b: 6) and evaluate them accordingly. Neoliberal economized states will include 'individuals who possess human capital or expertise [that] are highly valued' and exclude or marginalize those 'who are judged not to have such tradable competence or potential' (Ong 2006b: 7). For Ong, these rationalities of inclusion and exclusion are part of a neoliberal transformation in which citizenship is no longer the inescapable condition of possibility for the 'the right to have rights'. While this continues to be the case 'for asylum seekers and refugees for whom gaining citizenship in a host country is the most basic step towards being recognized as modern human beings', this no longer applies to a cosmopolitan elite of wealthy, educated and entrepreneurial individuals (Ong 2006b: 15). As Ong remarks:

> Expatriate talents constitute a form of movable entitlement [with or] without formal citizenship. Citizens who are deemed too complacent or lacking in neoliberal potential may be treated as less-worthy subjects. Low-skilled citizens and migrants ... are constructed as excludable populations in transit, shuttled in and out of zones of growth.... [C]ertain rights and benefits are distributed to the bearers of marketable talents and denied to those who are judged to lack such capacity or potential.
>
> (Ong 2006b: 16)

The beneficiaries of citizens-by-investment schemes should be considered, together with 'a class of global professionals armed with "world-class credentials"', as the expression of 'a new of form of global ranking based on human capital, mobility and risk-taking' (Ong 2006b: 154). Their capital should not be reduced to their cash, but encompasses their capacity to increase the cultural, human, and economic capital of the country, whether financially or through the (direct or indirect) creation of enterprises and jobs. As Maltese Justice Minister Owen Bonnici stated in 2016, the fact that 300 high net worth families have become part of Maltese society should be a source of pride because these people 'are successful ... lead lifestyles we can only imagine ... [and have] links we could not even dream of' (*Malta Independent* 2016). In a pervasive process of neoliberal economization that penetrates all aspects of human existence and subjects them to logics of competition, the value of these citizens is not merely financial, but it is also cultural as they represent a role model we should all look up to: the successful networked neoliberal entrepreneurial subject.

This argument challenges those perspectives (such as Shachar and Hirschl 2014 and Parker 2017) which draw a substantial distinction between citizenship in exchange for *capital* and citizenship in exchange for *human capital.* These views fail to recognize that the neoliberal transformation of citizenship may be at stake even when citizenship is not traded for cash, that is, even when it is not blatantly commodified in the traditional and narrower sense of the term. These views rest on an untenable distinction between capital and human capital that neglects how the inclusion of 'the wealthy' on the one hand and 'the talented' on the other is governed by the same neoliberal rationality of value. Yet, how pervasive is this neoliberal rationality and to what extent does it affect every instance of citizenship and related forms of inclusion, protection, and belonging?

3. The pervasiveness of neoliberalism

Ong argues that the neoliberal transformation of citizenship should not be considered a totalizing governmental rationality which has gone unchallenged. Several regimes of 'exception' variously grounded in 'religion ..., feminism, humanitarianism and other schemes of virtue' articulate contending views of citizenship through what she describes as, drawing on Collier and Lakoff, a 'counterpolitics of sheer life', namely, the deployment of forms of protection in the name of a shared humanity and global solidarity (Ong 2006a: 504). This 'counterpolitics', she suggests, has become an important source of entitlement for citizenship and citizenship-like rights and constitutes a relevant exception and challenge to neoliberal schemes of valuation and modes of belonging.

While Ong's argument that neoliberalism should not be regarded as the only rationality that shapes citizenship and the politics of belonging is certainly relevant, it overlooks how forms of inclusion based on human rights, shared humanity, and common solidarity may have been economized—that is, colonized and corrupted by neoliberalism, a rationality of government that 'invariably exists in an essentially parasitical relationship with those extant social formations with which it has an antagonistic relationship' (Peck, Theodore, and Brenner 2009: 96). This argument suggests that modes of inclusion seemingly based on human rights and shared solidarities may be the expression of neoliberal rationalities that value prospective citizens for their embodiment of moral or emotional capital.

To consider this argument, it is necessary to return to the concept of 'economization', particularly in the formulation advanced by Wendy Brown as the dissemination of 'the model of the market to all domains and activities—even where money is not an issue' (2015: 31). Economization, she emphasizes, differs from monetization. The fact that all spheres of life become informed by the logic of the market means that individuals and states alike will act according to logics of competition, strategic positioning, and maximization of value even in those instances when money may not directly or may only indirectly be at stake.

Brown (2016: 31) considers how dating through online dating companies is increasingly approached as an investment which entails targeting the right person through a careful process of evaluation and screening to maximize 'return on investment of affect'. The purpose of dating thus becomes generating an emotional (rather than financial) return. Similarly, a Facebook user may publish pictures or post comments not primarily to share their life experiences, but to accumulate 'likes' to improve their social ranking and benchmarking,[1] while the Twitter 'hashtag activist' may carry out their digital protest as a means of self-promotion. These are all instances of economization (of mating and socialization) in which entrepreneurial subjects enact strategies of capital enhancement that are not directly measurable in terms of monetization or economic growth.

In other cases, the economization of 'heretofore noneconomic domains activities' such as higher education and charitable work may still take place, even if the possibility of a monetary gain is at best an indirect and probabilistic one (Brown 2015: 31). Thus, in the neoliberal academia, university students are increasingly approaching knowledge not as a journey of discovery or process of transformation of the self, but as a purely instrumental endeavour which may result in a better social status and salary (Mavelli 2014). Likewise, charitable volunteer work may become the opportunity to strengthen one's CV, gain social approval, and improve one's chances of employment, rather than the possibility to genuinely connect with and help others (Brown 2015: 31).

According to Brown (2015: 10), the neoliberal rationalities that inform entrepreneurial subjects—namely, 'improving and leveraging' their 'competitive positioning and ... enhancing [their] ... monetary and nonmonetary portfolio value across all ... endeavours and venues'—are also 'the mandates, and hence the orientations, contouring the projects of neoliberalized states.' However, despite this homology between entrepreneurial individuals and states, Brown ultimately regards the neoliberal state as fundamentally concerned with economic growth. In line with economic theorists of the 'competition state' (see, for instance, Cerny 1997, 2010; Fougner 2006), she focuses on how the state has progressively relinquished or significantly scaled down its welfare functions and turned into what Cerny (quoted in Fougner 2006: 167) describes as 'a market player, that shapes its policies to promote, control, and maximise returns from market forces in an international setting.'

This argument highlights a limit of existing research on the neoliberalization of citizenship. This literature does not consider that neoliberal economization may prompt states to behave like entrepreneurial subjects trying to maximize not just their economic growth, but their non-monetary and non-economic capital value. States may approach prospective or existing citizens as capital which enhances their cultural, emotional, and reputational value. While the existing scholarship on citizenship- and residency-by-investment programmes

[1] As effectively portrayed in the not-so-alternative reality of the episode 'Nosedive' of the television series 'Black Mirror' (21 October 2016).

has partially analysed how the granting of citizenship to artists or athletes playing for national teams may be instrumental to 'enhance the collective pride, international reputation, and competitive standing of the political community' (Shachar and Hirschl 2014: 253), it has failed to appreciate that this phenomenon is governed by the same neoliberal rationality of citizenship- and residency-by-investment schemes. In different ways, both fields of research have focused on 'the wealthy and the talented' and neglected the extent to which forms of inclusion apparently based on human rights and shared solidarities—such as the humanitarian corridors for refugees—may also be the expression of a neoliberal rationality that values prospective citizens for their embodiment of moral or emotional capital.

Three main considerations follow. First, states' endeavours to attract talented and wealthy individuals are not a product of the retreat of the state and the domination of the market. Rather, these efforts are the expression of entrepreneurial states which treat the granting of citizenship as an investment aimed at attracting wealthy and talented individuals in order to strengthen the economic and financial competitiveness of the country.

Second, the fact that entrepreneurial states increasingly approach existing and prospective members as economic resources indicates that membership in a political community is no longer solely a function of one's own legal status (citizen, resident, refugee, asylum seeker, etc.), but of one's own endowment of human, economic, and financial capital. This means that neoliberalism is progressively blurring the boundary between citizens and residents and deconstructing the category of citizenship to the effect that it is no longer the necessary and sufficient condition of possibility for 'the right to have rights'.

Third, the neoliberal process of economization indicates that states will strive to maximize their capital value not just in economic and financial terms, but also in emotional and reputational terms, that is, even in those areas in which money is not at stake. States may approach prospective and existing citizens not just as human, economic, and financial capital, but also as a source of emotional, moral, and reputational value. This emotional value may not be confined to 'the talented and the brightest' but also to refugees and victims in need. This means that neoliberalism does not simply undermine the principles of reciprocity, fairness, equality, mutual participation, and solidarity that should inform political forms of citizenship by replacing these principles with economic ones. Rather, neoliberalism *rewrites* these principles in economic terms.

This argument, to be sure, differs from the Marxist critique that these principles reflect an overly *idealized* and *romantic* understanding of citizenship which neglects how the latter is 'strategically created, endorsed, and valorized by the collective membership of a national community or the political elites that claim to represent them' in order to 'cater to the particular historical context, political agendas, and economic needs of nation-states' (Bauder 2014: 320). My contention is not that these principles are the instantiation of a 'false consciousness' produced by states which have been 'captured' by the ruling economic and financial elites. Rather, I contend that the principles of reciprocity, fairness, equality, mutual participation, and solidarity which in theory underpin the status and institution of citizenship have been 'economized', that is, shaped from within by the economic logics of states which have embraced neoliberalism as a governmental rationality. The neoliberal economization of citizenship is thus contributing to the emergence of a distinctive neoliberal political economy of belonging. To introduce the contours of this emerging neoliberal belonging, Section 4 discusses a series of illustrations from New Zealand before returning the focus to Europe.

The case of New Zealand is particularly interesting because '[d]uring significant periods of its modern history, New Zealand has been hailed as the "social laboratory of the world"' (McClintock 1998: 497). The image of a robust welfare state that takes care of its people persists, despite three decades of neoliberal policies. These policies have transformed a country once at the forefront of welfare social reforms and workers' rights which championed state intervention into a significantly deregulated and privatized economy. On many fronts—from the dismantlement of labour rights, to regressive taxation, the scaling down of welfare provisions, the impoverishment of large sectors of the population, and the growing inequality—New Zealand has embraced neoliberalism all the way down (Marcetic 2017). With due caution, the cognitive dissonance at the heart of New Zealand's national narrative is reminiscent of that experienced by a European Union which, while priding itself as the land of 'human dignity, freedom, democracy, equality, the rule of law and respect for human rights' (Article 2 of the Treaty on European Union), has allowed thousands of undocumented migrants to drown in the Mediterranean, impoverished hundreds of thousands through austerity policies, and plunged Greece into a dramatic recession with a quarter of the population unemployed and almost half below the poverty line.

The case of New Zealand highlights the global reach and pernicious penetration of neoliberal rationalities into the logics and practices of citizenship in a polity characterized by a self-understanding grounded in collective solidarity and the alleged rejection of the market as a totalizing rationality. Contrary to the United States, where neoliberalism has become an accepted and almost uncontested dimension of the country's identity, New Zealand and Europe have seemingly resisted neoliberalism's onslaught by retrenching into the comforting narratives of the 'social laboratory' and the 'social model'. This has prompted resilient neoliberal rationalities to adapt, conceal, and disguise themselves in seemingly 'antagonistic … social formations' (Peck, Theodore, and Brenner 2009: 96), such as New Zealand's humanitarian discourses and practices that will be explored in Section 4. As will become clear in the following chapters, these discourses and practices, and the overall approach to citizenship as a regime governed by rationalities of value, bear striking similarities with logics, dynamics, and practices that we will observe in the European context. The case of New Zealand, therefore, offers crucial insights into the pervasiveness of the neoliberalization of citizenship in Europe.

4. Neoliberal belonging

In January 2017 it was revealed that German-born US billionaire Peter Thiel, the co-founder of Paypal, had been granted New Zealand citizenship in 2011. This news sparked controversy because Thiel did not meet the requirement for citizenship: he was not born in New Zealand, had not spent 70 per cent of the previous five years in the country (only visited it six times for short periods), and had not been granted refugee status. While New Zealand does not have a citizenship-by-investment scheme, its Citizenship Act includes the provision that 'the Minister [of Internal Affairs] may authorise the grant of New Zealand citizenship to any person … if … [deemed] in the public interest because of exceptional circumstances of a humanitarian or other nature relating to the applicant' (New Zealand Citizenship Act 1997). As the 145-page file on his citizenship application explains, Thiel was granted citizenship because of 'exceptional circumstances' related to 'his skills as an entrepreneur and his philanthropy', which included having donated NZ$1m to the Christchurch earthquake relief fund, being involved in a series of business ventures in New Zealand, and being committed to 'contribut[ing] to the existing entrepreneurial environment and further development of the venture capital market in New Zealand' (cited in Ainge Roy 2017). These factors, the document concludes, make Thiel's citizenship potentially beneficial for New Zealanders and for the country.

This case cannot be grasped from a perspective that draws a sharp distinction between schemes designed to attract capital and schemes designed to attract human capital, and that reduces the former to the 'prostitution' of citizenship (Parker 2017: 345). Thiel was capable of 'buying' his way in the country through a 'generous donation' even in the absence of a citizenship-by-investment scheme. Nonetheless, his contribution cannot be reduced to just one of 'cash', given that he already had a series of business ventures in the country (which had contributed to creating jobs), although these investments pre-date the granting of citizenship, which was therefore not strictly necessary for the country to be able to benefit from his investments. Thiel's story suggests that citizenship-by-investment programmes are only one manifestation—certainly one of the most visible and controversial—of a process of neoliberal transformation of belonging in which logics of commodification are part of a broader neoliberal entrepreneurial rationality that prompts states to assess, evaluate, and include/exclude migrants according to their multiple capital endowments.

From this perspective, the governmental rationalities behind Thiel's citizenship are not dissimilar from those informing schemes aimed at attracting human capital, such as the 2017 'Looksee' initiative launched by Wellington Regional Economic Development Agency (WREDA). This scheme invited 'the best and the brightest' from across the world (by paying their flight, accommodation, and sightseeing) to fill 100 highly qualified tech jobs in Wellington and encourage them to settle 'in a place with a lifestyle you never thought possible.' This scheme is also an expression of an underlying logic of commodification *even if* citizenship/residency is not being traded for cash but for human capital. This means that commodification is not exclusive to cash-for-passports programmes. Yet, the Thiel and the WREDA cases also suggest that what is at stake is not just a process of exchange epitomized by the commodification of citizenship and residency, but a broader redefinition of the meaning of belonging in which ideals of reciprocity, fairness, equality, and solidarity are reconfigured in economic terms.

A particularly interesting illustration of this dynamic is the case of Dimitri Leemans, a Belgian mathematics professor based at the University of Auckland who, in February 2016, had his 13-year-old autistic stepson denied residency on the grounds that he would constitute an unduly heavy burden for New Zealand's welfare system. Immigration New Zealand (cited in Ainge Roy 2016) explained that 'All migrants are required to have an acceptable standard of health so as not to impose undue costs and/or demands on New Zealand's health and/or special education services.' The professor, winner of several national awards, received numerous statements of support and solidarity from his peers. They are worth quoting in full.

> Astrid an Huef, president of the New Zealand Mathematics Society, said the departure of 'an outstanding mathematician' like Leemans would be 'a great loss for us and New Zealand.' 'The New Zealand mathematics community deeply regrets that we are losing our valued and talented colleague, Dimitri Leemans, under such sad circumstances. We have benefited greatly from his research expertise and teaching excellence.' University of Auckland vice-chancellor Stuart McCutcheon said Leemans was 'an example of the outstanding young academics we must have at the University of Auckland if we are to maintain our premier world ranking.'
>
> (cited in Ainge Roy 2016)

What emerges from these statements is not solidarity with the professor *and his stepson* for the fact that a child had been denied the right to stay due to a neurodevelopmental condition; it is not solidarity in the name of compassion, justice, universal dignity, shared humanity, the right to emigrate for people with disabilities, and against an accounting logic that objectifies individuals as a bundle of costs and benefits and excludes those who are considered to be lacking in human capital and to be a burden to the health and education system. Solidarity was in the name of the fact that, as a result of this decision, New Zealand was losing a 'valued and talented colleague', an 'outstanding young academic' who had contributed to the international competitiveness of the University and the country. Solidarity was primarily grounded in an instrumental economic rationality which has as its primary concern the 'value' of the academic as a measure of his contribution to the value, competitiveness, and ranking of the university and the country, and the fact that New Zealand was losing valuable human capital which would negatively affect its 'growth'. Solidarity was completely 'economized' (see Brown 2015: 22, 2016: 3).

This case may suggest that in a regime of neoliberal citizenship people with illnesses and disabilities will always be considered a burden and thus be excluded. After all, according to Nobel laureate Gary Becker (2011: 27), a pioneer in the study of human capital and behaviour through an economic lens (whose views will be explored at great length in Chapter 6), the list of people who should be denied the right to immigrate include 'obvious cases such as potential terrorists, criminals and people who are very sick and who would be immediately a big burden to the health system.' These groups have negative human capital attributes which make them potential threats to economic growth. However, to infer from this argument that neoliberal citizenship automatically excludes people with illnesses or disabilities would be a hasty conclusion.

Consider New Zealand's reaction to the death of Alan Kurdi. Shortly after this tragic event and following a public outcry, the government decided to welcome an extra 600 Syrian refugees in 2015/16 'and a further 500 over the next two financial years' (New Zealand Refugee Quota Programme 2015). In August 2016, it also set aside NZ$17.2m to fund support programmes, since as a result of their 'traumatic experiences … many of the refugees will need counselling and support services, [whereas] others will need help to manage a range of disabilities and chronic health conditions' (Health Minister Jonathan Coleman, cited in Stuff 2016). This case raises an important question. How is it possible to explain that New Zealand was reluctant to grant residency to an autistic child, but was willing to welcome and support hundreds of refugees in need of medical care?

It could be argued that New Zealand's stance reflects a well-established distinction between refugees and economic migrants. Whereas the former should be assessed and helped according to the principle of need, the latter should be evaluated solely in term of economic cost/benefits. To reinforce this point, it could be considered that New Zealand has a long tradition of welcoming refugees with disabilities (Saker 2010). For instance, in welcoming Asian refugees from Uganda in 1973, Prime Minister Norman Kirk insisted that New Zealand should be ready to accept 'a significant proportion of "handicapped" cases' (Beaglehole 2009: 107). This argument would lend support to Ong's (2006b: 22–4) view that contemporary rationalities of inclusion and exclusion encompass two contending paths: neoliberalism and ethical traditions of solidarity variously grounded in 'religion …, feminism, humanitarianism and other schemes of virtue'. The latter may challenge the economic rationality of the former by prompting states to welcome potentially 'defective' refugees in terms of human capital, who would constitute a burden for the welfare state.

However, as I suggested in Section 3, this argument neglects how forms of inclusion based on human rights, shared humanity, and common solidarity may be colonized and corrupted by neoliberalism. It neglects how these values may have undergone a process of economization and how—given the fact that economization cannot be reduced to monetization—entrepreneurial states may try to maximize not just their economic growth, but their non-monetary and non-economic capital value. Hence, they may evaluate prospective citizens—a few hundred Syrian refugees, in this case—as capital which may enhance their cultural, emotional, and reputational value even if this implies an economic cost.

In New Zealand, following Alan's death, 'Amnesty, the United Nations, Catholic bishops, former Prime Minister Helen Clark and local mayors publicly urged the Government to do more' (Vance 2015). Yet, the rationale for 'doing more' was not solely framed as necessary in order to relieve the suffering of Syrian refugees. For Labour leader Andrew Little, 'Kiwis' should keep up with their 'track record' of open borders for those in need because '[t]here is something in our nature—we are people of conscience and compassion—[we] offer help and do something about it' (Vance 2015). Similarly, for then Prime Minister John Key, New Zealand should do more because 'people want us to respond with extra people, they definitely want us to respond for Syrians' (*New Zealand Herald* 2015). These remarks invite us to consider how responding to the *demand* of compassion stemming from the emotional wave provoked by Alan's death required *supplying* New Zealand society with Syrian refugees in order to reproduce an ethical and compassionate self-understanding of New Zealand's people. Alan's death, in other words, contributed to turn Syrian refugees—specifically, a few hundred Syrian refugees with mental and physical disabilities—into a source of *emotional capital* which would contribute to strengthening the self-understanding of the moral value of the country.

To add a further layer to this argument, it is necessary to consider how the last few years have witnessed a progressive shift from human rights to humanitarianism (Ticktin 2006). This means that provisions of care for 'precarious lives' (Butler 2004) such as 'the lives of the unemployed and the asylum seekers, ... of sick immigrants and people with AIDS, ... of disaster victims and victims of conflict' (Fassin 2012: 4) have been increasingly linked and subordinated to their recognition as 'victims'. Abetted by the protean development of visual culture and social media consumption, humanitarianism has introduced a new language of compassion and emotions revolving around notions of 'suffering' and 'trauma' which has resulted in the construction of a 'new humanity' made of individuals who are legitimate as long as they are recognized as 'suffering bodies' (Ticktin 2011).

Miriam Ticktin (2011: 2, 4), for instance, has explored how the French so-called 'illness clause'—a humanitarian principle which grants residence to those already in the country who suffer from a life-threatening condition which would not be properly treated in their home country—has endowed the government with the power to decide what constitutes 'legitimate suffering' and has contributed to turn the 'suffering body' into a 'means to papers'. For Ticktin (2006: 35), this clause—which is a product of and contributes to reproducing a self-understanding of France as a 'global moral leader' and as the 'home of human rights'—has engendered 'a new politics of citizenship in France, a humanitarian space at the intersection of biopolitical modernity and global capital, in which contradictory and unexpected diseased and disabled citizens emerge.' Humanitarianism has instituted a new global 'meritocracy of suffering' (Clifford Bob, cited in Ticktin 2006: 34) which has resulted in the establishment of humanitarian corridors for certain categories of refugees, such as women and children, particularly if affected by physical and mental conditions, and the hardening of borders for able-bodied refugees.

Ticktin's argument resonates with Mezzadra and Neilson's (2013: 159) notion of 'differential inclusion', namely, how the modern process of 'disarticulation of citizenship' has resulted in a condition in which 'inclusion in a sphere, society, or realm can be subject to varying degrees of subordination, rule, discrimination, and segmentation.' However, whereas Mezzadra and Neilson deem differential inclusion a function of the neoliberal political economy of labour, Ticktin alerts us that inclusion may also be a function of humanitarianism. For her, humanitarianism represents a partial 'degeneration' (my term) of the human rights regime since it subordinates the universalism of human rights to the more particularist and selective discourses of emotions, charity, and compassion. My contention is that humanitarianism and, specifically, the establishment of humanitarian corridors for vulnerable refugees is a product of neoliberal citizenship, a regime of differential inclusion that deems vulnerable refugees to be a source of emotional capital which can strengthen the *humanity capital* of the country.

The fact that this choice may be potentially costly for the health system lends support to the argument advanced in this book that the market value of prospective citizens may not be reduced to their human, economic, or financial capital and to their capacity to contribute to the economic growth of the country. The process of economization turns emotions into a valuable source of capital with the effect that, in the neoliberal political economy of belonging, the possibility of inclusion may become a function of prospective citizens' capacity to strengthening the humanity capital and, more generally, the emotional identity and self-understanding of the country. States may try to maximize their value even in those instances when money is not at stake or even if this may have a negative impact in economic terms.

From this perspective, the physically and mentally disabled refugees taken by New Zealand should be considered the embodiment of an emotional capital instrumental to preserve and promote a national sense of collective pride, self-esteem, and moral-righteousness. Neoliberal citizenship makes it possible that, while residency for an autistic child from a relatively wealthy family is denied on the grounds that he would be a burden to taxpayers, a few hundreds or thousands of disabled refugees are welcomed, despite their potential cost, as a testimony to the country's humanity. It makes it possible that hundreds of thousands of refugees may languish in refugee camps in North Africa, Turkey, and Europe, or in offshore locations such as Christmas Island, and that hundreds may die every day in the attempt to cross border zones such as US–Mexican border or the Mediterranean because solidarity and empathy are now understood through the neoliberal lens of value.

Conclusion

In an important book on citizenship and migration published at the beginning of this century, Stephen Castles and Alastair Davidson (2000: viii) observed that '[p]orous boundaries and multiple identities undermine ideas of cultural belonging as a necessary accompaniment to political membership. There are increasing numbers of citizens who do not belong' and are perceived not to belong. For Castles and Davidson (2000: viii) the separation of cultural inclusion (belonging) from political inclusion (citizenship) and the progressive decline of the former represented a threat to 'the nation-state as a central site of democracy'. The main critique advanced by the existing literature on citizenship-by-investment programmes may be considered a continuation of this argument: political inclusion deprived of cultural belonging has emptied citizenship from within, with the effect that the political logic of citizenship has been progressively replaced by the economic logic of the market. The latter has reduced citizenship to a tradable commodity and erased any remnant of cultural belonging.

This chapter has advanced a different argument. Starting from an understanding of neoliberalism as a process of economization, it has discussed how neoliberalism has turned individuals and states into entrepreneurial subjects that aim to maximize their value, with the result that existing and most of all prospective citizens become increasingly perceived as sources of human and financial capital, and evaluated (and included/excluded) according to their capacity to contribute to the economic growth of the country. Yet, moving beyond existing accounts and fully embracing the implications of neoliberal economization, the chapter has explored the possibility that states may try to maximize their value not just in economic terms but also in emotional and moral terms. The argument was advanced that the growing mobility opportunities for wealthy and talented migrants epitomized by citizenship- and residency-by-investment schemes and the opening of humanitarian corridors for particularly vulnerable refugees are not disparate phenomena, but manifestations of the same neoliberal rationality of government. This rationality prompts states to include/exclude migrants according to their endowment of human, financial, economic, and emotional capital; that is, according to their capacity to contribute to the country's finances, economic growth, moral and emotional standing, and self-understanding.

The economization of emotions challenges the separation of cultural inclusion (belonging) from political inclusion (citizenship) described by Castles and Davidson. As I showed in Section 3, neoliberal rationalities of inclusion/exclusion are political—with the political shaped and informed by the logic of the market—and have an emotional dimension that transcends mere cost/benefit calculations. New Zealand's decision to welcome more Syrian refugees potentially 'defective' in terms of human capital and thus potentially costly in economic terms was outweighed by the refugees' endowment of emotional capital. In the wake of Alan Kurdi's death, welcoming them was instrumental to reproducing an ethical and compassionate self-understanding of the country and strengthening its *humanity* capital. Similarly, the exclusion of potentially valuable migrants, such as the non-British spouses of British citizens earning less than £18,600 a year, suggests that neoliberal citizenship may not be reduced to 'the ability to exchange something of sufficient market value' (Somers 2011: 26). The neoliberal political economy of belonging at the heart of neoliberal citizenship encompasses an emotional dimension that transcends mere monetary calculations, and yet is fully inscribed into neoliberal rationalities. As illustrated by the case of the Belgian professor whose autistic stepson was denied New Zealand residency, neoliberal citizenship does not replace the principles of reciprocity, fairness, equality, and mutual participation with economic ones: it rewrites them in economic terms.

At a closer look, the latter case also suggests that neoliberal citizenship can reinforce but also subvert the traditional categories of inclusion and exclusion as well as the degree of protection that individuals and groups will be accorded. While it reinforces the exclusion of 'undesirable others' such as the predominantly Muslim migrants from North Africa and the Middle East, it can also privilege them over a white Western boy provided that the migrants suffer from mental and physical disabilities which, under the circumstances previously considered, can make them valuable as victims. The power of subversion of neoliberal citizenship becomes even more evident if considered against the deep-seated and longstanding European anxieties about Islam, widely regarded as a backward culture incompatible with Western values of individualism and gender equality, unable to separate religion and politics, fundamentally prone to violence, and ultimately impossible to integrate in the framework of Europe's secular modernity (Mavelli 2012a). These anxieties appear to vanish if the Muslims in question are millionaires and billionaires, such as those residing in the UK, who enjoy family rights which are currently denied to British citizens married to non-British spouses.

As we have seen, the UK has not been alone in offering a privileged regime to wealthy foreigners. Several countries in Europe have combined their offer of citizenship and residency-by-investment schemes with particularly favourable fiscal regimes not available to ordinary citizens. This means that in a Europe anxious about the 'tide of Muslim refugees' washing up on its shores—a theme that I shall explore in greater detail in the following pages—a steady transfer of wealth and rights has been taking place from austerity-stricken citizens to wealthy foreigners able to buy their way into the country and benefiting from fiscal red carpets. Many of these wealthy foreigners are from Islamic countries and yet not regarded as a feral threat to the survival of Europe.

These considerations suggest that neoliberal citizenship does not simply rewrite the criteria of inclusion, exclusion, and protection, but also the very meaning of racism that often underpin them. The relation between neoliberal citizenship and racism will be the subject of Chapter 4. The focus will be on how the emotional value of refugees as a distinctive feature of neoliberal belonging crucially rests on what Michel Foucault labels biopolitical racism. To this end, the concept of humanitarianism introduced in this chapter will be further investigated, particularly when deployed in conjunction with the logic of securitization, thus resulting in a regime of governance often referred to as 'humanitarian government'. The argument will be advanced that humanitarian government is a manifestation of neoliberal citizenship that crucially relies on, and indeed promotes, biopolitical racism.

4

The emotional value of refugees

Introduction

One paradigm that has been increasingly employed to account for the rationalities of government of refugees and undocumented migrants is that of humanitarian government. This concept denotes the simultaneous deployment of humanitarian and security practices in the governance of vulnerable subjects in border zones. According to several scholars (Walters 2011; Vaughan-Williams 2015; Williams 2015; Little and Vaughan-Williams 2017), the concept of humanitarian government poses a critical challenge to Foucault's notion of biopolitics, and particularly to the idea of a shift from the traditional sovereign power 'to take life or let live' to the modern biopolitical 'power to foster life or disallow it to the point of death' (Foucault 1978: 138). Biopolitics, critics maintain, struggles to account for the construction of migrants as the simultaneous target of practices of humanitarianism and security because their aim is neither exclusively 'making live' or 'letting die' but a combination of both. Scholars of humanitarian government have therefore either analysed these practices as the expression of a 'minimalist biopolitics', whose goal is not to 'optimize and foster life', but 'simply holding off death' (Williams 2015: 17), or have supplemented Foucault's approach with new concepts in order to enable it to capture this apparent paradox (see Vaughan-Williams 2015; Little and Vaughan-Williams 2017).

In this chapter, I build on the important insights of this scholarship but challenge its reading of Foucault's biopolitics. I contend that the phenomenon of humanitarian government should be understood within the broader framework of neoliberal citizenship and that the 'precarious lives' (Butler 2004) of undocumented migrants are not the primary but only the secondary concern of this regime of governance. The primary referent object of humanitarian government is the biopolitical government and care of host populations through the humanitarian government of refugees. From this perspective, I advance two main arguments. First, the practices of humanitarianism and security that

Neoliberal Citizenship. Luca Mavelli, Oxford University Press.
 DOI: 10.1093/oso/9780192857583.003.0004

underpin the notion of humanitarian government are derivative of rationalities of value, namely, caring for a small group of refugees which are emotionally and morally valuable for the host population—as in the case of the physically and mentally disabled Syrians discussed in Chapter 3—while securitizing the rest, perceived as a worthless and threatening mass. Second, these rationalities of value are informed by a fundamental biopolitical logic that frames humanitarianism as instrumental to enhance the life and advance the well-being of host populations.

From this perspective, humanitarian government is a neoliberal rationality of citizenship that establishes which (and how) refugees must be welcomed and which ones must be rejected on the basis of their moral and emotional value. It follows that, as I shall discuss, neoliberal citizenship rests on a biopolitical form of racism that partially reinforces and partially subverts traditional forms of racism based on nationality, ethnicity, religion, colour, gender, and allegedly intractable cultural differences. The biopolitical racism of neoliberal citizenship incorporates traditional manifestations of racism and redraws the boundary between 'valuable' (to be included or differentially included) and 'not valuable' (to be excluded) according to the refugees' capacity to enhance the *biological* and *emotional* well-being of host populations by strengthening the latter's economic and moral/emotional capital.

To assess the relevance of this argument, three main cases will be explored. First, I will focus on the German response to the death of Alan Kurdi—the 2015 decision to open its borders to up to 800,000 refugees a year for several years—and compare it with the UK's (and New Zealand's) decision to 'invest' in a few thousand refugees. Despite an apparent difference, I will show how both cases are expressions of biopolitical logics of care of the host population, with Syrian refugees valued as a source of emotional capital in the British case and emotional *and* human capital in the case of Germany (a skilled workforce capable to support the welfare system). Second, I will discuss the so-called Dubs Amendment case which saw the UK falling short of its commitment to 'relocate and support unaccompanied refugee children from Europe' (Home Office 2016) when these minors emerged in the eyes of the British public as no longer a valuable source of emotional capital. Finally, I will consider several little-known *individual* stories of neoliberal citizenship across Europe in which undocumented migrants have been granted citizenship following particularly deserving actions, such as rescuing an endangered child or foiling a terrorist plot. I will show how these are instantiations of a neoliberal rationality in which the granting of citizenship is a biopolitical form of care of the host population that builds on and reproduces biopolitical racism.

In discussing these cases, and particularly the individual stories of Mamoudou Gassama, Lassana Bathily, Mahmoud Diallo, Gorgui Lamine Sow, and Ramy Shehata and Adam El Hamami, I embrace Elspeth Guild's call 'for the increased prominence of the individual in the study of migration' as a way of resisting the 'massifying statist language of "flows", "stocks" and "tidal waves"' (Peoples and Vaughan-Williams 2020: 207; see Guild 2009: 3–5). Whereas the regimes of power and knowledge rallied by this language will be analysed and challenged in the next chapter, the individual stories I recount in this chapter enable us to see how the rationalities of neoliberal citizenship are mobilized though the lived experiences of 'fellow human beings' (Vaughan-Williams and Pisani 2020: 670).

This focus on the individual is part of a recent and important turn in security and migration studies which has been variously described as 'vernacular' and/or 'everyday' security (Jarvis and Lister 2013; Croft and Vaughan-Williams 2017; Löfflmann and Vaughan-Williams 2018; Jarvis 2019; Vaughan-Williams 2021). My approach shares another feature with this turn: an emphasis on those whose 'voices are not being heard' (Vaughan-Williams and Stevens 2016: 54). My focus on the marginalized, the neglected, the excluded, the dispossessed, and particularly those who no longer have a voice because they have been killed or let die (crossing the Mediterranean, as the result of the perverse effects of austerity, or in underfunded hospitals and care homes as I shall discuss in Chapter 8) is a way of resisting their disappearance by exposing the tragic outcome of the rationalities of value that govern the neoliberal citizenship regime.

This chapter adds another layer to our understanding of these rationalities by elaborating on the relationship between neoliberal citizenship and biopolitical racism. In his 1978–79 lectures at the Collège de France, *The Birth of Biopolitics*, Foucault (2008: 22n) argues that biopolitics should be understood within the broader framework of neoliberalism. However, despite this remark and the very title of his lectures, Foucault never properly addressed this connection to the effect that 'how exactly Foucault understood the conjunction between biopower and late modern [neoliberal] capitalism' remains an 'unsolved puzzle' (Lemm and Vatter 2014: 5). My goal in this and the following chapters is to elaborate on this connection by using Foucault's conceptual categories as a 'toolbox' to explore how the notion of neoliberal citizenship, which subordinates the possibility of inclusion and protection to the capacity of the individual to enhance the economic or emotional value of the country, crucially entails a biopolitics of care of the host population which relies on and reinforces forms of biopolitical racism.

This perspective invites us to reconsider dominant approaches to biopolitics that have primarily focused on 'the emergence and governance of life in its biological existence' (Huysmans 2008: 177), and on how biopolitics has contributed to bring 'biological life (zoē) into the modalities of state power (bios)' (Little and Vaughan-Williams 2017: 12). While this focus on 'biological being' (Dillon and Reid 2009: 20), 'biological processes' (Hamilton 2018: 41), and on 'biological, corporeal, or even carnal regimes of power, rule, and force' (Debrix 2015: 151) is certainly essential, it has mostly overlooked how emotional concerns have been an equally important dimension of biopolitical governmentalities. Hence, the approach advanced in this chapter maintains that existing responses to the European refugee crisis are governed by biopolitical governmental rationalities of biological and emotional care of host populations performed through the humanitarian government of refugees.

The chapter is organized in four sections.[1] First, I discuss how the existing literature considers humanitarian government exclusively as the government of disenfranchised subjects, such as refugees and undocumented migrants, and deems biopolitics unable to account for the simultaneous deployment of logics of humanitarianism and security. Second, I explore how the humanitarian government of refugees is a manifestation of a biopolitical governmentality which aims to maximize the biological and emotional life of the host population. To this end, I discuss two largely neglected dimensions of biopolitics: its underlying 'differentialist' understanding of race and its concern with the emotional well-being of the population. Third, I consider how this conceptual framework advances existing understandings of the European refugee crisis by analysing the British and German responses to the plight of Syrian refugees following the death of Alan Kurdi. Fourth, I consider a series of cases from the UK, France, Spain, and Italy where the neoliberal granting of citizenship to deserving undocumented migrants has been used as an opportunity to reinforce traditional manifestations of racism.

1. The humanitarian government of refugees

The last few years have witnessed a novel phenomenon in international politics: 'the reinvention of the border as a space of humanitarian government'

[1] Sections 1, 2, and 3 of this chapter include extensive passages from 'Governing Populations through the Humanitarian Government of Refugees: Biopolitical Care and Racism in the European Refugee Crisis', *Review of International Studies* 43, no. 5 (2017): 809–832, which are reprinted with permission from Cambridge University Press.

(Walters 2011: 138). The emergence of the 'humanitarian border' signals the actualization of a domain in which traditional practices of 'militarization, securitization, and fortification of borders' (Walters 2011: 138) have been increasingly accompanied by forms of humanitarian care aimed at 'the preservation of life and the alleviation of suffering' (Didier Fassin, cited in Walters 2011: 138). Hence, the proliferation and externalization of borders (Brown 2010; Fassin 2011), the enforcement of systems of mandatory detention (Darling 2009; Mountz 2011; Bosworth 2014; Nethery and Holman 2016), the strengthening of deportation regimes (Walters 2002; De Genova and Peutz 2010), the deployment of sophisticated surveillance technologies (Amoore 2006), and the '"optimization of natural obstacles" for the purpose of migration control', have been increasingly accompanied by the 'proliferation of humanitarian aid and services' (Williams 2015: 13). These include search-and-rescue missions, 'migrant reception centers; agencies providing food, shelter, … medical care, [legal assistance and spiritual support]; the documentation of migrant fatalities and associated efforts to identify and repatriate remains' (Williams 2015: 13).

According to William Walters (2011: 139), these seemingly conflicting trends defy and exceed analytical frameworks which may read the humanitarian border as a way of 'compensating for the social violence embodied in the regime of migration control.' Indeed, this 'compensation' is not internal to sovereign power because although states and international governmental agencies are the main agents of border securitization, their contribution to humanitarian aid and services is often overshadowed by that provided by international non-governmental organizations. Equally, humanitarian government cannot be considered as an external 'compensation' performed by civil society because the humanitarian aid provided by NGOs has often resulted in dehumanizing securitizing practices (such as migrant detention), rather than challenging them, thus contributing to their perpetuation (on this latter argument see Walters 2011: 153).

For Walters (2011: 144) the humanitarian border represents 'a site of ambivalence and undecidability' characterized by practices of compassion and infliction of suffering, forms of neoliberal disciplining, acts of resistance and counter-conduct, and the constant, mutual co-optation of humanitarianism by security. These dynamics, he contends, exceed the capacity of biopolitics to fully grasp them. While they signal a condition in which life is the object of political management and intervention, Foucault's characterization of biopolitics as the power to 'make live and let die' seemingly struggles to account for a situation in which life is simultaneously targeted by humanitarian forces that aim to foster life and securitizing forces that negate it. To better understand Walters' critique, it is necessary to consider Foucault's argument in greater detail.

According to Foucault (2003), the modern biopolitical exercise of power over life entails two main forms of biopower: 'making live' and 'letting die'. Unlike traditional forms of sovereign power which manifested themselves through mechanisms of deduction of wealth, labour, services, and 'ultimately life itself', biopolitics encompasses a power of care and production whose main task is to 'incite, reinforce, control, monitor, optimize, and organize the forces under it: a power bent on generating forces, making them grow, and ordering them, rather than one dedicated to impeding them, making them submit, or destroying them' (Foucault 1978: 136). The goal of biopower has thus been variously described as 'enhancing', 'fostering', 'strengthening', and 'maximizing' life. However, Foucault (2003: 241) contends, the modern shift from sovereign power to biopower does not mean that 'sovereignty's old right—to take life or let live—was replaced, but it came to be complemented by a new right which does not erase the old right but which does penetrate it, permeate it.'

The biopolitical 'power to make live' is not an unqualified attempt to promote all forms of life, but only the life of the race/population cared for. This means that the biopolitical power to 'let die' and the traditional sovereign 'right to take life' are essential to make life live by marginalizing, segregating, or eliminating those internal deviant elements and external threatening 'others' who may put at risk the survival, flourishing, and well-being of the population. This is what Foucault calls biopolitical racism: a process of 'cleansing of the social body' (Lemke 2011: 43–4) that 'differentiates between worthy and unworthy forms of life' (Vaughan-Williams 2015: 43) and where the death of the latter is essential for strengthening the life of the former.

Foucault's account has been extensively used by migration scholars to analyse how securitizing practices which lead to the exclusion, abandonment, and death of refugees and undocumented migrants have often been linked to their biopolitical construction as a threat to the identity, culture, economy, and social well-being of the population (see for instance Doty 2011; Squire 2017). However, Foucault's argument has been considered limiting in the framework of humanitarian border practices which see the simultaneous affirmation and negation of life. Drawing on Peter Redfield, Walters describes these practices as expressions of a 'minimalist' or 'significantly attenuated biopolitics' confined to 'the provision of bare necessities' (Walters 2011: 155) whose main task is 'monitoring and assisting populations in maintaining their physical existence'

(Peter Redfield quoted in Walters 2011: 144), not enhancing, fostering, and optimizing their lives.

Jill M. Williams (2015) advances a similar argument in her ethnographic analysis of the increasingly securitized humanitarian border in Southern Arizona, USA. She argues that humanitarian practices, such as the transferring of undocumented migrants to local hospitals for medical care, are primarily a form of 'care enforcement' or 'contingent care': a 'minimalist biopolitics' whose main goal is not the long-term well-being of the migrants but providing the minimal amount of medical treatment necessary to ensure that they may be speedily deported and that 'death does not occur until after deportation' (Williams 2015: 17).

In discussing the French 'illness clause'—the humanitarian principle we encountered in Chapter 3 whereby those suffering from a life-threatening condition not properly treatable in their home country may be granted residence—Miriam Ticktin (2011) considers how humanitarian government subordinates the right to protection to the requirement of suffering. Humanitarian government constructs individuals as objects of care and compassion rather than equal citizens, thus prompting a process of 'biological involution' (Ticktin 2011: 11, 215). This results in the production of disabled subjects who are ultimately more valued and mobile than their 'able bodied' counterparts because they can become the object of a politics of compassion. In this regard, Ticktin (2011: 13) recounts the story of several HIV+ patients who stopped taking their medication once they received their residence papers, fearful that an improvement in their condition could undermine their right to reside in the country.

According to Fassin (2012: 226), although biopolitics and humanitarian government share an underlying politics of care and although humanitarian action employs biopolitical 'techniques of management of populations'—such as 'setting up refugee camps, establishing protected aid corridors … conducting epidemiological studies of infectious diseases'—they also have different goals. Biopolitics is primarily concerned with caring for and maximizing the life of the population *as a whole*. Humanitarian government, on the other hand, is a *politics of individual life* (Fassin 2012: 226). As such, it requires 'selecting those that have priority for being saved (for example, when drug supplies are insufficient)' (Fassin 2012: 226), or in the case of the Mediterranean refugee crisis, deciding which 'worthy lives' must be saved (even risking other lives to this end) in the name of the humanitarian imperative, and which 'unworthy lives' can be left to drown in the name of security (Basaran 2015).

Hence, humanitarian government rests on the concurrent deployment of logics of 'securitization and humanitarianism' which highlight a 'symbiotic relationship' between 'care and control', that is, between 'the humanitarian world (the hand that cares) and the police and military (the hand that strikes)' (Pallister-Wilkins 2015: 159; see also Agier 2011).

These remarks echo Walters' reflections on the humanitarian border. Humanitarian government is a 'significantly attenuated biopolitics' (Walters 2011: 150) since 'the life that is preserved is structurally marginalized and only maintained, not fostered' (Williams 2015: 17). The encroachment of humanitarianism and security turns humanitarian government into a space of contradictions characterized by acts of compassion and the deliberate infliction of suffering, neoliberal disciplining, practices of resistance, forms of counter-conduct, and the constant, mutual co-optation of humanitarianism by security and vice-versa (Walters 2011: 144). This complex field of interactions transcends mere processes of 'biopolitical reproduction', Walters contends, and calls for supplementing 'Foucault's toolbox' with new concepts (Walters 2011: 144, 158).

Taking up this challenge, Adrian Little and Nick Vaughan-Williams draw on Roberto Esposito's concept of (auto)immunity to grasp the ambivalence at the heart of humanitarian government. This is the idea that the protection of life requires the incorporation (in small doses) of that which represents a threat to life in order to develop immunity against it. For them, Foucauldian biopolitics primarily concerns the 'positive' goals of optimization and maximization of life, whereas humanitarian government as deployed in practices of compassionate borderwork is neither a 'straightforwardly "positive"' nor simply a '"negative" or thanatopolitical' 'biopolitical technology of power' (Little and Vaughan-Williams 2017: 18). Accordingly, biopolitics is unable to account for the capacity of humanitarian government 'to lead to "irregular" migrants' and refugees' dehumanisation and death' (Little and Vaughan-Williams 2017: 4). Conversely, Esposito's concept of (auto)immunity explains how the protection of life through the inoculation of threatening agents in excessive doses may result in 'an autoimmune crisis' (Little and Vaughan-Williams 2017: 19). From this perspective, humanitarian government is informed by 'an (auto) immunitary logic: the very lives that are identified as in need of protecting and saving can also become targeted by lethal apparatuses of security' (Little and Vaughan-Williams 2017: 19). This ambiguity is particularly evident in the Australian 'stop the boats' policy which claims, at once, to protect the migrants by abandoning them (Little and Vaughan-Williams 2017: 19).

The brief overview of humanitarian government literature carried out in this section suggests that: (1) humanitarian government concerns the government of disenfranchised subjects, such as refugees and undocumented/'irregular' migrants, through the simultaneous deployment of rationalities/practices of care and security; (2) these rationalities/practices are only partially captured by a biopolitical lens. In the remainder of this chapter, I wish to offer a contending perspective. Instead of regarding disenfranchised 'others' as the primary referent object of humanitarian government, my contention is that humanitarian government is primarily a biopolitical governmentality targeting host populations, whose aim is to maximize their biological and emotional well-being through the selective inclusion/exclusion of refugees. To advance this argument, in Section 2, I explore how this process of inclusion/exclusion rests on a biopolitical 'differentialist' understanding of racism and how biopower targets not just biological, but emotional life.

2. Governing populations through biopolitical racism

The perspectives discussed in the previous section emphasize the dimension of care and maximization of life at the heart of biopolitics. The biopolitical 'power to make live', however, is not an unqualified attempt to promote all forms of life, but only the life of the race/population cared for. For Foucault, the key dimensions of biopolitics, 'love and care' (Ojakangas 2005: 20), encompass and indeed are advanced through the 'negative' biopolitical power to 'let die' and the traditional sovereign 'right to take life' (Foucault 2003: 241). As Foucault (2009: 105) explains, with the emergence of biopolitical governmentality 'the problem of sovereignty is not eliminated; on the contrary it is made more acute than ever.' The reason is that the power 'to kill', 'take life', or 'let die' is essential to make life live by marginalizing, segregating, or eliminating those internal deviant elements and external threatening 'others' who may put at risk the survival, flourishing, and well-being of the population. Particularly with respect to the latter, biopolitical governmentality requires the active deployment of what Foucault describes as *state* or *biopolitical racism* in order to discriminate between 'threatening' and 'non-threatening' others.

For Foucault, biopolitical racism 'is an expression of a schism within society that is provoked by the idea of an ongoing and always incomplete cleansing of the social body' (Lemke 2011: 43–44). It is a governmental rationality that breaks the biological continuum of life by dividing it into 'superior/good' and 'inferior/bad races', and establishing a relationship in which the 'the death of the bad race, of the inferior race ... is something that will make life in general healthier' (Foucault 2003: 254). It follows that modern biopolitical racism is not exclusively and primarily 'an irrational prejudice, a form of socio-political discrimination, or an ideological motive in a political doctrine; rather, it is a form of government that is designed to manage a population' (Rasmussen 2011: 34) by raising the problem of 'foreigners' and 'deviants'. For Foucault, racism can be understood as a way to measure, assess, rank, intervene on, and distribute individuals in the domain of the living according to their endowment or absence of those biological qualities which can contribute to the well-being and flourishing of the population. Modern biopolitical racism is an essential component of biopower. It is 'a way of introducing a break into the domain of life that is under power's control: the break between what must live and what must die' (Foucault 2003: 254).

In the rest of this section, I build on Foucault's scattered remarks and argue that biopolitical racism, while shaped by traditional forms of racism based on nationality, ethnicity, religion, colour, and gender, also incorporates and partially transcends them. As Roxanne Doty (2011: 603) has perceptively observed, Foucault's approach to racism rests on a 'differentialist' perspective. This view deems 'race' a mobile category which is the product of the underlying governmental rationality—racism—that endows it with meaning according to shifting and evolving (bio)political circumstances (Doty 2011: 603). It follows that, from the perspective of biopolitical racism, the boundary that separates 'superior' and 'inferior races' is a tool of the biopolitical governmentality targeting the population rather than what delimitates its space of action.

This means that the boundary between 'superior' and 'inferior races' can be redrawn *beyond traditional forms of racism* (based on nationality, ethnicity, religion, colour, and gender) if members of the 'inferior races' are deemed instrumental to enhance the material and emotional life of the population. This suggests that practices of humanitarian government resulting in the acceptance of refugees do not have as their exclusive and primary goal the care of 'disenfranchised subjects', but the care and well-being of the host population. Humanitarian government, in other words, is first and foremost a biopolitical governmentality targeting host populations aimed at enhancing their emotional and material well-being. As such, it is an essential component of neoliberal citizenship.

To better understand this argument, it is necessary to consider how European anxieties about refugees have been exacerbated by the predominantly

Muslim identity of those seeking refuge. The widespread European perception of Islam as a backward, irrational, violent-prone religion that promotes terrorism and gender inequality, unable to distinguish between facts and beliefs, and unwilling to accept the separation between religion and politics (Mavelli 2012a) has fuelled traditional manifestations of racism mostly in the form of anti-Muslimism or Islamophobia (Halliday 1999; see also Betts 2016). For instance, several European countries (including Slovakia, Poland, Hungary, Bulgaria, and Cyprus) have repeatedly refused to take in refugees on the grounds that the latter's (alleged) Muslim identity would threaten their country's Christian identity (Wilson and Mavelli 2017: 3, 7). The media have indulged in representations of Muslim refugees as 'patriarchal, homophobic, violent threats to personal, national and international security' as well as '"rapefugees" and innate sexual predators following the attacks on European women in Cologne on New Years' Eve' (Fiddian-Qasmiyeh 2017: 207), as in the infamous *Charlie Hebdo* cartoon depicting a grown-up Alan Kurdi molesting women. However, despite these traditional manifestations of racism grounded in a deep-seated mistrust and suspicion of Islam, a number of Muslim refugees have been portrayed as 'good refugees' that should be welcomed.

As Elena Fiddian-Qasmiyeh (2016: 459) explains, Syrian refugees as a whole have been initially framed as 'good refugees', that is, as 'both legitimate and priority "candidates" for international protection' to the effect that they have been 'fast- tracked' and given priority over Iraqis and Afghans, who have been treated as 'second-tier refugees'. However, with the intensification of the crisis, the binary clichéd representation of 'good/deserving/real refugees' versus 'bad/undeserving/bogus refugees' has also been applied to Syrian asylum seekers. In particular, the figure of the 'good/deserving/real refugee' has been employed to describe 'women, children and male victims of violence who patiently wait in refugee camps to be rescued by British/European/Western saviours' (Wilson and Mavelli 2017: 7). Conversely, bad refugees are those who exercise agency by taking matters in their own hands and initiate the dangerous journey across sub-Saharan Africa and the Mediterranean to seek refuge in Europe. They 'challenge the script "refugee=victim"' (Wilson and Mavelli 2017: 7), exercise resilience beyond the limits established by neoliberal citizenship, and resist their sacrificial role.

These refugees have become a 'swarm of people coming across the Mediterranean' (UK Prime Minister David Cameron, cited in Wilson and Mavelli 2017: 7), '"queue jumpers" and "bogus asylum seekers" who are jeopardizing the protection claims made by "real" (i.e. "good") refugees' (Fiddian-Qasmiyeh 2017: 210), economic migrants, and potential terrorists who put at risk the survival of the nation. The 'good refugee', Fiddian-Qasmiyeh remarks, is epitomized by the hybrid figure of the weakened and dependent 'womanandchild', as per Cynthia Enloe's definition (Fiddian-Qasmiyeh 2017: 211). This figure of defenceless, resilient, apolitical and innocent victimhood, highly valued in 'the global meritocracy of suffering' (Clifford Bob, cited in Ticktin 2006: 34) has also occasionally been extended to vulnerable male figures. This is the case of Laith Majid, a Syrian refugee who in 2015 was pictured 'weeping in relief as he reaches the island of Kos holding his 7-year-old daughter in his arms and hugging his 9-year-old son' and was subsequently dubbed by the BBC as one of the 'faces of the migration crisis' (Fiddian-Qasmiyeh 2017: 212).

The 'good refugee' discourse draws on a series of racial and gender stereotypes: the defenceless Muslim woman (doubly victim of Islamic patriarchy and war), the innocent child (not yet corrupted by the ideology of Islam) and the de-sexualized and even feminized, and for this very reason, non-threatening Muslim man (the negation of the hypersexualized, violent, and fanatic Muslim). Similarly, the figure of the 'good refugee' rests on a paternalistic racism that reinforces notions of racial superiority, magnanimity, and moral righteousness and crystallizes the inequality and power imbalance between 'white' and 'brown' lives. From the view outlined in this chapter, the identification of certain Muslim groups as 'good refugees' signals the presence of a biopolitical bifurcation whereby protection for some 'womenandchildren' or 'menandchildren' becomes an exacerbation of racial prejudices and securitization towards those Muslims—male, single, healthy, and young who have already crossed or attempted to cross the Mediterranean—who escape the status of victim to be rescued and are perceived as economic migrants, sexual predators, and potential terrorists.

Hence, the deflation of racism towards 'sick Muslim refugees' and its exasperation towards 'other Muslim refugees' represents an instantiation of biopolitical racism that partially redraws the line between 'superior' and 'inferior races' because some members of the 'inferior races' are deemed instrumental to enhance the life of the host population. This biopolitical outlook raises a series of questions: What makes these 'sick' and 'feminized' refugees 'valuable' from a biopolitical perspective? How can they enhance and maximize the life of the populations hosting them?

A shared line of argument is that, from the perspective of biopolitical governmentality, 'valuable lives' are those that can be inscribed into neoliberal logics of entrepreneurship and resilience, responsibility and self-governance, security and risk, competition and inequality, consumption and accumulation, circulation and dispossession (Dillon and Lobo-Guerrero 2008, 2009; Dillon and Reid 2009; Nadesan 2010; Cooper 2011a; Lundborg and Vaughan-Williams 2011; Evans and Reid 2014; Chandler and Reid 2016). This view finds resonance in Foucault's understanding of biopower as an 'indispensable element' in the development of neoliberal capitalism, which would not have been possible 'without the controlled insertion of bodies into the machinery of production', 'the adjustment of the phenomena of population to economic processes' and the development of 'methods of power capable of optimizing forces, aptitudes, and life in general' (Foucault 1978: 141).

This argument rests on a widespread 'biological' understanding of biopolitics, what Vivienne Jabri (2007: 73) describes as 'the biologization of power', namely, the fact that with biopolitics, 'the basic biological features of the human species' become 'the object of political strategisation' (Dillon and Lobo-Guerrero 2008: 273). Life in its material, biological, and molecular dimensions becomes the object of a complex assemblage of biopolitical interventions aimed at its regulation, evaluation, hierarchization, entrepreneurialization, commodification, securitization, and, overall, neoliberal subjectification for the purpose of enhancing its strength, value, and productive and reproductive capacity. From this perspective, 'valuable lives' in biopolitical terms are those that can be transformed 'into value, in the form of commodity and capital' (Dillon and Lobo-Guerrero 2009: 2), and can *adapt* and *contribute* to the reproduction of the neoliberal biopolitical order, thus generating *surplus life* which may strengthen the life of the population (Vatter 2009).

It follows that sick 'womenandchildren' refugees—such as those that the UK has pledged to take in directly from camps in Syria's neighbouring countries—can hardly be considered 'valuable' in biopolitical terms: these 'defective bodies' are a burden for the welfare state, will not be able to generate biological surplus-life, cannot be integrated into neoliberal mechanisms of economic control, and cannot contribute to strengthening and maximizing the biological life of the British population. However, if a strictly biological reading of biopolitics is abandoned, it is possible to consider how sick 'womenandchildren' refugees may be 'valuable' from a biopolitical perspective, that is, capable of enhancing and maximizing the life of the populations hosting them. Ted Rutland (2015: 853) argues that an exclusive biological outlook displays 'an unduly narrow conception of biopolitics'. It neglects how biopolitics transcends 'the most basic biological or medical dimensions of existence' such as 'the health of the population; its longevity, growth, and decline; and its physical security' and encompasses a specific concern with the affective and emotional life of the population (Rutland 2015: 853), which is not merely derivative of biological interventions.[2]

According to this view, biopolitics does not just concern the material dispositions of the population in order to promote and advance its biological well-being. By the same token, biopolitics cannot be reduced to the cultivation of feelings of uncertainty, fear, anxiety, and insecurity in order to fashion resilient subjects capable of withstanding and adapting to the shocks of the neoliberal economic order (Dean 2014: 161), and in order to justify its power to kill or let die those members of the sub-species which represent a threat. Crucially, biopolitics also entails caring for and, therefore, intervening on, the emotional life of the population. This view is supported by a careful reading of Foucault's genealogy of biopolitics, particularly his remarks on *pastoral power* and the *police* (Ojakangas 2016).

The notion of pastoral power, mostly associated with early and medieval Christianity, revolves around the metaphor of God as a shepherd and encompasses a fundamental focus on the 'care of souls' (Gordon 1991: 8). For Foucault, pastoral power was exercised by the shepherd—the Church—over a flock, and endowed the shepherd with the task 'to provide continuous material and spiritual welfare for each and every member of the flock' (Ojakangas 2016: 78). Pastoral power was thus 'a beneficent power', a 'power of care' (Foucault 2009: 124–5) concerned with 'constantly ensur[ing], sustain[ing], and improve[ing] the lives of each and every one' (Foucault 1994: 307), and with providing 'spiritual direction' (Foucault 2009: 121). Its ultimate task was the spiritual 'salvation of the flock' and of every single sheep in the flock, with the effect that pastoral power was both an individualizing and massifying power (Foucault 1994). For Foucault, the seventeenth and eighteenth century saw a fundamental transformation in the logic and reach of the pastorate which ceased to be an exclusively religious phenomenon. It migrated to the political sphere and crucially shaped the first governmental rationality of the modern state, namely *raison d'État* (reason of state). The latter had as its goal the strengthening of the state through a technology of power focused on the unlimited regulation of its subjects, from their economic activity to their social behaviours through the 'unlimited objectives' of the 'police' (Foucault 2008: 7).

[2] Although there is a growing literature on the 'cultural politics of emotion' and 'emotions and world politics', this scholarship has largely overlooked the relationship between emotions and biopolitics and emotions as a constitutive dimension of biopolitics. See, for instance, Ahmed (2003) and Bleiker and Hutchison (2008).

With this term, Foucault does not understand 'exclusively the institution of police in the modern sense', but also, and possibly more importantly, a regulatory type of power concerned with 'the art of managing life and the well-being of populations' (Foucault 2009: 306). 'Police' thus stands for policy or 'science of policy'. Its main task is attending to the basic necessities of life of the population, providing them with an education and an occupation, making possible their orderly circulation, and ensuring the growth of their wealth and the preservation of their health. All these goals are instrumental for augmenting and enhancing the state's strength. To achieve this task, the police cannot just attend to the biological well-being of the population, but must also focus on 'individual felicity', on the 'well-being [of the population] beyond [mere biological] being', by 'procuring the happiness of its subjects' (Foucault 2009: 306). As Mika Ojakangas observes, even though the new rationality of government that underscores the biopolitical project relinquishes the goal of total control of *raison d'État* by introducing the principle of self-limitation of governmental reason, the concern with happiness and care for the emotional well-being of the population retains a central presence in the biopolitical episteme. This means that the 'ideology of the police' should be considered a crucial precursor of modern biopolitics (Ojakangas 2016: 31).

Recent research in human geography and cultural studies has emphasized how 'the affective life of individuals and collectives is an "object-target of" and "condition for" contemporary forms of biopower' (Anderson 2012: 28; see also Clough 2008 and Rutland 2015). Two main dynamics can be identified. First, 'capital extracts value from affect—around consumer confidence, political fears, etc., such that the difference between commodification and labor, production and reproduction, are collapsed in the modulation of the capacity to circulate affect' (Clough 2008: 16). Second, capital does not just extract value from affect. As part of the neoliberal process of economization of society, affect becomes a form of capital that is instrumental for governing the population. Promoting enjoyment, positive feelings, fulfilling emotions, and rewarding passions—in other words—caring for the emotional well-being of the population through the accumulation of constructive sentiments becomes a central biopolitical rationality of government.

From the perspective outlined in this section, humanitarian government does not primarily concern the government of disenfranchised subjects, but the biopolitical government of host populations through the humanitarian government of refugees. The latter, when recognized as emasculated innocent victims, can become biopolitically 'valuable lives' because they are instrumental to enhance and maximize the life of the host population by enticing positive feelings of compassion and moral righteousness. Hence, the Syrian refugees welcomed by New Zealand discussed in Chapter 3 can be considered the result of a 'differentialist' rationality of biopolitical racism that redraws the line between who must live, because they are deemed valuable from a neoliberal biopolitical perspective, and who must die. Biopolitical rationalities of care, both in their emotional and biological declensions, provide the measure of value in a neoliberal order and are therefore a central pillar of neoliberal citizenship. In Section 3, I will explore this argument with reference to the British and German responses to the plight of Syrian refugees following the death of Alan Kurdi.

3. Biopolitical care

The nature of biopolitical racism in the British context needs to be understood with reference to widespread socio-political anxieties about Islam and long-standing fears about Britain being 'swamped by people with a different culture', as Margaret Thatcher (in)famously declared in 1978, stating that it was necessary to 'allay people's fear on numbers' (cited in Smith 2010: 253). These concerns have shaped a refugee policy that, across different Conservative and Labour prime ministers, has shown a central preoccupation with 'bogus' and 'undeserving' asylum seekers threatening the identity, culture, wealth, and health of the British population and undermining the protection that should be offered to 'genuine refugees' (Smith 2010: 253). It is revealing that a 2003 poll for *The Times* indicated the number of asylum seekers as 'the most serious problem in Britain at present', whereas a study published a year later by the Information Centre about Asylum and Refugees (ICAR) highlighted that some of the key terms and expressions used by the popular press to describe asylum seekers and refugees included 'scrounger, sponger, fraudster, robbing the system', 'burden/strain on resources', 'illegal working, cheap labour', 'criminal violent', 'mob, horde, riot, rampage, disorder', 'a threat, a worry, to be feared' (Smith 2010: 261).

When it comes to the current refugee crisis, the construction of refugees as potentially 'bogus' and the expression of an 'inferior race' not worthy of protection that threatens the British way of life is epitomized by a series of statements by then Prime Minister David Cameron at the apogee of the emergency in 2015. In July, Cameron spoke of 'a swarm of people coming across the Mediterranean, seeking a better life, wanting to come to Britain because Britain has got jobs, it's got a growing economy, it's an incredible place to live' (BBC News 2015b). A month later, he reinforced the classic refrain of economic migrants disguised as refugees coming to the UK to steal jobs and depress wages by portraying them as burglars trying to 'break into Britain without permission' (*The Guardian* 2015b). During that summer, he repeatedly stressed that Britain had already taken its fair share of Syrian refugees—even though the UK has the lowest number of asylum seekers and the lowest rate of approval of asylum claims among the four biggest European countries (Eurostat 2017)—and would not be 'taking more and more refugees' as this could not be the answer to the crisis (David Cameron, cited in BBC News 2015c). However, the death of Alan Kurdi prompted Cameron to change his stance.

The picture of Alan's dead body washed ashore triggered a national debate, which was fuelled by a strong sense of identification. Thousands of emotional comments such as 'My god, that could be my child, who has the same colour hair, the same chubby legs' (Gunter 2015) inundated the media. Alan was the 'ideal refugee': a child, an innocent victim who would have deserved to be helped. Cameron was quick to embrace this emotional wave—'Anyone who saw those pictures overnight could not help but be moved and, as a father, I felt deeply moved by the sight of that young boy on a beach in Turkey', he declared (cited in Sky News 2015). He vowed that the UK would 'fulfil' its 'moral responsibilities' towards Syrian refugees by taking 20,000 of them directly from camps neighbouring Syria over a period of five years privileging 'the most vulnerable: … disabled children, … women who have been raped, … men who have suffered torture' (cited in BBC News 2015a).

From a humanitarian government perspective, the decision to take only sick children, women who had been raped, and men who had suffered torture would be considered an instantiation of the simultaneous deployment of two rationalities. The first rationality is one of care for a small group of 'sick bodies' who would be welcomed as objects of compassion, rather than equal citizens. The second rationality is one of security for the majority of refugees, for whom borders would be further hardened. Deploying both rationalities would be considered a case of temporary and ad hoc intervention which privileges an immediate compassionate response focusing on a few individual lives and which ultimately underscores autoimmune tendencies that negate the very lives that are claimed to be saved. From the perspective that I have articulated in this chapter, Cameron's decision to recognize and protect the humanity of some Syrian refugees was not just aimed at governing them, but also at governing the emotional well-being of the British population. The flurry of calls urging the government to act, in fact, raised a series of questions about British identity, the crisis of British values, and the extent to which Britain was failing the test of compassion.

Harshly criticizing 'the UK's dismal record on refugees', well below that of comparable nations in the European Union, the *Financial Times* wrote that 'there is a compassionate and humane streak in the British people that ought not to be underestimated. As Europe's refugee crisis develops, it is not the defensive crouch of Mr Cameron that Britons may come to admire but the courage and principle of Ms Merkel' (*Financial Times* 2015). 'British people are compassionate people who will want to play their part' wrote two Labour MPs (Stephen Timms and Lyn Brown) (*Newham Recorder* 2015), echoed by several Tory MPs who tweeted: 'We r nothing without compassion. Pic should make us all ashamed. We have failed in Syria. I am sorry little angel, RIP' (Nadhim Zahawi); 'The UK I know has always shouldered its burden in the world. DfID is doing life-saving work abroad but we can—& must—do more at home' (Ruth Davidson); 'We cannot be the generation that fails this test of humanity. We must do all we can' (Nicola Blackwood) (*Channel 4 News* 2015). Liberal Democrat leader Tim Farron labelled the government policy on refugee as 'morally wrong', while Scotland's First Minister Nicola Sturgeon urged to 'do more' (*Channel 4 News* 2015). On traditional and social media, the idea that 'British values require that we help Syrian refugees' gained a remarkable momentum.

Undoubtedly, Cameron's pledge to take in 20,000 Syrian refugees was a way of quelling public and political pressures, including from his own party. The focus on 'womenandchildren' refugees taken directly from Syrian camps drew on racial and gender stereotypes and displayed a paternalist racism which reproduced the refugees as helpless victims who should be rewarded for patiently waiting in camps, thus further condemning those who would decide to exercise agency and resilience by seeking refuge in Europe. Yet, Cameron's pledge was also instrumental to re-establishing the social imaginary of Britain 'as a moral nation ... fulfil[ling]... [its] moral responsibilities' (cited in BBC News 2015a), hence instrumental to governing the emotional welfare of the British population, whose consciousness was no longer pacified by the narrative of the 'bogus refugees' and their portrayal as an existential threat to the survival and well-being of Britain.

Biopolitical rationalities and racism partially redrew the line between who should live and who should die by constructing Syrian sick children, women who had been raped, and men who had suffered torture as 'valuable' refugees who could enhance and maximize the emotional life of the country by restoring a self-understanding of Britain as compassionate, moral, and caring. Cameron's humanitarian government of a tiny fraction of Syrian refugees was thus a way of governing the emotional well-being of the British population and enhancing its sense of self-appreciation and self-worthiness. Yet, as I shall discuss in the remainder of this section, this limited act of humanitarianism also responded to biological governmental rationalities of care aimed at securing the welfare of the population. To explore this argument, it is necessary to compare the British response to Alan's death to the German one.

Shortly after Alan's drowning, Germany decided to immediately allow in tens of thousands of Syrian refugees and vowed to welcome up to 800,000 refugees a year. Numerous explanations have been advanced for this landmark historical decision. These include: Germans' own experiences as refugees in the aftermath of World War II, when 12 million German citizens and people of German ancestry were expelled from Eastern European countries; historical guilt for the devastations of Nazism and the Holocaust; a reaction against mounting xenophobia; Germany's 'controversial role in the Greek debt crisis' (Schmidtke 2015) and the desire of Chancellor Angela Merkel to display a humanity which had been perceived as missing in the German imposition of draconian austerity measures on Southern Europe and particularly Greece; and Germany's commitment to save Europe by preventing a humanitarian catastrophe which would most likely destabilize the countries along the Balkan refugee route.

Other accounts have emphasized Merkel's own experience of growing up in East Germany. This translated in her rebuttal to Hungarian Prime Minister Viktor Orbán's hope that more fences be built across Europe: 'I lived behind a fence for too long for me to now wish for those times to return' (cited in Schmidtke 2015). Merkel's own vision of Christian justice, the result of her upbringing as the daughter of a socialist pastor, has also been considered as an important factor in her decision to open the German border. This vision, she argued, requires caring for those in need of help and the strangers 'standing in the rain before your door': 'We hold speeches on Sundays and we talk about values. I am the chair of a Christian political party. And then people come to us from 2,000 kilometers away and … you can't show a friendly face here anymore?' (cited in Feldenkirchen and Pfister 2016).

German openness to Syrian refugees should also be understood as part of a particularly welcoming refugee policy that, until 1992, was embedded in the constitution (Holmes and Castaneda 2016: 15). The subsequent restriction of this 'previously unqualified right' (Holmes and Castaneda 2016: 16) did not prevent Germany from being 'the largest receiver of Bosnian refugees' (Valenta et al. 2020: 166) in Europe during the 1992–95 Bosnian War and one of the primary destinations for refugees from Kosovo, Iraq, Afghanistan, and Somalia. The 'compassionate pragmatism' of German 'Willkommenskultur' (culture of welcome), also motivated by a desire to oppose the still glimmering embers of racism and xenophobia (Holmes and Castaneda 2016), has contributed to establishing a self-understanding of Germany as a moral leader, capable of expressing solidarity towards distant strangers in need and, in the words of German President Joachim Gauck, committed to 'do more ... better ... in respect of ... the rights we have and are committed to ... [and] together [with other European countries], as Europeans' (cited in Schwarz 2016: 63). The Syrian refugee crisis has resulted in the emergence of a growing 'emotional experience' and 'the formation of an affective block between refugees and large parts of the German population' (Karakayali 2016). The dissolution of the German border for hundreds of thousands of Syrian refugees was therefore an expression of a biopolitical governmentality which had as its target not only and possibly not primarily the Syrian refugees, but the German population, its identity and self-understanding, through the care of its emotional well-being.

This biopolitical care of emotions, however, is not the whole story of the German 'open-arms' policy. Biopolitical concerns regarding the *biological* well-being of the German population have been equally central. They encompass the idea, championed by Angela Merkel in her 2016 new year address, that 'countries have always benefited from successful immigration, both economically and socially' (*The Guardian* 2015a), and the view of the CEO of Daimler, a major German automotive corporation that: 'Most refugees are young, well-educated, and highly motivated—just the sort of people we are looking for' (a view shared by numerous other large German companies) (cited in McGregor 2015). These perspectives are the expression of a central biopolitical technology of government: managing and regulating the demographic trends of the population in order to ensure a constant homeostasis 'between resources and inhabitants' (Foucault 1978: 140). To place these statements in context, it is essential to consider that Germany's population is declining and ageing. Whereas the population of the UK is rising steeply (expected to rise from 64.1 to 80.1 million by 2060), Germany's is falling (expected to shrink from 81.3 to 70.8 in 2060) (Peston 2015). As a result, 'the dependency ratio (the proportion of expensive older people in the population relative to able-bodied, tax-generating workers) is rising much quicker in Germany than in the UK' (Peston 2015).

According to a report published by the Centre for European Economic Research, for Germany to be able to continue to provide support for non-working older people, it will need to have an annual net immigration of more than 200,000 skilled or semi-skilled people (ZEW 2014). This is expected to result in a significant economic gain considering that, in 2012, the 6.6 million foreign residents living in Germany generated a surplus (more taxes paid than social transfers received) of €22 billion, which is expected to reach €147.9 billion over their remaining life cycle (ZEW 2014). As German economy minister Sigmar Gabriel stated: 'If we manage to quickly train those that come to us and to get them into work, then we will solve one of our biggest problems for the economic future of our country.' In a similar vein, German labour minister Andrea Nahles remarked: 'We will profit from this, too' (cited in Bellon and Copley 2015). This argument has been explicitly couched in biological terms by finance Minister Wolfgang Schäuble, who warned that '[s]ealing ourselves off [from migrants] is what would ruin us, leaving us to degenerate through inbreeding' (Schäuble 2016), thus framing migration as an opportunity to strengthen the German 'race' (in biopolitical terms).

This biopolitical concern with the material well-being of the German population well illustrates the connections between neoliberal accumulation and biological reproduction—the inscription of bodies 'into systems of efficient and economic controls' described by Foucault—and how they are employed as a means to govern an ageing population and ensure its biological flourishing and well-being. It highlights how the rationalities of value of neoliberal citizenship are informed by a fundamental biopolitical logic in which humanitarianism and the recognition of the humanity of 'others' become instrumental to maximize the life and the well-being of host populations. This argument also suggests that the biopolitical governmentality of emotions is not merely derivative of biological preoccupations, but rather that emotional and biological concerns are mutually supporting and reinforcing forces at the heart of the biopolitical governmentality of populations.

This does not mean that the resulting regime of neoliberal citizenship eschews contradictions. Angela Merkel has been the object of growing internal criticism from multiple sectors of society, particularly right-wing and far-right movements and populist parties such as *Alternative for Germany*, which see the significant influx of refugees as a threat to German identity and cohesion—that is, to use Foucault's terminology, as a threat to the German 'race'. Similar criticisms have also been voiced by some (particularly Eastern) European countries which have accused Germany's open-door policy of exacerbating the crisis by providing migrants with an extra incentive to relocate to Europe, thus further encouraging the risk of an invasion. Interestingly, though, criticisms have also been raised by more moderate, centrist, and event leftist sectors of society and political parties, both within Germany itself and in Europe.

The main accusation has been that such an indiscriminate policy of hospitality has contributed to stir xenophobia and racism and prop-up support for extreme right-wing parties.

The irony of this accusation should not go unnoticed: a country that rejects refugees on the grounds that a more welcoming approach will foster racism and xenophobia is already one that has fallen prey to racism and xenophobia. Yet, this irony does not simply signal a logical paradox, but the extent to which neoliberal citizenship is tied with a double knot to biopolitics: neoliberal citizenship entails a biopolitics of care of the host population which rests on and reinforces biopolitical racism. Caring for the host population through the care of some refugees requires stigmatizing, marginalizing, devaluing, and ultimately classifying as threatening and inferior the rest of the refugees and, at times, some of the refugees cared for when they are regarded as not as valuable as was originally thought. From this angle, the criticisms levelled against Merkel's open-door policy do not signal an underlying incoherence or a deep-seated weakness of the regime of neoliberal citizenship. Quite the opposite, these tensions are internal to its logic. The logic of value that establishes the degree of protection that certain individuals or groups should be granted rewrites as well as amplifies traditional manifestations of racism. This argument will be further explored in Section 4 through a discussion of the Dubs Amendment case in the UK and several little-known individual stories of neoliberal citizenship from France, Italy, and Spain.

4. The market value of refugees

Compared to Germany, the British humanitarian government of Syrian refugees has resulted in a much more limited reappraisal of the meaning and boundaries of biopolitical race. Their evaluation as valuable members of society who could positively contribute to the emotional well-being of the British population has been offset by their disqualification as biologically valuable in view of Britain's different demographic trends. Britain's resolution to take 20,000 refugees over five years compares very poorly with other European countries, and Germany in particular, which just in the single weekend prior to Cameron's pledge took 18,000 Syrian refugees, and, following Alan's death, over a million. In the UK, the combined emotional-biological biopolitical apparatus has redrawn the racial divide between who must live and who must die by excluding able-bodied migrants deemed unnecessary to support the economy and its welfare provisions and including a small number of extremely vulnerable subjects. This has contributed to validate Britain's self-understanding as moral, compassionate, capable of empathizing with distant strangers and of fulfilling its 'moral responsibilities', as David Cameron put it.

Yet, vulnerability alone is not sufficient to guarantee access to the system of protection of neoliberal citizenship. Vulnerability has no intrinsic value: it is a commodity for which there must be a demand to be able to generate emotional capital. Hence, its value is a function of supply and demand. A limited availability of vulnerability—particularly if properly packaged, as in the graphic image of Alan's lifeless body face down on the shore or in the promotional stunt of the 20,000 Syrian victims sourced at the origin—can boost the value of suffering. Conversely, an oversupply of vulnerability, such as that carried by overloaded and overcrowded vessels crossing the Mediterranean crammed with migrants can lead to a fall in demand, as this suffering is deemed not just worthless, but even dangerous to the point of requiring its securitization. By the same token, a high demand of vulnerability can lead to market failures if the kind of vulnerability supplied does not meet the expectations of the consumers. This is what happened in the UK in the aftermath of Alan's death.

Following the emotional wave, in May 2016, the Parliament approved the so-called Dubs Amendment to the Immigration Act which committed the government to bringing to the UK several unaccompanied minor refugees from various European countries. While the exact figure was not specifically set, the proposal and ensuing debate suggested that at least 3,000 refugee children would be welcomed under this scheme (Addley 2017). The amendment was named after its proponent, Lord Alfred Dubs, a Labour peer who arrived in the UK as a 6-year-old in 1939 thanks to the *Kindertransport*, a mission which relocated about 10,000 Jewish children from Germany, Austria, Czechoslovakia, and Poland, thus saving them from Nazi persecution. The Dubs Amendment was framed from the start as a morally noble and caring initiative which epitomized the compassionate and altruistic spirit of Great Britain, and the magnanimity and kindness of its people who fifty years on were still ready to fulfil their moral duties by rescuing innocent victims in danger. A general atmosphere of support surrounded the campaign. Even conservative tabloids traditionally hostile to migrants and well versed in their stigmatization as the source of all the evils of British society expressed their approval (see McLaughlin 2018).

The suffering of the displaced children to be rescued by the UK became a commodity in high demand. Their suffering was turned into valuable emotional capital which would enable the children to be granted protection under the regime of neoliberal citizenship. At the same time, this neoliberal inclusion mobilized a powerful wave of biopolitical racism towards the children's parents, regarded as irresponsible and morally corrupt for not taking care of their offspring. This 'fed into the demonisation of asylum-seekers as bad parents, a recurring theme of anti-asylum discourse in Britain as well as other countries' which further reinforced the sense of moral worth and value of the British public, which would 'step in as substitute parents' (McLaughlin 2018: 1760). The emotional value of the children—the quintessential embodiment of innocence—was thus boosted by a double condition of suffering: that of displacement and that of perceived parental abandonment which epitomized the moral depravity of undocumented migrants. The children could therefore be doubly rescued and, by being placed in the caring hands of Great Britain, would be prevented from becoming like their morally decayed parents.

However, in October 2016 when the first batch of child refugees arrived, they failed to meet the expectations of their clients. 'These don't look like "children" to me', conservative MP David Davies tweeted (cited in McLaughlin 2018: 1763), capturing the sense of disappointment of the British public. The latter expected cute, little, cuddly victims the size of Alan and instead was delivered young adolescents, many of whom unashamedly displayed signs of puberty (facial hair, muscles, height). This raised the terrible suspicion that the British public had been tricked and its hospitality abused, with some politicians and pundits calling for dental examinations or the use of face-recognition apps to ascertain their real age (McLaughlin 2018: 1763). Biopolitical racism was extended to the alleged 'children' refugees received, who became the embodiment of the cunningness and deceitfulness of 'bogus refugees' who had once again abused the generosity and magnanimity of the UK, thus providing further evidence, if needed, to the case for the securitization of undocumented migration.

Regrettably, this defective batch could not be returned, but at least it would be possible to stop ordering more of the same. Hence, in February 2017, after only 350 children had been relocated to the UK, the scheme was closed. Against critics who objected that the number fell considerably short of the 3,000 originally considered, the Home Office replied that the 'the specified number of 350 children … reasonably meets the intention and spirit behind the provision' and that its termination was also in the interests of the safety of children as it was acting as a 'pull factor' and was thus 'incentivising' children to make the dangerous journey across Europe (cited in Addley 2017). This argument, once again, rests on a paternalistic racism: refugees are irresponsible to the point of endangering their own lives, hence it is our responsibility to prevent this from happening by stopping a scheme which may encourage them to come to Europe.

This reasoning performs a paradoxical inversion whereby inaction is the best course of action: in order to save child refugees stranded in Europe it is necessary to leave them stranded. The neoliberal biopolitical perversity of this logic will be explored in Chapter 5, where I consider how the suspension of search-and-rescue missions in the Mediterranean in 2014 was de facto a policy of 'saving refugees by letting them die'. For the time being, it is sufficient to observe that the limited endeavour to save a very tiny fraction of victim-refugees—the expression of a neoliberal biopolitics of care of the British population—eventually resulted in the further stigmatization, devaluation, and securitization of the refugees as a whole as the sample received did not meet the expectations of the British public. The emotional capital of the child refugees was regarded as not valuable enough to guarantee their protection as human beings. While the scheme was formally reopened at the end of December 2018, following the pressure of Lord Dubs and NGOs such as Safe Passage (2018), according to the information available at the time of writing no further children have been relocated under its provisions.

So far, we have seen how the protection and recognition of humanity granted to certain *vulnerable groups* can become a function of neoliberal logics of emotional value that mobilize and amplify biopolitical racism. In the remainder of this section, I wish to consider how this dynamic can also apply to *non-vulnerable individuals* who became protagonists of commendable actions for which they were rewarded with citizenship. The first case to consider is that of Mamoudou Gassama in France. Gassama was an undocumented migrant from Mali who, in May 2018, was hailed as a hero and subsequently granted French citizenship after he climbed the façade of a four-storey building and brought to safety a 4-year-old boy dangerously hanging from a balcony. The video of his heroic gesture can be seen on YouTube as his act of bravery was filmed by numerous astonished bystanders. The remarkable dexterity, physical strength, and courage shown by Gassama earned him the nickname of 'Spider-Man of the 18th arrondissement', from the name of the district of Paris where the event took place.

The celebration of Gassama as a national hero was unanimous. Marine Le Pen, president of the right-wing *Rassemblement National* (formerly *Front National*), well-known for its anti-immigration and anti-Muslim stances, publicly supported the naturalization of the 'hero Mamoudou' (Geisser 2018: 4). However, Le Pen was also quick to emphasize that this should not make us forgetful of the numerous other migrants who commit crimes and should be deported to their countries of origins (Geisser 2018: 4). Gassama, she basically argued, should be considered an exception to the rule of the criminal and delinquent (African and Muslim) migrant. Although more understatedly, the exceptional nature of Gassama's naturalization was also stressed by French President Emmanuel Macron. During his meeting with Gassama at the Élysée Palace, Macron praised his behaviour as 'exceptional', as 'an act of bravery and strength that has drawn everyone's admiration' (cited in Poole 2018). Yet, he also stated that this would not change French immigration policy: 'We can't just give papers to everyone who comes from Mali, from Burkina' (cited in Poole 2018). Indeed, France's immigration policy had just been changed earlier in the year with the introduction of numerous measures aimed at discouraging asylum applications, increasing the length of administrative detention, facilitating the process of deportation, and strengthening the regime of border controls (see Bristow 2018).

The recognition of Gassama as human and therefore worthy of protection—as opposed to the undistinguished and threatening mass of undocumented migrants to which he belonged before rescuing the child—is made possible by a neoliberal biopolitical economy of belonging that rewrites the meaning of being a hero and of suffering. As Akram Belkaïd (cited in Geisser 2018: 7) observes, Gassama was already a hero *before* saving the child. He had left home, crossed the Sahara, passed through Libya and its detention camps, undertook the dangerous journey across the Mediterranean—and like him, many thousands of others who would deserve to be regularized. In a neoliberal citizenship regime, however, the journey undertaken by undocumented migrants is not regarded as heroic and emotionally valuable. This suffering is too dispersed, extended, difficult to imagine, and ultimately undocumented. It cannot be packaged in a 30 seconds YouTube video that can be quickly consumed and shared on Facebook, Twitter, or WhatsApp. To be valuable, suffering must be 'selected, mediated and instrumentalized' (Esther Benbassa, cited in Geisser 2018: 6), and preferably embodied by women, 'womenandchildren', children (such as Alan Kurdi), or young male adults but only when the latter behave like Hollywood superheroes.

For Esther Benbassa (cited in Geisser 2018: 6), Gassama is first and foremost 'our good conscience': his act of bravery quells our sense of justice and makes us believe that, by granting citizenship to one undocumented migrant, we are being generous, forthcoming, caring, and good-hearted towards destitute strangers. Quite the opposite, Gassama's rescue 'anesthetizes and makes us insensible to the suffering of thousands of other exiles languishing in misery' (cited in Geisser 2018: 6; my translation from French). Hence, in another perverse inversion, the heroic act of saving a child committed by Gassama does not just overshadow his (heroic) suffering in the dangerous journey to Europe, but is also weaponized against his former fellow undocumented migrants. The message is simple: your suffering is worthless and so are you, hence you do not deserve protection; to be recognized and treated as human you have to entertain us, make us feel better, increase our sense of moral righteousness and national pride, behave like a superhero; you have to contribute to the biopolitical emotional and/or material value of the country by turning your courage into a valuable commodity.

The case of Gassama is not an isolated one. In 2015, Lassana Bathily, a Malian citizen who had been living in France since 2006 and was on a waiting list to become a permanent resident, was celebrated as a hero and granted French citizenship (French Government 2015). He worked as a shopkeeper in a kosher supermarket in Paris which was attacked by two Islamic State terrorists on 9 January 2015 (two days after the *Charlie Hebdo* shooting which left twelve people dead). Bathily saved several people by hiding them in a cold storage container in the basement. In January 2019, Mahmoud Diallo, an undocumented migrant from Guinea, was also described as a hero and granted asylum status after he rescued a woman from an assault by a man who had attacked her with a knife (Seale 2019). Spain has also had its undocumented migrant hero, Gorgui Lamine Sow, an undocumented migrant from Senegal. In December 2019, Sow rescued a man on a wheelchair trapped inside a house on fire by climbing on to a second-floor balcony, hoisting him over his shoulder, and bringing him to safety. His actions, reminiscent of Gassama's, have been captured by a series of photos which have triggered a strong emotional wave. Sow was granted permanent residency a month later as a reward for his 'act of courage and service to the community' (InfoMigrants 2020a).

The final illustration I wish to discuss in this section is a recent case that occurred in Italy, where an extraordinary act of courage did not automatically translate into the granting of citizenship because of the resistance engendered by traditional racism—although, as I shall discuss in a moment, this resistance was eventually overridden by biopolitical racism. The story is that of Ousseynou Sy, a 47-year-old Italian bus driver of Senegalese origins who, on 20 March 2019, hijacked the school bus he was driving and kidnapped the fifty-one children onboard. He threatened their lives for 40 minutes and eventually set the bus on fire. One of the children, 13-year-old Ramy Shehata, managed to hide his mobile phone and with the help of 12-year-old Adam El Hamami, succeeded in alerting the authorities and providing them with precise information about their whereabouts and conditions. This information proved vital to avert a tragedy. The police successfully managed to intercept the bus, arrest Sy (who was later to explain his actions as a retaliation for Italy's immigration policy which had caused the 'death of thousands'), and bring all the pupils to safety.

The two boys were acclaimed as heroes. They were invited to popular talk shows and to meet high ranking police officers and institutional representatives, and were conferred the Gold Medal for Civil Valour, one of the most important Italian honours, which is awarded for 'acts of exceptional courage manifesting civic virtue'. A growing public, political, and media movement demanded their naturalization as Italian citizens. In fact, at the time of the event, Ramy and Adam were not Italian citizens. Despite being born in Italy, they were born from, respectively, Egyptian and Moroccan immigrant families. According to Italian law, they would only be eligible to apply for citizenship at eighteen. While support for their naturalization was strong and widespread, there were nonetheless significant sectors of the population that, inflamed by right-wing politicians and media, opposed it on the grounds that citizenship is a matter of 'blood' and 'descent', not place of birth.

Then deputy Prime Minister and Interior Minister Matteo Salvini, also leader of the populist and xenophobic *Lega* (the leading party in Italy at the time) remarked its opposition to the *ius soli* principle (citizenship by place of birth) and maintained that, in the case of Ramy, the conditions for granting citizenship were not in place due to the alleged 'significant' criminal record of one of his relatives. Citizenship is a serious matter and should not be awarded lightly, he warned, particularly when serious offences have been committed (ANSA 2019a). Salvini's unqualified allegation appeared as a smear campaign aimed to please his political constituency, which he had long fed with massive doses of anti-immigrant and anti-Muslim sentiment and resentment. The 'Ramy affair', however, proved to be more challenging than usual for his traditionally racist and generally effective strategy.

Although Ramy was the son of a Muslim immigrant, he was also a child and a hero, who actually spoke Italian with the same inflection and accent of his fellow and 'properly Italian' pupils whose rescue he had contributed to. Moreover, the accusations uttered by Salvini were too vague and did not concern Ramy, but only a relative. Even for the hard-core Lega enthusiast, it was difficult to identify Ramy with the much-hated figure of the Muslim immigrant. Salvini's constituency was split, and many of his traditional supporters regarded his opposition to Ramy's citizenship as unjustified. After a few days of dwindling declarations, Salvini eventually performed a U-turn: 'I am in favour of awarding Italian citizenship to Ramy', he stated, 'because it is as if he was my son and has demonstrated to have understood the values of this country' (ANSA 2019b, my translation from Italian).

What made Salvini forget about the alleged criminal record of Ramy's relative, to the point that Ramy turned from (despised) son of Muslim Egyptian immigrants to 'his own son'? Reportedly, in the wake of the bus hijacking, his communication and media team had been carefully monitoring Facebook posts, tweets, Instagram photos, YouTube videos, and blogs to capture the public sentiment about Ramy. This analysis suggested that those who supported the naturalization of Ramy were a majority, not just in the country as a whole but also among Salvini's voters. There was, in other words, a clear *demand* for the granting of Italian citizenship to Ramy, to which Salvini eventually responded. The biopolitical rationality of neoliberalism decreed that Ramy was worthy of recognition as a proper Italian citizen because of his emotional value and despite his Muslim immigrant heritage and the opposition of a consistent minority of the public and media pundits.

Neoliberal citizenship thus partially overrode and partially reinforced traditional manifestations of racism. As the debate on Ramy's citizenship settled, the focus moved onto Sy, the perpetrator of the hijacking, with Salvini embracing the growing demand that he be stripped of the Italian citizenship he had recently gained as a long-term resident of the country. Ultimately, neoliberal biopolitical citizenship reproduced the divide between 'good migrant' and 'bad migrant' in a market logic of supply and demand: grant citizenship to the hero Ramy and deprive of citizenship the hijacker Sy, a criminal who is also not properly Italian given his Senegalese origins. This case, like the others analysed in this section, once again shows that neoliberal citizenship rewrites the meaning of protection, inclusion, and belonging according to logics of value and irrespective of the nominal status of being a citizen. The value in question transcends monetary, financial, and economic determinations. It ultimately concerns boosting the pride, moral worth, and sense of self-esteem of the population by attending to its biopolitical care and well-being through the care of a few and selected 'others'.

Conclusion

According to Foucault, pastoral power is a crucial formation in the genealogy of biopolitics. Pastoral power is both a massifying and an individualizing power concerned with the well-being of the whole flock and of every individual sheep in the flock (Foucault 2009). The shepherd must ensure the material and spiritual well-being of the flock in order to guide every single one of them to salvation. This task, though, may require, 'accepting the sacrifice of a sheep that could compromise the whole. The sheep that is a cause of scandal, or whose corruption is in danger of corrupting the whole flock, must be abandoned, possibly excluded, chased away, and so forth' (Foucault 2009: 169). The modern rendering of this rationality of government is neoliberal biopolitical citizenship, with biopolitical considerations of care fully inscribed in and governed by neoliberal logics of value. In this regime of inclusion, exclusion, and differential inclusion, biopolitics is not just concerned with the population as a whole—as Fassin argues—but also with individual lives.

The UK decision to take in a small number of children, women who had been raped, and men who suffered torture directly from Syrian camps displays a concern with individual lives, but also suggests, beyond existing accounts of humanitarian government, that the primary target of this biopolitics of care has not been Syrian refugees but the British population and its emotional well-being following the death of Alan Kurdi. The same biopolitical care of host populations can be observed in relation to the cases of the Dubs Amendment in the UK, Gassama, Bathily, and Diallo in France, Sow in Spain, and Ramy in Italy. These cases also showed how the neoliberal logic of value that extends the protection, membership, and inclusion that individuals or groups will be granted simultaneously rewrites and amplifies traditional manifestations of racism. This points to a fundamental connection between neoliberalism and biopolitics, with the latter materializing in the two complementary and mutually supportive dimensions of biopolitical care and biopolitical racism.

Biopolitical care vehiculates the neoliberal logic of value, both in its material and emotional declensions, beyond and irrespective of entrepreneurial attempts of individuals and populations 'to turn whatever they have at their disposal into a relatively valuable asset' (Feher 2020: 157). In the case of Germany, an ageing population combined with a distinctive historical legacy have contributed to the biopolitical evaluation of Syrian refugees as 'valuable lives' which could contribute to the emotional and material well-being of the country. Biopolitical racism, on the other hand, performs two main functions. First, it rewrites traditional manifestations of racism by making possible the inclusion of Ramy as an Italian citizen. His value as a hero trumps his 'original sin' of being the offspring of a Muslim immigrant family. Second, biopolitical racism reinforces traditional manifestations of racism, as with the stigmatization of those Muslim immigrants who 'fail' to behave like heroes, through the establishment of a biopolitical type of relationship between 'worthy' and 'unworthy' individuals. In this relationship the death of the latter will contribute to strengthen and improve the life of the former in the same way that the biopolitical inclusion of 'worthy' foreigners, strangers, and undocumented migrants will.

In Foucault's description of pastoral power, the unwanted 'other' that threatens to corrupt 'the whole flock must be abandoned, possibly excluded, [and] chased away.' Neoliberal biopolitical citizenship brings this to a whole new level not just by chasing away the economically worthless stranger, but by demanding its sacrifice, in the same way that it can demand the sacrifice of the nominal citizen—the poor, the marginalized, the week, the vulnerable, the unresilient—for the sake of the market and of those healthy neoliberal citizens who thrive under its rule. Chapter 5 continues the excavation of the biopolitical racism of neoliberal citizenship by looking in detail at the moral and economic justifications behind the killing or letting die of the neoliberally unworthy, less valuable subjects.

5

If Europeans want to live, refugees must die

Introduction

In the classic *Metaphors We Live By*, George Lakoff and Mark Johnson (2003 [1980]) argue that metaphors are not just literary devices or figures of speech, but systems of meaning that shape the way in which we as individuals and groups think about the world and act upon it. This argument appears ominously relevant in the European refugee crisis. The rising number of people who, over the last few years, have endeavoured to cross the Mediterranean on overcrowded and often unseaworthy vessels in order to escape poverty, war, and persecution (almost two million over the last five years, with a million alone in 2015; UNHCR 2020) have been variously described as: 'a swarm', 'a flow', 'a flood', 'a rising tide', 'an invasion', 'a tidal wave', and a 'stream of migrants inundating Europe' threatening its economic, social, cultural, and religious foundations.

The construction of refugees as an amorphous mass of sub-humans which embodies a feral threat to the survival and well-being of Europe powerfully evokes biopolitical racism. The 'power to *foster* life' requires excluding, containing, and possibly disposing of those individuals and groups which represent a threat to the survival and well-being of the population. Biopolitical racism 'establish[es] a relationship between my life and the death of the other', Foucault (2003: 255) argues, by framing and justifying the killing or 'letting die' of the 'the bad race, of the inferior race' as 'something that will make life in general healthier: healthier and purer.' In this chapter, I argue that in the European refugee crisis this biopolitical relationship has tragically become: if Europeans want to live, refugees must die. My goal is to investigate the moral and biopolitical economy which makes it possible and 'necessary' to sacrifice the undocumented migrants coming to Europe to guarantee the survival of the host populations and enhance their life and well-being.

So far, we have established that neoliberal citizenship governs the degree of inclusion, protection, and recognition of humanity that an individual or a

Neoliberal Citizenship. Luca Mavelli, Oxford University Press.
 DOI: 10.1093/oso/9780192857583.003.0005

group will be granted according to their economic or emotional value. We have also considered that neoliberal citizenship ascribes the lack of such value to inner deficiencies of individuals and groups—namely, their lack of resilience and incapacity to comply with the neoliberal logics of the market—rather than to structural conditions of inequality and exploitation. Neoliberal citizenship activates a process of blaming and scapegoating, with blame transferred from the market to vulnerable groups, and then from—and by—one vulnerable group to the other. This regime establishes that the 'unworthy' refugees will have a subtractive impact not just on the country's economy, but on its cultural mores and religious beliefs—particularly in Europe where the categories of 'undocumented migrants' and 'Muslims' tend to overlap (Casanova 2006a: 76)—and on social cohesion, by raising the level of conflict and xenophobia.

To understand why this subtractive effect is of such magnitude to require the sacrifice of refugees as necessary for Europeans to survive, we need to look at the socio-political 'imaginary of catastrophe' (Aradau and Van Munster 2011) in which the rationalities of value and politics of scapegoating of neoliberal citizenship are mobilized. This imaginary is an offshoot of neoliberalism as a crisis-driven regime of governance. As discussed in Chapter 2, the 2008 financial crisis has introduced a fundamental transformation 'of neoliberal rationalities and technologies', that is, a new regime of government that naturalizes 'the inevitability of catastrophe' (Dean 2014: 159–60). Whereas a crisis-driven mode of governance authorizes the use of exceptional measures, a catastrophe-driven one makes exceptional measures necessary and inescapable to avoid annihilation. The neoliberal slogan 'there is no alternative' (T.I.N.A.) is a product of this imaginary: a magnified crisis-driven mode of governance. In the neoliberal-biopolitical imaginary of catastrophe, the meaning of sacrifice is not confined to giving up part of one's wealth, well-being, and life for the sake of the market and its thriving citizens. Sacrifice requires killing, letting die, and accepting to die to preserve the existence of the market and its related neoliberal life.

To advance this argument, I focus on the largely neglected connection between biopolitics, economics, and imaginaries of catastrophe. Arguably, this neglect reflects a limit of Foucault's argument (one which has trickled down to the copious literature it has inspired), namely, that '[w]hen it comes to the way in which the calculations of [neoliberal] political economy are manifest in the [biopolitical] governance of both individuals and the populace as living beings, neither Foucault's lectures on governmentality nor the rest of his work offers more than scattered, fragmentary remarks' (Bröckling 2011: 248). This limit is particularly evident in Foucault's failure to connect his early 1970s economic reflections on the 'anthropology of finitude' (Foucault 2002 [1970]: 280) with his late 1970s explorations of a 'constitutive connection between the biopolitical regulation of life and an "economical government"' (Bröckling 2011: 248). Differently said, Foucault's exploration of neoliberal theory and practice of government in which 'society [is] regulated on the basis of and in terms of the competitive market economy' (Foucault 2008: 160) does not explicitly take into account his early 1970s reflections on the economic limits of human existence.

To address this gap, in Section 1, I theorize biopolitics as the manifestation of an underlying 'anthropology of natural finitude' that informs a neoliberal bioeconomy of scarcity, the condition of possibility of a catastrophe-driven mode of governance. To this end, I draw on a recent stream of research that emphasizes how the notion of population advanced by the English cleric and scholar Thomas Robert Malthus (1766–1834) crucially inspires Foucault's approach (Tellman 2013; Dean 2015). In particular, I explore how neoliberal biopolitics encompasses an underlying 'bioeconomic necessity' (Dean 1991: 120, 149) that frames 'civilized populations' as being constantly exposed to the existential threat of 'savage populations' and their unrestrained tendency to reproduce beyond the available means of subsistence. While the most visible expression of this catastrophic threat—the scarcity of resources caused by overpopulation—is economic and material, the genesis of the problem is moral. Incapacity, indolence, irresponsibility, and lack of foresight make the savage underclass responsible for its own condition.

From this perspective, helping the 'savages'—be they the poor, the homeless, the migrants crossing the Mediterranean, or the debased citizens of austerity—by throwing them money, a blanket, or a lifejacket will only contribute to perpetuate and amplify their distorted and twisted behaviours, with the effect of endangering society as whole. The relevance of this argument is explored in Section 2 by looking at the 2014 decision of the European Union to suspend search-and-rescue (SAR) missions in the Mediterranean on the grounds that these missions are a 'pull factor' and thus encourage more migrants to undertake the dangerous journey and risk their lives. In particular, I show how neoliberal citizenship has turned SAR missions into Malthusian 'perverse incentives' which exacerbate the very problem—deaths at sea—that they would want to address. This portrayal has made the policy of saving refugees by letting them die socially and politically acceptable and performed a paradoxical subversion whereby an act of compassion and solidarity becomes one that feeds irresponsible behaviour and risks damaging society to the point of catastrophe.

In Section 3, I discuss how the idea of saving refugees by letting them die is not a paradox, but the natural offspring of a mode of solidarity that I label 'neoliberal humanitarianism', which is the correlate of neoliberal citizenship. This is a form of solidarity appropriated, colonized, and rewritten by neoliberalism in which exposure to death becomes a market signal that resilient migrants are supposed to correctly interpret as a negative incentive to undertake the dangerous sea crossing. Neoliberal humanitarianism is a Malthusian-inspired biopolitical rationality of government that erases the moral distinctions between security and solidarity—because it frames preventing migrants from crossing the Mediterranean as instrumental to saving their lives—and the moral divide between saving lives and sacrificing them—because the sacrifice of lives is required to save the lives of other undocumented migrants and, most of all, of Europeans citizens.

In Section 4, I consider how this sacrifice is justified by the framing of the sacrificed as savages who fail to comply with the requirements of neoliberal citizenship. Their labour is not required and their expanding presence exceeds the boundaries decreed by the neoliberal bioeconomy of scarcity. These savages carry with them the spectre of catastrophic overpopulation: a bioeconomic anxiety caused by the 'tide' of 'uncivilized' and irrationally 'prolific' refugees who are precipitating Europe in a calamitous condition of scarcity characterized by lack of jobs, falling incomes, shrinking public services, and—overall—a seismic reduction of life chances. I conclude by suggesting that the sacrificial apparatus outlined in this chapter points to a fundamental process of sacralization of the market as a core component of the neoliberal citizenship regime.

1. Bioeconomy of scarcity

For Foucault, the emergence of biopower is the product of a growing acquisition of power by the State over the biological life of individuals. This entails a reconceptualization of 'man' from body to species or population, a process that is underscored by the modern 'postevolutionist theme of the struggle for existence' (Foucault 2003: 80). War conceived as a perpetual and necessary condition of power—and, therefore, as a structuring force of states and societies—'is no longer a battle in the sense that a warrior would understand the term, but a struggle in the biological sense: the differentiation of species, natural selection, and the survival of the fittest' (Foucault 2003: 80). As we saw, with the process of neoliberal economization, the biopolitical notion of population becomes inscribed into logics and metrics of value that partially transcends social, cultural, national, or ethnic understandings of race. The biopolitical racism at the heart of neoliberal citizenship is a way of separating 'valuable' from 'less valuable' individuals, where value is a measure of an individual's or a group's capacity to enhance and maximize the economic or emotional capital of the population. The sacrifice of 'unworthy' foreigners and internal 'deviants' is thus an essential component of the neoliberal biopolitical order.

What justifies the practice of killing or letting die in such an order? Foucault does not really address this question. He fails to systematically address the relationship between neoliberalism and biopolitics and does not seem primarily concerned with the search for motivations. While he occasionally refers to the role of ideology, material interests, conflicting values, and diverging conceptions of the good, his main focus lies with how these motivations may be experienced in a biopolitical order in which 'entire populations are mobilized for the purpose of wholesale slaughter in the name of life necessity' and 'massacres have become vital' (Foucault 1978: 137). Although Foucault does not elaborate on the notion of life-necessity in his writings on biopolitics (Tellman 2013; Dean 2015; see also Bröckling 2011), he offers some scattered but important remarks on this concept in his early 1970s writings, particularly in *The Order of Things* (2002 [1970]). Here he links the idea of life-necessity to the problem of scarcity as a central dimension of the modern economy (Tellman 2013).

'In the Classical analysis of wealth', Foucault (2002 [1970]: 278) writes, 'scarcity was defined in relation to need', that is, as a relative absence, but not as a structural limitation of what could be obtained from the use of land, labour, and capital. However, the demographic expansion of the population no longer made it possible to 'subsist on the spontaneous fruits of the land', and compelled human beings to find new land for cultivation, extract more resources from the earth, and develop more efficient forms of production and exploitation of labour (Foucault 2002 [1970]: 279). These transformations take place 'under the threat of death' because 'any population that cannot find new resources is doomed to extinction' (Foucault 2002 [1970]: 279). Hence, Foucault (2002 [1970]: 279–80) contends, '[w]hat makes economics possible, and necessary ... is a perpetual and fundamental situation of scarcity', namely, an underlying 'anthropology of radical finitude' crucially linked to 'the biological properties of a human species, which, as Malthus showed ..., tends always to increase unless prevented by some remedy or constraint.' The *homo oeconomicus* of this bioeconomy of scarcity is 'not the human being who represents his own needs to himself, and the objects capable of satisfying them; he is the human being who spends, wears out, and wastes his life in evading the imminence of death' (Foucault 2002 [1970]: 280).

This argument is significantly different from the one Foucault advances in *The Birth of Biopolitics* (2008). Here he describes modern political economy as a 'method of government that can procure the nation's prosperity' through the limitation of governmental action (Foucault 2008: 13, 30). At the core of this idea is the liberal notion—most famously captured by Adam Smith's *invisible hand*—that the pursuit of individual interests will result in the promotion of the collective good (Foucault 2008: 280). Liberal economy thus differs in three main respects from the economy of scarcity. First, liberal economy rests on the idea that the market is capable of achieving an equilibrium that will result in the maximization of individual and collective goals. This equilibrium is completely missing in the economy of scarcity in which the expansion of the population always tends to exceed the limited resources available.

Second, the *homo oeconomicus* of liberal economy seeks to maximize their interests through 'truck, barter and exchange' (Smith 1957 [1776]: 12) or, in a more neoliberal fashion, to maximize their own capital value through self-investment and competition (Foucault 2008: 226–9; Brown 2015: 17). The (neo)liberal *homo oeconomicus* differs from the *homo oeconomicus* of the economy of scarcity who struggles to survive and is constantly exposed to the catastrophic threat of death. Third, in the neoliberal economy the 'constitutive connection' between biopolitics and the economy—although only tangentially addressed by Foucault—sees the former playing a central role in the establishment of the latter through 'the controlled insertion of bodies into the machinery of production' and 'the adjustment of the phenomena of population to economic processes' (Foucault 1978: 141). Foucault, however, does not explore the 'constitutive connection' between biopolitics and economy of scarcity.

My contention is that in an economy of scarcity the task of neoliberal biopolitics is to 'incite, reinforce, control, monitor, optimize, and organize the forces under it' (Foucault 1978: 136) through two main routes. First, neoliberal biopolitics establishes the narrative that those external threatening others or internal deviant citizens—be they undocumented migrants or debased citizens of austerity—consume more resources than they produce and therefore are responsible for an impending catastrophe. This narrative is instrumental to concealing the responsibility of the wealthy neoliberal subjects (for instance, those responsible for the 2008 financial crisis) that through appropriation, dispossession, and moral hazard have contributed to create the very debased subjects they now blame. Second, neoliberal biopolitics deploys 'security mechanisms' (Foucault 2003: 246) which guarantee the survival of the population by ensuring that its multiplication takes place through the selection of the most economically and emotionally valuable and the contextual elimination of less valuable subjects.

According to Ute Tellman (2013) and Mitchell Dean (2015), the fact that Foucault does not offer any substantive reflection on this biopolitics of scarcity stems from the fact that he misses a fundamental rupture in the genealogy of the concept of population, namely, that represented by Malthus' famous idea of a catastrophic disequilibrium 'between the rate of growth of the population and the rate of growth of its means of subsistence' (Dean 2015: 20). In his (in)famous *Essay on the Principle of Population*, Malthus (1992 [1803]: 4) argues that '[p]opulation, when unchecked, increases at a geometrical ratio. Subsistence increases only in an arithmetical ratio', thus posing a fundamental problem of survivability linked to the catastrophe of overpopulation. For Malthus, the main cause of this fundamental disequilibrium is not the stinginess of nature or the barrenness of the land, but the natural inclinations of populations to grow, proliferate, and expand at a ratio that will always exceed the capacity of the earth to produce the necessary livelihood.

In this situation, Malthus (1992 [1803]: 20) contends, 'the increase of the human species can only be kept down to the level of the means of subsistence by the constant operation of the strong law of necessity', namely, by a condition of deprivation and 'severe want' that temporarily re-establishes a balance between population and means of subsistence. One of the most controversial political implications of this argument was Malthus' staunch opposition to the English Poor Relief Act of 1601. This law established that each parish should 'provide relief to those in need from sickness, old age, absence of parental support, or unemployment as long as they had legal "settlement" in the locality' (Somers and Block 2005: 266). Malthus considered that this act encompassed an underlying contradiction as it encouraged the poor to proliferate and multiply, and thus amplified the very problem—poverty—it was intended to address.

For Margaret Somers and Fred Block (2005: 265), at the core of Malthus' argument lies what they describe as 'the perversity thesis', namely, 'the assertion that policies intended to alleviate poverty create perverse incentives toward welfare dependency and exploitation, and thus inexorably exacerbate the very social ills that they were meant to cure.' For them, however, the 'perversity thesis' is itself the expression of an underlying perversity: blaming the poor for their own condition and exempting the ruling political and economic elites from responsibilities. This logic transmutes the decision of denying assistance to the poor from 'cruelty' to 'compassion' (Somers and Block 2005: 266), hence as a morally laudable action.

To better understand Somers and Block's critique, it is necessary to consider that for Malthus poverty is primarily a moral problem, not a problem of resources. It is the result of irresponsible individuals who 'live from hand to mouth' (Malthus 1992 [1803]: 101), that is, of individuals who are completely absorbed by the satisfaction of immediate needs and pleasures to be unable to plan, organize, and project themselves in the future. Hence, throwing more resources at the poor will only make things worse by encouraging them to proliferate and multiply in the framework of a culture of dependence which will bring 'ever-expanding levels of irresponsible sexuality, sloth, and moral degradation' (Somers and Block 2005: 271). This dependable mass of destitute beings will worsen the problem of overpopulation, bringing further pressure on already limited and overstretched resources, with potentially catastrophic effects on the well-being of society. Hence, Malthus (1820: 279) concludes, it is 'quite obvious' that 'the knowledge and prudence of the poor themselves, are absolutely the *only* means by which any general and permanent improvement in their condition can be effected.'

Malthus' catastrophic theory of population is thus the product of an economy of scarcity, which is in turn engendered by a moral problem: the incontinence, lust, and lack of foresight of the poor who are to blame for their own condition. Yet, Malthus' argument is also seminally biopolitical in that it understands the poor as a threat to the survival, growth, and well-being of the population. Accordingly, it establishes what Foucault would describe as a racist 'biological-type relationship' in which '[t]he more inferior species die out, the more abnormal individuals are eliminated, the fewer degenerates there will be in the species as a whole, and the more I—as species rather than individual—can live, the stronger I will be, the more vigorous I will be' (Foucault 2003: 255). This biopolitical relationship is also a moral relationship based on a bioeconomy of scarcity and catastrophe that informs and shapes neoliberal citizenship.

As Ute Tellman (2013: 135) has convincingly argued—yet without drawing any connection with Foucault's notion of biopolitical racism—for Malthus 'the question of population is tied to a colonial hierarchy that differentiates between dangerous "savage" and economic "civilized" life' in which the former represents a constant threat to the latter to the point that their 'right to live' should not be taken for granted. And indeed, in his first edition of the *Essay on the Principle of Population*, Malthus did not shy away from advancing the controversial view that the poor should not be automatically granted the 'right to live'.

> A man who is born into a world already possessed, if he cannot get subsistence from his parents on whom he has a just demand, and if the society does not want his labour, has no claim of right to the smallest portion of food, and, in fact, has no business to be where he is. At nature's mighty feast there is no vacant cover for him. She tells him to be gone, and will quickly execute her own orders ... if these guests get up and make room for him ... the order and harmony of the feast is disturbed, the plenty that before reigned is changed into scarcity.
>
> (Malthus 1992 [1803]: 249)

These remarks suggest that while Foucault almost completely ignored Malthus' catastrophic theory of population (save for the very brief remark in *The Order of Things* discussed earlier in this section), his biopolitical argument is consistent with and, indeed, may have been implicitly informed by Malthus' economic account. I therefore disagree with Tellman's and Dean's view that Foucault completely misses the Malthusian rupture in the genealogy of the concept of population. Although largely underdeveloped, this rupture is implicitly present in Foucault's notion of biopolitical racism. As I have shown, it is possible to connect Foucault's account of biopolitics with his earlier reflections on the economy as a product of an 'anthropology of finitude', and ground his frugal reflections on biopolitics and sketchy remarks on biopolitical racism on a bioeconomy of scarcity that makes the killing or letting die of foreigners and deviants a life-necessity and a central feature of neoliberal citizenship.

This argument does not suggest a tension between Foucault's early writings on the 'anthropology of finitude' and the economy of scarcity and his later writings on neoliberalism. Quite the opposite, it indicates that the politics of value and care at the heart of neoliberal biopolitics cannot be pursued solely through an art of government in which 'society [is] regulated on the basis of and in terms of the competitive market economy' (Foucault 2008: 160), that is, through self-interested and self-oriented entrepreneurial subjects whose interests naturally coalesce thanks to a Smithian *invisible hand*. The existence of the neoliberal society also depends on the elimination of those 'uncivilized' internal deviant elements and external threatening 'others' who 'live from hand to mouth', whose labour may not be wanted, and who reproduce and proliferate at a rate of growth that vastly exceed that of the economy. The neoliberal order and neoliberal citizenship thus crucially rest on the deployment of biopolitical racism in the awareness of the existence of a fundamental biopolitical economy of necessity, scarcity, and catastrophe associated with the threatening presence of 'uncivilized populations'.

In Section 2, I explore how this argument provides a powerful framework to account for the biopolitical injunction that *if Europeans want to live, refugees must die*. Focusing on the suspension of search-and-rescue missions in the Mediterranean to discourage prospective undocumented migrants to embark on the dangerous sea crossing, I explore how this strategy of deterrence constructs refugees as fundamentally irrational, irresponsible, and uncivilized—hence, as ultimately to be blamed for their own fate—while presenting the suspension of SAR missions as a responsible act of compassion of the superior, civilized Europeans. SAR missions have been turned into a Malthusian perverse incentive to the effect that, in a paradoxical inversion, letting the refugees die is presented as a way of saving them.

2. Saving refugees by letting them die

On 3 October 2013, a boat carrying hundreds of undocumented migrants from Libya to Italy capsized off the Italian island of Lampedusa. Almost 400 people lost their lives in what was, at that time, the worst shipwreck of recent years (this ominous record was tragically broken less than a year later when more than 500 people died off the cost of Malta and then again on 19 April 2015, when a migrants' boat capsized off the coast of Libya, killing an estimated 700 people). In Italy, the dramatic testimonies of the survivors, underwater images and footage showing hundreds of bodies trapped in the sunken boat (including that of a couple embracing each other), and the photos of hundreds of coffins (many of them child-size) lined-up in the hangar of the airport of Lampedusa found ample coverage in the media. Then Italian Prime Minister Enrico Letta took many symbolic steps to address public calls for more humane approaches to undocumented migrants. He proclaimed a day of national mourning, stated that the victims of the Lampedusa disaster would be considered Italian citizens, and that it was 'fundamental to apply the pope's appeal launched in Lampedusa: "Never again"' (cited in Salerno 2015; Rygiel 2016).

More concretely, on 18 October 2013, Letta presided over the launch of *Mare Nostrum*, a search-and-rescue (SAR) operation almost entirely funded by Italy that saw the deployment of ships, helicopters, and airplanes up to the Libyan coastline in order to help migrant boats in distress and prevent deaths at sea. *Mare Nostrum* was extremely successful. Over one year, it rescued more than 150,000 people (UNHCR 2014). Yet, on 31 October 2014 it was terminated and replaced by *Triton*, a EU-funded operation run by Frontex (the European Union's borders agency) with a third of the budget of *Mare Nostrum*, less naval and aerial capabilities and, most of all, a much more limited mandate which did not include SAR operations up to the Libyan coast, but only border patrolling within 30 nautical miles of Italian shores.

The decision to phase out *Mare Nostrum* and replace it with *Triton* was officially framed in humanitarian terms. In August 2014, a Frontex report stated that 'with the disappearance of the naval assets in the area [*Mare Nostrum* vessels operating in proximity of the Libyan coast], considerably fewer migrants would risk departing in bad weather and the prices of the sea-trips would rise due to the fact that more fuel and food/water would be needed for a longer trip.' In an intervention at the EU Parliament in September 2014, Frontex's executive director Gil Arias-Fernández explained that 'the smugglers have abused of the proximity of the operation to the Libyan coast to … put more people on the sea, with … less fuel, less food, less water on the vessel … [on the] assumption that they will be rescued very soon … [all of which] increases the risk for the migrants' (cited in *Death by Rescue* 2015).

The representation of SAR missions as Malthusian 'perverse incentives' which contributed to create the very problem they were supposed to address by endangering undocumented migrants rather than helping them received a strong political endorsement shortly afterwards. In October 2014, the UK announced that it would no longer support search-and-rescue missions in the Mediterranean because it considered them 'an unintended "pull factor" encouraging more migrants to attempt the dangerous sea crossing and thereby leading to more tragic and unnecessary deaths' (UK Foreign Office, cited in Travis 2015). This perspective was widely embraced by other European countries and became the rationale for phasing out *Mare Nostrum*.

In a Malthusian fashion, this argument—which will later also be used to justify the end of the Dubs scheme as we saw in Chapter 4—focuses on the 'perversity' of the incentive (SAR missions). It conceals the structural 'push factors'—such as poverty, war, and persecution, as well as the political responsibilities of the EU and its Member States—which make refugees undertake the dangerous journey. Accordingly, it implicitly points to the underlying 'irresponsibility' of refugees who entrust their lives to reckless smugglers for a journey that has caused more than 20,000 deaths since 2014 (InfoMigrants 2020b). This argument performs a dual construction: of refugees as fundamentally irresponsible—and therefore as existentially dangerous—and of the UK and the EU, which quickly embraced the UK position by phasing out *Mare Nostrum*, as responsible civilized actors primarily concerned with the well-being of the refugees. These constructions rest on the underlying perversity of the 'perversity thesis' which justifies the biopolitical 'killing' or 'letting die' of refugees as a moral act of compassion, as a way of saving them. The sacrifice of some uncivilized irresponsible refugees becomes necessary to 'save' other refugees by deterring them from undertaking the dangerous journey to Europe; hence, by preventing them from attempting to escape their condition of poverty and destitution. Yet, most of all, their sacrifice is required by neoliberal citizenship to prevent the arrival of economically unworthy individuals, and thus guarantee the survival and well-being of Europe.

This sacrifice is facilitated by the remarkable capacity of the perversity thesis to create an inverted mirror image of reality. The widely circulated pictures of overcrowded vessels crossing the Mediterranean bursting with migrants, the bodies amorphously amassed one on top of the other gasping for air or a life jacket, has inverted the terms of the moral question at stake. Rather than triggering feelings of piety and solidarity, and calls for the restoration of human dignity, these graphic images have become an ominous warning of a looming invasion, a taste of what is to come if Europe continues to toy with its (alleged) naïve, woke 'doo-goodism'. The undocumented migrants have become a savage overpopulation that should make us aware of the catastrophic risk of rescuing and allowing them in. Unlike the scarce, properly packaged, and therefore valuable suffering of Alan Kurdi's heartbreaking photo, the oversupply of suffering embodied by this desperate and for the most part black mass of humanity generates repulsion. They may have crossed continents under the most precarious of conditions and withstood unimaginable hurdles, but these are no heroes like Mamoudou Gassama rescuing a child in the glory of a YouTube video (see Chapter 4, Section 4). They are just surplus lives: unwanted and unvaluable. In this construal, the fact that this condition of uncivilized debasement and dehumanizing overconcentration of 'bare lives' is also, crucially, the responsibility of a Europe which has securitized migration, tightened its immigration rules, and drastically reduced access to asylum procedures is completely forgotten.

In the uncritical Malthusian consumption of the images of overpopulated vessels, even pregnant women—actually, pregnant women more than others—become a threat. Their pregnancy becomes the stigma of a savage irresponsibility: getting pregnant in such uncertain and dangerous times and then putting their life at risk while carrying a life inside. This unwelcomed resilience conceals another and more dangerous threat: the mass of children born from prolific immigrants. They will invade the European public space without sharing its fundamental values, beliefs, and civilized manners. What will these children become? The satirical French magazine *Charlie Hebdo*, whose staff was decimated in the tragic 2015 terrorist attack, raised this question with respect to Alan Kurdi in a cartoon published in June 2016. 'What would have he become had he had the chance to grow up?' asked the magazine. A sex offender, a rapist, or more precisely a 'rapefugee' is the answer that emerges from the drawing of an adult monkey-looking Alan chasing women.

While this miserable cartoon was—rightly so—extensively criticized for its racism, xenophobic stereotyping, and Islamophobia, the hypocrisy should not go unnoticed that many of those who felt outraged by the portrayal of Alan as a savage sexual predator are the same who support the suspension of SAR missions: a 'let them drown' policy that implicitly rests on the same perception and treatment of undocumented migrants as less-than-human. Arguably, among the many who question *Charlie Hebdo* for its callousness and cold-heartedness, are those who, in the comments sections of online articles covering the numerous tragedies in the Mediterranean, write: 'These People leave their countries at their own risk and peril and if they are so crazy to brave danger they should face the Music [sic] and if they at last find death, it is only their fault if they come to a bad end'; 'If you feel that it's your fault I and others certainly do not feel that it is ours. These irresponsible ILLEGAL immigrants know what dangers they will face so let them face the consequences'; 'Honestly these people flee their own mess, their wars were to get rid of their dictatorship ... sorry but it is NOT our fault' (cited in Wilson and Mavelli 2016: 267).

The suspension of SAR missions did not go unchallenged. Heated criticisms were raised by human rights organizations and sectors of civil society. Michael Diedring, former secretary of the European Council on Refugees and Exiles (ECRE), described the European approach to the crisis as that of a person 'walk[ing] by a river and see[ing] a child being pulled away by the current and think[ing]: "I'll let the child drown because then the other kids will know that they shouldn't fall into the river"' (ECRE 2014). Similarly, United Nations Rapporteur on the rights of migrants François Crépeau denounced that the 'appalling' logic behind the phasing out of *Mare Nostrum* 'bank[s] on the rise in the number of dead migrants to act as deterrence for future migrants and asylum seekers' (cited in *Death by Rescue* 2015). These criticisms notwithstanding, the biopolitical logic of 'letting die in order to deter' has continued to be implemented through a series of official policy documents and informal communications.

For instance, in a leaked private letter entitled: 'Concerns about engagement of Frontex deployed assets in activities outside the operational area' sent in November 2014 by Frontex's director Klaus Roesler to the director general of Italy's Immigration and Border Police, 'concerns' were raised about the possibility that *Triton* assets could be deployed outside the 30-mile patrol area off Italy's coast (*Death by Rescue* 2015; Statewatch 2017). In another example of moral inversion, the concern had nothing to do with the ineffectiveness of this move to save lives but quite the opposite. In reality, the letter intimated that a 'satellite phone call [from a suspected vessel in distress] is not per se a SAR event ... actions should be taken to investigate and verify ... and only afterwards, and in case of distress, activate other maritime assets.' As Zach Campbell (2017) remarks, with *Triton*, Frontex is 'deliberately not patrolling the area where most of the shipwrecks occurred' and its 'quibbling with definitions of distress' is purposefully designed to delay, if not prevent, SAR interventions beyond the designated area.

Unsurprisingly, the end of *Mare Nostrum* did not result in a reduction of migrant arrivals and deaths. Arrivals rose from 216,000 in 2014, to over a million in 2015, and 370,000 in 2016, whereas the number of deaths in the Mediterranean steadily rose from 3,283 in 2014 to 4,054 in 2015, and 5,143 in 2016 (Statista 2020a; see also IOM 2020), with one of the worst tragedies to date taking place on 19 April 2015 (well after the end of *Mare Nostrum*) when more than 800 people lost their lives off the cost of Libya (UNHCR 2014, 2020; IOM 2017, 2020; Missing Migrants 2017). These figures question the idea that SAR missions may act as a 'pull factor'/'perverse incentive'. They suggest that 'the intensification of crossings ... resulted from deeper regional political factors' (*Death by Rescue* 2015) concerning the growing destabilization and insecurity of the North African region (particularly Libya) and the Middle East (particularly Syria), which both preceded and succeeded *Mare Nostrum*.

The Malthusian logic of SAR missions as perverse incentives was once again employed by Frontex in 2017 to mobilize a scathing attack against private missions carried out by NGOs. Since the second half of 2015, a growing number of NGOs had begun to carry out SAR missions in the Mediterranean, thus 'filling the gap' left by Italy and the EU. Initially, NGOs benefited from widespread public support in view of their 'crucial contribution to mitigating the loss of life at sea' (Cusumano 2017: 91). It is estimated that in 2015, the three NGOs operating in the Mediterranean rescued 20,063 migrants, whereas in 2016 this figure had gone up to 46,796, with fourteen NGOs' vessels involved (Cuttitta 2018: 633). Yet, within a year, the positive climate surrounding NGOs' had progressively turned sour, marred by accusations of aiding and abetting smuggling and of putting migrant lives at risk by encouraging human traffickers to use unseaworthy rubber dinghies with limited water and fuel.

It started in the *Financial Times* (2016), in December 2016, with an article based on a confidential report from Frontex, the European Border and Coast Guard agency, which alleged that NGOs rescuing migrants in the Mediterranean may be abetting smuggling. A few weeks later, new Frontex director Fabrice Leggeri stated that by 'picking up migrants ever closer to the Libyan coast', NGOs were encouraging 'traffickers to force even more migrants on to unseaworthy boats with insufficient water and fuel', with the effect of supporting traffickers' business and putting more migrant lives at risk (*The Guardian* 2017). In February 2017, a Frontex Risk Analysis report (2017) suggested a connection between the high number of migrants crossing the Mediterranean route in 2016 (181,459), the highest number of deaths ever recorded (5,083), and the rise of NGOs' involvement in search-and-rescue (SAR) operations from 5 per cent to 40 per cent in the second half of the year. NGOs' SAR missions, the report stated, encourage migrants to undertake the dangerous sea crossing 'since they are aware of and rely on humanitarian assistance to reach the EU', and thus are contributing to worsen 'the safety of migrants and refugees' (Frontex 2017).

NGOs' SAR missions, the report continued, 'unintentionally help criminals achieve their objectives at minimum cost, strengthen their business model by increasing the chances of success' (Frontex 2017). They also inspire migrants and refugees to undertake the dangerous sea crossing, as they are 'encouraged by the stories of those who had successfully made it in the past' (Frontex 2017). This has resulted in the worsening of their safety and, 'most significantly', in an 'increasing number of fatalities' (Frontex 2017). These arguments have become part of a broader campaign of 'de-legitimization and criminalization' that has seen the active involvement of 'high-level politicians, and the media' (*Blaming the Rescuers* 2017). NGOs have been accused of colluding with people smugglers, supporting illegal immigration, acting as 'taxi cabs for migrants', and 'aiding and abetting the invasion of Europe' (see Floris and Bagnoli 2017). This 'has also led to the opening of several exploratory inquiries by prosecutors in Italy' (*Blaming the Rescuers* 2017) and the drafting and enforcement of a code of conduct by the Italian government that severely limits the humanitarian independence of NGOs, for instance, by forcing them to accept the presence on their vessels of armed police. The combined effect of these policies and societal pressures has forced many NGOs to significantly scale down and, in some cases, even halt their operations.

As the discussion carried out in this section suggests, the Malthusian-inspired neoliberal biopolitics of saving refugees by letting them die thrives on a paradox, on a fundamental tension that posits the killing or letting die of the refugees—their sacrifice—as necessary to make them live. It could be argued that this tension disqualifies the very humanitarian element at the heart of this policy, which is solely the hypocritical manifestation of a strategy of deterrence primarily concerned with the protection of the European neoliberal life. Alternatively, from the perspective of humanitarian government articulated in the previous chapter, saving refugees by letting them die may be regarded not as the result of a plain hypocrisy but of an 'autoimmune crisis' in which 'the very lives that are identified as in need of protecting and saving can also become targeted by lethal apparatuses of security' (Little and Vaughan-Williams 2017: 19).

In Section 3, I offer a third argument: the policy of saving refugees by letting them die is the natural offspring of an economized mode of solidarity and biopolitics of care that can be described as 'neoliberal humanitarianism'. This argument, to be sure, does not aim to ascribe a positive moral value to a policy that, it should be clear from the above, I consider morally despicable. My aim is to show how solidarity and humanitarianism are appropriated, colonized, and rewritten by neoliberalism to the effect that the policy of saving refugees by letting them die is the product of an ultimate (however twisted) rationality of care.

3. Neoliberal humanitarianism

In Chapter 4, I began to investigate the connection between neoliberalism and biopolitics by showing how neoliberal citizenship encompasses a biopolitical logic of care of the population aimed at maximizing its economic and emotional value. I also considered how neoliberal citizenship mobilizes biopolitical racism in order to exclude 'worthless' individuals and groups which are regarded to have a subtractive impact on the economic or emotional value and well-being of the population. My argument was that the regime of differential inclusion that governs the refugee crisis is a manifestation of the neoliberal-biopolitical care of host populations. In this section, I argue that these same rationalities are also, *secondarily*, forms of biopolitical care of refugees and an expression of neoliberal humanitarianism. Yet, my contention is that the care in question does not concern those who are included and granted protection, but those who are excluded.

This argument may appear counterintuitive. After all, I have been arguing that biopolitical racism needs to be understood in the framework of a neoliberal bioeconomy of scarcity characterized by the threat of catastrophe caused by the moral failure of savage populations. Hence, any attempts to help them—from giving money to the poor to rescuing migrants stranded in the Mediterranean—will be a Malthusian 'perverse incentive' that only aggravates the problem it aims to solve. This may suggest that the policy of saving refugees by letting them die is simply a strategy of deterrence and a rather pitiful way of masking our indifference and lack of care for the fate of the vulnerable. However, this would be a hasty conclusion that does not take into account how biopolitics needs to be understood within the framework of neoliberalism, and therefore, how the notions of enhancing, optimizing, and fostering life take shape in and meaning from a distinctive neoliberal context. To understand how neoliberalism rewrites the meaning of strengthening and maximizing life, we need to go back to and expand the analysis of the neoliberal rationalities of government (governmentalities) introduced earlier in the book.

Neoliberalism is a political rationality based on the principle of minimum government and a regime of subjectification aimed at the production of self-regulating subjects. Neoliberal governmentality can be described as a way of 'governing at a distance' by establishing and managing 'the conduct of conduct' (Foucault 1994; see also Gordon 1991: 2)—or, following Talal Asad's (2006: 521–2) insightful characterization, as the government's power to teach 'the subjects in its care about what counts as real, and what they themselves really are, *in order to* better govern them by letting them govern themselves.' At the heart of neoliberal governmentality, Foucault contends, lies a process of economization of state and society, namely, the application of market competition to all spheres of human activity with the effect that the market becomes a principle of 'formalization for both the state and society', as well as the individual (Foucault 2008: 117). The neoliberal society rests on the assumption that the market is the best mechanism to promote individual autonomy, collective growth, and the efficient allocation of goods and services in a range of domains—from politics to the family, to education.

The (alleged) greater autonomy that characterizes the neoliberal citizen, however, comes with a fundamental reconfiguration of provisions and services from shared duties, societal responsibilities and collective goods, to individual commodities. Education and healthcare, to take two examples, are less and less understood as collective goods which are the responsibility of society as a whole. They are purchasable assets in which individuals decide to invest according to their possibilities, personal circumstances, opportunity costs, and strategic goals (maximizing one's life chances, individual career opportunities, or financial returns; see Mavelli 2014). Accordingly, the progressive privatization of education and healthcare has not just been the product of 'retreating states' making space for private market actors, but of entrepreneurial states that have actively reconfigured the meaning of and reorganized these sectors according to market-based logics of competition.

It follows that neoliberalism cannot be reduced to 'the state's organization of its own retreat' (Dardot and Laval 2013: 2). It is a rationality of government actively pursued by states and, more broadly, political institutions that aims to promote the economization of all domains of human activity in the belief that this will maximize autonomy, efficiency, individual interests, and collective value. For this reason, Foucault (2008: 145) maintains, in neoliberalism '[g]overnment must not form a counterpoint or a screen ... between society and economic processes' with, for instance, 'welfare or suchlike policies', in order to correct what may be regarded as 'the destructive effects of the market on society' (Foucault 2008: 145). Quite the opposite, neoliberal government must create, preserve, encourage, and support market competition and remove those 'screens' such as 'welfare policies' which may curb individual initiative, prevent entrepreneurship, and encourage irresponsible behaviours. Hence, from a neoliberal perspective, welfare mechanisms such as provisions for the poor are 'perverse incentives'. They magnify the very problem they want to address by 'discouraging work and self-reliance' and by 'seduc[ing] people in a life of dependency' that can 'be transmitted from parent to child, who may come to see welfare as the social norm' (USA Domestic Policy Council, cited in Somers and Block 2005: 234).

Foucault's considerations have prompted some scholars to reduce biopolitical care to the welfare state and thus to infer a fundamental tension between neoliberalism (with its dismantlement or scaling down of the welfare state) and biopolitics. M. G. E. Kelly (2015: 16), for instance, argues that a progressive shift 'from a race-based national biopolitics, to a micro-exclusionary form of biopolitics' based on wealth is resulting in 'a delegitimisation of the biopolitical care of the poor'. 'Biopolitics', he (2015: 16) contends, 'seems, indeed, to be increasingly subordinated to the [neoliberal] market.' Similarly, Mika Ojakangas (2005: 28) asks whether we are witnessing the collapse of the biopolitical society at the hands of a neoliberal globalization that 'takes place without bio-political considerations of health and happiness of individuals and populations.' In comparing Foucault's 'positive' account of biopolitics with Agamben's 'negative' one, he argues that '[t]he bio-political paradigm of the West is not the concentration camp, but, rather, the present-day welfare society and, instead of *homo sacer*, the paradigmatic figure of the bio-political society can be seen, for example, in the middle-class Swedish social-democrat' (Ojakangas 2005: 27). For Ojakangas, the welfare state represents the ultimate manifestation of biopolitics and therefore the neoliberal attack on the welfare state signals a fundamental crisis of the 'positive' biopolitical goal of 'fostering' and 'maximizing' life.

Ojakangas acknowledges that the biopolitical task of enhancing life precedes the twentieth-century development of the welfare state. He also concurs that biopolitics should be understood as a major epistemic break in the transformation of the logic of power—from the sovereign power 'to *take* life or *let* live' to the biopolitical power 'to *make* live or *let* die'—which has been interpreted and implemented differently by the various 'forms of governmentality [that] have held sway at different times and in different places throughout history' (Lawrence 2018: 43). These different governmentalities include pastoral power, *raison d'état*, the 'police state', liberal mercantilism, and liberal welfarism (Foucault 2009). Yet, Ojakangas maintains, with neoliberalism the 'care of life', which constitutes the 'kernel' of these different rationalities of government, is completely undermined.

Arguments such as Kelly's and Ojakangas' overlook Foucault's idea that biopolitics should be understood within the framework of neoliberalism. In a neoliberal order, the life and well-being of the population will be enhanced by the selective openness and closure of borders—welcoming economically and emotionally valuable migrants and excluding unworthy ones—as well as by the elimination of those 'perverse incentives'—such as welfare provisions—which allegedly contribute to poverty, social vulnerability, and economic debasement. Hence, to the extent that neoliberalism frames welfare provisions as perverse incentives that are ultimately detrimental to the well-being of the population, their neoliberal removal, even if it aggravates poverty, social vulnerability, and economic debasement, is an act of biopolitical care aimed at 'enhancing', 'strengthening', and 'maximizing' life by fostering responsible and entrepreneurial individuals.

This suggests that there is no tension between neoliberalism and biopolitics. Neoliberalism is a political project that envisages and strives to establish a population of individualized, independent, autonomous, self-regulating, self-reliant, and resilient subjects responsive to market signals and informed by a cost/benefit rationality who may be able to maximize their life chances in a plurality of domains—from education to work, leisure, and health. The removal of safety nets—welfare provisions, unemployment benefits, pension plans, free healthcare, public housing, free education, minimum wage—is designed to strengthen entrepreneurial resilient responsibility by increasing the amount of risk and degree of uncertainty in the life of neoliberal subjects. Neoliberalism aims to enhance life *by* constantly exposing it to threats and potentially death.

This exposure brings us back to the notion of resilience discussed in the second chapter. The proliferation of this concept in political discourse and policy making can be interpreted as a further entrenchment of neoliberalism in the connective tissue of society. Resilience is a form of 'embedded neoliberalism' that reinforces and normalizes the idea that individuals are ultimately responsible for their social and economic security (Joseph 2013: 38). Hence, in neoliberalism 'the only role for government is that of facilitation and enablement of more adaptive and capable individual choices—a system of techniques and practices of so-called "good governance", held to enable the better and more efficient use of markets and market-based forms of choice-making as a necessary requirement for the instauring of adaptive capacities socially' (Chandler and Reid 2016: 4; see also Chandler 2014a and 2014b). The result is that, through the notion of neoliberal resilience, 'the complex, unknowable and forever dangerous landscapes that define the topos of contemporary politics' turns the 'dangerousness of life' from a 'threat' to life to 'its condition of possibility' (Evans and Reid 2013: 87).

What this argument does not consider is that the neoliberal 'belief in the necessity and positivity of human exposure to danger', which is central to the narrative of resilience (Evans and Reid 2013: 84), is ultimately the expression of a biopolitical technology of care aimed at the construction of autonomous, independent, empowered, and responsible neoliberal citizens. From a neoliberal perspective, this 'enhancement' of life can only be pursued by constantly exposing life to danger, catastrophe, and possibly death. Neoliberalism thus performs a remarkable ideological inversion that turns welfare provisions from condition of possibility to threat to life. If welfare provisions—the screen between society and the economy—encourage individual irresponsibility and a deleterious path of dependency that ultimately reverberates with tragic consequence on the wealth and well-being of society as a whole, then their removal is an act of care. With neoliberalism, biopolitics transcends mere positive/negative renderings because its negative dimension—the exposure of life to threats, catastrophe, and death—is the very condition of possibility for the maximization of life. This of course implies that the neoliberal care of life comes at a cost in terms of disenfranchisement, poverty, and possibly death for those individuals—and sectors of the population—who fail or are incapable of reading the market and respond to its signals.

The European response to the refugee crisis is a product of this neoliberal rationality. This response has not been characterized by the 'rolling back of the state'—that is, the unwillingness of EU member states to carry out SAR missions and their subsequent 'privatization'—but by an active intervention to prevent these missions being carried out by private actors. Preventing NGOs' SAR operations should not be solely understood as an exercise of 'the right of governments to control their borders and exercise sovereignty' and thus to determine 'who will enter the country and under what circumstances' (Maley 2003: 188), but as a product of a neoliberal biopolitical rationality that applies market logics to the management of the refugee crisis. Specifically, the goal of scaling-down state-led and preventing NGOs' SAR missions is to eliminate 'perverse incentives' which could cause 'market failures', that is, the arrival of more refugees than those that Europe is willing to care for, and thus preventing more deaths in the Mediterranean. The scaling down of SAR missions is therefore a 'market signal' that aims to encourage potential undocumented migrants to carefully evaluate their life chances and take responsibility for their own decisions in a context characterized by increased levels of risk.

The biopolitics of saving refugees by letting them die is ultimately the product of a *neoliberal humanitarianism* that, through market signals, aims to maximize the life chances of prospective migrants by exposing them to death in order to discourage them from undertaking the dangerous sea journey. Prospective migrants are treated as neoliberal resilient subjects who should correctly read and respond to market signals—the 2014 Frontex report emphasized how the suspension of SAR missions should be 'properly planned and announced well in advance'—and accept personal responsibility for their incapacity to properly do so. In this neoliberal humanitarianism there is very limited collective responsibility of European governments and institutions to save those drowning at sea because 'the only role for government' is, to reprise Chandler and Reid's (2016: 4) argument, 'that of facilitation and enablement of more adaptive and capable individual choices' through a 'more efficient use of markets and market-based forms of choice-making.'

Undocumented migrants are thus expected to behave as neoliberal resilient subjects, yet to be resilient within the framework and boundaries of neoliberalism. This means that their resilience cannot manifest itself in the dangerous endeavour to seek a better life across the Mediterranean, but only in stoically and patiently waiting in refugee camps to be rescued by the magnanimous 'white Western saviour' (as in the case of the 20,000 refugees that the UK has promised to take following the death of Alan Kurdi). Those who disregard and contravene this neoliberal disposition must be sacrificed for the sake of their fellow undocumented migrants, who will therefore be dissuaded by undertaking the same course of action, and for the sake of European citizens, who will be spared the arrival of economically and emotionally unworthy migrants. This suggests that in the government of the refugee crisis there has not been a shift from solidarity to security, but the *economization* or *marketization* of solidarity towards refugees crossing the Mediterranean.

Hence, in neoliberal humanitarianism there is no tension between security and solidarity because preventing migrants from crossing the Mediterranean is instrumental to saving their lives: it is a humanitarian act of care. There is also no tension between saving lives and sacrificing them, because sacrifice is necessary to save lives and preserve the neoliberal life of European citizens. And the fact that lives are lost in this process is ultimately deemed necessary because those who are dying are not even, to go back to Arendt, just human beings without political status, but individuals who have been expelled 'from humanity altogether'. Indeed, they are savages, whose labour is not wanted and who stubbornly insist to live and reproduce themselves at a rate that vastly exceeds that decreed by the neoliberal economy of scarcity. These savages are dangerous because, as I shall discuss in Section 4, they bring with them the spectre of catastrophic overpopulation.

4. Catastrophic overpopulation

The suspension of SAR missions has taken place in a context of mounting European anxieties about an 'invasion' of undocumented migrants. The fear of 'a tidal wave of refugees engulfing Europe' has authorized the suspension of SAR operations as the enactment of the Malthusian 'strong law of necessity'. The latter, as discussed, underpins the very logic of biopolitical racism as manifested in the idea that letting the uncivilized refugees die—their sacrifice—is necessary to prevent that they may destroy the life, livelihood, and well-being of Europe. This fear of catastrophic annihilation has received slightly different declensions across Europe.

In Italy, the country that together with Greece has seen the highest number of arrivals of undocumented migrants (181,000 in 2016 and over 660,000 during the last five years; Statista 2020b), the term 'invasion' has become a regular occurrence in the political debate. The almost daily disembarkation of refugees on Italian shores together with the collapse of Italy's birth rate (the lowest in Europe) have prompted cries of a looming 'population disaster', 'demographic death spiral', and 'replacement of population' (Meotti 2017). A 2015 United

Nations report entitled 'Replacement Migration: Is It a Solution to Declining and Ageing Populations?' suggests that in 2050 a third of Italy's population may be made up of 'foreigners', also as a result of the higher fertility rate of the foreign-born population (UN 2015). This report has received wide media coverage and contributed to fears of demographic catastrophe. These fears have been exacerbated by high-levels of unemployment, stalled economic growth, and declining welfare provisions due to severe austerity measures. This has heightened hostilities towards undocumented migrants, who are increasingly portrayed as an uncivilized Muslim tide that is undermining Italy's Christian identity, as a horde of fake asylum seekers who are grabbing jobs, welfare provisions, school and hospital places which should be for Italians, and as 'an army of invaders' who are threatening the very existence of the country.

In France, the fear of catastrophe is well captured by the literary success of *The Camp of the Saints* (*Le Camp des Saints*) by Jean Raspail (1994 [1973]). This dystopian novel, originally published in 1973, describes the collapse of France and the West by unrestrained 'Third World' migration. Between 2011 and 2016, the novel topped the best-seller list and has been taken by many in France and in the West (including French right-wing presidential candidate Marine Le Pen and former US President Donald Trump's alt-right political advisor Steve Bannon) as an ominous and sombre depiction of the catastrophic implications of the current 'migrant invasion'. The story of the book revolves around an army of 'kinky-haired, swarthy-skinned, long-despised', miserable, poor, and sexually promiscuous Indians who sail *en masse* to France, the land of 'milk and honey', in order to steal a share of the 'white man's [hard earned] comfort' (Raspail 1994 [1973]: 98, 36). This 'single, solid mass' of lazy, debauched, and morally deprived 'teeming ants' resembling a 'gigantic beast with a million legs and a hundred heads' (Raspail 1994 [1973]: 98, 17) eventually succeeds in colonizing and destroying France first and then the West as a whole, by exploiting the latter's kindness towards seemingly disadvantaged populations.

As Jean-Marc Moura (1988: 123) observes, at the heart of the novel lies a French 'neo-Malthusian ideological complex' that captures Malthus' worst fear: the geopolitical catastrophic collapse of the civilized at the hands of the barbarians. The choice of the Indians as the epitome of uncivilized populations is not casual. Raspail wanted to ground his dystopian narrative into the alleged 'scientific [and ethical] neutrality of Malthus' theory of population' (Leisinger and Schmitt 1994: 48). For this reason, he considered, using 'nearby North Africans or Arabs' would have prompted a 'false debate about racism and anti-racism in French daily life' (Raspail, cited in Dalmia 2016). This 'precaution' has not sheltered the book from accusations of racism and has not prevented a contemporary reading of the novel in overtly Islamophobic and Orientalist terms, with Raspail's 'Indians' as a metaphor for backward, lazy, irrational, prolific, and threatening Muslims who are 'submerging' Europe and turning it into a 'Eurabia'.

As these vignettes suggest, in France and Italy the fear of catastrophe associated with uncivilized migrants has been expressed through a mixture of *traditional racism*, mostly revolving around the Muslim identity of the refugees, and Malthusian-inspired neoliberal *biopolitical racism*, seemingly grounded in the scientific laws of population. As discussed in Chapter 4, biopolitical racism incorporates, amplifies, and partially rewrites traditional forms of racism according to the perceived economic and emotional value of individuals and populations. Compared to traditional racism, which is 'irrational' and 'backward', biopolitical racism is rational, pragmatic, forward-looking, and capable of normalizing and authorizing 'slaughter in the name of life necessity' (Foucault 1978: 137).

To better appreciate how biopolitical racism differs from traditional forms of racism and how it rests on a Malthusian-inspired neoliberal economy of scarcity, it is useful to focus on the UK, the country in Europe which, according to a recent Pew Research poll (Wike, Stokes and Simmons 2016), has the less 'unfavourable view of Muslims'. In the UK, fears about the 'tidal wave of migrants' have often been codified privileging biopolitical racism over explicitly Islamophobic racism—hence with an emphasis on the negative impact of unskilled and semi-skilled migrants on jobs, public services, and security, rather than with a primary focus on the civilizational threat posed by Muslim migrants. Arguably, this attitude has been favoured by the construal of the EU and its people as 'different' and 'inimical' by important sectors of British society, a trend that has been strengthened in the aftermath of the Brexit referendum. This, to be sure, does not mean the absence of Islamophobia, but its incorporation into a broader regime of biopolitical racism governed by neoliberal rationalities of value and anxieties concerning overpopulation. The remainder of this section focuses on this latter dimension and its relevance for further understanding the British decision to no longer contribute to SAR missions in the Mediterranean.

In 2010, a cross-party group including Labour and Conservatives MPs as well as civil society figures such as the former Archbishop of Canterbury Lord Carey issued a 'Declaration on Population'. The Declaration warned that '[o]ver the next 25 years the [UK] population will increase by 10 million' mostly (70%) due to an out-of-control immigration (White 2010). This will have a significant negative 'impact on our public services, our quality of life and on the nature of our society', putting at risk its 'future harmony' by fuelling extremist views and placing 'a strain on public services' (White 2010). Getting immigration under control by bringing it 'to the levels of the early 1990s—that is less than 40,000', the Declaration concluded, is essential to avert the potential catastrophic effects of overpopulation (White 2010).

In a Malthusian fashion, this Declaration did not just express concerns about overpopulation, but about overpopulation caused by migrants. It depicts their contribution to UK economic growth as negligible, if not negative, as it is not expected to translate into more public resources to invest in schools, hospitals, and public services. A further illustration of the biopolitical and moral economy of scarcity that frames migrants as mere consumers of wealth is a 2013 Home Office report that assessed the 'impact of immigration on British communities' (Swinford 2013). The report warned that 'refugees and low-skilled immigrants are creating overcrowding, fuelling community tensions and putting pressure on the NHS [the National Health Service]' as the former tend 'to suffer from depression, anxiety and mental illness', whereas the latter often 'suffer from tuberculosis, HIV and Hepatitis B' (Swinford 2013). Refugees and migrants are also more prolific than native British people—which creates 'additional demands for midwifery, maternity and health visiting services'—and have a poor level of English—which results in longer GP appointments (Swinford 2013). The report offered similar arguments to assess the impact of migrants on school and other public services. It concluded by warning that, in the absence of proper restrictions on immigration, communities will be damaged and services overstretched.

This report offers a remarkable instantiation of Malthusian reasoning. Malthus' savages were marked by 'perpetual diseases', were short and monstrous, with 'protuberant bellies', 'large heads' and 'covered with filth and vermin'; they lived 'hand to mouth' and always 'pressed hard' against the limits of available means of livelihood, with no foresight and concern for the future (Malthus 1992 [1803]: 43ff). In a similar fashion, refugees and low-skilled migrants are presented as an amorphous mass of uncivilized savages who are physically and mentally impaired, unable to speak properly, and incapable of producing wealth, only capable of consuming it. They are weak, and yet dangerous as a mass in constant expansion due to their irresponsible sexual reproductive behaviours. In a bioeconomic framework of scarcity, they have a catastrophic negative impact on 'on a range of services, from the queue for social housing ..., to hospital, maternity and GP services as well as education, public transport, the environment [due to a higher demand of homes which "adds to pressures on our countryside and the green belt"] and the general transport infrastructure' (Migration Watch UK 2016).

These Malthusian considerations have repeatedly punctuated British political discourse. Consider former Prime Minister David Cameron's depiction of undocumented migrants as a 'swarm' and a 'bunch' trying to 'break into Britain without permission' to get 'a better life' because 'Britain has got jobs, it's got a growing economy, it's an incredible place to live' (BBC News 2015b; *The Guardian* 2015b; *The Independent* 2016a). This is reminiscent of France, and the West more broadly, as the land of 'milk and honey' described by Raspail. Similarly, former Secretary of State William Hague (2015) stated that the European migrant crisis is 'a mere gust of the hurricane that will soon engulf Europe': a symptom of a more fundamental problem of overpopulation in Africa and west Asia that is spilling over into Europe (just like Indian overpopulation spilled into France, as in Raspail's story). Former Prime Minister Theresa May is no exception to this script. For her, the UK is 'a country of remarkable population stability' which is threatened by the 'millions of people in poorer countries who would love to live in Britain' and the hundreds of thousands who actually made it to the UK, forcing 'thousands of people ... out of the labour market' and worsening the housing crisis and the overcrowding of public schools (*The Independent* 2016b).

Arguably, these Malthusian reasonings have crucially fuelled 'Britain's obsession with net migration' (Semmelroggen 2016) and prompted the 2010 Conservative pledge to cut migration to the tens of thousands. Indeed, it is the very existence of such a target—a central feature of the Brexit referendum debate—that has shaped Britain's response to the refugee crisis (Griffith 2016) and prompted it to opt out of search-and-rescue operations in the Mediterranean. At the heart of this decision thus lies a Malthusian-inspired neoliberal biopolitical moral and political economy in which the uncivilized savages emerge as a feral threat to the survival and well-being of the British population. In such a bioeconomic framework of scarcity the moral course of action is dictated by necessity. Saving the 'swarm' of refugees irresponsibly risking their lives in the Mediterranean will only increase the 'flood' that will submerge the UK and Europe. From this perspective, neoliberal biopolitical racism—'making live' my population by 'letting die' the inferior race—is the only sound economic and moral course of action.

Conclusion

Well before the eruption of the European refugee crisis, neo-Malthusian ecologist and philosopher Garrett Hardin (1974, 1980) famously argued that nations should be considered like 'lifeboats'. Whereas wealthy nations/lifeboats are 'full of comparatively rich people', poor nations/lifeboats are overcrowded. As a result, 'the poor fall out of their lifeboats and swim for a while in the water outside, hoping to be admitted to a rich lifeboat' and 'benefit from the "goodies" on board' (Hardin 1980: 172). This poses a considerable ethical problem: 'What should the passengers on a rich lifeboat do?' For Hardin, welcoming the poor would eventually sink the wealthy boats, because, as neoliberal economist Milton Friedman once said: 'You can't have free immigration and a welfare state', and because the poor lack the reproductive continence of the rich (Hardin 1988: 186). Welcoming a rapidly expanding mass of poor would eventually result in the elimination of the wealthy host, with the effect that wealthy nations/lifeboats would disappear and the whole world would turn catastrophically poor. Hence, letting the poor drown may be the only economically and morally viable course of action (Hardin 1974, 1980, 1988).

This chapter has investigated how Malthusian reasonings of this kind have contributed to establish the biopolitical injunction *if Europeans want to live, refugees must die* as a morally and politically acceptable response to the refugee crisis and the Mediterranean as a border zone where the death of undocumented migrants becomes essential to making Europeans live. I explored how Foucault's notions of biopolitics and biopolitical racism rest on a Malthusian bioeconomy of scarcity which frames 'civilized populations' as constantly exposed to the existential threat of 'savage populations' and their unrestrained reproductive tendencies beyond existing means of subsistence. This view provides a fundamental moral and economic justification for letting savage populations die, but also engenders a perverse reversal whereby letting the refugees die becomes a way of saving them. The resulting neoliberal humanitarianism frames undocumented migrants as neoliberal resilient subjects who must be compliant with and responsive to market signals. Their failure authorizes their expulsion from the neoliberal order. Neoliberal humanitarianism thus erases the tensions between security and solidarity, and saving lives and sacrificing them, as the sacrifice of the migrants is an act of solidarity necessary to save lives.

This analysis advances our understanding of the relationship between neoliberalism and biopolitics and its relevance for neoliberal citizenship in two significant ways. First, it establishes a crucial connection between Foucault's early 1970s economic reflections on the 'anthropology of finitude' and his late 1970s exploration of the liberal (and neoliberal) art of government as based on the model of the competitive market economy. In particular, reconsidering Foucault's notion of biopolitics in light of Malthus' theory of population and economy of scarcity suggests that liberal biopolitical governmentality cannot be reduced to governing 'the conduct of conduct' (Foucault 1994), namely, to the promotion of forms of self-government through the construction of self-interested and self-oriented entrepreneurial subjects whose interests will naturally coalesce as if guided by a Smithian *invisible hand*. The existence of neoliberal society also depends on sheltering it from 'uncivilized populations' who 'live from hand to mouth', whose labour may not be wanted, who reproduce themselves at an economically unsustainable level. Neoliberal citizenship thus crucially relies on the deployment of biopolitical racism, that is, on the idea that sacrificing inferior populations may be necessary for my population to survive, prosper, and thrive. In the European refugee crisis, the deployment of biopolitical racism has become *if Europeans want to live, let the refugees drown*.

Second, the arguments advanced in this chapter suggest that blaming the refugees for their own suffering should not be solely considered a strategy of deflection of official responsibilities, as recent contributions to the literature have pointed out (Doty 2011; Williams 2015; Squire 2017, 2020), but part of a neoliberal biopolitical rationality which performs a dual construction: of refugees as fundamentally irresponsible for risking their lives in the Mediterranean and Europeans as responsible civilized actors crucially concerned with the well-being of refugees to the point that their decision to stop SAR missions is portrayed as a humanitarian effort aimed at saving lives. Indeed, it is the very representation of SAR missions as 'perverse incentives' that reinforces the moral deficiency of the refugees as subjects beyond redemption, as helping them will only amplify their 'perverse' attempt to seek refuge. In this framework, saving refugees by letting them die is not just a perverse act of solidarity that has turned the Mediterranean into a graveyard, but also a way of establishing contending subjectivities: the civilized Europeans and the uncivilized refugees.

This analysis departs from traditional readings of Malthus, such as Hardin's. These readings conceal themselves behind the veil of a bioeconomy of scarcity to justify the fact that not guaranteeing the 'right to live' to the poor, the refugee, the destitute, the disenfranchised other, however unpalatable, may be the only economically and morally viable course of action. The analysis carried out in this chapter reveals that the perspective should be reversed. The Malthusian bioeconomy of scarcity at the heart of the biopolitical injunction if Europeans want to live, refugees must die has emerged not just as a problem of overpopulation and limited resources, but of overpopulation and overstretched resources caused by uncivilized populations. Even more importantly, the analysis suggests that, even reversing the perspective, the market, with its bioeconomy of scarcity, remains an autonomous and independent variable, namely, the measure, metric, and condition of possibility of life. We thus end up with a final, perverse moral inversion: it is the market that is sacred, not life, and it is the market that decides who must live and who must die. This inversion will be the focus of the next two chapters.

6

Sacred market, sacrificial lives (I)

Introduction

In this chapter, I theorize the process of commodification as one of sacralization of the market and explore its relevance for the rationalities and practices of neoliberal citizenship. In broad terms, commodification can be described as the possibility of trading goods and services for profit. For Marxist scholars, what makes commodification central to the modern neoliberal project is its colonization of all areas of life—areas which were originally spared from the economic logic of the market. Over the last century, there has been a progressive commodification of public goods and services such as railways, healthcare, forests, land, water, parts of the ocean (with the creation and sale of fishing rights), air (with the sale of carbon emissions), incarceration and immigration (with the privatization of prisons and immigration detention centres), as well as the commodification of food (take-away meals replacing cooking), entertainment (with socialization increasingly mediated by social media, thus becoming fully inscribed in a logic of profit), and the body (with DNA patents and the privatization of genetic data) (Leys 2012).

According to Colin Leys (2012), 'the dominant process underlying the transformation of life in all societies, since at least the mid-nineteenth century, is the conversion of things and activities into commodities, or commodification.' For David Harvey (2005: 160), neoliberalism has further accelerated and expanded the capitalist process of 'commodification of everything' by opening up 'new fields for capital accumulation in domains hitherto regarded off-limits to the calculus of profitability', including that of human relationships. The totalizing 'commodification of everyday life' is often described through the concept of 'cash-nexus'. Originally coined by nineteen-century Scottish historian Thomas Carlyle, this term has been popularized by Marx and Engels (2008 [1848]: 37–8) in *The Communist Manifesto* to describe the commodification of labour. By turning the labour of workers into a tradable commodity, Marx and Engels state, capitalism 'has drowned the most heavenly ecstasies

Neoliberal Citizenship. Luca Mavelli, Oxford University Press.
 DOI: 10.1093/oso/9780192857583.003.0006

of religious fervour, of chivalrous enthusiasm, of philistine sentimentalism, in the icy water of egotistical calculation'; it has 'resolved personal worth into exchange value', with the effect of leaving 'no other nexus between man and man than naked self-interest, than callous "cash payment"' (Marx and Engels 2008 [1848]: 37–8).

Historian Bruce Mazlish (1989: ix–x) argues that the 'cash-nexus' denotes the modern 'omnipresent substitution of money for personal relations' and the resulting pervasive 'sense of dislocation' stemming from the 'feeling that all connections other than the monied one between Man and Man (and between Man and Nature, and between Man and God)' have 'been broken'. Leaving aside the gendered language, this concept captures a fundamental aspect of the modern neoliberal era, namely, the idea that money has become the epistemic framework of meaning and significations, scheme of valuation, and universal measure of the worth that we ascribe to the most disparate spheres of human activity and, indeed, to other human beings.

However, as a framework for understanding the process of commodification of life, the 'cash-nexus' has two limitations. First, it reduces value to cash, money, or exchange-value (which is ultimately translated into a monetary form when traded on the market), and therefore neglects non-monetizable forms of value. As previously analysed, with neoliberal citizenship the value of refugees may transcend their capacity to contribute to the economic growth of the country. Indeed, despite their negative economic value, particularly vulnerable refugees may be regarded, under certain circumstances, as the embodiment of valuable and non-monetizable forms of emotional capital that strengthen the sense of pride, worth, and moral self-understanding of the country. Commodification, therefore, needs to be understood within the broader neoliberal rationality of economization, namely, the dissemination of 'the model of the market to all domains and activities—even where money is not an issue' (Brown 2015: 31).

Second, equating commodification to the 'cash-nexus' reduces it to a process of attachment of a price tag to every aspect of our being in the world. However, in a larger acceptation, to the extent that commodification is 'the insertion of a product of human labor into a system of exchange such as capitalism', it can also be understood as the 'removal of an object (or person) from a (theoretical) realm outside the social relations of production and its seemingly forcible incorporation into market relations' (Sammond 2007: 609). What happens, then, when the 'commodification of everything' leaves no domain outside that of market relations? A 'cash-nexus' approach and, indeed, most approaches to commodification cannot answer this question as they focus on the individual elements in the structure of commodification, rather than the structure itself. My goal in this chapter is to explore this epistemic, structural dimension of commodification by raising the following question: What happens to citizenship and the related system of protection and exclusion when the neoliberal market becomes the hegemonic and totalizing framework of meanings and significations to the point that everything is commodified? The thesis I advance is that the market is sacralized and life is sacrificed on its altar.

To entertain this argument, we need to begin with the observation that commodification is often theorized as the inverse of the process of consecration or sacralization (Agamben 2007). As philosopher Giorgio Agamben (2007: 73) considers, for Roman jurists, '[s]acred or religious were the things that in some way belonged to the gods. As such, they were removed from the free use and commerce of men; they could be neither sold nor held in lien, neither given for usufruct nor burdened by servitude.' To 'belong to the gods' does not exclusively mean to belong to an otherworldly domain. For Immanuel Kant, for instance, feelings of piety, compassion, solidarity, dignity, and empathy should be regarded as sacred because, albeit experienced and practised immanently, they belong to the transcendental domain of universal morality. Accordingly, commodification occurs when practices, institutions like citizenship, or human beings themselves are removed from the sacred domains of justice, equality, and solidarity—or, more precisely, when these domains are desacralized and inscribed into a system of market relations. As we saw in Chapters 3 and 4, neoliberalism does not undermine the principles of reciprocity, fairness, and mutual participation, but rewrites them in economic terms.

By desacralizing these principles—or profaning them, as per Agamben's terminology—through their incorporation into the market system, the totalizing process of commodification leaves no outside domain from which the neoliberal market can be questioned or challenged. The paradoxical result is that the 'commodification of everything' entails the very sacralization of the market as a transcendent domain that, following Émile Durkheim's (1995 [1912]: 44) classical definition of the sacred, is 'set apart and forbidden', hence turned into a source of truth and revelation that cannot be subjected to rational scrutiny, but only worshipped. For Agamben, the 'capitalist religion' ends up performing a process of sacralization of the market. In this chapter, I explore how the neoliberal totalizing process of commodification has prompted the sacralization of the market and the profanation of life, with the effect of shaping a neoliberal understanding of citizenship that frames immigrants as disposable commodities. To advance this argument, this chapter will investigate the visions of citizenship of leading neoliberal thinkers Milton Friedman and Gary Becker. This focus requires some clarifications.

As Dieter Plehwe (2009: 14) observes, from the onset, 'neoliberalism was anything but a "pensée unique"', but a 'thought collective' which 'drew on different theoretical approaches'. Over the years, neoliberalism's global reach, adaptive capacity, hegemonic tendencies, parasitical inclinations, and colonizing rationalities have turned it into an 'almost bewildering array of local trajectories, contingent forms, and hybrid assemblages' (Peck, Theodore, and Brenner 2009: 96). Traditional attempts to identify different strands of neoliberalism sometimes privilege a tripartite classification that includes the Austrian School, the Chicago School of economics, and the German ordoliberal approach (which was briefly discussed in Chapter 2). More often, though, a bipartite classification is adopted. This pits the 'positivist' strand of neoliberalism embodied by the Chicago school, which includes Friedman and Becker, against the 'subjectivist' approach championed by the Austrians, most famously represented by neoliberal founding father Friedrich Hayek.

While both schools share the idea that market-based competition rewards ingenuity and innovation, maximizes individual and aggregate utility, and enables the efficient circulation and allocation of capital, they rely on completely different theories of knowledge. Whereas for the Chicagoans markets exist in a condition of equilibrium and transmit all relevant objective information, for the Austrians knowledge cannot be formalized in mathematical models because it is 'tacit, private, subjective, and decentralized' (Bagus 2016). Accordingly, whereas the former uses history as a source of data to make predictions about the future, for the latter the complex dynamic interactions of the market escape recurrence and make forecasts impossible. It follows that whereas the Chicagoans favour some degree of political intervention to preserve the correct and smooth functioning of the market (particularly when it comes to the money supply), for the Austrians any intervention aiming at guaranteeing the stability of the market is meaningless, if not altogether counterproductive, given the dispersed and subjective nature of knowledge (Bagus 2016).

These differences are reflected in how these neoliberal perspectives adopt different modalities of sacralization. Friedman and Becker, as I shall discuss in Sections 2 and 3, sacralize the market by championing a totalizing process of commodification, whereas Friedrich Hayek (analysed in Chapter 7), sacralizes the market through a subjectivist epistemology of knowledge that turns the market into a source of revelation. These differences remind us that neoliberalism 'is neither singular nor constant in its discursive formulations, policy entailments and material practices' (Brown 2016: 4) and that it exists in different forms and socio-political contexts. They caution us from treating neoliberalism as a monolithic and unified phenomenon. At the same time, these differences should not make us lose sight of the fact that neoliberalism in its various conceptual declensions and practical manifestations finds unity and coherence in an underlying process of sacralization of the market and profanation of life which, to borrow Weber's (2003 [1905]: 17) famous formulation, is one of the 'most fateful force[s] in our modern life'.

As usual, the discussion proceeds in four main steps. First, I discuss Agamben's idea of the sacralization of the market as opposed to the classic idea of the secularization of the market, most famously advanced by Max Weber. In Sections 2 and 3, I look at the immigration proposals and related neoliberal citizenship regimes envisioned by Friedman and Becker. In Section 4, I show how these approaches are expressions of a bioeconomy of necessity concerned with the scarcity of valuable immigrants. The exclusion or expulsion of 'worthless' migrants will emerge as a process of disposal that, while seemingly turning them into waste, sacrifices and sacralizes unwanted migrants to the market with the effect of often re-inscribing them in the process of commodification.

1. Secular market?

Agamben's idea of commodification as a process of consecration of the 'capitalist religion' needs to be understood against the backdrop of Weber's influential contending thesis of the secularization of the market. This, in turn, requires us to dwell on Weber's understanding of religion and the sacred. For Weber, religion is not a timeless dimension of the human condition, but the first systematic attempt to address 'the experience of the irrationality of the world' (Weber 1946 [1919a]: 123). 'Irrational' for Weber (1946 [1919a]: 122) is a 'world of undeserved suffering, unpunished injustice and hopeless stupidity.' By acting as a rationalizing framework of meaning, religion performed three main purposes: serving as an epistemological framework that could account for the unknowns that surround life; explaining the 'unjust suffering' and 'unequal distribution of individual happiness' (Weber 1946 [1915]: 353); and act as a system of intersubjective moral norms. The sacred is thus, at its inception, an attempt to rationalize the irrational of the human condition. Ironically, however, 'the general result of the modern form of thoroughly rationalizing the conception of the world and of the way of life ... has been that religion has been shifted into the realm of the irrational' (Weber 1946 [1915]: 281). As a result, science and bureaucratic rationality have progressively replaced religion as the hegemonic rationalizing framework of the modern order.

For Weber, this process can be vividly observed in the emergence of modern capitalism. In *The Protestant Ethic and the Spirit of Capitalism* (2003 [1905]), he famously argues that the main driver behind the development of capitalism is ascetic Protestantism. In particular, he maintains that the Calvinist notion of predestination—the idea that economic and social success may be taken as an indication of future salvation decreed by God—acted as a transcendent and disciplinary force that encouraged a virtuous and sober behaviour compliant with religious precepts. The ascetic Protestant way of life thus has its origins in a religious calling. Yet, the advancement of scientific rationalism engendered a process of secularization (which Weber refers to as 'disenchantment') that resulted in a progressive separation of the spheres of religion, morality, and the sacred from that of the economy. Accordingly, the original rationale for the process of capitalist accumulation—the Calvinist sacred calling—was progressively replaced by the 'iron cage' of capitalism, namely, 'the technical and economic conditions of machine production' and 'care for external goods'—that is, mass consumption—'which today determine the lives of all the individuals who are born into this mechanism ... with irresistible force' (Weber 2003 [1905]: 181).

It follows that capitalism for Weber is a secularized version of the Protestant ethic. It is a regime of norms, practices, and aspirations devoid of sacred religious meanings and governed by a bureaucratic rationality that is ultimately an 'iron cage' that locks modern individuals into a 'meaningless' pattern of accumulation and consumption. Hence, from Weber's perspective, the idea that the market may be considered sacred and neoliberal capitalism akin to a religion is simply misplaced as capitalism is the ultimate embodiment of secularism and modern markets are the ultimate secular institutions. This view is powerfully articulated by Jürgen Habermas in his recent critique of the secular market order.

For Habermas (2008: 111; see also Habermas et al. 2011), secularization is the expression of a process of instrumental rationalization that has enslaved individuals in the impersonal and dehumanizing forces of 'markets and administrative power'. For this reason, he (2008: 107) argues, recovering the moral intuitions of faith becomes essential to counter a secular modernization that has replaced 'domains of life that used to be held together by norms' with market 'mechanisms of instrumental action guided by individual preferences' and the 'uncontrolled dynamics of the global economy'. Habermas thus advocates a postsecular shift, namely, a new role for religion in the public sphere as a source of inspiration for moral action. As he explains, religion has a 'semantic potential' that 'can "help us express our best moral intuitions without burning the bridges to secular languages and cultures". We should respect the "power of articulation" of religious language and recover the "regenerative power" it offers for a "dwindling normative consciousness"' (Habermas, cited in Harrington 2007: 544).

Habermas' account can be read as a continuation of Weber's thesis and attempt to reverse its tragic outcome. For Weber, one of the consequences of the 'irrationalization' of religion has been the rise of the 'iron cage' of secular bureaucratic rationality as embodied by the capitalist market system. For Habermas, to oppose this degeneration, the solution is to recover from religious traditions some universally valid moral and 'sacred' principles—that is, principles which should be freed from the totalizing logic of the market and returned to their original autonomous domains. Following Habermas, then, the idea that neoliberalism may be considered a form of religion is at best impressionistic—and therefore lacking any analytical value—and at worst deceptive, because the neoliberal market is the ultimate embodiment of the secular order.

A different reading of Weber is offered by Bethany Moreton (2009), who focuses on the case of the United States. In her celebrated *To Serve God and Wal-Mart*, she argues against those dominant interpretations of Weber's thesis that see in the exponential acceleration of twentieth-century mass consumption the ultimate manifestation of the secularization of the Protestant ethic. To argue that 'American Protestantism lost the battle' and that '[s]alvation gave way to self-realization', she argues, would be to miss the growing relevance of 'the new Christian right of the 1970s and 1980s' and how it contributed to shape a 'powerful counterculture' that 'combined religious efforts to regulate sex', family values, communal life, ideas of citizenship, and understandings of the role of government 'with an equally religious celebration of material comforts, self-expression, technological innovation, and secular success' (Moreton 2009: 87–8, 156).

For Moreton (2009: 86–8), what the new Christian right has managed to accomplish is nothing less than '[s]anctifying capitalism and consumption under Christianity' with the effect that, in a reversal of the trajectory described by Weber, '[s]elf-realization placed salvation back into the centre of American public [and economic] life.' In her account, this dynamic is vividly illustrated by the retailer giant Wal-Mart. 'People within the orbit of Wal-Mart,' she explains, 'learned to revalue shopping as selfless service to family, and service in turn as a sacred calling. In this context, the salient identity became not citizen-consumer nor worker of the world, but Christian servant' (Moreton 2009: 101). This view departs from Habermas and Weber as it suggests that the modern neoliberal order continues to be sustained (at least in the USA) by the Protestant ethic, whose 'sacred calling' is now the duty to 'consume' and 'helping others consume' (Moreton 2009: 107, 101).

Unlike Habermas, Moreton frames the market as a means to salvation through the process of mass consumption rather than an expression of anomic and dehumanizing secular rationalities. However, like Weber and Habermas, she regards the market as a fundamentally secular institution governed by principles of profit, risk taking, and entrepreneurship, whose ultimate rationale is generating material welfare and rewards. Like Weber and Habermas, therefore, she does not consider the possibility that the sacralization of mass consumption engendered by the 'commodification of everything' may have also resulted in a process of sacralization of the market.

To entertain this possibility, we need to turn to Agamben's idea of commodification as sacralization. Agamben's starting point is a 1921 unfinished and fragmentary note entitled 'Capitalism as Religion' written by Walter Benjamin. Benjamin (2004 [1921]: 289) maintains that capitalism is not 'a religiously conditioned construction', as Weber argues, but 'an essentially religious phenomenon' that ultimately reproduces the same semantic register of established religious traditions. For Benjamin, secularization—'the suppression of religion by Enlightenment reason'—did not result in the overcoming of religion, but 'left a blank space to be filled' which was occupied by capitalism as a new form of religiosity (Racy 2016: 89).

Taking his cue from Benjamin's fragment, Agamben (2007) argues that capitalism mimics religion in that pushes 'to the extreme a tendency already present in Christianity', namely, 'it generalizes in every domain the structure of separation that defines religion' (Agamben 2007: 81). In the case of religion, the separation in question is that between sacred on the one hand and secular/profane on the other. The profane should be understood as an extreme form of the secular. Secularization retains some of the original force of the sacred, albeit in a secular form—for instance, modern readings of human rights based on the notion of shared humanity are secularized versions of Christian understandings of the idea that human beings are created in the image of God. Conversely, profanation 'neutralizes what it profanes'—consider how the totalizing commodification of citizenship subordinates the right of protection to the value of individuals and populations irrespective of their shared humanity.

In the capitalist framework, the separation between sacred and secular/profane becomes that between things-in-themselves and things as commodities. In its extreme forms, capitalism engenders a totalizing process of commodification that does not simply secularize objects and subjects by inscribing them into an epistemic framework seemingly independent of religious justifications. Capitalism desacralizes or profanes literally 'everything that is done, produced, or experienced', including 'the human body', 'sexuality', and 'even language' by embedding it into the logic of the market (Agamben 2007: 81). Capitalism completely subdues and collapses the religious separation between sacred and profane (Agamben 2007: 81), 'to the point that there is nothing left to separate.' By investing all spheres of human activity, capitalism behaves like a religion in reverse. Whereas religion is 'that which removes things, places, animals, or people from common use and transfers them to a separate [sacred] sphere', capitalism is that which transfers these objects to a separate profane sphere (Agamben 2007: 74). The outcome is paradoxical though: 'an absolute profanation without remainder [which] now coincides with an equally vacuous and total consecration' (Agamben 2007: 81). By profaning/commodifying everything, Agamben (2007: 82) concludes, 'the capitalist religion in its extreme phase aims at creating' the market as an 'absolutely unprofanable', that is, sacred entity.

This means that through the commodification of everything the market becomes the overarching and foundational dimension of all aspects of human existence, whose logics, rationalities, and schemes of valuation become indistinguishable from those of the neoliberal market. It means that the market cannot be questioned or challenged, even if it creates inequality, produces misery, and fails to deliver prosperity and growth. To appreciate the significance of this argument, it is useful to briefly consider Pope Francis' (2013) critique of the existing economic order as articulated in his first Apostolic Exhortation, Evangelii Gaudium (The Joy of the Gospel), which offers a remarkable illustration of Agamben's argument. For Francis, there is a fundamental tension between the 'outcomes' of the current economic system and the 'faith' that supports its existence. The present 'economy of exclusion and inequality' kills as it rests on Darwinian logics that foster exploitation and indifference to human suffering (Pope Francis 2013: 45).

> How can it be that it is not a news item when an elderly homeless person dies of exposure, but it is news when the stock market loses two points? ... Can we continue to stand by when food is thrown away while people are starving? ... Today everything comes under the laws of competition and the survival of the fittest, where the powerful feed upon the powerless. As a consequence,

> masses of people find themselves excluded and marginalized, without work, without possibilities, without any means of escape.
>
> (Pope Francis 2013: 45)

Hence, Francis continues, how is it possible that despite these tragic outcomes, people continue to believe in 'trickle-down theories' and their capacity to bring 'greater justice and inclusiveness in the world'? (Pope Francis 2013: 48) The problem, he argues, is that 'the prevailing economic system' has been 'sacralized', the 'deified market' has 'become the only rule' (Pope Francis 2013: 48). For Francis, this has been made possible by the reduction of 'man' [sic] 'to one of his needs alone, consumption'. The 'unbridled consumerism' of 'today's economic mechanism', he observes, has contributed to turn 'human beings' into 'consumer goods' (Pope Francis 2013: 46–50), that is, into commodities. Francis' remarks on the 'sacralization' of the economic system, on market 'competition and the survival of the fittest', on the neoliberal creation of a 'throwaway culture' which produces indifference and 'leftovers', should be considered in the wake of the disillusionment following the 2008 financial crisis.

This crisis—which until the coronavirus outbreak had triggered the worst recession since the Great Depression—raised the expectation that there would be a shift toward a 'post-neoliberal regime'—a shift that eventually did not take place (Konings 2016: 268; see also Cooper 2011b; Dean 2014). Even more, in the aftermath of the crisis, the key features of neoliberalism—competition, inequality, privatization of profits and socialization of losses, the centrality of the market mechanism for the allocation of essential goods and services, and (particularly in the case of Europe) austerity—have been strengthened rather than weakened. For Francis, this outcome is ultimately the result of an act of faith in the 'deified market' and 'in the sacralized workings of the prevailing economic system' (Pope Francis 2013: 48). These have decreed 'the absolute autonomy of the marketplace' over which states do not have the right 'to exercise any form of control' (Pope Francis 2013: 47).

This argument resonates with Agamben's view that the conflation between life-in-itself and life-as-commodity erases the boundary between the sacred and the profane. Life is no longer sacred as it is objectified, commodified, exchanged, and consumed in the name of a market logic which has been donned an aura of sacredness that invests all domains of existence. For Francis and Agamben, the neoliberal market is not a secular space—as Weber, Habermas, and (in a slightly different fashion) Moreton suggest—but one that, through the commodification of everything, has been sacralized through the profanation of life. In Section 2, I employ this perspective to analyse the immigration proposals and related visions of neoliberal citizenship of leading neoliberal thinkers Milton Friedman and Gary Becker.

2. Chicago-style citizenship (I)

In a book tellingly entitled *Why Government Is The Problem* (1993: Cover), outspoken neoliberal economist and 1976 Nobel prize winner Milton Friedman argues that '[t]he major social problems of the United States—deteriorating education, lawlessness and crime, homelessness, the collapse of family values and the crisis in medical care—have been produced by well-intended actions of government.' Friedman treats government intervention, however inspired by morally laudable goals, as a Malthusian perverse incentive that ends up worsening the problems it aims to solve. The solution he advocates is rolling back the state and rolling out the market. The capacity of the latter to create and distribute wealth, maximize utility, and provide services—hence, strengthening education, healthcare, and the family, while reducing social exclusion and crime—stems from the market's reliance on 'positive economics'. This is 'in principle independent of any particular ethical position or normative judgments' as it focuses on 'what is', not 'what ought to be' (Friedman 1953: 4). 'The great virtue of a free market system', Friedman (1993: 19) states, 'is that it does not care what color people are; … what their religion is; it only cares whether they can produce something you want to buy. It is the most effective system we have discovered to enable people who hate one another to deal with one another and help one another.'

For Friedman, the value of an individual or a group is their capacity to trade something of sufficient value: it is the economic and emotional capital that I discussed in Chapters 2 and 4. He therefore regards immigration as valuable. The immigrants who made it to the USA in the nineteenth and early twentieth centuries, he contends, for the most part managed to improve their condition, developed 'a better life for them and their children', and at the same time contributed to the economic growth of the country (Friedman, cited in Peron 2018). However, he continues, this regime of (relatively) free immigration would not be sustainable now because, 'it is one thing to have free immigration to jobs. It is another thing to have free immigration to welfare. And you cannot have both if you have a welfare state, if you have a state in which every resident is promised a certain minimal level of income, or a minimum level of subsistence, regardless of whether he works or not, produces it or not' (Friedman, cited in cited in Peron 2018).

Friedman believes that hard working immigrants are valuable as they can be net contributors to economic growth provided though that they are not entitled to 'a pro-rata share of the pot … or even to a low level of the pie' as this would mean 'a reduction of everybody to the same, uniform level' (cited in Peron 2018). Hence, the solution he advocates is more illegal immigration. Illegal immigration from Mexico, he suggests, 'is a good thing. It's a good thing for the illegal immigrants. It's a good thing for the United States. It's a good thing for the citizens of the country. But, it's only good so long as it's illegal' (cited in Peron 2018). The reasoning is remarkably simple: welfare provisions are perverse incentives which encourage people to immigrate. Remove them and loosen immigration requirements and what you will have is more illegal immigration: a disposable workforce that cannot claim any benefit or protection. Illegal immigrants will come for jobs (rather than welfare provisions) 'that most residents of this country are unwilling to take. They [will] provide employers with the kind of workers that they cannot get' (Friedman, cited in Peron 2018). And even if they are not entitled to any 'share of the pot' these 'hard', 'good workers' will be 'clearly better off' (Friedman, cited in Peron 2018).

Friedman's world is a marketplace in which people have no intrinsic identity, value, or morals that transcend the logics of competition, maximization, and accumulation. Their preferences are uniquely dictated by the system of economic incentives in place and the attempt to maximize their economic value. Perverse incentives like welfare provisions encourage immigrants to maximize their utility at the expense of the host society. The removal of these incentives by severing the link between residency and welfare provisions as in a condition of illegal immigration will prompt a 'win–win' situation, Friedman claims that illegal immigrants would be happy to become a disposable labour commodity and host populations would be happy to have more disposable labour for the production of the commodities they 'want to buy'. In this sacralized market-world, Friedman believes, illegal immigrants will be 'clearly better off' even if they have no sick pay, job security, minimum wage, legal protections, maternity leave, insurance, or pensions; even if they work in hazardous activities without proper health and safety standards and can be fired at any moment without warning. Friedman completely disregards the inequality, exploitation, precarization, insecurity, and fear stemming from an illegal condition. The migrant is ultimately a commodity, whose value resides in their capacity to produce commodities for the consumer-citizens of the host society.

Friedman's immigration proposal is a graphic illustration of the process described by Agamben whereby commodification performs 'an absolute profanation without remainder' which ends up in a 'total consecration' of the market. The resulting regime of neoliberal citizenship is an ominous reminder of Pope Francis' warning that 'unbridled consumerism' has turned human beings into commodities and is revealing of how neoliberal citizenship conceals its biopolitical racism behind the alleged objectivity of its rationalities. In fact, Friedman's goal could be achieved legally by subordinating the eligibility for welfare provisions to a longer period of residency to prevent immigrants from 'taking' from the system before they have contributed enough to it through their taxes. Hence, what is at stake in Friedman's argument is not simply the seemingly technical claim that 'you cannot simultaneously have free immigration and a welfare state', but the neoliberal desire to reduce immigrants to pure commodity labour-power which can be exploited, disposed of, and discarded if and when no longer needed. To this end, Friedman needs the state's coercive powers of incarceration and expulsion (illegal immigrant workers can be threatened with deportation), and more broadly the government's power to separate the domains of the legal and the illegal. It is the very constitution of an illegal space that enables the exploitative commodifying logics of the market to run unhindered.

These considerations raise questions on Friedman's claim that neoliberalism is colour and religion blind because it is only interested in the people's capacity to 'produce something you want to buy'. If this is the case, why does his proposal discriminate between insiders and outsiders, members and strangers? Why are immigrants denied the opportunities and protections granted to citizens? The answer could be that citizens should benefit from the wealth created by their parents. However, once again, this does not require keeping immigrants in a condition of precarious 'illegality'. It would be sufficient to place legal restrictions on the possibility of accessing welfare provisions until it is considered that the immigrant has significantly contributed to the 'welfare pot'.

This brings us to a final and even more fundamental consideration: why does Friedman treat the welfare pot as limited to the effect that even sharing 'a low level of the pie' with the immigrants would mean 'a reduction of everybody to the same, uniform level' (cited in Peron 2018)? What about the Syrian immigrants taken by Germany after the death of Alan Kurdi? They were regarded as a valuable source of emotional and human capital because they are expected to become net welfare contributors to a system fatigued by an ageing population. Numerous studies from a variety of countries including the USA indicate that legal immigration generally provides an economic benefit to the host countries both in terms of net fiscal contribution and filling gaps in the job market, not to mention the role that highly skilled immigrants often have in advancing the international competitiveness of the host country.[1] Why does Friedman seemingly discard the possibility that migrants may contribute to increase the size of the 'welfare pie'?

In fact, Friedman does not discard this possibility for the highly skilled migrants, the wealthy foreigners, and the ultra-high net worth individuals we encountered in Chapter 3. In his account, the incapacity to increase the size of the 'welfare pie' is a prerogative of 'Mexicans', a shorthand for a poor, vulnerable, powerless, and exploitable labour commodity, who therefore deserve the privilege of illegality. This distinction is reflective of the biopolitical racism of neoliberalism—despite Friedman's depiction of the latter as a science versed in the positivist method, concerned with 'what it is', and free from ethical burdens. The racist case for exclusion and the neoliberal case for inclusion ultimately produce the biopolitically racist compromise of including the 'Mexicans' 'differentially' in a condition of illegal subjugation. Yet, there is also another unacknowledged strand of reasoning in Friedman's argument about the incapacity of 'Mexicans' to contribute to welfare provisions. This is a fundamental neoliberal belief in the problem of Malthusian scarcity, and thus the idea that the expansion of the population always exceeds the limited resources available.

The scarcity in question is for Friedman that represented by welfare resources which are under threat by the uncivilized immigrants who, due to perverse incentives like the promise of a slice of the 'welfare pie', will depredate it as if there was no tomorrow. It does not matter that this is an oversimplistic and misleading explanation of the complex reasons behind the decision to migrate and that this argument disingenuously neglects the important contribution that immigrants make to the state's coffers. Welfare scarcity is ultimately a fetish in the sacred order of the market that enables Friedman to reduce immigrant labour to a mere commodity and advocate its illegalization. This process of dispossession of dignity and desacralization of life is not just shaped by a biopolitical racism that separates 'valuable' from 'less valuable' individuals and frames the latter as a threat to the survival and well-being of the population. It is also informed by a biopolitics of care in the same way that, as we saw in Chapter 5, the decision to suspend search-and-rescue missions in the Mediterranean is the expression of a neoliberal humanitarianism aimed at

[1] To consider a very famous recent example, Uğur Şahin and Özlem Türeci are German citizens born from Turkish immigrants who, through their German company BioNTech, have developed the first approved messenger RNA-based vaccine against COVID-19.

maximizing the life chances of prospective migrants by discouraging them to undertake the dangerous sea journey.

To better appreciate how neoliberalism can suspend search-and-rescue missions or advocate a condition of illegality for migrants and regard these actions as humanitarian, it is helpful to dwell on Friedman's understanding of racism. For Friedman racism is not a belief in the existence of races and in the superiority of one's own race, the ascription of negative qualities to members of other races or, in its biopolitical declension, a relationship that frames the death of the inferior race as something that will improve the life and well-being of my population. It is merely a matter of individual preferences or 'taste'. Hence, he argues, preferring to hire a white person instead of a black one is no different from preferring jazz to blues or pasta to bread. While he hastens to say that this does not mean that 'all tastes are equally good' (Friedman 2002: 110), nor that people should be treated differently because of the colour of their skin, he nonetheless considers that the best course of action to tackle racism is letting the market do its job and solve the issue. As a matter of fact, Friedman explains, racism is anti-economic:

> A businessman or an entrepreneur who expresses preferences in his business activities that are not related to productive efficiency is at a disadvantage compared to other individuals who do not. … [Similarly,] '[t]he the man who objects to buying from or working alongside a Negro, for example, thereby limits his range of choice. He will generally have to pay a higher price for what he buys or receive a lower return for his work. Or, put the other way, those of us who regard color of skin or religion as irrelevant can buy some things more cheaply as a result.
>
> (Friedman 2002: 109)

However, what about the case of a shop-owner who hires white clerks instead of black ones not because of personal preferences, but simply to cater for 'the tastes of the community'? Should the state intervene with anti-discrimination laws? Absolutely not, Friedman contends, because the consumers are clearly 'willing to pay' for this 'service' and by not catering to their needs the shop-owner would be economically damaged. What about the perpetuation of racism then? Since employers 'have an incentive … to try to find ways of getting around the preferences of their consumers or of their employees if such preferences impose higher costs upon them' (Friedman 2002: 112), eventually this will result in a hiring policy based exclusively on merit rather than the colour of the skin. This argument, however, is rather vague and does not really explain how letting the sacred logic of the market rule would contribute to eliminate racism, particularly if consumers continue to be willing to pay a premium to be racist in the same way that jazz lovers are willing to pay a premium to listen to their favourite music at the Blue Note in New York rather than on YouTube.

Friedman nonetheless displays an unshakeable faith in the capacity of the market to deliver us from all evils, including racism. His approach not only completely neglects how capitalism thrives on racism—from the process of primitive accumulation, to accumulation by dispossession (Harvey 2005, 2010, 2014a), to the biopolitical racism mobilized by neoliberalism explored in this book—but turns the relationships between capitalism and the market on its head by claiming that rolling out the market and rolling back the state will eventually eliminate racism as an anti-economic deviancy. The result is a paradoxical reversal whereby letting racism go unchallenged is a form of biopolitical care of the population, but crucially also of those who are at the receiving end of racism, in the same way that encouraging illegal immigration is a way of caring for the poor 'Mexican' immigrants. All these groups are dehumanized and reduced to disposable labour commodities in a neoliberal citizenship regime that transcends and merge biopolitical care and racism. And yet, this desacralization is ultimately a consecration as their bodies and lives are sacrificed on the altar of the market to manufacture the commodities that, to use Friedman's (1993: 19, 2002: 112) words, 'you want to buy', including discrimination, a service 'for the consumers that the consumers are willing to pay' for.

3. Chicago-style citizenship (II)

Neoliberal economist Gary Becker was a student of Friedman, whom he regarded as 'by far the greatest living teacher' he had 'ever had'. Becker was deeply influenced by Friedman's approach and indeed shares his overall neoliberal outlook, with some interesting differences though when it comes to immigration and citizenship. A Nobel prize winner in 1992, Becker is most famously known for radically extending and applying the logics of the market to virtually all domains of human existence and behaviour. He argues that all spheres of life—from family to education, mating, reproductive behaviours, patterns of consumptions, modes of interaction—and social phenomena—such as crime, deviance, addiction, immigration—should be understood as the product of market rationalities and dealt with accordingly.

For instance, parents and criminals (to take two of his most famous examples) should be regarded as entrepreneurial subjects who respond to market incentives and aim to maximize their utility. Becker maintains that parents ultimately see the family as an economic firm in which the choice of the number of children is a function of the maximization of welfare of the whole household. Hence, their decision to finance their children's university education is based on an economic calculus on the return that this investment in human capital will bring (better jobs and higher salaries, which would also translate into better care for themselves in their old age given their children's increased wealth) (Becker 1993 [1964]; see also 1973, 1974, 1976, 1993 [1981]). Similarly, for criminals, the decision to commit a crime is informed by the system of sanctions in place, with too low or too high a punishment as a positive incentive because the potential criminal would have too little or nothing to lose (Becker 1968).

Becker's approach is both explanatory and normative. It is explanatory as it considers that 'behaviours apparently motivated by love, dependence and aesthetic taste can be explained economically' (Newheiser 2016: 5). This does not mean that individuals are just cold-hearted utility maximizing machines, nor that individuals are always rational and do not randomly deviate from this behaviour, but that, taken in their aggregate and collective manifestations, social phenomena can be best explained through economic behavioural patterns. Becker's approach is normative because—very much like Friedman—he suggests that the marketization of all domains of human existence can contribute to the maximization of individual and collective wealth, greater allocational and distributional efficiency, and to address some of society's most compelling social problems, from unemployment, to crime, to discrimination against minorities and women, to the shortage of organs for transplant.

As Guy Sorman (2014) observes, Becker sees 'markets everywhere'. This means that he sees human beings as entrepreneurial subjects responsive to economic incentives and constantly striving to increase their human capital in order to maximize their existing and prospective value. For Foucault (2008: 226), the neoliberal subject envisioned by Becker is the epitome of the 'homo oeconomicus as entrepreneur of himself' whose behaviour is informed by an endless chain of cost–benefit calculations. Foucault was extremely captivated by this facet of Becker's argument—a captivation that some have mistakenly interpreted as an endorsement of Becker's view (for a discussion see Newheiser 2016). This fascination led Foucault to precipitously argue that the main feature of neoliberalism is not commodification, but 'a social fabric in which precisely the basic units would have the form of the enterprise', namely 'a society that is not orientated towards the commodity and the uniformity of the commodity, but towards the multiplicity and differentiation of enterprises' (Foucault 2008: 149). What Foucault failed to consider is that by seeing 'markets everywhere', Becker also saw commodities everywhere.

For instance, in a 1965 paper, 'A theory of the allocation of time', Becker (1965: 496) famously argues that the family is a 'a small factory' because 'it combines capital goods, raw materials and labour to clean, feed, procreate and otherwise produce useful commodities', that is, children. For Becker (1965: 496), children are 'non-purchasable household commodities ... who are consumed by parents/family who, in turn, create the demand for them.' Parents are thus entrepreneurial subjects who use commodities—'market-purchased goods and services, their own time, and human capital and other environmental variables' (Becker 1993 [1964]): 7)—to produce children-commodities that satisfy their own demand. The only difference between children-commodities and diaper- or milk-commodities is that the former are non-tradable. Why? The reason is not moral, but purely technical. A market for children would suffer from a problem of asymmetric information that ultimately would make it non-viable. As Becker (1993 [1981]): 140–1) explains, 'parents would be more likely to put their inferior children rather than their superior children up for sale or adoption if buyers were not readily able to determine quality.'

In view of this 'market fundamentalism' that treats the market as a sacred framework of existence in which life-commodity is bought and sold, it should come as no surprise that Becker regards citizenship as a commodity that should be subjected to the laws of supply and demand. For Becker (2011; Becker and Lazear 2013), existing mechanisms to manage migration, residency, and citizenship are inefficient as they are not based on the most important rationale that pushes people to migrate: improving their socio-economic condition. The migrant should be considered 'an investor', or as Foucault (2008: 230) puts it, 'an entrepreneur of himself who incurs [economic, moral, and social] expenses by investing to obtain some kind of improvement.' For Becker, states should capitalize on this natural entrepreneurial inclination of migrants either by auctioning the right to immigrate (setting a fixed quantity and variable price) or by selling it at a fixed price (and variable quantity, depending on the demand of the country).

Selling citizenship and residency would have two main benefits. First, it would encourage the migration of only the more talented and skilled individuals capable of earning enough money to repay the cost of citizenship or residency. Hence, selling the right to immigrate would contribute to improve the stock of human capital of the country. Bringing in 'more people with skills, vision and a drive to improve themselves' would result in 'innovation, business creation, increased employment and higher wages' (Becker and Lazear 2013). Second, the revenues coming for the sale of citizenship/residency would contribute to cut the deficit (Becker 2011). Becker suggests that if the USA were to sell the right to immigrate for $50,000 to the roughly one million people that every year enter the country, the US would earn revenues for 50 billion dollars. By reducing the deficit, this money would facilitate lowering taxes, which in turn would contribute to boost growth. Hence, the sale of citizenship/residency would be beneficial for both states and immigrants. States would benefit from a higher growth rate and many potential immigrants would be offered a possibility that under current regulations they are often denied.

Citizenship for sale would thus contribute to fix three main shortcomings of existing immigration regimes. First, and crucially departing from Friedman's argument, Becker (1993) maintains that current regimes often reward illegal immigration 'while entry is denied to millions who stoically wait their turn for the right to enter legally.' Second, existing regulations privilege migration linked to family reunification and for humanitarian reasons, rather than economic migration. Third, and this is a charge against all countries that employ a points-based system to manage migration, states rely on the mistaken assumption that they are capable to determine the amount and type of skills that their economy needs. For Becker (2011: 64), however, the points-based system is simply centralized and state-led 'manpower planning', which he considers to have a very bad track record. Hence, it would be generally beneficial to eliminate the points-based system and encourage economic migration in a framework where the right to migrate has a price and thus raises the human capital investment required.

Becker's argument has been the object of four main objections. First, how would the scheme work for those individuals who have the skills, but not the money to purchase citizenship/residency? Second, how would it contribute to protect the welfare state from those migrants allured by welfare benefits and other economic goods provided by wealthier countries? Third, given that potential terrorists could purchase the right to immigrate, would not such a scheme pose a potential threat to national security? Fourth, would not a citizenship-for-sale scheme be objectionable from a moral point of view? For Becker (2011: 31), the first problem, the fact that many skilled migrants would not have the money to buy citizenship/residency, could be solved by a system of loans modelled on the mechanism of student loans. Immigrants could simply borrow the money and pay off the loan through a monthly deduction on their salary. For the scheme to work with low-income jobs (such as healthcare professionals or nurses), it would be a matter of setting a price commensurate to the average level of salaries in the country (Becker 2011).

In relation to the protection of the welfare state, Becker (2011: 29) distances himself from Friedman's advocacy of illegal immigration and maintains that the selection induced by an entry price would result in young and most likely healthy individuals, who would likely be net contributors to the welfare system. Having said that, Becker also argues that—and this interestingly constitutes an answer to the third question concerning potential terrorist threats—'the sale of slots must be coupled with strong enforcement of the laws' (Becker and Lazear 2013) in order to prevent entrance to 'obvious cases such as potential terrorists, criminals and people who are very sick and who would be immediately a big burden to the health system' (Becker 2011: 27). In relation to the final objection, the morality of selling citizenship/residency, for Becker this is no less fair (and, indeed probably fairer) than existing criteria, such as birthright, family reunifications, and points-based systems.

For Becker, the sacralization of the market translates into a regime of neoliberal citizenship in which human capital is the true and only measure of the value and worth of the individual. As a result, Becker groups together 'potential terrorists, criminals and people who are very sick'. They have negative human capital attributes which make them threats to economic growth—by carrying out terrorist attacks that depress the market or criminal activities that affect levels of consumptions, or by simply being 'a big burden to the health system'. Conversely, whoever may be willing to pay to obtain citizenship or residency (apart from the above groups) is potentially the bearer of positive human capital that may benefit the country as price will act as an effective mechanism of selection. Hence, unlike Friedman, Becker understands immigrants not as disposable labour power, as a commodity required for the production of other commodities, but as the embodiment of tradable and multiple sources of human capital. Indeed, for Becker the sale of citizenship/residency serves the purpose of attracting both human and financial capital.

This is premised on the neoliberal assumption of an ultimate convertibility between human skills, knowledge, and know-how on the one hand and capital on the other. This is not simply a 'cash-nexus', but a more mediated equivalence mired in the logic of economic growth. Any form of human capital—even those of artists, seemingly 'indifferent to money and working for the sake of being creative'—can ultimately result in a positive economic contribution to the country (Becker 2011: 45). The citizenship- and residency-by-investment programmes discussed in Chapter 3 represent a rather imperfect approximation of Becker's proposal. Their cost is set too high, which makes them available only to the super-rich, and their primary purpose is to attract capital, rather than human capital. Becker, on the other hand, wants to 'democratize' the sale of citizenship by commodifying human capital in all its forms.

The neoliberal profanation of life and its subordination to the sacred logic of market value thus reaches, in Becker, new heights. Whereas Friedman's argument is informed by a more traditional state-centric distinction between members entitled to welfare provisions and poor immigrant strangers as disposable labour power, for Becker the distinction between members and strangers, internal and external, is further eroded and rewritten in biopolitical terms. This means that for Becker the regime of protection of neoliberal citizenship is a function of the economic value of the individual as human capital, and this value is partially independent of one's citizenship status. Non-citizens can become citizens if they are talented, skilled, healthy, willing to pay a fee, and work hard. Conversely, existing citizens who are poor and not particularly talented, might need to renounce their physical integrity and sell one of their organs to generate the income required for their survival. This is what Becker suggests in his controversial proposal for a market for organs (Becker and Elias 2007, 2014).

As is often the case with neoliberal reasoning, the argument is striking simple. Every year thousands of people die waiting for a kidney transplant because of an insufficient number of donors. Waiting time to receive a kidney is, on average, four years. During this time the prospective recipient is on dialysis, with negative implications for their quality of life and at a considerable cost for the community. All these issues stem from the fact that the demand for kidneys vastly exceeds the supply. Accordingly, 'establishing a market for organs', that is, 'paying donors for their organs would finally eliminate the supply–demand gap' (Becker and Elias 2014). Becker acknowledges that such a market would be considered '"immoral" because it involves the "commodification" of body parts' and because it would be the poor who would for the most part put their organs up for sale (Becker and Elias 2007: 21).

However, to the first accusation, Becker replies that the current system lets people die in the vain hope that a kidney may become available one day, hence it should be considered equally if not more immoral. To the second accusation, which is the one that concerns us most, Becker responds by reversing the logic of the argument. Not to allow poor people to sell their organs would not prevent them from experiencing deprivation, severe want, suffering, desperation, and exploitation. Quite the contrary, such a prohibition would mean depriving the poor 'of revenue that could be highly useful to them' (Becker and

Elias 2007: 21). Moreover, he adds, 'the organs of low-income individuals who use drugs or have AIDS, hepatitis, or other serious illnesses would be rejected. So probably the healthy poor and middle classes would actually provide most of the organs for live transplants under a market incentive system' (Becker and Elias 2007: 21).

This argument offers a concise illustration of the biopolitical care and racism at the heart of Becker's vision of neoliberal citizenship. In the same way that Friedman frames the discrimination of black people and poor Mexican immigrants as a form of biopolitical care of the population and black people and poor Mexican immigrants themselves, so Becker regards the exploitation of the poor as a source of organs as beneficial for those in desperate need of an organ and for the poor donor themselves. The latter, despite their lack of tradable skills or talents, are enabled to raise some cash and contribute to their well-being and that of the community as a whole. This argument rehearses the neoliberal humanitarianism of 'saving refugees by letting them die' explored in the previous chapter. In the neoliberal order, suspending search-and-rescue missions and letting refugees drown, reducing undocumented migrants to labour power in a condition of illegality, and encouraging the poor to sell their organs are all expressions of a neoliberal biopolitical rationality of care of host populations and, paradoxically, of refugees, undocumented migrants, and the poor themselves.

In Becker's neoliberal citizenship regime, the poor are not coerced to sell their kidneys as coercion conceals itself behind the allegedly free system of market incentives. As Foucault (2008: 259; see also Newheiser 2016: 7) reminds us, neoliberalism is neither 'an exhaustively disciplinary society', nor one in which 'a mechanism of general normalization and the exclusion of those who cannot be normalized is needed.' It is the internalization of the sacred logic of the market which makes the 'healthy poor' valuable as organ-sellers and disqualifies the 'sick poor' as neoliberal citizens as they have nothing to sell. The internalization of the sacred logic of the market turns the 'healthy poor' into the epitome of the neoliberal entrepreneurial subject: the 'homo oeconomicus' who is 'for himself his own capital, … his own producer, … the source of [his] earnings' (Foucault 2008: 226). This entreprenurialization requires the commodification of the healthy poor and their body parts. This profanation shifts the sacredness of life and the body from the domain of God to that of the market. And yet, at the same time, it is also a consecration that brings the poor into the domain of the sacred. Through the sacrifice of one of their body parts, the 'healthy poor' can save the life of a sick person in need and fulfil their duty as neoliberal citizen.

4. Scarcity, waste, and sacrifice

The logics of commodification and sacralization that inform Friedman's and Becker's arguments are a response to the fundamental problem of scarcity encountered in Chapter 5. As we saw, the neoliberal homo oeconomicus is not just the one who pursues growth and the unbounded satisfaction of desire, but also the subject troubled by the scarcity of resources caused by the excess or overabundance of 'savage populations'. Neoliberal citizenship thus mobilizes biopolitical racism in a logic of bioeconomic necessity aimed at forestalling the risk of catastrophe. Whereas Friedman focuses on the scarcity of the 'welfare pot' and how it is threatened by an oversupply of legal immigrants—hence his case for illegal immigration—Becker concentrates on the problem of the overabundance of immigrants and the need to identify and select the most valuable ones—hence his proposal for a system of market incentives (the citizenship/residency fee and the exclusion of sick immigrants) to ensure that those included may provide a positive contribution to the economic growth of the country.

As Becker's argument indicates, the problem of scarcity can be considered as the other side of a problem of overabundance or surplus. For both Friedman and Becker there are simply too many potential immigrants. In the absence of mechanisms of containment, this surplus of immigrants would flock en masse to the wealthiest countries (such as the USA) to take advantage of their 'generous' welfare provisions. While some immigrants can be taken in and properly civilized through market incentives—by subjecting them to a condition of illegality for Friedman or to the servitude of debt for Becker—there is simply an excess of them that needs to be rejected and excluded. In its basic form, this is the problem of 'surplus populations', which was identified by Marx over a century and a half ago. According to Marx, capitalism has its own 'law of population', namely, 'capitalist accumulation … constantly produces, and produces indeed in direct relation with its own energy and extent, a relatively redundant working population, i.e. a population which is superfluous to capital's average requirements for its own valorization … a surplus population' (Marx 1976: 782). Hence, '[t]he greater the social wealth, the functioning capital, the extent and energy of its growth, and therefore also the greater the absolute mass of the proletariat and the productivity of its labour, the greater is the industrial reserve army' (Marx 1976: 798; see also McIntyre 2011; Tyner 2013).

For Marx, poverty and hunger are not the result of a natural condition in which the population 'increases at a geometrical ratio' whereas the means of subsistence grow at an 'arithmetical ratio', as Malthus argues, but of a distinctive tendency of the capitalist system of production. The expansion of the 'power of capital' creates a 'mass' of 'surplus population'. This means that in capitalism the problem of scarcity is derivative of the more foundational problem of surplus, excess, and abundance. As Todd McGowan (2016: 85) observes, '[t]he capitalist economy enters into crisis not through scarcity but through overproduction, the production of an excess of commodities with a paucity of consumers for these commodities.' A telling example is the 2008 financial crisis, with 'an excess of houses' and not enough people able 'to pay for them' (McGowan 2016: 86). In relation to the argument explored in this chapter, the problem is that neoliberal capitalism produces an excess, an oversupply of commodity-migrants for which there is no demand. The migrants who are excluded, who die in the attempt to cross the US–Mexican border and the Mediterranean are 'surplus populations'. Yet, they are often regarded as being in excess in a slightly different way from that envisaged by Marx.

Marx regarded surplus populations as internal and necessary to the mechanics of reproduction of capitalism. They are a 'reserve army of labour' constituted by 'floating', 'latent', and 'stagnant' labour forces that, by lacking secure employment and suffering the effects of unstable and precarious occupations, move by different degrees in and out of the labour market (Marx 1976: 794). These workers serve two main purposes in the capitalist economy: putting downward pressure on wages and breaking the unity of the labour force (Rajaram 2018: 630), both of which contribute to strengthening the hegemonic power of capital. By contrast, the commodity-migrants for which there is no demand are increasingly regarded as superfluous to the needs of capital reproduction to the point of constituting 'a mass of humanity structurally and biologically redundant to global accumulation and the corporate matrix' (Mike Davis, cited in Yates 2011: 1679). This argument has been taken to suggest that unwanted migrants, growing sections of the population of developing countries, and debased citizens of wealthy nations who have seen the progressive erosion of their rights and standards of living, have all become populations in excess who are superfluous to the reproduction and needs of capitalism. The notions of 'wasted lives', 'humans-as-waste', 'wasted humans', and 'waste populations' (Bauman 2004; Yates 2011) strive to capture this seemingly momentous transformation of capitalism and how it has resulted in the 'excessive' production of marginalized, unwanted, undesired, disposable, and precarious lives. These analyses often draw their conceptual underpinnings on Agamben's figure of homo sacer (see Bauman 2004: 26; Tyner 2013: 706).

Homo sacer is an ancient category of Roman law that designates an individual whose existence is outside the spheres of the secular and the sacred. Homo sacer 'is simply set outside human jurisdiction' to the effect that he can be 'killed with impunity' and his death will not constitute homicide (Agamben 1998: 52, 47). At the same time, this death will not bring homo sacer into the sacred 'realm of divine law', which means that he cannot be sacrificed to the gods. To understand this argument, we need to remember that 'sacrifice always sanctions the passage of something from the profane to the sacred, from the human sphere to the divine' (Agamben 2007: 74). Homo sacer thus experiences a double exclusion: 'both from the ius humanum and from the ius divinum' or, differently said, 'both from the sphere of the profane and from that of the religious' (Agamben 1998: 52). This places homo sacer in a condition of extreme vulnerability and debasement. His life can be disposed of without sanctions and yet his killing does not constitute sacrifice, that is, 'consecration to the gods' (Agamben 1998: 52). This consecration (however posthumous), would make homo sacer deserving of universal moral feelings of piety, compassion, solidarity, and empathy—all of which he is denied.

The bare life of homo sacer is thus regarded as waste and treated as such: in the same way that people throw away garbage and then forget about it until it is time to dispose of the new garbage (Rathje and Murphy 2001: 45–6); in a cycle of recurrence and repetition that at best strikes as an uneventful annoyance that at regular intervals needs to be dealt with. The bare life of homines sacri is a cycle of reproduction and disposal, yet filled with struggle, desire, hope, misery, and desperation that goes largely unnoticed. Bare lives should therefore be regarded as surplus populations in an even more diminished sense than that originally envisaged by Marx. Whereas for Marx the sacrifice of surplus populations translated into the strengthening of capital, bare lives–waste populations are also denied this meagre and paradoxical consolation. Their death is not sacrifice as it does not contribute to enhance the neoliberal market and therefore does not consecrate them to the glory of economic growth and creation of value. Bare lives–waste populations are unwanted commodities: to dispose of them is not to commit desecration or sacrifice as they are worthless in the biopolitical economy of neoliberal citizenship.

At a close reading, this argument might appear to be in contradiction with the one I have advanced so far, namely, that neoliberal citizenship entails a fundamental sacrificial component and that unwanted undocumented migrants (like debased citizens of austerity) are sacrificed and expected to sacrifice to guarantee the reproduction of the sacred neoliberal order. It is the very sacredness of the market, I argued earlier in the book, which makes the lives of less economically valuable populations sacrificial. By sacrificing themselves for the market (by dying at the border, accepting a pay cut, not protesting austerity measures), these lives become economically valuable, and therefore sacred for the market. However, if Agamben is right and bare lives are not sacrificial, does it mean that unwanted migrants and refugees cannot be considered bare life? This is not the case, as for Agamben 'refugees can be seen as the ultimate "biopolitical" subjects' who 'are reduced to "bare life": humans as animals in nature without political freedom' (Owens 2009: 567). Refugees and undocumented migrants are the ultimate manifestations of homines sacri. Does this mean, then, that so far I have used the notion of sacrifice improperly, with reference to subjects who actually cannot be sacrificed? This question, to be sure, is not purely theoretical, but has a distinctive applied implication for the way we understand the role of 'bare lives'/'waste populations' in the biopolitical economy of neoliberal citizenship.

To claim that 'bare lives'/'waste populations' cannot be sacrificed means that their status as unwanted commodities makes them economically worthless. Paradoxically, however, this would also mean that they can escape—albeit at the extreme cost of their lives—the logic of valuation of neoliberalism and thus place themselves beyond the reach of power of the market. It is here, I think, that Agamben's argument—and that of those writing of waste populations in his wake—falters. The unwanted migrants who die in the attempt to cross the US-Mexican borders, are left drowning in the Mediterranean, or should be rejected according to Becker because sick and therefore burdensome for the welfare state are not worthless. Very much like waste, they have a negative value, which is not the same as being worthless.

Waste is a negative externality, that is, a collective cost and by-product of the process of production and consumption. Waste needs to be properly disposed, otherwise it will pollute the land, poison the water, and spread diseases. Over time, however, waste has been increasingly reframed from cost to valuable commodity, resource, factor of production, and source of profit. A whole economy of waste management, recycling, and transformation aimed at the production of energy, glass, plastic, fertilizers, and many other commodities has flourished. Waste has been economized. Its very excretion from the body of society has become a process of re-incorporation into the neoliberal market system of production and consumption, with the effect of turning waste into a valuable source of profit. The same logic applies to unwanted migrants.

Very much like waste, immigrants are a negative externality of the exploitation and inequality of neoliberal capitalism. If untreated—that is, if allowed to circulate freely—immigrants will pollute the culture, poison the moral, deplete the welfare state, and spread the diseases of unemployment and economic recession. Immigrants are thus not worthless but have a negative value. Their necessary excretion from the healthy body of society makes imperative their re-incorporation in the neoliberal order as commodities that may feed the profits of a series of interconnected markets.

The most visible market is probably the immigration-industrial complex. As Ruben Andersson (2014) insightfully argues, state efforts to curb illegal immigration have resulted in the creation of an 'illegal immigration industry' to the effect that the process of 'bordering Europe' has turned into a 'business'. While most accounts have focused on the repressive side of the securitization of migration, Andersson (2014: 6) highlights how efforts to curb illegal immigration—from the traditional use of border guards, 'military planes, helicopters, satellites, and patrol boats' to the recent employment of more sophisticated technologies such as 'intelligent fences', eye scanners, surveillance cameras, drones, databases, satellites, radars and advanced information systems—have a distinctively 'productive' side. 'Migrant illegality', he observes, 'is processed, "packaged", presented, and ultimately rendered profitable' (Andersson: 2014: 6). This argument could suggest that, were states to follow Friedman's prescriptions—decriminalizing illegal immigration, relaxing border controls, and allowing in more illegal immigrants—'immigrants-as-waste' would disappear and so would the immigration-industrial complex. The commodification of migrants as waste would be replaced by the arguably 'healthier' (in Friedman's view) commodification of migrants as labour power. This argument, however, neglects two crucial factors.

First, the condition of illegal immigration, however tolerated and encouraged, is itself a partial excretion from the body of society, whose 'healthy' part is made by entitled, legal citizens. Consider the extensive use of illegal immigrants in the fruit and vegetable picking industry in southern Italy. They provide a crucial service and play a key role in the agricultural economy and are subjected to conditions of extreme exploitation and deprivation—working for ten hours in a row under the sun for 3 euro per hour, being regularly abused and beaten by their employers, forced to live in barracks with no electricity or running water, constantly threatened with being denounced to the authorities for their illegal status. This indicates that their positive economic value only to a limited extent compensates their negative value as polluting waste. They are bare lives in Agambeian terms as they can be (and often are) killed almost with impunity like the undocumented migrants left drowning in the Mediterranean. Yet, they are not bare lives because they are sacrificed on the altar of the market. Their sacrifice enables us to purchase more fruit and vegetables at a lower cost, in the same way that the sacrifice of the undocumented migrants dying in the attempt to cross the Mediterranean or the electrified fences in the Spanish enclave of Ceuta and Melilla are feeding the immigration-industrial complex, providing jobs for those who work in this sector as well as satisfying the need of security for the healthy, legal, and entitled population.

The second factor to consider is that illegal immigration produces another market—one which is completely neglected by Friedman and considerably larger than the immigration-industrial complex identified by Andersson—that of right-wing populism. Political leaders such as Donald Trump in the USA, Marine Le Pen in France, Matteo Salvini in Italy, and Viktor Orbán in Hungary need immigrants to sustain their political platforms. Immigrants are the raw material, the commodity-waste they rely on in order to deliver their promise of a country free of polluting and poisonous aliens. In its basic formulation, their populism is a movement of double opposition that pits the people against an internal enemy—the elites—and an external one—the immigrants. These 'others' are thus essential for the reproduction of their populist project. The supply-chain of the political offer of populism thus crucially rests on what it promises to eliminate. The undocumented migrant, the potential 'rapist' clandestine who threatens women and social security, not to mention our morals and Christian beliefs, is simultaneously bare life as he can be killed with impunity in the Mediterranean, in the Sonora desert, or across the Australian shores, but is also not bare life as his life will feed the market and contribute to its growth and multiplication.

From this perspective, the death of Alan Kurdi was a sacrifice that benefited a plurality of markets. Some of the aforementioned populist leaders took it as an opportunity to consolidate their consensus by satisfying public demands with a slight increment in the intake of Syrian refugees. For the press it was an opportunity to sell stories on 'womenandchildren' refugees that increased their clicks, traffic, and made them more attractive for the advertisement industry. For the broader public, it satisfied their need to feel compassionate, moral, caring, and able to connect with the destitute (however, only if embodied by the dead body of a child). The death of Alan Kurdi was thus a commodity, part of a process of commodification of life and sacralization of the market, whose value stemmed from its alleged scarcity, namely, the fact that it was packaged and sold as if he was the only migrant child to have died at the hands of Europe's callousness. Finally, the deaths of the thousands unnamed and unaccounted migrants also have some degree of sacredness because their overabundance signals another form of scarcity—of our welfare, our culture, our jobs. By sacrificing them, we also make them sacred, as their death will enable us to grow healthier and stronger.

Conclusion

Kim Rygiel (2016) argues that the act of death transgresses the logic of modern citizenship. With death, the refugees and undocumented migrants that in life were treated as disposable 'bare lives', are forcefully re-inscribed into the domain of biopolitical care of the state. 'In the moment of death', Rygiel (2016: 549) explains, 'the state becomes responsible for ensuring that certain rights of the dead are provided including the provision of ethical care, the right to be identified, preparation of the body for burial, and the return of bodies and belongings to relatives.' The paradoxical result is a form of empowerment that sees 'the dead migrant' transcending the 'categorization of legality/illegality' and acquiring 'a legal subjectivity and status denied to him or her in life' (Rygiel 2016: 549). A similar argument is advanced by Vicki Squire (2017: 513), who considers how 'the treatment of the dead functions as a means of compensating for (yet not redressing) biophysical violence' as well as ensuring the latter's reproduction. In particular, through the process of identification and burial, the state is forced to grant the migrants some of the dignity it denied them in life. Both accounts share Agamben's view of refugees as 'bare lives', but ultimately depart from this account by suggesting that with death these lives are ultimately recognized, albeit only partially and tragically belatedly, a sacred human status.

The perspective I advanced in this chapter challenges this reading by arguing that while refugees and undocumented migrants are bare lives in the sense that they can be killed almost with impunity, their death does not grant them a sacred human status, but a sacred market status. The fact that 'the dead refugee/migrant … must be identified, by first recovering the body, followed by providing an identity through a name, DNA and/or a person's history' (Rygiel 2016: 549) is not dissimilar to the identification of the undocumented migrants who are then locked up in immigration detention centres run by private corporations for a profit. In both cases, identification does not stand for recognition of human dignity. The excretion of migrants from the healthy body of society through death or imprisonment is a simultaneous re-incorporation into the rationalities of value of neoliberal citizenship, which therefore exceeds the 'disposing of the discredited' (Feher 2020).

Their negative value is neutralized through death and commodified as a factor of production that feeds the immigration-industrial complex, the political platforms of right-wing populists, the media hungry for drama and novelty, and the public's desire to scapegoat, blame, condemn, and yet be confirmed in its moral integrity and superiority. The suffering of the undocumented migrants, if properly packaged in recognizable 'womenandchildren' refugees, can be commodified as an act of piety and generosity that will boost the moral pride and sense of worth of the country welcoming them. Hence, as we saw in the fourth chapter, caring for physically and mentally disabled refugees becomes a way of caring for the emotional well-being of the population. We can now say that this biopolitical care crucially rests on the neoliberal commodification of the lives of the refugees.

This commodification instantiates the commodification of migrants advocated by Friedman and Becker. Their sacralization of the market requires the migrants to be kept in a condition of illegality (Friedman) and the exclusion of sick migrants who will be a burden on the welfare state (Becker). Yet, the sacralization of the market engendered by the totalizing process of commodification also partially transcends these requirements. Once properly packaged and marketed, there is no difference between healthy, sick, and dead migrants. They all respond to different needs and cater for different segments of the market as part of a logic of market differentiation. Hence, the migrants dying at the border, the illegal immigrants praised by Friedman and exploited as labour force, the legal immigrants that in Becker's view should pay a fee to enter the country, are all commodities in a regime of sacralization of the market. As such, they are sacred in the sense that they can be sacrificed and their sacrifice can contribute to increase the value of different markets. Their life is not governed by principles of universal rights, human dignity, and shared humanity, but by an economic metric of supply and demand that is crucially mediated by the principle of scarcity.

This principle transcends the nominal fact of being a citizen. In the regime of neoliberal citizenship envisaged by Friedman, black citizens whose services are in scarce demand are required to accept their condition of debasement and subjugation. Similarly, in the neoliberal citizenship envisioned by Becker, poor citizens whose organs are in high demand due to their scarcity may be required to sell them. In both cases, the right to life, integrity, protection, and dignity is a function of a metric of value that encompasses both economic and emotional dimensions. The scarcity of migrant victims—such as Alan Kurdi—and migrant heroes—like Mamoudou Gassama, Lassana Bathily, Gorgui Lamine Sow, Ramy Shehata and Adam El Hamami encountered in Chapter 4—makes them valuable as precious emotional capital. This scarcity, however, is not natural, but purely artificial as there are many more victims and heroes than those acknowledged and recognized by the metrics of neoliberal citizenship.

For the surplus victims and surplus heroes that do not make it to this status, there is the forceful incorporation into the market of waste, as part of a political economy of life that makes it impossible to escape the dictates of neoliberal citizenship. From this perspective, the market is not secular as Weber, and more recently Habermas and Moreton maintain. The market is sacred as suggested by and beyond Agamben, as the totalizing process of commodification makes all living beings—and particularly those debased, excluded, marginalized, unwanted, undesired, disposable, and precarious lives—sacrificial. Their sacrifice sanctions their passage 'from the profane to the sacred, from the human sphere to the divine' (Agamben 2007: 74) in a remarkable inversion in which life is profane to the point where its only way to acquire sacredness is by totally surrendering itself to the sacred market.

7

Sacred market, sacrificial lives (II)

Introduction

In this chapter, I explore a second trajectory of the process of sacralization of the market. This is based on the idea that the market encompasses an almost mystical and transcendent complexity that vastly exceeds human comprehension. To introduce this argument and its relevance for neoliberal citizenship, we can start with a series of statements by leading scholars in the immediate aftermath of the 2008 financial crisis. For renowned historian Eric Hobsbawm, 'a sort of theological free-market ideology' had dominated the thirty years prior to the crisis (cited in Peck, Theodore, and Brenner 2009: 99). Shortly afterwards, economist and Nobel Prize winner Joseph Stiglitz (2009: 346) offered a similar remark: '[f]rom a historical point of view, for a quarter of century the prevailing religion of the West has been market fundamentalism.' Over this time, Stiglitz contends, the Western approach to the market 'was not based on economic science or historical evidence.' Thatcher in the UK and Reagan in the USA, Stiglitz continues, revived 'some old [economic] ideas' and myths, such as Adam Smith's notion of the invisible hand, which justifies the pursuit of 'self-interest and the maximization of profits' on the grounds that this would miraculously translate into greater 'societal well-being' (Stiglitz 2009: 345).

For Fred Block and Margaret Somers, what has been variously described as 'neoliberalism', 'laissez-faire', or 'free market ideology' should more properly be labelled 'market fundamentalism'. This term, they (2014: 3) argue, 'conveys the quasi-religious certainty expressed by contemporary advocates of market self-regulation' and a mode of reasoning based on 'revelation' rather than 'empirical verification', which is akin to that of religious fundamentalists. The remarkable resilience of neoliberalism—its capacity to survive the crisis and thrive despite being widely regarded as the main culprit for the worst recession since the Great Depression until the recent crisis caused by the coronavirus pandemic—has prompted a multiplication of depictions of

Neoliberal Citizenship. Luca Mavelli, Oxford University Press.
 DOI: 10.1093/oso/9780192857583.003.0007

neoliberalism as religion, system of belief, 'kind of faith' (Graeber and Piketty 2014), and 'theology disguised as social science' (Petrella 2008: 127).

These characterizations emphasize an 'elective affinity' between belief in an institutionalized religion and belief in the neoliberal market, and question the very secular nature of the latter. Following Freud, it could be argued that this affinity is the product of 'an epistemological approach that privileges myth and the unquestioned authority of doctrinal tradition over evidence acquired through independent rational inquiry' (Hewitt 2014: 7). Yet, neither Stiglitz, Block and Somers, nor the others who have increasingly hinted at the religious nature of neoliberalism have attempted to explain the causes of the ascendancy of this epistemological approach. Existing commentaries have remained largely impressionistic, and mostly concerned with emphasizing that, although the 2008 financial crisis may 'have represented a kind of theological crisis for the neoliberal belief system' (Peck, Theodore, and Brenner 2009: 99), it has not undermined a widespread dogmatic belief in the neoliberal market.

Undeniably, the initial expectation that a crisis of this magnitude would engender a 'post-neoliberal' shift has progressively vanished (Konings 2016: 268; see also Crouch 2011; Harvey 2010; Schmidt and Thatcher 2013). Governments' responses to the crisis have often consisted of more neoliberal policies, such as austerity measures and welfare cuts, bailing out with public money the financial actors responsible for the crisis, and encouraging the further penetration of mechanisms of competition, privatization, commodification, and neoliberal re-regulation in new social and political domains. The almost unchallenged authority of neoliberalism is even more puzzling given the ontological mutation of neoliberal capitalism from crisis-driven to catastrophe-driven regime of governance explored earlier in the book. Hence, is it the case that neoliberalism—as a rationality of government, economic theory, scheme of valuation, and framework of political and social relations—has acquired an almost 'sacred status' to the effect that it now commands a quasi-religious authority, even despite its inability to deliver prosperity and growth?

Whereas in Chapter 6 I focused on the totalizing process of commodification as a mechanism of consecration of the market, in this chapter I explore a different and complementary trajectory of sacralization: the construction of the market as an entity that, following Durkheim's classical definition of the sacred, is 'set apart and forbidden' and thus cannot be questioned or challenged unlike secular/profane things. This task will be carried out in two main steps. In the first two sections, through an extensive engagement with Friedrich Hayek, I show how this sacralization stems from the ascription to the market of a transcendent complexity, unknowability, and capacity of coordination that combine to vastly exceed human comprehension. The result is a regime of neoliberal citizenship that mixes secular and religious registers and relies on belief. Unlike the consecration engendered by commodification in which neoliberal capitalism mimics the structure of separation of religion and absolutizes it, the sacralization of the market based on its (alleged) unfathomable complexity rests on a distinctive 'leap of faith' into the unknown. The resulting vision of neoliberal citizenship is a rendering of Malthus' theory of overpopulation that glorifies suffering and justifies the sacrifice of less valuable individuals as necessary for the reproduction of the neoliberal market order.

In Sections 3 and 4, I explore how the bioeconomy of necessity at the heart of neoliberal citizenship rests on the institution of scarcity as a fundamental category that establishes uncertainty, insecurity, desire, and envy as essential for economic growth and justifies oppression and exploitation as conditions for peace. The threat of scarcity acts as a powerful disciplining tool that is not confined to material resources but also encompasses moral, social, and political values. In the neoliberal process of economization performed by the sacred market, these values become a scarce resource threatened by the overabundance of migrants. This external excess of migrants mirrors an internal excess: that of the impoverished and debased citizens of austerity. The connection established by scarcity, I will show, challenges one of the most established assumptions concerning the fear of migrants: this fear is not grounded in difference but in sameness. It is the fear that our worshipping of the market as a transcendent entity that cannot be questioned or challenged will make us become like them.

This argument advances the investigation of the 'mystique of complexity' introduced in the second chapter by exploring how neoliberal citizenship disarticulates, rearticulates, and deploys the categories of sacred and secular in order to subordinate the sacredness of life to that of the market. To this end, the sacred needs to be questioned in its dynamic interaction with secularism, given the mutually constructed nature of sacred and secular (Scherer 2013: 8; see also Casanova 1994: 20; Hurd 2004: 238, 2017; McCutcheon 2007). Once again, it is helpful to draw on Agamben's (2011) insights. For the Italian philosopher, there are two possible ways of understanding secularism. The first one is the Weberian approach, which understands secularization as a process of replacement: secular forms of rationality progressively replace religious ones, with the effect of compressing the domain of the sacred. Secularism is therefore a condition characterized by the public triumph of science, reason, and critique over belief, emotions, and dogma, which are confined to the private sphere.

This view implicitly informs the quotes in the opening paragraphs of this chapter. They frame neoliberalism as a kind of religion, and thus as the expression of irrational beliefs and uncritical thinking, and suggest that neoliberalism is a glitch, a bug, a malfunction in the rational secular path of modernity.

A different and more sophisticated approach, Agamben (2011: 4) contends, consists of understanding the process of secularization not as a 'concept', but as a 'signature' [*segnatura*]. A signature is 'something that in a sign or concept marks and exceeds such a sign or concept referring it back to a determinate interpretation or field, without for this reason leaving the semiotic to constitute a new meaning or a new concept' (Agamben 2011: 4). The distinctive feature of signatures is that they 'move and displace concepts and signs from one field to another (in this case, from sacred to profane, and vice versa) without redefining them semantically' (Agamben 2011: 4). Following this view, secularism is not a static state of affairs caused by a shift from a theological to a secular episteme and where the presence of religion should be considered a sign of secularism's crisis. Rather, secularism is an epistemic framework whose semantic register prompts a constant process of blurring, displacement, and renegotiation between secular and sacred declensions.

This perspective, to be sure, does not suggest that there is 'an identity of substance between theology and modernity, or a perfect identity of meaning between theological and political [or economic] concepts' (Agamben 2011: 4). Rather, what Agamben (2011: 4) emphasizes is that there is a 'particular strategic relation that marks political [and economic] concepts and refers them back to their theological origin.' His approach thus extends Carl Schmitt's famous theological-political paradigm—'All significant concepts of the modern theory of the state are secularized theological concepts'—to the economic domain (Agamben 2011: 2). For Agamben (2009: 40), the idea of secularization as signature 'does not merely express a semiotic relation between a *signans* [theological concept] and a *signatum* [the secular market]; rather, it is what—insisting on this relation without coinciding with it—displaces and moves it into another domain, thus positioning it in a new network of pragmatic and hermeneutic relations' in which '*signum* and *signatum* exchange roles and seem to enter into a zone of undecidability.'

Building on this argument and on the idea of 'blurred boundaries' between the secular and the religious (Mavelli 2012a, 2012b; Hurd 2017; see also Casanova 2006b; Göle 2010; Lynch 2011; Scherer 2013), I argue that the power of neoliberalism stems from being a secular rationality of government that continuously evokes religious meanings and significations. Neoliberalism displaces and redraws the boundary between sacred and profane, and appropriates an aura of sacredness while concealing itself behind an authoritative secular rational façade. Hence, the neoliberal market bears, displays, and strategically mobilizes the 'signatures' of a religious/sacred episteme to the effect that, rather than being a secular entity at the service of the sacredness of life, it has become a sacred entity in itself. In this epistemic framework, neoliberal citizenship is the measure of the worth and value of life as well as a distinctive act of faith in the sacred workings of the market.

1. Sacred complexity

Hayek is often regarded as 'the single most important neoliberal economist' (Gaffney 2017: 124). Nobel Prize winner in 1974, Hayek's 'subjectivist' strand of neoliberalism has received increasing attention in recent scholarship and policy discussions. His views have inspired existing debates on the shift from neoclassical equilibrium theory to processes of permanent adaptation, and on risk governance and the impossibility for states to place themselves 'outside the logic of risk and speculation' through centralized knowledge (Konings 2016: 278). Over the last two decades and particularly in the aftermath of the 2008 financial crisis, Hayek's views have progressively turned from 'minor tradition' to major analytical perspective (Cooper 2011b; see also Walker and Cooper 2011; Konings 2014) to the point of challenging the hegemony of the 'positivist' Chicago School of Economics, which for many scholars and observers has long represented the ultimate embodiment of neoliberalism (see, for instance, Klein 2007).

The 'subjectivist' and 'positivist' strands of neoliberalism share the idea that market-based competition rewards ingenuity and innovation, maximizes individual and aggregate utility, and enables the efficient circulation and allocation of capital. However, they differ on the limits and possibilities of market regulation and intervention. Whereas the Chicago School considers that a certain level of intervention may be necessary to preserve the correct and smooth functioning of the market (particularly in relation to the money supply), for Hayek (2005 [1944]: 210; see also 1945, 1952, 1967, 1989) the idea that human beings may govern the market in order to improve its functioning is the expression of an 'erroneous rationalism', namely, the mistaken presumption that human minds may have greater computational capacity than the market. Hayek regards markets as 'complex systems' comprising an extraordinary high number of variables that greatly exceed the human capacity to grasp them in their totality. At the same time, markets also have an innate and spontaneous capacity to produce order, progress, and growth (Hayek 1967; see also Walker and Cooper 2011). Hence, any human attempt to intervene on the market will negatively affect its performance and, as I shall discuss in a moment, potentially threaten our freedom by establishing new forms of tyranny.

Tyranny is for Hayek a direct consequence of the hubris of scientific knowledge. By claiming an unprecedented ability to grasp and successfully intervene upon the complexity of the market, scientific rationalism endows 'other men' in the guise of communist dictators, socialist planners, leftist redistributionists, and central bankers with the 'arbitrary power' to compress our freedom (Hayek 2005 [1944]: 204–5). It follows that the only way to escape the 'serfdom of the individual' and defend our liberty 'rests chiefly on the recognition of the inevitable ignorance of all of us' (Hayek 2011 [1960]: 80), namely, on the recognition that individuals only possess scattered fragments of knowledge and that government cannot overcome the inherent unknowability of the market. For Hayek, relinquishing the myth of scientific knowledge is not a cause for despair because '[t]here is not much reason to believe that, if at any one time the best knowledge which some possess were made available to all, the result would be a much better society. *Knowledge and ignorance are relative concepts*' (Hayek, cited in Mirowski 2013: 66; emphasis mine).

Hence, to preserve our freedom, we need to embrace the idea that the market is fundamentally unknowable in its totality and that the market has an endogenous agency that transcends our individual and collective agency, which is precisely what makes knowledge and ignorance relative. To preserve our freedom, Hayek intimates, it is paramount to *believe in the truth of the market* in very much the same way that 'men in the past' used to believe in the truth of religious traditions. As Hayek explains:

> It was men's [sic] submission to the impersonal forces of the market that in the past has made possible the growth of civilization.... It does not matter whether men in the past did submit from beliefs which some now regard as superstition.... The refusal to yield to forces which we neither understand nor can recognize as the conscious decisions of an intelligent being is the product of an incomplete and therefore erroneous rationalism. It is incomplete because it fails to comprehend that co-ordination of the multifarious individual efforts in a complex society must take account of facts no individual can completely survey.
>
> (Hayek 2005 [1944]: 210)

Hayek (1989: 137) admits that this faith in the market is ultimately not 'verifiable or testable'. Yet, he maintains, the very advancement of progress and civilization is also the product of 'beliefs which are not true ... in the same sense as are scientific statements and which are certainly not the result of rational argumentation' (Hayek 1989: 137). These beliefs or 'symbolic truths,' as Hayek (1989: 137) describes them, by citing *The Book of Genesis*, have forcefully encouraged 'their adherents to "be fruitful and multiply and replenish the earth and subdue it" (Genesis 1, 28).' Indeed, he concludes, 'nonfactual beliefs' have been essential for the establishment of 'the extended order that we now enjoy' to the effect that 'now the loss of these beliefs, whether true or false, creates great difficulties' (Hayek 1989: 137).

It can be inferred that for Hayek the Weberian process of *disenchantment*—the shift from religious rationalism to scientific rationalism and the related downgrading of 'belief' to the sphere of the irrational—threatens the advancement of human civilization. Weber's (1946 [1919b]: 139) famous idea that, with modernity, 'there are no mysterious incalculable forces that come into play, but rather that one can, in principle, master all things by calculation' becomes for Hayek the very condition of possibility for the 'erroneous rationalism' (Hayek 2005 [1944]: 210) and 'pretence of knowledge' (Hayek 1989) that pose a grave threat to human freedom. Hence, to be free and to advance our material and civilizational well-being, we have no choice but to bow to the inscrutable mysteries of the market by abandoning our 'pretence of knowledge' (Hayek 1989), confessing our ignorance, and letting ourselves be guided by the wisdom of a superior intellect—the neoliberal market—whose impenetrable design we can neither understand nor grasp in its totality.

Hayek's idea of the neoliberal market offers a remarkable instantiation of secularization as signature. His approach mixes secular and religious registers. It blurs the divides between science and faith, facts and beliefs, the secular and the religious as well as the practical and moral divide between knowledge and ignorance. In an almost mystical and transcendent turn, it gestures towards the unknowability and inscrutability of the market, thus asking for an act of faith in its inherent goodness. Yet, this act of faith is justified in purely secular-rational terms concerning the epistemological limits of scientific knowledge. The result is a process of dislocation of religious *signa* and secular *signata* that constantly blurs the boundary between sacred and profane, thus producing what Agamben would describe as 'a zone of undecidability'. The neoliberal market is sacralized, and yet its sacralization does not seemingly rest on revelation, but on a secular rationality that reveals the inherent epistemological limits of our capacity to know due to the sheer complexity of the market. And yet again, at a closer look, Hayek's secular scientific reasoning also crucially encompasses an element of revelation concerning the natural goodness of the market. As Néstor Míguez, Joerg Rieger, and Jung Mo Sung perceptively observe:

> [I]f it is true that we cannot sufficiently understand the factors and dynamics of the market so that we can intervene in it, how can we know that the market always produces beneficial effects or that it is essentially a 'force for good'? Is knowing that the market always produces beneficial effects not a pretension of knowledge of the market? Since one cannot prove this providential character of the market, we have here a 'leap of faith' in the affirmation of the essentially beneficent quality of free market.
>
> (Míguez, Rieger, and Sung 2009: 82)

This, however, does not mean that Hayek's neoliberalism resembles a religion. The ultimate justification for trusting the market is the expression of an eminently scientific and secular rational argument: our epistemological incapacity to fully grasp the complexity of the social world in its sheer intricacy. However, through a 'leap of faith', this secular approach ends up advocating trusting the market as a benevolent entity capable of delivering economic growth and advancing the pathway of human civilization. This reasoning performs a paradoxical subversion whereby it is rational to have faith in the market—even when the market delivers crisis, shocks, and failures—and it is irrational not to have faith in the market—as this would express a 'pretence of knowledge' that clashes with secular registers. In Hayek's account, secular and religious registers are inextricably mixed and '*signum* and *signatum* exchange roles and seem to enter into a zone of undecidability' (Agamben 2009: 17). The neoliberal market thus emerges simultaneously as a sacred and profane space that draws strength on competing frames of authority, and results in a power that transcends both secular and religious registers. To further appreciate this argument, it is useful to consider Hayek's fascination with scholasticism, a facet of his thought that has been largely neglected.

Scholasticism was the medieval system of thought based on ontological realism. It deemed the world as the expression of a universal and timeless order established by God, and God as 'ordained power', namely, as a superior Being embodying infinite love and goodness who would not act outside the law he had himself established (Oakley 1998: 445; see also Gillespie 2008 and Mavelli 2012b). For scholasticism, the world was the manifestation of divine love and reason, and knowledge was the attempt to grasp an external reality. This endeavour required both the rational faculties of the individual and faith in God, as well as a recognition that this attempt would always be limited and partial as God's knowledge and wisdom (as projected and manifested in the order of creation) would always incommensurably exceed that of human beings.

When it comes to the market, and particularly to the price mechanism, this theological view shaped the idea that 'the just price depends on so many particular circumstances that only God can know it, and that consequently, for human purposes, the just price is the price spontaneously established by the social process; in other words, the market price' (Huerta De Soto 2010: 66, note 9). Hence, prominent Jesuits argued that '*pretium iustum mathematicum, licet soli Deo notum*' and '*quas exacte comprehendere et ponderare Dei est, non hominum*', namely, only God knows and can determine the just price through the market, not human beings (Huerta De Soto 2010: 66, note 9). This view crucially shapes Hayek's idea of the market. In *Law, Legislation and Liberty*, he approvingly cites several late scholastic Jesuits to support the argument that only the market-God knows.

> [T]hese ancestors of ours thought and 'acted under a strong impression of the ignorance and fallibility of mankind,' and ... argued that the precise 'mathematical price' at which a commodity could be justly sold was only known to God, because it depended on more circumstances than any man could know, and that therefore the determination of the 'just price' must be left to the market.
>
> (Hayek 1998: 21)

Yet, Hayek's commitment to scholasticism goes deeper than an endorsement of the market as a transcendent and superior intellect. In fact, he embraces all the way the idea that the market-God is the ultimate expression of goodness, even if we may not be able to see it. This argument becomes clearer if we compare Hayek with Adam Smith, widely regarded as the father of economic liberalism. Although Hayek's notion of 'spontaneous order' has often been described as a modern and even 'secularized' rendering of Adam Smith's 'invisible hand' (see, for instance, Konings 2016: 279), the latter should be more properly understood as an expression of that nominalist thought that crucially challenged and undermined medieval scholasticism. For nominalism, the scholastic idea that God could be constrained by his own actions and therefore that his power was limited was untenable. This, in turn, meant that for nominalism the world could not be considered the expression of a transcendent and benevolent order. This theological shift represents for many (Gillespie 2008; Elshtain 2008) a crucial moment in the process of secularization as it opened up the space for human autonomy and self-assertiveness in all domains of human existence including the market, which could no longer be considered a spontaneous and God-regulated order.

Hence, whereas for Hayek, the market is a partially inscrutable, transcendent, and ultimately benevolent domain able to determine the 'just price' of things, Smith considered that price-setting dynamics are socially constructed rather than natural, and therefore market prices are often higher than natural prices. In particular, Smith maintained that prices reflect relationships of power and powerlessness, privilege and exploitation: 'People of the same trade seldom meet together, even for merriment and diversion, but the conversation ends in a conspiracy against the public, or in some contrivance to raise prices' (Smith 1979 [1776]: 232). For Smith the market is self-regulating only within a robust moral and legal framework that prevents abuses and excesses. As he puts it in *The Theory of Moral Sentiment* (2010: 309), 'Concern for our own happiness recommends to us the virtue of prudence, concern for that of other people, the virtues of justice and beneficence; of which the one restrains us from hurting, the other prompts us to promote that happiness.' For Smith, in other words, the 'invisible hand' (which, it is also worth mentioning, only figures three times in his writings) could only deliver prosperity if a certain moral and political oversight—the human planning so much feared by Hayek—was in place.

These considerations suggest that Hayek's view of economic order *is not* 'a more fully secularized version of Adam Smith's notion of the invisible hand' (Konings 2016: 279). While Hayek's reasoning for trusting the market seemingly draws on a scientific argument—the epistemological limits of our knowledge—the ultimate justification is a 'leap of faith' in the market as a sacred benevolent entity. The neoliberal market is a superior intellect that vastly exceeds our capacity to understand, let alone govern its complexity, and that ultimately delivers prosperity and growth if left untouched by human intervention or attempt at regulation. What understanding of citizenship does stem from this neoliberal view? To answer this question, we need to discuss Hayek's apparent rebuttal of Malthus' theory of overpopulation. As will become clear in the next section, this does not constitute a rejection of the bioeconomy of necessity and an unconditional endorsement of the 'right to live'. Quite the opposite, I will show how for Hayek the 'right to live' is a function of an individual's economic value and their capacity to contribute to market prosperity and growth.

2. The 'calculus of lives'

Hayek's refutation of Malthus' thesis of overpopulation begins with a telling quote from Adam Smith: 'The most decisive of the prosperity of any country is the increase of the number of its inhabitants' (Hayek 1988: 120). For Hayek (1988: 121), the idea that 'population growth threatens worldwide pauperisation' no longer holds. While relevant at the time of Malthus, when the 'homogeneity of labour' could translate into a 'reduction of . . . marginal productivity', nowadays diversification and specialization of labour yield increased productivity and returns (Hayek 1988: 122). The growth of the proletariat is a striking illustration of this transformation. Turning Marx's argument on its head, Hayek (1988: 123) maintains that the expansion of this class is not an indication of the pauperization and exploitation of labour, but of the fact that the process of growth engendered by capitalism 'benefits the larger number of the poor more than the smaller number of the rich.' The capitalist system of free markets has the merit of having 'brought into being and kept millions alive who otherwise would not have lived at all and who, if they had lived for a time, could not have afforded to procreate' (Hayek 1988: 123).

The second consideration Hayek advances is that the population problem is not global, as Malthus suggested, but distinctively regional. It primarily concerns those backward populations in the peripheries of the world who 'practice customs of procreation stemming from circumstances outside the market economy where, for instance, the first response of poor people to a slight increase of wealth had been to produce a number of descendants at least sufficient to provide for them in their old age' (Hayek 1988: 129). Moreover, this tendency of backward populations to reproduce 'beyond the volume at which accumulated capital could still be currently reproduced' (Hayek 1988: 125) has been encouraged by the development aid provided by wealthy countries. In advancing this argument, Hayek employs two classic Malthusian tropes: that of savage populations who have a tendency to reproduce beyond their means of subsistence and that of the perverse incentives which encourage this reproduction. Unlike Malthus, though, who sees the 'savages' as almost irredeemable, Hayek (1988: 129) argues that the advancement of the market economy re-establishes a balance as the poor of the world will progressively imitate the wealthy of 'the growing commercial centers' and embrace the latter's more sober and market-compliant reproductive behaviours.

For Hayek (1988: 127), then, the 'specialisation brought about by division of labour, knowledge and property, but also by some individual accumulation of new forms of capital' has made possible the growth of population, which in turn has enabled the further advancement of capitalism. Hence, any increment in population growth must be in harmony with the unfathomable order of the market. Indeed, Hayek argues that the market economy prevailed 'over other types of order because it enabled those groups that adopted its basic rules the better to multiply' (Hayek 1988: 132). This means that '*the calculation in market values is a calculation in terms of lives:* individuals guided by this calculation did what most helped to increase their numbers' in accordance with the market (Hayek 1988: 132, emphasis in original). It follows that 'serious problems may arise if we attempt indiscriminately to preserve all human lives everywhere' (Hayek 1988: 125) through 'perverse' incentives, be they foreign aids or national welfare provisions. Any such attempt will put at risk the very extended order that the market economy has been able to establish and hampers its prospects of growth. It follows that to preserve the liberal order, we cannot shy away from the 'calculus of life', that is, from the ascription of economic value to each and every life and the ensuing need of 'sacrificing a few [less valuable] lives in order to serve a larger number elsewhere.' In the liberal order, Hayek states,

> not that all individual lives [can] be regarded as equally important. It may be more important to save the life of the doctor … than to save the lives of any particular one of his patients: otherwise none might survive. Some lives are evidently more important in that they create or preserve other lives. The good hunter or defender of the community, the fertile mother and perhaps even the wise old man may be more important than most babies and most of the aged. On the preservation of the life of a good chief large numbers of other lives may depend. And the highly productive may be more valuable to the community than other adult individuals.
>
> (Hayek 1988: 132)

Despite his avowed rejection of Malthus' theory, Hayek ends up embracing not just its most important tropes—the 'savages' and the 'perverse incentives'—but also its very denial of the indiscriminate right to live. Hayek replaces Malthus' law of nature with the law of the market, which becomes endowed with the power to decide who must live and who must die. Those who must live are the most economically valuable members of the community. Hayek thus retains and, if anything, amplifies the Malthusian bioeconomy of necessity. As has been observed, in Hayek's world the market 'is elevated to an order "beyond rational comprehension" and requires a code of morality ultimately based on the fear of hunger' (Polanyi-Levitt and Mendell 1989: 30). As Hayek explains, 'our morals are materialistic, not idealistic and must be so because their first function is to keep us alive' (Hayek, cited in Polanyi-Levitt and Mendell 1989: 30). In this framework, citizenship as the right to have rights becomes entirely a function of an individual's economic value, and thus of their capacity to be fully inscribed in and contribute to the growth of the market. Those who fail in this endeavour must be sacrificed for the greater good of the market and of the neoliberal citizens who live by and thrive under its rule—and possibly through death they will be able to achieve the sacredness they failed to obtain in life by feeding the growing economies of the undesirables discussed in Chapter 6.

But there is more. Hayek's neoliberal bioeconomy of necessity exceeds the biopolitics of who must live and who must die as it foregrounds and justifies a whole new biopolitical economy of suffering. The unreserved acceptance of the transcendent law of the market requires us to unconditionally abide by its pronouncements even when these materialize in crisis, unemployment, shocks, austerity measures, furloughs, and the likes. The reason, Hayek explains, is that any human attempt to correct the occasional inefficiencies of the market, 'even in the midst of crisis free fall', will fail because 'the market always surpasses the state's ability to process information' (Mirowski 2013: 54). Moreover, any such intervention will result in an existential threat to our autonomy. Rather than seeking protection from the uncertainties, crises, and shocks of the market by putting our fate in the hands of 'other men' (Hayek 2005 [1944]: 210), we should embrace the market wholeheartedly, even in phases of market crisis. In fact, what may appear as inefficiencies or market failures are actually phases of adjustment that will eventually deliver equilibrium and growth.

As usual, Hayek's explanation draws on a mixture of secular and religious registers characteristic of the 'secularization as signature' proposed by Agamben. He combines rational argumentations concerning the hubris of modern rationalism—what has been variously described as 'epistemology of limited knowledge' (Walker and Cooper 2011: 149), 'epistemology of ignorance' (Friedman 2005), 'epistemological scepticism' (Sharpe 2009), and 'epistemological subjectivism' (Selgin 1988)—and a distinctive leap of faith in the ultimate goodness of the market and its capacity to eventually deliver us from the evils of uncertainty, scarcity, and poverty. Hayek's bioeconomy of necessity requires a faithful acceptance of whatever hardship the market may hold for us. It therefore implicitly relies on the categories of resilient and sacrificial citizenship encountered in Chapter 2.

As we discussed, resilient citizenship is not an unqualified attempt to adapt and bounce back, but one that can only take place within the policed boundaries of the biopolitical racism of neoliberalism. Hence, for undocumented migrants to be resilient is not to seek a better life by attempting the dangerous sea crossing of the Mediterranean, but to stoically wait in refugee camps to be rescued by the magnanimous 'white Western saviour'. For the debased citizens of austerity, to be resilient is to stoically adapt to and cope with precariousness, casualization, underemployment, and welfare cuts. In this scenario resilience and sacrifice become virtually indistinguishable and suffering becomes a normal, natural, and even necessary dimension of life as suffering alone can bring forward the ingenuity, resourcefulness, entrepreneurial spirit, and ultimately the resilience required to succeed and thrive in the existing economic order.

Neoliberalism is replete with narratives that celebrate suffering as good and necessary for economic growth. Consider the late Apple founder and former CEO, Steve Jobs, who once famously declared: 'I didn't see it then, but it turned out that getting fired from Apple was the best thing that could have ever happened to me. The heaviness of being successful was replaced by the lightness of being a beginner again, less sure about everything. It freed me to enter one of the most creative periods of my life' (cited in Byrne 2011: 97). Here the biblical narrative of Israel's rise and fall translates into the disciplined acceptance of the logic of resilience as dictated by the neoliberal market. In Jobs' account, being fired was the result of both individual incapacity and complacency: incapacity to properly manage success and its complacent acceptance. At the time of his 'fall', Jobs could not see how Providence would have turned this event into a 'blessing'. As the Bible recites: 'a righteous man may fall seven times and rise again' [Proverbs 24: 17], and for the righteous man—for the one who deserves it—it is good 'to be afflicted' as this will enable him to learn 'God's decrees' [Psalm 119: 71]. Neoliberalism establishes suffering as an acceptable and almost desirable dimension of life, and Hayek's rendering is no exception.

> In the market as conceived by Hayek ... there is much suffering: people do not find work or lose their jobs, companies go bankrupt, suppliers are abandoned by long-time clients, speculators play for high-stakes and lose everything, ... et cetera. Decreed by blind fate, these sanctions are unjustifiable, unpredictable, incomprehensible. Yet, wisdom consists in abandoning 'oneself to

> the obscure forces of the social process'—a process driven by a beneficent spontaneity and endowed with a knowledge that is inaccessible to any individual subject.
>
> (Dupuy 2002: 198)

What does 'abandoning oneself to the obscure forces of the social process' mean for Hayek? It means embracing a resilient and sacrificial adaptation of the self in the belief that the mysterious and ultimately beneficent market will eventually reward the suffering and deliver salvation-growth. In blurring the divide between the secular and the religious, Hayek's neoliberalism operates like Benjamin's capitalism: not as 'a religiously conditioned construction', but as an almost 'religious phenomenon' that, while seemingly retaining a secular and rational façade, tends to reproduce the same semantic register of established religious traditions. From this perspective, Hayek's economic theology of the market can be read as a theodicy.

The term theodicy comes from the combination of two Greek words: *theos* [God] and *dike* [justice] and can be translated as both 'God's justice' and 'justification of God'. These two questions are interconnected because the idea of God's absolute goodness and justice clashes with the presence of evil, injustice, and suffering in the world. Max Weber, who developed one of the most penetrating sociological analyses of the problem of theodicy, characterizes it as follows: 'How is it that a power which is said to be at once omnipotent and kind could have created such an irrational world of undeserved suffering, unpunished injustice and hopeless stupidity?' (Weber 1946 [1919a]: 122) For Weber, religious doctrines such as the original sin, the principle of the corrupt nature of humanity, the idea that evil is a necessary corollary of God's gift of free will, predestination, reincarnation, or a better life in heaven, are all attempts to address the seeming paradox at the heart of God's justice. These doctrines strive to account for the evils of the human condition by inscribing them in cosmological, theological, and teleological narratives in which injustice, fear, insecurity, and suffering acquire meaning as part of a larger order of creation and are not just the outcome of an ultimate randomness (Mavelli 2016: 121). These doctrines make violence and suffering meaningful and justifiable as expressions of God's inscrutable justice (Weber 1946 [1919a]: 123).

In Hayek's account, the neoliberal market replaces the transcendent God to the effect that when the market-God delivers shocks, crises, and failures, these are framed as part of an inscrutable plan which will eventually deliver prosperity and growth. Hence, in the same way that God created Man in his likeness, as the Book of Genesis recites, so Hayek moulds the neoliberal market in the image of God—and specifically in the image of the God of scholasticism, namely, as a superior Being embodying infinite generosity and goodness who acts according to a divinely ordained plan that, however impenetrable to the human mind, is the expression of divine love and reason. Hence, the suffering caused by the market is not random; it is not in vain; it is not the product of a regime of inequality and exploitation, or of the violence of class, racism, and gender. Suffering *by* the market is part of an unfathomably larger scheme of creation, and thus should be more properly understood as suffering *for* the market: as a necessary and inescapable sacrifice that holds the promise of a future reward in the form of liberation from evil, plentifulness, and abundance.

Yet, as Weber alerts us, the task of theodicy is not just that of justifying (and enabling the reproduction of) the misery of the status quo for the lower classes, but of providing ideological legitimation for inequality. Indeed, a fundamental function of theodicy is also to explain the absence of evil for the 'fortunate'. The 'theodicy of suffering', Weber maintains, should always be considered in conjunction with the 'theodicy of good fortune', whose goal is to persuade the fortunate and, most of all, the miserable that they deserve their condition and merely experience their due. For Weber (1946 [1922]: 271), religions have contributed to rationalizing the inequality between groups or classes on behalf of 'all ruling men, the propertied, the victorious, and the healthy' by 'treating suffering as a symptom of odiousness in the eyes of the gods and as a sign of secret guilt.' Good fortune and suffering are ultimately the expression of God's justice.

The 'calculus of life' endorsed by Hayek is a neoliberal scheme of valuation that rationalizes the theodicies of suffering and good fortune through the seemingly undisputable principles of necessity and the greater good. It establishes that the lives of the 'highly productive' and of those on whom other lives depend are more valuable to the community and thus in need of greater protection. However, what is a 'highly productive' life? Is it that of the CEO who creates value for his shareholder through the casualization of labour or is it the trade union activist who fights the race to the bottom in labour standards? Are more lives dependent from the former or from the latter? Similarly, which is more valuable: the life of the CEO of a company of the immigration-industrial complex that boosts profits by manufacturing the ultimate type of drone to spot and prevent the arrival of undocumented migrants or the NGOs activist who carries out search-and-rescue missions in the Mediterranean to bring the same migrants to safety? Are more lives dependent on the former or on the latter?

In Hayek's world, the market exercises no constriction, hence the casualized worker will have chosen such employment possibly because, as neoliberal advocates maintain, 'self-employed people, even on low incomes, have higher job satisfaction than full-time employees' (Welsh 2016). Moreover, irrespective of the individual preferences, the casualized worker will ultimately be experiencing what he or she deserves. Similarly, as we saw in Chapter 5, neoliberal thinking considers that the undocumented migrants should correctly interpret market signals—the suspension of search-and-rescue missions—and refrain from putting their lives at risk. If they defy the market and place themselves on a precarious boat, and eventually drown, they will have merely had their due. From Hayek's neoliberal scheme of valuation, it can be deduced that the lives of CEOs are more valuable than those of trade unionists—who should not exist in the first place, given that the market is the domain of freedom—and of NGOs activists—who endeavour to save lives that are not worth saving. Hayek's conclusion is remarkably similar to that shared by Friedman and Becker: the value of life is a mere economic calculus in which moral considerations of universality, shared humanity, and intrinsic dignity of the individual have no place.

3. The value of scarcity and the scarcity of values

To fully understand how the 'calculus of life' has become a fundamental feature of neoliberal citizenship, in both its 'positivist' and 'subjectivist' declensions, we need to consider that Hayek, Friedman, and Becker share a fundamental preoccupation with the problem of scarcity. At first sight, this observation may seem unremarkable. After all, it is generally assumed that the 'foundation of economy activity' and modern economic thinking rests on scarcity. This is exemplified by a much-quoted, almost century-old definition by economist Lionel Robbins (1932: 15–16): 'We have been turned out of Paradise. We have neither eternal life nor unlimited means of gratification. Everywhere we turn, if we choose one thing we must relinquish others—scarcity of means to satisfy given ends is an almost ubiquitous condition of human behavior. ... Economics is the science which studies human behavior as a relationship between given ends and scarce means which have alternative uses.' This definition takes scarcity as natural, given, 'quasi-ontological' (Tellman 2015: 24; see also Tellman 2017), and as the inevitable product of our human finitude.

However, a small group of scholars has challenged this understanding by arguing that scarcity is a relatively modern invention, it is not natural but 'socially instituted' (Dumouchel 2014: xi), and a fundamental engine of the mechanism of capitalist reproduction. As Nicholas Xenos (1989: 3) persuasively observes, the concept of scarcity should be distinguished from that of scarcit*ies*. Human beings have always confronted scarcities—of food, water, energy, and healthcare—as a result of droughts, famine, floods, and diseases. These scarcities were based on the notion of absolute material needs and concerned the very survival of the population. While these scarcities continue to exist—each year over 3 million children die from undernutrition and malnutrition (UNICEF 2021), whereas 1.5 million die of vaccine-preventable diseases (WHO 2015), and about 829,000 people die from diarrhoea as a result of the scarcity of safe drinking-water and sanitation (WHO 2019)—they have been compounded, particularly for the wealthy countries of the global North, by the emergence of *scarcity* as a relative condition grounded in individual and collective desire. As Xenos (1989: 5) observes 'once a degree of relativity is allowed, the distinction between needs and desires becomes difficult to maintain'.

As a result, in the relatively affluent societies of the global North, sacrificing undocumented migrants by not saving them, causing their death, or reducing them to servitude in a condition of illegality has become a 'necessity' that stems from the desire to guarantee our standards of living. This, in turn, originates from the desire to keep at bay the fear that undocumented migrants *could* affect our standards of living. Biopolitical racism thrives on this conflation and the arguments of Hayek, Friedman, and Becker are a striking evidence of this moral and analytical ambiguity. They all rely on and endorse a bioeconomy of necessity, but what they present to us as necessity is not survival per se, but the survival, reproduction, and expansion of the neoliberal order and of its regime of consumption. This is reflective of a broader societal ambiguity which, as considered in Chapter 5, has seen the growing construction of migrants as a 'flow', 'flood', 'rising tide', 'invasion', and 'tidal wave' that threatens Europe's economic and cultural survival. Is this threat grounded in need—as allowing more migrants in will allegedly make many of us jobless and cause the collapse of the welfare state, with a devastating impact on social cohesion—or in desire—as more legal immigrants will supposedly have a negative impact on our consumption or longing for a culturally, racially, and religiously homogenous society?

The answer, to be sure, does not really matter, and not just because the 'subtractive' hypothesis concerning the impact of migrants on society is highly questionable. What matters are the rationalities that lead neoliberal capitalism to strategically re-invent and mobilize a desire-driven scarcity to guarantee its reproduction and expansion and how this contributes to the construction of sacrificial neoliberal citizens in a sacred market. I would like to consider three rationalities in particular. First, as Paul Dumouchel (2014) explains, scarcity is ambivalent. It is instituted both as a threat to the social order, as people fight each other for limited resources, but also as its condition of possibility, as a state of scarcity is regarded as a powerful positive incentive (as opposed to the Malthusian 'perverse incentives') that will encourage people to work, trade, invest, compete, and cultivate their entrepreneurial spirit.

The institution of scarcity can materialize in a variety of ways. Early in the book, we considered the case of former British Prime Minister Cameron's frontal attack on the welfare state, which he regarded as guilty of having fostered a culture of 'welfare dependency' that 'for years has paid British people not to work' (cited in Burnett 2017: 218). The scarcity created by welfare cuts—that is, austerity—would, according to the Tory establishment, prompt people to work harder and take economic responsibility for themselves. A more forceful rendering of this view is provided by some hardcore supporters of Brexit. A few months before the June 2016 referendum, billionaire Peter Hargreaves (who endorsed and bankrolled the Brexit campaign) stated: 'Brexit would be the biggest stimulus to get our butts in gear that we have ever had.... We will get out there and we will be become incredibly successful because we will be insecure again. And insecurity [i.e. the scarcity of security] is fantastic' (*The Guardian* 2016).

Neoliberal capitalism establishes uncertainty, insecurity, 'envy, desire, and pride [as] the driving forces behind economic growth', and turns economic activity grounded in 'the most brazen exploitation' and the 'oppression of the weak by the strong' into a necessary condition for social peace (Dumouchel 2014: 6). This is not only necessary, but commendable as the sacrifice of the weak and the poor will save us from the destruction of society as whole. For Dumouchel (2014: xii), 'The sacred is organized around rituals that seek to restore the troubled social order ... and obligations that tie agents and groups to one another for their own protection while simultaneously providing an outlet of permissible violence that they can exert outside of the group.' The neoliberal market is sacred as it provides a series of legitimate outlets—such as the neoliberal citizenship regime—in which violence can be exercised and life can be legitimately sacrificed.

Second, the neoliberal unrestrained logic of consumption and related totalizing process of commodification is premised on 'the boundlessness of desire' which has engendered the 'proliferation of social needs' (Xenos 1989: 5). Desire and need merge in a process of consumption and commodification that promises to deliver us from the scarcity that capitalism itself has contributed to institute. The totalizing process of commodification becomes a consecration of the market as a response to the evil of scarcity through a process of multiplication of desire that makes the problems of scarcity increasingly more acute.

Once again neoliberalism becomes indistinguishable from theodicy: it simultaneously institutes and feeds the evil of scarcity by multiplying the sources of desire while constructing narratives of consumption-salvation. However, this salvation—the realization of our desires through consumption—is an impossible achievement, as the newly acquired commodity will only make all the more evident the condition of scarcity in which the subject finds itself enmeshed, thus reactivating an endless cycle of consumption sustained by the promise of an impossible redemption from scarcity (Xenos 1989; McGowan 2016).

Third, scarcity is fundamental for the creation of value. As commodity theory explains, '[a]ny commodity will be valued to the extent that it is scarce, unavailable, or difficult to attain' (Brock 1968: 246). The value of immigrants as a commodified labour force or a source of emotional capital is a function of their limited availability. It is therefore the very rationality of valuation of the sacred market that decrees that only a handful of immigrants can be regarded as heroes and deserve our sympathy. For one Mamoudou Gassama who rescues a child hanging over a balcony, there are thousands (including Gassama himself) who risked their lives through desert, war, violence, and rough seas to bring themselves and their loved ones to safety. Yet, the overabundance of the latter makes them less valuable and not heroes, and condemns them to honour the market solely through their participation in the economy of waste. For one Alan Kurdi, whose plight was captured and conferred visibility by a graphic shot, there are thousands of other children who have departed in silence. It is the scarcity of the former that consecrated—and profaned—Alan's death to the commodified consumption of social media and condemned to oblivion thousands of child refugees.

The totalizing commodification of everything does not spare life and makes individuals subject to the desire-driven principle of scarcity. The child refugees who were brought to the UK in 2016 under the auspices of the Dubs scheme were indeed anticipated as desirable because they were scarce—unlike the overabundant 'flood' of undifferentiated immigrants—and because they would boost the sense of moral worth, compassion, and self-esteem of the British people (unfortunately, as we saw, these commodity-children turned out to be 'faulty' as they resembled adults). What we have not considered so far, and what has been largely neglected by the critical literatures on scarcity and commodification, is that it is not just resources and lives that have become valuable if only experienced in a context of scarcity but also *values*. This is a natural outcome of the neoliberal process of economization, which is characterized by the extension of the logic of the market—and thus of the principles of economic value, competition, inequality and, crucially, scarcity—to all spheres of human activity.

Consider how one of the distinctive implications of the growing presence of Islam in Europe has been the re-discovery of Europe's Christian—or Judeo-Christian—roots and the re-activation of a sense of Christian identity (Mavelli 2012a). Scholars have debated whether this re-appropriation of Christianity in a secular Europe should be regarded as evidence of the 'glimmering embers' of a tradition and dimension of identity and belonging that has never really abandoned Europe (Katzenstein 2006: 2) or as an instrumental and even calculated political move that appropriates Christianity as a floating signifier to oppose the 'ultimate other' of Islam (Marzouki, McDonnell, and Roy 2016). From the perspective articulated in this chapter, the re-awakening of a Christian identity is the product of a reckoning of its scarcity. The presence of seemingly abundant Muslims does not simply make them less valuable, and increases the value of Christianity, but engenders a specific competition for the scarce resources of identity and belonging. These values are in short supply and Muslim immigrants are seen as competitors that threaten to further deprive Europeans not just of their scarce material resources but also of their ideational ones. It is not by chance, then, that migrants in general—and Muslim migrants in the West and Europe in particular—are seen to embody a range of threats that span across the material and ideational spectrum.

For French *Rassemblement National* leader Marine Le Pen, the contemporary influx of migrants to Europe resembles the 'barbarian invasions' of the fourth century. She argues that, while a catastrophic globalization 'has ravaged the French economy' and 'jobs have faded away', 'immigrants have flooded in, many of them Muslim immigrants, from North Africa' (cited in Nail 2016; Cooper 2017). 'They are draining resources, rejecting French values and transforming the culture' (cited in Cooper 2017). The overabundance of surplus migrants is presented as both a material and civilizational threat. In Germany, the right-wing party *Alternative for Deutschland* has explicitly stated that Germany rests on 'Judeo-Christian and humanist foundations' and that 'Islam does not belong to Germany' as it is incompatible with its 'legal system and culture' (Biskamp 2018). Eastern European countries have most vocally raised the question of the Muslim identity of the refugees. Viktor Orban, the Hungarian Prime Minister, has stated: 'Islam does not belong to Europe': 'Those arriving have been raised in another religion, and represent a radically different culture. Most of them are not Christians, but Muslims' and every single one of them 'poses a public security and terror risk' (cited in Wagenvoorde 2017: 70).

Similar remarks have been made by political leaders in Slovakia, Poland, Bulgaria, and Cyprus, with Czech president Milos Zeman warning that 'Muslim refugees won't respect local laws and mores. Instead, he warned, they would seek to implement Sharia law' (Chadwick 2015).

In all these accounts, the European fear of Muslim migrants reflects European preoccupations with the paucity of its religious identity, the scarcity of its religious resources, the exiguity of its civilizational roots. The migrant Muslim becomes a competitor for scarce ideational resources, and this competition activates a powerful theodicy that identifies the migrant, and specifically the Muslim migrant, as the ultimate scapegoat. While neoliberalism claims that scarcity forces people to take responsibility for themselves, it actually encourages a projection of responsibility. As McGowan (2016: 201) observes, '[t]he benefit of scarcity lies in the justification that it provides: if it weren't for the scarcity, we believe, we could access the ultimate satisfaction.' As a result, '[t]he idea of scarcity allows us to continue to see ourselves as externally limited rather than internally limited subjects' (McGowan 2016: 202). Yet, by promising to deliver us from the evil of scarcity, neoliberalism reroutes this failure away from itself. Hence, responsibility for the failure of our satisfaction ultimately lies with the migrant. Our scarcity becomes the responsibility of the overabundance of migrants—not of our political choices, political leaders, and of our economic and financial establishment.

At the peak of the refugee crisis in 2015, Matthew Carr (2015) observed that '[w]hen immigrants drown by the hundreds in the Mediterranean we are taught that in a way it's their fault too, because they should not have come to take resources that were needed for "our own people" in a time of austerity.' We can now add that their fault is also representing a threat to our culture, identity, and religion, namely, to our scarce ideational resources. We thus end up with a bitter irony. Right-wing populist parties that advocate the closure of borders and curtailment of asylum rights as necessary for the preservation of our culture, identity, and economic well-being are contributing to nurture the very scarcity of ideational and material resources they claim to fight. Their politics of scapegoating is a way of projecting onto refugees and undocumented migrants the effects of the neoliberal rationality of scarcity and, by exempting it from responsibilities, of perpetuating its 'creative destruction'.

4. Fear of difference or fear of sameness?

The notion of scarcity, we have established, is central to the rationalities of reproduction of neoliberalism and neoliberal citizenship. By acting as a framework of incentives, justification for the boundlessness of consumption, and mechanism for the creation of value, scarcity subjects to its rule not just material objects but ideas. The scarcity of resources compounded by the scarcity of values brings legitimacy to the bioeconomic necessity of sacrificing less valuable lives—be they undocumented migrants or debased citizens of austerity—to preserve the sacred marked and the lives of those who thrive under its rule. There is yet another dimension of the notion of scarcity that must be considered: the extent to which it subverts traditional ways of conceptualizing and explaining the fear of immigrants. Existing accounts generally converge on the argument that refugees and undocumented migrants are perceived as a threat because they are regarded as different—whether culturally, religiously, economically, socially, or ethnically. The underlying idea is that difference prompts conflict, which means that sameness produces peace. In this section, I challenge this reading and show how the 'sameness' caused by scarcity is the main source of fears of the immigrant 'other'.

The seemingly intuitive and uncontroversial view that difference prompts conflict has gained growing legitimacy in both public and academic circles and has been embraced by very different thinkers. In international relations, it has been propped up by popular theses such as Samuel Huntington's (1996) *Clash of Civilization* and its idea that civilizational differences revolving around culture and religion—hence the fear of the cultural and religious 'foreigner'—are the main sources of conflict in the post-Cold War world. In philosophy and social theory, Jacques Derrida is at loggerheads with Huntington's bellicist 'model of cultural abjection' which, as Michael Shapiro (2016: 200) observes, 'fails to appreciate the historical contribution of "the foreigner" to constructive criticism of systems of national authority.' And yet, while Derrida (2000) argues that we should consider the immigrant stranger not as a threat but as an opportunity to question and challenge our established ways of being and acting in the world, his starting premise is similar to Huntington's: difference feeds fear and conflict. Let me briefly consider this argument in greater detail.

For Derrida (cited in Caputo 2000: 276), at the heart of the 'crimes against hospitality that are endured by the wayfarers and hostages of our times, day after day incarcerated or expelled, from concentration camps to detention camps, from border to border' there is the fear of 'otherness', that is, the radical difference of the stranger. Our reaction, Derrida maintains, should not be giving in to this fear, but actually confronting and embracing it by taking a leap of faith in the name of God. The 'otherness' of undocumented migrants should be regarded as a way of encountering God. Welcoming the stranger should therefore be conceived as an experience of 'holiness' that produces 'an excess of transcendence' (Derrida, cited in Caputo 2000: 284, 298), that is, a crucial moment of deconstruction that enables us to transcend our fears and subvert who we are and the world we live in. Hence, Derrida (2000: 25) maintains, we should conceive of hospitality as an absolute, unconditional gift to the radically different 'absolute, unknown, anonymous other'. We should open our hearts and homes and offer them a place 'without asking of them either reciprocity ... or even their names' (Derrida 2000: 25).

Hospitality, Derrida maintains, must be unconditional to the point that we must be willing to question our material and ideational certainties, both individually and collectively. As he puts it, hospitality is 'an interruption of the self' and 'the deconstruction of the at-home; deconstruction is hospitality to the other' (Derrida 2002: 364). Absolute hospitality thus involves the willingness to take a risk, to embrace the threat that welcoming the 'other' may change us forever, even lead to the dissolution of who we are as individuals and as a community. By reframing undocumented migrants from potential threat to emissaries of God, Derrida's political theology of hospitality posits a forceful challenge to neoliberal citizenship and its economic framework of valuation. However, by framing undocumented migrants as expressions of a radical alterity, Derrida does not reject the axiom difference-conflict but only its inevitability. As a result, and however ethically inspiring, Derrida not only fails to problematize the concept of difference, but ends up performing its metaphysical sacralization in the Durkheimian sense of the term, namely, he conceives of 'difference' both as an object of veneration—an opportunity for a critical deconstruction of the self—and as something 'apart and forbidden', as a given that cannot be questioned.

This approach unwittingly reinforces and essentializes the divide between 'host' and 'guest', 'member' and 'stranger', 'citizen' and 'non-citizen' (see Squire and Darling 2013: 63) and thus the very 'difference' that for many is the cause of our (allegedly justified) fear of undocumented migrants. To an extreme, by portraying immigrants as radically different, the only thing that this approach can offer against biopolitical racism is a leap of faith in the inherent goodness of difference, not a sustained questioning and deconstruction of the idea of difference itself. More specifically, Derrida's argument prevents us from considering that what we may be afraid of is not something *beyond* ourselves, but something *in* ourselves that undocumented migrants reveal and make visible. Hence, it prevents us from entertaining the possibility that what we may be afraid of is not difference, but sameness. To explore this argument, we need to return to the concept of scarcity and consider that, as Dumouchel (2014: 4) reminds us, material and ideational scarcity 'forces people's desires to converge on the same objects and sets us against one another in necessary rivalry.' Scarcity erases differences by creating an ultimate sameness that 'condemns us to war' (Dumouchel 2014: 4). If not an inherent cause of conflict, what is difference then?

According to René Girard, difference is a system of established hierarchies and recognized social roles which keep in check the conflicts arising from mimetic desire by acting as a mechanism of external mediation. Mimetic desire is the condition whereby we imitate or desire the desires of others, with the effect that our collective desires converge on the same material or ideational objects. This creates a potential for conflict that can be amplified by a condition of scarcity because we will compete against each other for the same scarce resources (Girard 1987: 85–6, 1966: 120; Palaver 2013: 61–3, 141). As Wolfgang Palaver (2013: 61) explains in relation to Girard's argument, as the world turns seemingly more egalitarian and traditional social hierarchies, roles, and structures crumble, 'the metaphysical distance between desiring subject and model diminishes', with the effect that 'the potential for rivalry and violence increases. The more negligible this distance becomes, the more probable it is that mimesis will end in rivalry and violence' (Palaver 2013: 61). For Girard, this transformation is insightfully captured by Alexis de Tocqueville in his book *Democracy in America*. For Tocqueville:

> When all the privileges of birth and fortune are abolished, when all professions are accessible to all, and a man's own energies may place him at the top of any one of them, an easy and unbounded career seems open to his ambition and he will readily persuade himself that he is born to no common destinies. ... The same equality that allows every citizen to conceive these lofty hopes, renders all the citizens less able to realize them; it circumscribes their powers on every side, while it gives freer scope to their desires ... [because] they have opened the door to universal competition.
>
> (Tocqueville, cited in Palaver 2013: 61)

These words are remarkably prescient of the current neoliberal order which has replaced traditional hierarchies and structures with a self-disciplining mechanism of competition underpinned by a logic of unbounded desire. The original promise of neoliberalism was the satisfaction of desire—in the form of market equilibrium, economic reward, material growth, and virtually unlimited consumption—in exchange for a social order based on individualism, greed, envy, and rivalry. The satisfaction of desire would act as a mechanism of social coordination and regulation which channels violence into fierce neoliberal competition. However, as we saw earlier in the book, marked by a relentless pattern of crises, poor economic growth, declining social mobility, and growing inequality, neoliberalism has increasingly relinquished the 'triumphalist narrative' (Dean 2014: 161) of being able to generate material wealth that would trickle down to the poorest parts of society or the poorest countries. As Mitchell Dean (2014: 161) observes, neoliberalism's primary focus is now to 'fashion ways to make individuals, communities, systems and organizations fit for rigors of the catastrophe yet to come.'

In this 'neoliberalism of crisis' or 'neoliberalism of catastrophe', the promise of satisfaction of desire is no longer sufficient to channel violence into extreme individualism, greediness, envy, and market competition as neoliberalism is manifestly unable to deliver on its promise of growth for the masses—it can only deliver this promise for the few. Violence thus requires a new outlet, a new target, a new sacrificial victim, a scapegoat as Girard would describe it. This role has been assigned to the refugees and undocumented migrants. To this end, what neoliberalism has done, is not to increase the difference between Europeans and undocumented migrants; quite the opposite, neoliberalism has reduced this distance, it has established a new proximity by creating a class of socially destitute and economically marginalized Europeans who, particularly over the last ten years, have seen their wealth, social opportunities, standards of living, and possibilities of consumptions sharply declining. Neoliberalism has instituted a race-to-the-bottom egalitarianism, a new equality of the poor, the debased, and the unwanted irrespective of their citizenship status.

This perspective suggests that the European refugee crisis has not been governed by the fear of difference, but by the fear of sameness. The undocumented migrant has become the mirror image, the mimetic double of the impoverished European subject: in different ways, they are both uprooted, poor, marginalized, and at the mercy of forces they often do not understand let alone control. The fear of sameness at the heart of the European responses to the refugee crisis has been deliberately constructed and socially engineered through neoliberalism and, particularly in the aftermath of the 2008 financial crisis, through neoliberal policies of austerity. As we know, the effects of austerity have been quite dramatic. In 2017, it was estimated that '22% of the EU population are at risk of poverty or social exclusion—this includes 25% of all children in Europe, 23% of women, 18% of those over 65; 7% of Europeans live in severe material deprivation; 17% of Europeans live on less than 60% of their country's median household income; 9.3% of Europeans live in households where no one has a job' (European Commission 2017).

The significant impoverishment of large sections of the European population has been accompanied by a sustained growth of inequality, with a significant increase of the concentration of wealth in the hands of the richest strata of society. Of course, the impact of austerity has been uneven across Europe. It has been tougher on southern European countries—in particular on Greece, where the harsh package of austerity measures has caused social devastation. The impact of austerity has also been particularly exacting on those countries which had a relatively higher level of public debt compared to the rest of the Eurozone, namely, Portugal, Ireland, Italy, Greece, and Spain, often derogatorily described with the acronym 'PIIGS'. The neoliberal policies of austerity have contributed to establish a remarkable identity and a close proximity between the European dispossessed and the refugees flowing to Europe.

Yet, their sameness does not rest solely on their social displacement, economic disposability, and material destitution. The European dispossessed by austerity and the refugees flowing to Europe have become Girardian 'mimetic doubles' because both groups have become the object of stigmatization in public opinion and the target of a neoliberal theodicy that considers them responsible for their own condition. The European dispossessed have been increasingly portrayed 'as if they were responsible for their situation and if social protection was a luxury in times of austerity' (Cavero and Poinasamy 2013: 10). The undocumented migrants have been described either as 'fake' or as responsible for their forced displacement and for robbing Europeans of their scarce resources in a time of austerity. Austerity has reduced the distance between the European dispossessed and the refugees with the effect of collapsing the distinction between citizens and strangers in need and rewriting the notions of citizenship, human rights, refugee protection, and duties of hospitality in neoliberal terms. Austerity has engendered competition for scarce resources—homes, jobs, health services, and welfare provisions—to the point that the refugees, rather than the European economic and financial elites, have been blamed for these shortages. Refugees have been turned into the ultimate scapegoats of Europe and its financial crisis.

As Girard (2001: 11) reminds us, 'The principal source of violence between human beings is mimetic rivalry, the rivalry resulting from imitation of a model who becomes a rival or of a rival who becomes a model.' In the European refugee crisis, refugees have been successfully constructed as rivals who come here to rob us of our scarce resources and any who attempt to resist this narrative—by showing or practising a more human model of solidarity and a more compassionate politics of hospitality—have been increasingly branded as demonstrating political correctness, weakness, do-goodism, a lack of identity, wokeness, naivety, left-wing elitism, Marxism, a lack of love for one's country, a betrayal of one's own people, privileging strangers over members, philo-Islamism, and so on. Equally, the dominant narrative has managed to turn the rival refugee into a model—hence the portrayal of the refugees as benefit scroungers, who are allegedly given privileged access to health services, schools, and other welfare provisions that are often denied to native Europeans. Neoliberal austerity has managed to instil in the European dispossessed the desire for the desires of the refugees—disentitled strangers who are seemingly offered the good life they are denied—and has managed to create an artificial scarcity that, following Girard (1996: 10), has established these two groups 'as each other's conflictual doubles or 'twins''.

In such situations, Girard (1996: 10) warns, 'hierarchies' and established social roles 'disintegrate' and 'prohibitions are transgressed'. The refugee emerges as responsible for the misery and the deprivation of the European dispossessed and thus becomes the scapegoat, the surrogate victim that needs to be immolated and sacrificed in order to save Europe. Yet, Girard (1996: 13) adds, 'A scapegoat effect that can be acknowledged as such by the scapegoaters is no longer effective, it is no longer a scapegoat effect. The victim must be perceived as truly responsible for the troubles that come to an end when it is collectively put to death.' The sacrifice of undocumented migrants and of debased citizens of austerity thus becomes no one's responsibility and the seemingly natural and accepted outcome of neoliberal citizenship: a regime characterized by a bioeconomy of necessity governed by scarcity which is in turn the expression of a sacralized market. The latter, as we learned from Hayek, transcends out capacity of comprehension and we can only bow to its inscrutable workings and resiliently wait for its promise of redemption. The market cannot be questioned or challenged even when it delivers failures, crises, and shocks and even when it demands us to sacrifice 'distant strangers' or fellow citizens.

Conclusion

In this chapter, I have further advanced my exploration of the sacralization of the market by discussing how neoliberalism is a rationality of government whose power and resilience rest on its capacity to appropriate religious beliefs, modes of revelation, and frameworks of transcendence. In particular, focusing on Hayek, I showed that the sacralization of the market is not just the outcome of an unbridled process of commodification that undermines the sacred/profane separation, but of a fundamental condition of unknowability which requires that we submit to the transcendent mysteries of the market. As part of this analysis, I strived to offer a new reading of Hayek's neoliberalism by showing how it mixes secular and religious registers, blurs the divide between knowledge and ignorance, and eventually demands an act of faith in the market's ultimate goodness even when the latter delivers crises, failures, and shocks. For Hayek, the hubris of thinking that the market may be understood, managed, and acted upon will inevitably result in the 'the nemesis of the planned society', namely, in the decline of reason as manifested in the compression of freedom and the reduction to serfdom.[1]

Whilst this analysis builds on Hayek's rendering of neoliberalism—which has acquired growing explanatory, normative, and practical relevance in the aftermath of the 2008 financial crisis—its relevance transcends the disciplinary boundaries of his neoliberal subjectivism and offers crucial insights to grasp the transformation of neoliberalism and neoliberal citizenship. As I stated earlier in the book, the different theoretical strands and practical manifestations of neoliberalism should not distract us from the fact that neoliberalism finds unity and coherence in an underlying process of sacralization of the market and profanation of life. By ascribing to the market a transcendent unknowability, complexity, and capacity of coordination, neoliberalism turns it into a sacred entity that cannot be questioned or challenged. The neoliberal market thus emerges as an Agambeian 'zone of undecidability' that sacralizes the market through a profane secular reason. The latter encourages the acceptance of revelation—the inherent goodness of the market—as the only rational course of action.

This analysis has important implications for neoliberal citizenship. First, the sacralization of the market makes the recognition and protection that an individual may receive a function of the 'calculus of life', that is, of their economic value. The neoliberal 'leap of faith' in the unknown of the market ultimately results in a modern reinterpretation and endorsement of Malthus' theory of overpopulation. Neoliberal citizenship celebrates suffering and justifies the sacrifice of less valuable individuals as necessary for the reproduction of the neoliberal market order. This process, I have shown, is crucially underpinned by the institution of scarcity as a fundamental category that glorifies uncertainty,

[1] Nemesis was the Greek goddess of retribution that punished acts of hubris against the gods. 'Hubris of Reason' and 'The Nemesis of the Planned Society' were the titles of the two main sections that Hayek originally envisaged for *The Abuse and Decline of Knowledge* (see Ebenstein 2014: 107).

insecurity, competition, envy, and boundless desire as foundations of a peaceful order. The channelling of violence into an economic system that has been turned into the overarching framework of our existence makes us fearful and concerned not just for our scarce material resources but also for our limited ideational resources. Undocumented migrants thus become a double threat, as they threaten to deprive us of our wealth and culture, and become the mirror image of an internal threat, namely, the debased and impoverished citizens of austerity. Both groups become scapegoats, responsible for our condition of material and moral deprivation.

This connection reveals not just how neoliberalism crucially relies on and mobilizes biopolitical racism, but also how our fear of the 'immigrant other' is crucially a fear of ourselves. The undocumented migrant may seemingly appear as a symbol of difference but is actually a reminder of sameness. Migrants are a reminder of what we could become, and are actually becoming, through a neoliberal citizenship that knows no value and entitlement other than those stemming from the economic value recognized by a sacred market which cannot be questioned or challenged. In this framework, undocumented migrants are not external and foreign to us, *they are us*. They are a reminder of the precariousness and sacrificial nature of our lives—or more precisely—of the lives of nominal citizens who have experienced a compression of their entitlements and standards of living at the hands of the sacred logics of the market. Where does this compression, this curtailment, this deprivation end? When do the debased citizens of neoliberalism become internal migrants, internally displaced people who can be sacrificed on the altar of the market? When do they become unwanted to the point that they can achieve sacredness only through their sacrificial immolation to the economies of waste? These questions will be explored in Chapter 8 that focuses on the neoliberal sacrificial citizenship of the COVID-19 pandemic.

8

The sacrificial citizenship of COVID-19

Introduction

On 8 April 2020, at the peak of its first wave of coronavirus infections, Italy took the unprecedented step of declaring its seaports 'unsafe' for the docking of migrant rescue boats 'for the entire duration of the health emergency' (Tondo 2020). It was not the first time that Italy had closed its ports to NGOs' vessels as part of a broader European attempt to discourage search-and-rescue missions carried out by non-state actors. Indeed, similar closures had been a regular occurrence between mid-2018 and mid-2019, when right-wing-populist leader Matteo Salvini was Minister of the Interior. Yet, what was crucially different this time was the rationale for the closure. Salvini accused NGOs of collusion with human traffickers and portrayed undocumented migrants as a threat because culturally, religiously, and ethnically different and because, he claimed, they commit crimes and bring diseases, such as tuberculosis and scabies, which have long been defeated in Europe (Rizzuti 2019). The narrative of undocumented migrants as plague spreaders had already been debunked by the United Nations High Commissioner for Refugees among others (UNHCR 2016). The ministerial decree of a nominally more migrant-friendly government went even further in challenging Salvini's narrative. Unwittingly, it stated that the Italians represented a potential biological threat to the migrants, rather than the other way round.

Admittedly, Italy's decision had very little to do with the care of migrants. It was at best the expression of an incapacity to offer refuge at a time of acute crisis and, at worst, an attempt to exploit the pandemic outbreak to continue a policy of securitization of migration and selective closure and opening of borders (Italy has been at the forefront of rolling out fiscal red carpets to attract wealthy foreigners). Either way, the consequences of this act did not take long to materialize. A few days later, on Easter Sunday, it emerged that a boat in distress carrying dozens of migrants without food and water had been wandering aimlessly for days between the Italian island of Lampedusa and Malta,

Neoliberal Citizenship. Luca Mavelli, Oxford University Press.
© Luca Mavelli (2022). DOI: 10.1093/oso/9780192857583.003.0008

which had also closed its ports due to the coronavirus outbreak. Both countries had denied help. By the time the vessel managed to return to Tripoli with the help of a Libyan fishing boat, twelve people had died (Scavo 2020). Through its regime of neoliberal citizenship, Europe had once again stated the principle that to enable the reproduction of its neoliberal life it was willing to sacrifice 'worthless' migrants.

By this time, however, the sacrifice of undocumented migrants was no longer enough to quell the thirst of the neoliberal market order. The COVID-19 pandemic outbreak had seeped deeply into the heart of Europe and engrossed itself in the cracks opened by neoliberal austerity. What had to be sacrificed now was not just wandering denizens but ordinary citizens. These include the old, the sick, the weak, the poor, ethnic minorities, low paid workers often employed in the gig economy carrying out essential jobs (drivers, garbage collectors, shopkeepers, delivery workers), as well as those on the frontline of the epidemic (doctors, nurses, and care and sanitation workers). By the time the latest slaughter of undocumented migrants had been consumed, a number of citizens in Europe, the USA, Brazil, and elsewhere in the world had been turned into internally displaced sacrificial citizens. This chapter explores how neoliberal citizenship has shaped the response to the first wave of the coronavirus pandemic (February–July 2020).

We previously saw how neoliberalism, instead of seemingly increasing the difference between Europeans and undocumented migrants, has established a new proximity by creating a class of socially destitute and economically marginalized Europeans who have experienced a sharp decline in their wealth, social opportunities, and standards of living. Neoliberalism has instituted a race-to-the-bottom egalitarianism, a new equality of the poor, the debased, and the unwanted irrespective of their citizenship status with the effect of eroding the distinction between citizens and strangers in need in relation to the duty of care and protection. In this process, the sacrifice of undocumented migrants has not translated into better care for Europeans as apologists of populism would want us to believe with slogans such as 'Italians', 'French', and 'British first'. Rather, it has resulted in the establishment of neoliberal citizenship as a method and metric of valuation that, irrespective of nominal statuses, places the 'economically valuable' first and turns large sections of the population into sacrificial citizens.

The pandemic has further radicalized the nature and extent of this sacrifice, which is no longer the disciplined acceptance of a pay-cut, of a lack of sick pay, of a furlough scheme, of precariousness, and of an overall worsening of labour and life conditions. Neoliberal citizenship now requires the *generalized* acceptance of suffering and death as inevitable conditions of a sacralized bioeconomy of necessity. The latter, over the years, has instituted an artificial condition of scarcity through the scaling down of healthcare provisions while simultaneously reducing the capacity of large sections of the population to build the necessary excess (of money, time, space, safety, and job security) required to confront such a crisis. Ultimately, the neoliberal citizenship regime has successfully established the idea of a trade-off between life and market. Only a certain number of lives can be saved because saving too many lives will undermine the proper functioning of the market (see Barnett 2020). This does not mean that the neoliberal state has relinquished its biopolitical duty of care of the population. The population cared for has shrunk further and it is increasingly constituted only by those regarded as the most economically valuable, for whom the less valuable have to be sacrificed. The neoliberal citizenship of COVID-19 has significantly expanded the category of those who can be sacrificed to include a new group: elderly care homes residents.

In Europe and North America, during the first wave of the pandemic (February–July 2020), almost half of all COVID-19 deaths were care home residents (Comas-Herrera et al. 2020). These deaths were not just the inevitable outcome of the unknowns of an unprecedent event and of the complexity of governing a growing ageing population. Elderly citizens, particularly those with physical and mental disabilities, were framed and treated as surplus populations. In a typical neoliberal fashion, this desacralization of life in the shadow of the sacralization of the market has been presented as the inevitable and regrettable outcome of an original condition of scarcity. Indeed, as I shall discuss, the COVID-19 pandemic *is* a neoliberal crisis of scarcity: of intensive care beds, of ventilators, of personal protective equipment (PPE), of testing equipment, of qualified and properly trained staff. This scarcity, however, is not natural but socially instituted. It is the product of years of underfunded public healthcare infrastructure, of just-in-time managerial approaches aimed at saving costs at the expense of the capacity of the system to build the necessary redundancy to confront a crisis, of the casualization of care workers, of the worsening of their working conditions, and of the relentless privatization of healthcare.

This scarcity has placed Hayek's 'calculus of lives' (albeit without any public reference to Hayek) at the forefront of social and political debates. Doctors have been drafting 'ventilator triage guidelines', namely, the rules of allocation for the limited number of ventilators available based on a patient's capacity to successfully overcome the illness. Politicians, economists, and pundits have assessed the benefits of lockdown against the negative effects of its prolonged adoption on the economy. They have debated how the economic cost of the lockdown should be assessed against the cost of saving lives. In these debates, lives are ranked and their value measured against the sacred domain of the market. In the neoliberal citizenship of coronavirus, lives are sacred only insofar as they are strong enough to survive with scarce health provisions and the imperative of preserving the neoliberal order. Once again, in a remarkable reversal, the market order emerges as a sacred entity, rather than a secular one at the service of the sacredness of life.

These arguments will be explored in four steps. First, I consider how governing the pandemic has been framed as a trade-off between saving markets and saving lives. I focus in particular on the case of the UK, whose delayed response to the crisis and short-lived biopolitical attempt to establish 'herd immunity' typify the sacrificial logics at the heart of neoliberal citizenship. Keeping my focus on the UK, in Section 2, I explore how the two trajectories of sacralization of the market discussed in Chapters 6 and 7—totalizing commodification and the ascription to the market of a transcendent capacity of coordination—have resulted in the careful institution of scarcity (of hospital beds, PPE, ventilators, doctors, and nurses) which has contributed to turn the pandemic into a catastrophic crisis and certain categories of citizens into sacrificial citizens.

In Section 3, I discuss how scarcity in the face of coronavirus has not created a condition of 'sameness' as scholars such as Agamben and Žižek argue. Quite the opposite, scarcity has amplified the system of biopolitical differences that underpins the neoliberal citizenship regime and contributed to reinforcing and establishing new categories of surplus citizens. In Section 4, I focus on what I regard as the most important and at the same time neglected group of surplus citizens created by the pandemic: the elderly in care homes. I will show how their sacrifice bears striking resemblances with that of migrants in refugee camps, and how it represents an even more extreme expression of neoliberal citizenship, as their sacrifice no longer requires the moral justification of an alleged guilt.

1. Saving markets or saving lives?

On 12 March 2020, following mounting accusations of inaction, UK Prime Minister Boris Johnson held a much-awaited press conference. He informed the country that the COVID-19 pandemic was 'the worst public health crisis for a generation' as a result of which 'many more families are going to lose loved ones before their time' (*The Guardian* 2020a). This ominous warning was followed by a seemingly strikingly inconsequential plan: a series of light-touch recommendations for the elderly and those who displayed symptoms to stay at home. Schools, business, public transport, and the country overall would run almost as usual. The next day, Sir Patrick Vallance, England's chief scientific adviser, further explained that letting the virus run its course without enforcing lockdown measures would contribute 'to build up some kind of herd immunity so more people are immune to this disease and we reduce the transmission, at the same time we protect those who are most vulnerable to it' (*Financial Times* 2020).

This approach raised considerable criticism. China had just managed to flatten the curve of contagion through a series of strict lockdown measures. Italy, at the time the worst-hit country in Europe, had enforced a national quarantine a few days earlier. It had already reached a death toll of over a thousand and its health system, despite a higher number of intensive care beds than the UK (Rhodes et al. 2012), was struggling to cope. The media reported dramatic accounts of doctors forced to choose which patients to save due to the shortage of life-saving equipment, and who described the situation as a 'war'. Moreover, the very notion of 'herd immunity' was questioned by most of the scientific community which emphasized how it was a condition achievable only through mass vaccination, not by letting run amok a potentially lethal virus for which, at the time, there was no vaccine. The government's decision appeared as irresponsibly risking the life of hundreds of thousands of people.[1] A few days later, pressed by criticisms and seemingly prompted by a report from Imperial College London, which estimated the number of deaths in the order of 250,000 with the existing measures (Ferguson et al. 2020), the government backtracked. It claimed that 'herd immunity' was never its policy in the first place and enforced a late lockdown. Yet, doubts have been raised on the government's true intentions.

Shortly after this policy U-turn, it surfaced that at the end of February, at a private event, Johnson's chief adviser, Dominic Cummings, had presented the government's approach as 'herd immunity, protect the economy, and if that

[1] The same willingness to take risks would also inform the UK's speedy coronavirus vaccine approval at the end of 2020 and the decision in March 2021 not to suspend, like most European countries, the AstraZeneca vaccine on concerns that it could cause blood clots. In this case, the UK's willingness to take risks as opposed to the more 'precautionary approach' of most EU countries paid off. At the end of May 2021, the UK was 'leading the [European] race to herd immunity' with over 55 million vaccinations, followed by a more populous Germany with only slightly over 40 million, and almost doubling an equally populous France (Harris 2021). It should also be noted, *in passim*, how the vaccination campaign has been economized: it has been turned into a race governed by the principles of competition, inequality, and greediness. Indeed, in March 2021, Prime Minister Boris Johnson reportedly told a group of Conservative MPs that '[t]he reason we have the vaccine success is because of capitalism, because of greed, my friends' (BBC News 2021).

means some pensioners die, too bad' (*The Guardian* 2020b). While this claim was vigorously denied by the government, in February and March, Johnson had declared that 'coronavirus should not be allowed to segregate the market' and that a possible course of action would be to 'take it all in one go and allow the disease ... to move through the population, without taking as many draconian measures' (cited in Cooper and Furlong 2020). It is clear from these statements that the government was reluctant to implement quarantine measures which would negatively impact the economy. Indeed, the idea of a trade-off between saving lives and saving the market had already entered the public debate. A few days before Johnson's momentous press conference, the economic editor of BBC News stated that 'It is seen in policy circles that there may be a trade-off between limiting the spread of the virus and economic impact', whereas leading epidemiologist Roy Anderson opined that 'you can't both minimize mortality and minimize economic impact, so the government has to make a clear decision about what is their primary policy objective in the mitigation strategy adopted' (BBC World at One 2020).

Following to the letter the neoliberal script, the British government considered of paramount importance protecting the economy from the shock of a shortage of labour and demand that a lockdown would cause. It implicitly embraced the (Hayekian) idea that the market has a superior problem-solving capacity that vastly transcends human comprehension and that any attempt to intervene upon its functioning, unless aimed at preserving its conditions of existence, will fail and make a crisis worse. As discussed, according to the neoliberal credo, any such intervention, however well-intended, will result in perverse incentives of Malthusian memory. Hence, in the same way that the response to the refugee crisis was the suspension of search-and-rescue missions, regarded as a perverse incentive/pull factor that would encourage more people to undertake the dangerous sea journey and risk their life, so did the first response to the coronavirus pandemic became a strategy of inaction/herd immunity.

The subsequent decision to backtrack from this policy and enforce a lockdown should not be read as a disavowal of the neoliberal sacredness of the market. Indeed, the lockdown triggered a multiplication of ominous warnings at government, corporate, and societal level that a prolonged suspension of economic activity would have even more life-devastating consequences than the virus. This neoliberal defence has materialized in arguments such as 'If the coronavirus lockdown leads to a fall in GDP of more than 6.4 per cent more years of life will be lost due to recession than will be gained through beating the virus' (*The Times* 2020) and 'Covid-19 presents stark choices between life, death and the economy' (*The Economist* 2020a). The neoliberal magazine *The Economist* (2020b) admitted that there is conflicting evidence on the impact of economic recessions on mortality rates, and epidemiological research suggests that the lethality of certain pathologies—such as drug dependence and lung cancer—decreases with higher unemployment rates. Indeed, the worst modern economic crisis to date, the 1929 crash, saw an overall decrease in mortality. Yet, *The Economist* warned, when 'by the summer', a third of GDP will have been lost, markets will have tumbled, investment will have been delayed, and skills will have decayed, 'even if many people are dying, the cost of distancing could outweigh the benefits' (*The Economist* 2020b).

Emboldened by the statements of then US President Donald Trump—who had repeatedly stated that the 'cure' (the lockdown) may be 'worse than the disease' and that an economic recession will kill more than the virus—apologists of neoliberalism have produced countless 'calculi of life' (how much it would cost to save a life). They have celebrated the examples of countries such as the Netherlands—which after embracing the notion of herd immunity repackaged it as 'intelligent lockdown' (a selective closure of certain activities to minimize the impact on the economy)—and Sweden—the only country in Europe not to impose a lockdown in response to the COVID first wave.[2] They have vocally called the government to end the lockdown because 'spending £350 billion to prolong the lives of a few hundred thousand mostly elderly people is an irresponsible use of taxpayers' money' (Young 2020). These callous proclamations have prompted critics to denounce a mounting 'epidemiological neoliberalism' that 'literally puts profit before people' (Frey 2020) and a neoliberal 'eugenic logic' that regards the economy as 'more important than people's health' (Laterza and Romer 2020). These accusations are often shrugged off by arguing that the idea of a trade-off between saving the economy and saving lives is partially misleading as there is no economy without life and life draws on the economy for its nourishment (see for instance Costabile 2020).

Is this enough to dispel the accusation that the rejection, delay, or loose and partial implementation of lockdown has resulted in 'violence against the weak and the poor: elderly and disabled people, homeless people, refugees and

[2] There has been extensive discussion on whether Sweden's 'gamble' may have 'paid off' (Cohen 2020). The latest available research at the time of writing suggests that 'a 9-week lockdown in the first half of 2020 would have reduced infections and deaths by about 75% and 38%, respectively' and 'would not have caused much additional output loss' (Born, Dietrich, and Müller 2021: 1). As of 16 May 2021, Sweden had 139.79 COVID deaths per 100,000 people. This is less than Italy (205.69) and the UK (191.57), the two worst hit countries in Europe in absolute terms, yet it is remarkably higher than its neighbouring countries Norway (14.53), Finland (16.84) and Denmark (43.11), which all implemented early lockdown measures (Statista 2021b).

people with severe health conditions—many of whom are likely to also have a lower socio-economic status because of the correlation between poverty and illness' (Frey 2020)? Does the entanglement of economy and life exempt a free market, unregulated approach to the pandemic from the charge that for the 'herd' to survive 'other "weaker" members of society need to be sacrificed'? (Laterza and Romer 2020). Definitely not, but the issue of the entanglement of economy and life warrants further consideration to fully understand the governmental rationalities of the pandemic and the extent to which they have contributed to fully radicalize the neoliberal citizenship regime. To this end, a brief detour to the Greek debt crisis discussed in the second chapter is required.

The culturally racist and moralizing narrative that blamed the Greeks as lazy, incompetent, and fiscally lax (in order to conceal the responsibilities of the banking sector and morph a private debt crisis into a public debt crisis) was often accompanied by organic metaphors. In particular, it was frequently argued that by lying about their economic credentials and over-indulging in welfare spending, the Greek had infected with their toxic debt the 'monetary and financial lifeblood of the [European] economic body' (see Langley 2014: 68). The metaphor of money, finance, and, more generally, capital as 'the lifeblood that flows through the body politic of all those societies we call capitalist' (Harvey 2010: vii) draws on a deep-seated social imaginary that dates back to Aristotle (Langley 2014: 68) and explains how the financial threat is ultimately perceived as a biological threat. By infecting the bloodstream of Europe, Greece also infected its heart, namely, the banks, endowed with the task of pumping blood/money. In a sense, the Greek crisis was akin to a potential pandemic. It threatened to slow down and possibly suspend the blood flow, thus depriving of oxygen neoliberal capitalism and neoliberal life.

This argument highlights the biopolitical centrality of banking and, more broadly, of the neoliberal economic order, to the life, security, and well-being of the population. As Paul Langley (2014: 81) observes in relation to the 2008 financial crisis, the latter was not conceptualized and governed as a crisis concerning the functioning, reliability, and efficiency of the market, but primarily 'as a problem of solvency of banking'. Accordingly, the main goal was not to reform the market, but to restore circulation in order to allow the continuation and reproduction of the neoliberal 'financialized life' (Langley 2014: 98). The 'affective' compenetration of banking and life, Langley observes, was highlighted by a number of leading politicians and bureaucrats. Hank Paulson, then US Secretary of the Treasury, warned about the link between 'a frozen financial system' and the American people's 'reduced values in their retirement and investment accounts' (cited in Langley 2014: 98).

Gordon Brown, then UK Prime Minister, was even more explicit: '[b]anks aren't just economic entities, they are woven into the fabric of all our lives, vital to savers, to mortgage holders, to businesses and to ordinary families everywhere. And this isn't abstract, this is about the conversations mothers and fathers will be having on their sofas tonight once they have put their children to bed' (cited in Langley 2014: 98). Like the 2008 financial crisis, the Greek sovereign debt crisis was conceptualized and governed 'as a problem of solvency of banking'. Yet, in the Greek debt crisis, there was no need to publicly stress the banking–life connection in order to justify the bailout of private companies with public money. The possibility to identify a clear biopolitical cause and threat, the Greek population, provided legitimacy for a punitive bailout which established a biopolitical connection between the need for Greece to embrace austerity and the survival and well-being of the European population.

A biopolitical logic of care prompted European states to rescue the banks in order to secure the neoliberal life of the European population by transferring inequality, poverty, and social devastation to the Greek people. Accordingly, the Greek bailout saw political power, that is, European states, acting as biopolitical agents of mediation, coordination, and regulation that intervened to govern a neoliberal crisis. European governments intervened to 'establish an equilibrium, maintain an average, establish a sort of homeostasis, and compensate for variations within this general population and its aleatory field' (Foucault 2003: 246). This neoliberal-biopolitical apparatus introduced three 'break(s) into the domain of life that is under power's control' (Foucault 2003: 254). The first one is that between Europe—which had to continue to flourish, proliferate, and expand—and the Greek people—left with the social devastation of an overwhelming debt. The second break is that between wealthy Europeans, who survived the socialization of debt of the Eurozone crisis almost unscathed (with some of them also benefiting and profiting from it), and those debased citizens who suffered most of the consequences of austerity. The third one is between Europe and the migrants who became the target—the scapegoat—of the social resentment caused by austerity.

This governmental biopolitical apparatus blamed and punished the Greeks, the poorest strata of the population and the undocumented migrants for a socio-economic crisis primarily caused by the banking sector in a neoliberal citizenship regime of mounting inequality. The ensuing prolonged crisis of scarcity was governed through the neoliberal deployment of biopolitical racism. These three groups were established as a threat to the survival and well-being of Europe and its populations and punished with a series of measures (austerity, suspension of search-and-rescue missions) that caused thousands of unnecessary deaths, thus prompting a biopolitical 'cleansing of the social body' (Lemke 2011: 43–4). The laissez-faire response to the pandemic encapsulated by the controversial notion of herd immunity, by the 'calculus of life', by the late implementation of lockdown measures, and by calls for its early lifting or substantial reduction are all expressions of the same neoliberal citizenship regime, yet with an important difference: the neoliberal citizenship of the coronavirus pandemic has partially made the process of scapegoating independent from the ascription of blame. Let me elaborate.

In the cases of the Greek sovereign debt crisis, the imposition of austerity measures, and the refugee crisis, the resort to biopolitical racism has been facilitated by the process of scapegoating. The Greeks could be blamed for having irresponsibly created a debt that threatened the stability of Europe; the undocumented migrants for corrupting European identities and mores, and for being competitors for scarce resources at a time of austerity; the debased citizens of austerity for being akin to the Malthusian poor, hence for their morally debauched reliance on society for their sustenance. In a formulation that reproduces the theodicy of suffering discussed in the previous chapter, these groups have been portrayed as responsible for their own condition. Their suffering and death have thus been downgraded from violence inflicted on them to a condition that they merely brought upon themselves.

This neoliberal-biopolitical apparatus draws on a classical trope of the scapegoating process, namely, the fact that the scapegoat, however wrongly, is perceived to be guilty and therefore deserves to be sacrificed. As Wolfgang Palaver (2013: 189) reminds us, in a relation of scapegoating 'the guilt belongs to the victim as a quasi-ontological attribute, and the victim's presence in the community is sufficient to bring about a spread of the crisis' because, Girard (1986: 24) maintains, the victims are chosen 'for everything that suggests their guilty relationship with the crisis.' The centrality of the (imagined) notion of guilt to the process of scapegoating is also a crucial dimension of the exercise of pastoral power, the precursor of modern neoliberal biopolitics. As discussed in Chapter 4, pastoral power requires 'accepting the sacrifice of a sheep that could compromise the whole. The sheep that is a cause of scandal, or whose corruption is in danger of corrupting the whole flock, must be abandoned, possibly excluded, chased away, and so forth' (Foucault 2009: 169). The killing or letting die of biopolitical racism ultimately demands a belief in some form of guilt of the sheep.

The neoliberal response to the current coronavirus pandemic has brought the exercise of biopower onto a terrain that partially severs the link between the scapegoat and guilt. The fact that the 'sheep' to be sacrificed to save the 'herd' are the old and the sick, which have had no role in the spreading of the plague and indeed are universally recognized as its first innocent victims, signals a further and remarkable step in the process of sacralization of the market and radicalization of the neoliberal citizenship regime. Before fully exploring this argument later in the chapter, we need to discuss how the seeds of this sacrifice did not just blossom in the scrambled, delayed, and inchoate response to the pandemic, but have matured over a much longer period of time, which created the condition of possibility for this crisis to emerge as one of scarcity.

2. A crisis of scarcity

On 23 March, ten days after the 'herd immunity' press conference, the British government announced the enforcement of a full lockdown. All large gatherings would stop, shops selling nonessential goods would close, and people should stay at home and would be allowed to leave only for medical needs and to buy food. The reason for these measures which had so far been resisted was that, as Johnson explained, '[w]ithout a huge national effort to halt the growth of this virus, there will come a moment when no health service in the world could possibly cope; because there won't be enough ventilators, enough intensive care beds, enough doctors and nurses' (CNBC 2020). The new slogan of the government was 'Stay Home, Protect the NHS [National Health Service], Save Lives'.

The double irony of this slogan should not go unnoticed. The underfunding and privatization of the National Health Service in Britain have long been contentious political issues, with the Conservatives particularly keen on pursuing the marketization of 'the largest and oldest publicly funded healthcare system in the world' (Welch 2018: 43). The message 'protect the NHS' is a staple of those who for years have opposed cuts and privatization. Following the typical parasitical approach of neoliberalism—which does not erase and replace other domains, spheres of values, and meanings, but colonizes and rewrites them from within—the government did not just appropriate this message, but also perverted its original sense. As has been observed, 'the new usage of the phrase means to protect the NHS from being overwhelmed by the people it is meant to serve' (Pushkar 2020). It implies that the shortages of intensive care beds, of staff, of personal protective equipment (PPE) are a natural affliction independent of government's actions that requires a collective act of responsibility.

This formulation encompasses a dissimulated Malthusian reasoning. In the same way that for Malthus the population would always end up exceeding the means of subsistence because it increases at a 'geometrical ratio' rather than at an 'arithmetical' one, so the government's 'protect the NHS' slogan implies that the exponential growth of the pandemic has inevitably outpaced the resources of the NHS and other health services. Hence, the scarcity of beds, ventilators, doctors, and nurses, is not the government's fault, which could not anticipate an epidemic of this magnitude. However, the last two decades have been disseminated of warnings of a pandemic to come (the SARS, the swine flu, the bird flu, the MERS) which have been neglected by most countries. In May 2021, the Independent Panel for Pandemic Preparedness and Response (2021) established by the World Health Organization concluded that the 'outbreak became a pandemic' as a result of this neglect, of the adoption of a 'wait and see' approach instead of the implementation of 'an aggressive containment strategy', and of the limited funding initially available. In the UK, this national and international failure was compounded and aggravated by a healthcare system which had long been struggling with budget cuts.

In December 2019, the photo a four-year-old boy wearing an oxygen mask and hooked to an intravenous drip in a Leeds hospital made the headlines. The child was lying on the floor on a pile of coats. The image sparked outrage and a debate over the shortage of hospital beds. It emerged that, over the previous ten years, the number of hospital beds had shrunk by 17,000 (Grierson 2019). While this came as a surprise to the broader public, it was no news for those who had been studying and denouncing the critical state of the NHS. As early as 2012, warnings were raised on the number of intensive care beds in the UK, which at 6.6 per 100,000 were almost half of the European average of 11.5 and remarkably below the 29.2 of Germany (Rhodes et al. 2012).

The shortage of hospital beds has been compounded by that of doctors, nurses, and care workers. According to the Royal College of Nursing, in December 2019, and in England alone, there was a shortage of nurses of about 40,000. This shortage has been ascribed to declining salaries in real terms—a result of austerity measures—and reliance on a foreign workforce (18 per cent) which has been increasingly discouraged to work in the UK by restrictive immigration policies—a result of the 2010 pledge of the Conservative government to 'reduce net migration from the hundreds of thousands to the tens of thousands' a year (May 2010). The Brexit referendum in 2016 has further aggravated the shortage. Due to uncertainty and a hostile climate towards foreigners, the number of nurses from the EU has significantly declined, 'from 6,382 in 2016–17 to 805 in 2017–18' (Siddique 2020; see also Metcalf 2016).

Doctors are also in short supply: 'with 2.8 doctors per 1,000 people, compared with an average of 3.5 doctors across the OECD, the UK shortage is second only to Poland' (Skopeliti 2019). As in the case of nurses, the reliance on a foreign workforce (which amounts to 29 per cent of doctors) has been worsened by immigration caps. A 2019 report by the Organisation for Economic Co-operation and Development (OECD 2019: 3) on the state of healthcare in the UK noted how health spending was lower than that of 'similarly wealthy countries' and that '[s]ince 2008, budgets have not kept pace with growing demand for services, leading to increased waiting times and provider deficits.' This has resulted in greater 'mortality rates from preventable and treatable causes ... than in other high-income EU countries' and in 'workforce shortages' that 'threaten the sustainability of the health system' (OECD 2019: 3). In short, the report argued, 'the health system faces increasing demand with historical underfunding and recruitment deficits', all of which raise warnings on its resilience (OECD 2019: 18).

This scarcity of NHS staff is not natural. It has been carefully instituted through neoliberal policies of austerity, a neoliberal immigration regime, and the decision to leave the EU, which have turned foreign doctors, nurses, and health workers into the embodiment of overlapping and conflicting forms of capital: valuable human capital that positively contributes to the NHS and yet negative emotional capital for many 'Brexiters', who consider them as 'strangers' who have a negative impact on the country's culture and wealth (see Chapter 3). This approach to NHS staff has not spared the very structure of the NHS, which has been increasingly reorganized according to neoliberal market rationalities with catastrophic consequences. In particular, the growing adoption of the managerial principles of outsourcing and just-in-time procurement in the NHS supply chain is the main culprit for the shortage of PPE—gowns, masks, goggles, and respirators—during the early stages of the pandemic. This shortage, which has been described as 'a crisis within a crisis' (Tolhurst 2020), is widely regarded as responsible for the death of dozens among health and social care workers which could have otherwise been avoided.

The privatization of the NHS supply chain began in 2006. The strategy has been that of centralizing the system of procurement (instead of leaving each Trust to cater for its own supply) and outsourcing it to private contractors in order to reduce operational costs, achieve greater bargaining power, and increase efficiency through a just-in-time approach that would reduce inventory stockpiles (Hall et al. 2020). This would result in projected savings of '£2.4 billion ... over seven years up to 2022, and annual savings of £615 million thereafter' (Hall et al. 2020: 6). The outcome of this reorganization has been the creation of a complex chain—producers, wholesale supplier, procurement specialists, and logistic experts—which has had the effect of 'distancing NHS trusts from suppliers of equipment', to the effect that the Department of Health and Social Care (DHSC), while still nominally in charge of the NHS supply chain, has no effective control over it (Hall et al. 2020: 14). With the global surge of the coronavirus pandemic, the system showed its striking limitations.

Worldwide, medical equipment suppliers had long relocated or outsourced low-margin production, such as PPE, to countries like Mexico and most of all China in order to take full advantage of lower labour costs (Cartwright 2020). However, as a result of the pandemic, production in several areas of China partially stopped or was significantly scaled down, with the effect that the supply shrank, prices skyrocketed, and the global scramble for PPE became 'utter, cutthroat chaos' (CBC 2020). Having underestimated the gravity of the pandemic, the UK entered the worldwide competition for PPE at a later stage when most of the deals had already been made. Struggling to boost the stock of protective equipment, the UK embarked upon a series of public stunts, such as sending a military plane to collect PPE in Turkey (save for later discovering that most of this material was not compliant with health and safety standards). Most importantly, though, behind the curtains, the government instructed suppliers to ration the demand among NHS trusts (Hall et al. 2020: 8). Suppliers, in turn, sent an automated messageto NHS trusts desperate for PPE stating that 'Orders placed for excessive order quantities may be subject to automatic system reduction' (Hall et al. 2020: 8). The reorganization of the NHS supply chain according to market rationalities thus ended up prompting a series of perverse inversions.

First, a market system designed to increase efficiency by delivering just-in-time eventually interfered with the market in one of the worst possible ways, that is, by rationing the supply. Second, it has placed the Department of Health and Social Care at the mercy of market forces, which are now 'responsible' for the health and safety of NHS workers and the effective allocation of scarce resources. But of course, private contractors cannot be held responsible for public health—no more than, for instance, Amazon can be held responsible for public health by selling face masks to customers. Private companies have an incentive to sell PPE, but no duty to ensure that they do not run out of stock (see Barnett 2020: E139). This should be the responsibility of elected governments. In the ideal world of neoliberalism, the transcendent capacity of coordination of the market and the monetary incentives it provides should be enough to guarantee that private suppliers do not run out of stock. However, the COVID pandemic proved neoliberal supporters spectacularly wrong:

privatization, delocalization, outsourcing, and just-in-time, combined with traditional neoliberal cuts to welfare provisions have resulted in a condition of scarcity of PPE, hospital beds, and health professionals.

This scarcity, to be sure, is far from being unique to the UK. Italy, the country with the second highest Covid death toll in Europe (121,177) after the UK (127,538) (as of 2 May 2021; Statista 2021a), has also experienced a significant reduction of intensive and semi-intensive care beds, which since 1996 have been almost halved. Healthcare expenditures have also declined, with Italy spending 3.428 USD per capita, well below the 3.992 USD OSCE (Organization for Security and Co-operation in Europe) average (Aghilar 2020). All these figures have considerably worsened in the aftermath of the 2009 Eurozone crisis and the adoption of austerity measures. It is estimated that between 2011 and 2016, 'healthcare expenditures relative to GDP dropped from 9.0 to 8.8% despite a growth in population from 59.2 million to 60.7 million people over the same period' (Solty 2020).

In the USA, the country with the world's highest death toll as of May 2021, 'more than half of counties have no intensive-care beds at their disposal' and '29 million people have no health insurance' (Solty 2020). The country has also experienced an acute shortage of ventilators, which has led numerous pro-market commentators to admit that 'profit-driven decisions' have significantly impaired US capacity to fight the coronavirus outbreak (Zeballos-Roig 2020). And yet, the very failure of the market logic has prompted more market response, as graphically epitomized by the competition between US states to secure PPE. As summarized by Ohio Governor Mike DeWine 'You've got 50 states and the federal government all chasing the same companies. It's crazy' (cited in Zeballos-Roig 2020).

These considerations should not be taken to suggest that material scarcity will automatically translate into a crisis. Greece is a remarkable example here. Despite the draconian austerity measures imposed upon the country which 'caused healthcare expenditures to drop by 22.4 per cent between 2011 and 2016' (Solty 2020) and have resulted in an increase in mortality across all age segments (Global Burden of Disease 2016 Greece Collaborators 2018), as of May 2021, Greece has one of Europe's lowest death tolls in relation to the population and it has been successful in containing the epidemic (97.47 deaths per 100,000 population, contra 200 in Italy and 191 in the UK; Statista 2021b). Various explanations have been advanced to account for this seemingly unexpected situation. These include: effective leadership; the collaboration of the oppositions to ensure national cohesion; a collective sense of unity and responsibility due to Greece's recent and ongoing struggle with the austerity crisis; and an acute sense of the weaknesses of the healthcare system due to years of austerity measures, which made evident the need to avoid mass hospitalization and resulted in the enforcement of a very early lockdown.

Greece's success indicates that scarcity, apart from not being a natural condition, cannot be reduced to an objective state of affairs. As Dumouchel (2014: xi) reminds us, scarcity concerns the rules of 'distribution, access, and responsibility, … none of which is naturally given.' This point is clearly articulated by Karl Polanyi in *The Great Transformation* (2001 [1944]) where he argues that the notion of self-regulating markets has caused their social disembeddedness, namely, markets act as autonomous entities that increasingly shape social relations. This has significant implications for how the principles of 'generosity' and 'reciprocal obligations' are understood. In 'primitive societies', where markets are at the service of the social rather than being its conditions of possibility, '[t]he individual's economic interest is rarely paramount' to the effect that in a case of famine 'the community keeps all its members from starving unless it is itself borne down by catastrophe' (Polanyi 2001 [1944]: 48). For Polanyi (2001 [1944]: 172), '[i]t is the absence of the threat of individual starvation, which makes primitive society, in a sense, more human than market economy, and at the same time less economic.'

Time and further research will tell whether Greece's successful management of the coronavirus pandemic may be ascribed to a partial rejection of the sacralization of the market. While a 'primitive' deployment of the principles of 'generosity' and 'reciprocal obligations' may have contributed to this success, this argument should not be overstated for two reasons. First, an increase of solidarity and reciprocal obligations among Greeks has come at the expense of the securitization, hardening of attitudes, and biopolitical racism towards migrants. Second, Polanyi's idea of solidarity in 'primitive societies', while capturing an important aspect of the 'great transformation' performed by capitalism, is also a partially romanticized reading of the pre-capitalist world. For the purposes of this book, though, the case of Greece, seen through the lenses of Polanyi and Dumouchel, suggests that scarcity is not an objective state of affairs. It is certainly a material condition, yet one whose effects depend on its appropriation and deployment by the neoliberal citizenship regime in order to discipline individuals in the acceptance of inequality, competition, suffering, and death. As such, scarcity plays an essential role in the logic of reproduction of neoliberalism. As the competition engendered by the shortage of PPE indicates, scarcity has contributed to strengthening rather than weakening the market logic governing PPE production and distribution.

Moreover, as discussed in Chapter 7, scarcity is essential for the creation of value, as there is an inverse relation between the two. Scarcity activates the cycle of desire and neoliberal capitalism constantly re-invents and mobilizes a desire-driven scarcity to guarantee its reproduction. The very scarcity of PPE, both for health providers and individual consumers, has turned certain products, like face masks in the early stages of the pandemic, into some of the world's most desired commodities. Indeed, the PPE market is estimated to almost double over the next five years, reaching 'USD 92.5 billion by 2025' (Vynz Research 2020). As David Harvey (2014b: 335) observes in relation to Marx's argument in the *Grundrisse*, 'capital can't abide a limit, it has to turn it into a barrier which it then circumvents or transcends.' The shortage of PPE is a market failure, a limit that neoliberalism has turned into a barrier to circumvent and from which profit can be extracted.

This process of circumvention rests on the double process of sacralization of the market previously explored: the ascription to the market of a capacity of coordination that vastly transcends human comprehension and a totalizing logic of commodification that treats life-saving medical supplies like any other commodity. The market becomes an apodictic source of truth even if it fails to supply PPE and even if, arguably, PPE is manifestly different from other commodities as its shortage has biopolitical implications of life and death. In the sacralized system of the market, however, this difference is invisible. On the website of Unipart, the firm in charge of the NHS supply chain logistics, there is a section entitled 'Lessons for Health Logistics from the Automotive Sector' which advocates the extension of the principles governing the logistics of automotive parts to medical equipment (Hall et al. 2020: 23). What makes life-saving medical equipment commensurable to car parts is the establishment of the market as a sacred entity, as the measure, metric, and condition of possibility of life. It is the market that is sacred, not life, and it is the market that decides who must live and who must be sacrificed in order to enable its reproduction.

As I shall discuss in Section 3, this sacrifice is governed by a biopolitics that constantly rewrites the meanings and implications of difference and sameness. To this end, I will question the oft-repeated claim since the beginning of the pandemic that 'we are all in this together' and challenge Agamben's notion of bare life as the theoretical conceptualization of this underlying 'togetherness.' Agamben's philosophy of sameness, I will argue, misses a distinctive feature of the biopolitical governmental rationalities of neoliberal citizenship: the constant creation of difference in a regime of inequality.

3. Biopolitics of difference and sameness

With the coronavirus pandemic, the much used and abused trope 'We are all in this together' has been revived as an enunciation of a newly discovered egalitarianism of crisis. We are all human, the reasoning goes, and so we are all the same when exposed to the biological threat of the virus and its catastrophic economic consequences, irrespective of our age, class, race, and gender. Except that this is false. Epidemiological studies have established that age is a crucial factor of risk that increases exponentially the possibility of death, particularly if associated with pre-existing health conditions, such as diabetes, obesity, and hypertension. Many of these conditions are often the product of lifestyles and eating habits that reflect class-based divides. Other comorbidities of COVID-19, such as asthma, inflammatory lung disease, and coronary heart disease are linked to air pollution, which tends to be higher in areas inhabited by low-income people. Numerous analyses indicate that 'the most deprived areas in England and Wales have been hit twice as hard by the coronavirus outbreak compared to the wealthiest areas' (*New Scientist* 2020).

These areas often have a higher percentage of people from black, Asian, and minority ethnic (BAME) communities, which are emerging as being 'disproportionately' affected by the pandemic (Kirby 2020). While these groups are more exposed to some of the chronic health conditions which have been identified as the 'most important comorbidities linked to COVID' (*The Lancet: Diabetes & Endocrinology 2020*), it is also the case that people from ethnic minorities are 'more likely to live in more densely populated areas and housing, to use public transport more, and to work in lower paid service jobs without sick pay, meaning they would be more likely to go to work under all circumstances, increasing the risk of exposure' (Kirby 2020: 548). Overall, it has been established that '[t]here is a clear class divide in the COVID-19 death rate, with working class jobs such as carers, taxi drivers, security guards and retail assistants clearly worse affected than middle and upper class jobs who can much more easily self-isolate and work from home' (Williams 2020). With the exception of doctors, nurses, and dentists, 'managerial and professional occupations are less at risk' (Williams 2020).

Gender has also been identified as a significant factor of risk. While on average more men than women die of coronavirus, the lockdown has resulted in a surge of domestic abuse and domestic abuse killings (Kellam 2020). The pandemic has also had a distinctive impact on refugees and undocumented migrants. Governments have used the crisis to further pursue policies of securitization of migration either by denying the docking of migrant rescue boats or by refusing to comply with previously agreed-upon commitments such as, in the case of the UK, taking 'children from Greek camps threatened by Covid-19' (Townsend 2020). Moreover, by discouraging undocumented migrants to report any medical condition for fear of 'being reported to immigration authorities and deported' (Pertek, Phillimore, and McKnight 2020), the pandemic has further increased the already significant health risks they experience due to 'high geographical mobility, instability, living in overcrowded conditions, lack of sanitation, and lack of access to decent healthcare or vaccination programmes' (Norwegian Refugee Council 2020).

Even lockdowns have been experienced in radically different ways. As Marxist economist Alfredo Saad-Filho (2020: 480) observes with reference to the first lockdown, 'the uber-rich moved into their yachts, the merely rich fled to their second homes, the middle class struggled to work from home . . . , and the poor, already having worse health, on average, than the privileged, either lost their earnings entirely or had to risk their lives daily to perform much praised but (needless to say) low-paid "essential work" as bus drivers, care workers, nurses, porters, shopkeepers, builders, sanitation officers, delivery workers, and so on.' If anything, lockdowns have contributed to amplifying and consolidating already existing disparities between groups, further revealing positions of privilege and conditions of exploitation.

These brief remarks indicate that we are *not* all in this together and that the impact of the pandemic must be read through a complex matrix that takes into account class, race, gender, and the related dimensions of power and privilege. This complexity, however, seems to have been partially lost in the political philosophies of the pandemic that have been produced so far, which have often been oblivious to this exacerbation of inequality. Indeed, the pandemic has been understood as some sort of 'great leveller' whereby 'we are all the same' or, as philosopher Slavoj Žižek (2020: 5) claims, 'we're all in the same boat now.' This approach has engendered a series of 'future of humanity' analyses as if the pandemic had suddenly erased differences and transcended inequality to the point of creating a homogeneous and cohesive 'humanity' that shares the same risks, preoccupations, and interests.

Žižek (2020: 39, 70), for instance, argues that the pandemic may pave the way for 'an alternate society' that pursues 'global solidarity and cooperation' through the partial abandonment of 'market mechanisms' and the embracing of a 'reinvented Communism.' Bruno Latour (2020) asks whether the pandemic, which 'has changed the living conditions of all the inhabitants of the planet,' may be regarded 'as a dress rehearsal for the next crisis,' namely climate change. Agamben (2020a, 2020b, 2020c, 2020d), on the other hand, has offered a more pessimistic assessment. In his view, the response to the pandemic has been an opportunity that governments have exploited to advance a global regime of surveillance and the state of exception. In the remainder of this section, I concentrate on Agamben's claim and its limitations. This view, I contend, rests on an undue neglect of the institution of biopolitical difference as a central dimension of neoliberalism and neoliberal citizenship. The result is that critiques such as Agamben's are unable to see how one of the primary achievements of this health crisis has been the enlargement of the category of surplus citizens.

In a series of newspaper articles and blog posts published during the first wave of the pandemic, Agamben (2020a) argues that this crisis was 'invented' by governments with the purpose of instituting a series of exceptional measures—lockdowns, social distancing, and quarantines—whose primary purpose is to curtail individual and collective freedoms. The seemingly 'disproportionate response' to the virus, he continues, is a product of 'the growing tendency to use the state of exception as a normal governing paradigm' (Agamben 2020b). For Agamben this paradigm has reached its apogee with the so-called 'war on terror'. Now that the terrorist threat has significantly lost traction 'as a justification for exceptional measures, the invention of an epidemic could offer the ideal pretext for broadening such measures beyond any limitation' (Agamben 2020b). The institution of these measures undermines life in its very social and ethical foundations and ultimately reduces life to 'bare life'. In order to guarantee our mere biological survival, Agamben (2020c, 2020d) contends, we are willing to sacrifice our freedom of movement, our human relationships, and even our right and duty to assist the dying and leave them to be cremated or buried without a proper funeral.

Agamben's account has been questioned on a number of grounds. It gets dangerously close to being a conspiracy theory and shares the same virus-denialism of populist leaders like Trump and Bolsonaro (Christiaens 2020). It implicitly endorses the initial 'herd immunity'/market inaction of countries such as the UK, the Netherlands, and Sweden (Christiaens 2020). It overstates the divide between bare life and ethical/social life by neglecting that 'bare life and political life converge in citizenship, with the right to have rights itself dependent on the right to life' (Rygiel 2011: 94; see also Christiaens 2020; Berg 2020). It overlooks how the sacrifice of the lockdown is not for mere biological survival but precisely to preserve those relations, affects, and loves that make life worth living (Berg 2020). It ignores the fact that the problem has not been too much government in the form of a state of exception, but too little government as manifested in a crisis of scarcity. It has been suggested that Agamben's problematic analysis is ultimately a misapplication of his own theoretical argument to a case that differs significantly from the 'war on terror' (Berg 2020). My contention is that the limitations of Agamben's analysis have deeper roots in the underlying 'biopolitics of sameness' or 'togetherness' that underpins his famous philosophy of the 'camp'. This approach seriously impairs our capacity to recognize the sacrificial rationalities of neoliberal citizenship.

According to Agamben (1998), the camp is the paradigm of a modern condition of subjection to sovereign power that reduces life to 'bare life'. It is not 'an historical fact and an anomaly belonging to the past' (Nazi concentrations camps, for instance), but 'the hidden matrix and nomos of the political space in which we are still living' (Agamben 1998: 95). The camp signals the crisis of the modern nation-state whose three constitutive elements—land, order, and birth—can no longer provide a stable foundation for political communities. The camp is a condition that we virtually all share, although it mostly concerns those 'growing sections of humankind [who] are no longer representable inside the nation-state' such as refugees and undocumented migrants (Agamben 2000: 20). The camp is a regulatory mechanism whose purpose is 'to assume directly the care of the nation's biological life' by reducing life to 'bare life' (Agamben 1998: 174–5). 'Bare life' can be 'acted upon, controlled, constrained, confined and eventually disposed of in suspension of the law as a prerogative of sovereign power' (Wilson and Mavelli 2016: 268; Agamben 1998: 99).

For Agamben, the suspension of the rule of law—the state of exception—only exists in relation to the sovereign production of a system of codified norms, which can nonetheless be suspended at any time. This means that the camp is not a space outside the State, but one that 'is included solely through the exclusion' and that rule and suspension of the rule exist in a general space of 'indistinction' (Ojakangas 2005: 7). Accordingly, the distance between those within and outside the camp is not as great as one may initially imagine. As Mika Ojakangas (2005: 8) remarks, 'to the extent that in our age the state of exception comes more and more to the foreground as the fundamental political rule, as Agamben claims, then we are all living, at least virtually, in the state of exception.' For Agamben (2005), the creation of the juridical category of enemy combatant to whom the Geneva convention does not apply or the use of administrative indefinite detention during the 'war on terror' of the early 2000s are illustrations of how all lives are *virtually* bare lives divested of any juridical protection. 'We are all virtually *hominess sacri*', Agamben (1998: 99; emphasis in original) contends, who can all be killed with impunity without being sacrificed, by virtue of a state of exception that has become the norm.

In Chapter 6, I questioned the argument that bare lives are not sacrificial. I showed how they can be and are sacrificed on the altar of the market, since their excretion from the body of society is also a process of re-incorporation into the neoliberal market system of production and consumption, either through their elimination as a source of negative value and/or their incorporation as a factor of production that feeds the immigration-industrial complex. I now want to question the underlying biopolitics of sameness—the idea that 'we are all virtually *hominess sacri*'—that underlies Agamben's perspective. My starting point is not new. The critique that '[w]e are not all susceptible to being rendered to bare life' and that 'survivability results from the violent intersectionality of gender, "race", ... sexual orientation' and class has long been made (Tyner 2013: 707). I wish to expand this critique in light of Foucault's remarks on the logic of inequality within neoliberalism and my earlier considerations on the fear of difference and sameness towards undocumented migrants (Chapter 7, Section 4).

We previously considered (Chapter 4) how for Foucault biopolitics is deployed within the framework of neoliberalism understood as a process of economization that extends the principle of competition to all domains of human existence. Competition, Foucault argues, is ultimately a 'game of differentiation', whose primary purpose is to establish inequality as a rationality of government. Inequality presupposes difference, which is essential to support competition as a principle of self-government, yet it also seemingly creates a level playing field because 'inequality is the same for all' (Foucault 2008: 143, citing ordoliberal thinker William Röpke). Difference in a regime of inequality is thus 'a kind of general regulator of society that clearly everyone has to accept and abide by' (Foucault 2008: 143). In this framework, the function of biopolitics is to evaluate, hierarchize, and rank lives according to their value, establish the related degree of protection that they should be granted, and decide who should be sacrificed for the sake of the survival and well-being of the population.

The biopolitical divide between valuable, less valuable, and unworthy lives at the heart of neoliberal citizenship is thus a dynamic process marked by the endless recreation of difference in a framework of inequality in which new individuals and groups are identified as sacrificeable or deserving protection (or some degree of it). Inevitably, this process also entails the creation of new forms of sameness. Consider the proximity created by austerity policies between Greek citizens, debased citizens of austerity, and undocumented migrants discussed in Chapter 7. Poor citizens have increasingly been perceived as less valuable individuals who represent a threat to the survival and well-being of Europe, and therefore less deserving of protection and ultimately sacrificeable to enable the reproduction of neoliberal life. While this is an instance of race-to-the-bottom egalitarianism characterized by the biopolitical downgrading of poor citizens almost to the level of migrants, we have also encountered cases of upgrading, which have for the most part been conditional on the recognition of emotional value. This is the case of the Syrian refugees accepted by Western countries in the aftermath of the death of Alan Kurdi (Chapters 3 and 4), or the cases of Gassama, Bathily, and Diallo in France, Sow in Spain, and Ramy and Adam in Italy (Chapter 4), all of whom turned from undesired sacrificial others to valuable heroes deserving of protection.

Agamben's misreading of the response to the COVID-19 pandemic is the product of a static biopolitics of sameness that turns us all into potential bare lives subjected to the unrestrained power of the Leviathan. This approach is unable to account for the mobility and transmutability of a neoliberal citizenship regime shaped by the logics of economic profitability, emotional value, class, race, and gender and designed to constantly foster inequality for the creation of new formations of difference and sameness. The result is that Agamben reduces the impact of the pandemic to one of undifferentiated restriction of freedom, reduction to bare life and normalization of the state of exception. This approach is oblivious to the different impact that the pandemic has had on different groups.

This is particularly the case with respect to one group: the elderly. In commenting on the Italian government decision to partially lift the lockdown in April 2020 while retaining most of the restrictions for the over-seventies, including that of staying home, Agamben regarded this as a case of unjustified discrimination which would end up depriving the elderly of their freedom and condemning them to isolation without effectively contributing to their well-being. In Section 4, I evaluate this claim. My argument is that rather than suffering an undue restriction of their freedom as Agamben maintains, the elderly in many countries have been abandoned to their destiny to the point of becoming sacrificial victims like the undocumented migrants.

4. Surplus citizens

As of October 2020, more than 25,000 care home residents had died from COVID-19 in the UK. This accounted for 44 per cent of all COVID-related deaths (Comas-Herrera et al. 2020). In Italy, out of a total death toll of 36,000, about 30,000 were over 70 and half of them had died in care homes (Di Feo et al. 2020; Epicentro 2020). In Spain the percentage was even higher: 63 per cent, with 20,000 deaths among care home residents from a total of 33,000 (Troya 2020; Comas-Herrera et al. 2020). This figure stands at 46 per cent in France, 41 per cent in the USA, 75 per cent in Australia, and an even more staggering 80 per cent in Canada (Comas-Herrera et al. 2020). Overall, conservative estimates place the number of COVID-19 related deaths in care homes in Europe at around 40–57 per cent during the first three months of the pandemic (Williams 2020b), with a marginal decrease since May/June 2020. These disconcerting figures vastly exceed the 'some pensioner[s]' who would end up dying anticipated by Dominic Cummings. They unequivocally indicate that the elderly, and particularly the most fragile among them, are those hit the hardest by this health crisis. However, and perhaps surprisingly, this carnage has largely gone unnoticed. In the flurry of political debates, news frenzy, and data storm triggered by the virus, the elderly have made only a late and relatively scant appearance.

In the UK, deaths in care homes were not reported and added to the total death toll until the last week of April 2020. As Williams (2020b) observes, this has 'allowed beleaguered governments to present apparently flattening curves to worried or hostile publics.' While statistics have later emerged, this 'silent massacre' has remained for the most part a marginal question. After all, these people are old, often incapacitated, no longer socially useful, and unable to contribute to the economy. They are a burden on families and states. They consume private and public wealth and absorb scarce resources—beds, ventilators, doctors, and nurses—which could and should be directed to save more young and productive lives.

These ideas have been voiced by politicians and commentators alike, and not just in relation to the elderly in care homes but to the elderly tout court. In Italy, for example, whilst considering that most COVID victims were elderly patients and calling for an age-specific lockdown strategy which spared the younger population, Liguria Governor Giovanni Toti stated that older people are 'for the most part in retirement, not indispensable to the country's productive effort' (cited in D'Emilio 2021). Meanwhile, in the UK, a prominent *Telegraph* columnist opined that 'from an entirely disinterested economic perspective, the COVID-19 pandemic might even prove mildly beneficial in the long term by disproportionately culling elderly dependents' (Warner 2020). The elderly have little economic or emotional capital to offer unless dead, just like most of the undocumented migrants who have also been dying in the order of thousands over the last few years and for the most part in a context of neglect, indifference, silent approval, and, more often than not, vocal celebration.

Indeed, it is estimated that, between 2014 and 2018, 56,800 undocumented migrants worldwide (and 20,000 alone in the Mediterranean) have lost their lives (Hinnant and Janssen 2018). This is an extremely conservative figure that does not take into account the tens of thousands who have disappeared during their journey, whether swallowed by the Mediterranean or buried by the sands of the Sonora desert, who have not been reported missing, whose journey has never been detected by the authorities, and whose remains have never been found (Hinnant and Janssen 2018). The deaths of the elderly in care homes and undocumented migrants in border zones are not natural and inevitable occurrences which it would have been impossible to avoid. Even factoring in the complexity of governing a growing ageing population and a refugee crisis, these deaths could have been prevented. They are the result of a crisis of scarcity which has been deliberately instituted.

In the case of the undocumented migrants, as we saw with reference to the Mediterranean, it was first the decision to suspend search-and-rescue missions and then the deliberate effort to obstruct NGOs' efforts to carry out such missions that have created the scarcity of resources which has cost thousands of lives. This scarcity, of course, stems from a scarcity of solidarity that frames undocumented migrants as competitors for scarce material and ideational resources and thus as a threat to the life, prosperity, and well-being of Europe. As such, the undocumented migrants have been sacrificed because they are deemed guilty.

In the new phase of neoliberal citizenship ushered in by the coronavirus pandemic, the link between sacrifice and guilt has been almost totally severed. The elderly in care homes have been sacrificed without being ascribed any guilt, but only a negative economic value that frames them as a hindrance to the sacred workings of the market, particularly at a time of crisis. Their sacrifice is the outcome of a neoliberal metric of valuation that, by progressively informing the privatization and commodification of elderly care, has eventually resulted in a condition of scarcity. This process has affected most (though not all) OECD countries. Provisions have progressively shifted from a logic of care to one of profit, causing a growing reliance on a downsized, poorly trained, and mostly precarious workforce. Hence, in many countries, 'medical attendants, such as registered nurses, have been replaced or downgraded in care facilities, and the ratio of assistants to those left has ratcheted upwards' (Williams 2020a). As Owain Williams (2020a) observes, this has resulted in 'routine reporting of elder abuse, neglect, dehydration and malnutrition, and so on, in care homes. These cases all point to the fact that regulation of aged care is often a net with big holes, and firms become adept in gaming the system to mask deficiencies arising through lack of care or downward cost pressures.'

In Italy, for example, private aged care homes must comply with a staff ratio that ensures that each guest is provided with at least 901 minutes of assistance per week (Di Feo et al. 2020). This rather obscure figure acquires its tragic relevance if compared with that of Italian prisons, where the current staff ratio means roughly 1,053 minutes per prisoner. Elderly in care homes thus receive less assistance than prison inmates (Di Feo et al. 2020). The progressive transformation of care homes into 'warehouses' concealed from the public gaze has been steadily happening over the last thirty years. In Lombardy alone (the Italian region most hit by the pandemic), the level of care home staff has shrunk by about 20,000 units between 2009 and 2016, which corresponds to a reduction of roughly 20 per cent of the workforce (Di Feo et al. 2020).

In the UK, a series of recent reports warned of an all time high level of vacancies and turnover in the care sector, with a shortage of nursing staff reported by almost half of care homes, with the effect that they increasingly rely on less qualified agency staff (Knight Frank 2019). This state of affairs has been accentuated by Brexit, since almost 10 per cent of workers in adult social care are from the EU and the number of EU citizens in the UK has significantly declined since the referendum (McKenna, Baird, and Holmes 2019). These shortages are not unique to the UK and Italy but affect other countries in Europe such as Spain and Sweden. The shortage of staff has been accompanied by an increasing lack of qualification and experience in the workforce and growing precarization. With the pandemic outbreak, these factors, compounded by the shortage of PPE, of oxygen and other medical supplies, of resident doctors, and by the lack of testing for coronavirus, have become a deadly mixture for elderly patients, particularly when combined with the use of them as a 'political escape route and a health systems pressure valve' in the pandemic (Williams 2020b). As Williams observes:

> Not only have governments in the UK and USA, in France, Canada, and Spain, been passive or active in letting people die in long term care, many countries and authorities actively discharged elderly patients in hospitals into long term care facilities. In Italy, Spain and the USA, there are multiple instances, if not systemic policies, where sick care home patients were being turned away from hospitals. Politically, it seems that those deaths were politically convenient if they just disappeared, to became silent causalities of the normal attrition of our elderly in care.
>
> (Williams 2020b)

In the UK, a few days after the 'herd immunity' announcement, NHS England requested hospitals to 'urgently discharge' patients in order to vacate 15,000 beds to better face the coronavirus outbreak (NHS 2020a). At around the same time, Public Health England (PHE) identified 'a massive spike' in respiratory diseases which could be linked to Covid-19 (Clarke 2020). The government not only decided to ignore this information, but also did not make the testing of patients to be discharged mandatory (NHS 2020a). As a result, 25,000 patients, many of whom were arguably positive with COVID-19, were released into care homes (Lintern 2020). In Italy, a similar process allowed the pandemic to spread like 'fire in a haystack' and kill thousands of elderly patients (Di Feo et al. 2020). Unwittingly, care home staff also contributed to spread the disease. The fact that many of them are on zero-hours contracts means that they would often be rotating between different residences to make up enough hours, and they effectively facilitated the process of contagion. It also meant that care home staff who fell ill would often 'continue to attend because of a lack of sick pay or dependence on meagre incomes' (Williams 2020b). However, the opposite also happened, with staff falling ill and not turning up for work (Williams 2020b). This resulted in dramatic scenes of abandonment.

In Spain, the army had to intervene in numerous care homes which had been completely deserted by staff, with guests either dead or left in a total state of abandonment, in some cases 'literally bathed in faeces' (Kassam 2020). In Canada, residents of various care homes were found 'dehydrated … lying listless in bed, unfed for days, with excrement seeping out of their diapers' (Williams 2020b). In Italy, the shortage of staff prompted many care homes to tie elderly residents to their beds (Di Feo et al. 2020). Ironically, the shortage was further fuelled by the government's attempt to fill the scarcity of nurses in hospitals through a vast hiring scheme. The perverse outcome of this initiative was that many staff in precarious employment left for permanent hospital positions, further worsening the staff to resident ratio in care homes. In the UK, cases of elderly guests abandoned 'in squalor and filth', 'dirty', with 'stained and unclean clothes', hungry, thirsty, and 'malnourished' had already been reported before the onset of the pandemic (Scott 2019). With the coronavirus outbreak, more accounts of squalor and neglect have surfaced, with reports of care home residents 'covered in dried faeces' and 'necrotic' open wound infections (Booth 2020; BBC News 2020).

These deeply disturbing images are reminiscent of the Malthusian savages 'covered with filth and vermin' and evoke those of Europe's most infamous refugee camp: the so-called jungle near the city of Calais in the north of France. The abject conditions of this overpopulated site, which was eventually demolished in October 2016, have been extensively documented, with makeshift tents placed on a polluted wasteland marked by a lack of running water, toilets, and proper cooking facilities (Davies, Isakjee, and Dhesi 2017). In 2016, at the apogee of the refugee crisis, witnesses observed how this state of affairs forced 'many residents to openly defecate near to where they lived and prepared food, adding to the wretched nature of this makeshift encampment and its related health risks' (Davies, Isakjee, and Dhesi 2017: 1276). In the camp infections thrived. Migrants suffered from gastrointestinal parasites, scabies (that, contrary to what Salvini claims, was not brought in by migrants, but caught in Europe), and gangrene worsened by the lack of sanitation and medicines. Another crucial problem was the scarcity of food. Migrants responded by rationing the meagre portions they received. Yet, without fridges to properly store leftovers, rationing became a breeding ground for further infections (Davies, Isakjee, and Dhesi 2017).

According to Thom Davies, Arshad Isakjee, and Surindar Dhesi (2017: 1269, citing Davies and Polese 2015: 38), the Calais camp epitomizes the 'hidden violence of abandonment': it is the expression of a biopolitics of inaction that can be placed on a continuum with the 2014 decision to stop search-and-rescue missions in the Mediterranean. Throughout this book, we have seen how the biopolitics of inaction rests on a series of perverse inversions: to save undocumented migrants, let them drown; to save child refugees stranded in Europe, leave them stranded; to help the poor, it is better not to provide any welfare provision as this will result in Malthusian perverse incentives; to fight racism, Friedman tells us, it is better not to intervene with laws protecting vulnerable groups as these will fail to achieve the desired outcome and prompt an undue restraint on individual freedoms; to promote growth, defenders of austerity argue, cut the state's budget; to protect us from the coronavirus pandemic, pursue herd immunity or, at worst, minimize lockdowns, even if this entails sacrificing the elderly and the weakest (reportedly, in October 2020, shortly after begrudgingly approving a second lockdown, Boris Johnson stated: 'No more fucking lockdowns—let the bodies pile high in their thousands'; *The Guardian* 2021). These inversions are ultimately the product of a 'master inversion' at the heart of neoliberal citizenship that sacralizes the market and makes life conditional upon its economic and emotional value, turning less valuable lives into sacrificial ones.

The biopolitics of inaction of neoliberal citizenship is thus a way of governing through market rationalities that revolve around incentives, competition, and inequality. Yet, as discussed in Chapter 3, the market is not a natural entity that organically emerges from the state's withdrawal. It is an artificial and fragile system that needs to be instituted and requires constant government intervention to ensure its smooth functioning (as Foucault (2008: 121) reminds us, in the neoliberal order, 'one must govern for the market, rather than because of the market'). The institution of scarcity is one such government intervention, which in turn requires biopolitical racism to separate 'valuable' from 'less valuable' lives, where value is a measure of an individual's or a group's capacity to enhance and maximize the economic or emotional capital of the population. The sacrifice of the 'unworthy'—whether nationals or foreigners—is an essential component of the neoliberal citizenship regime.

With the coronavirus pandemic, elderly citizens in care homes have been turned into sacrificial citizens on a par with debased citizens of austerity and undocumented migrants, even though their sacrifice no longer requires the moral justification of an alleged guilt. The elderly in care homes have become surplus citizens: an excess of unproductive and burdensome individuals in whom it is not worth investing, for whom there is no demand, and whose death can alleviate the problem of scarcity—of beds, ventilators, PPE, and economic resources overall. Marx (1976: 782) regarded surplus populations as those which are 'superfluous to capital's average requirements for its own valorization' and yet still serve a purpose by placing downward pressure on wages and breaking the unity of the labour force. In the advanced phase of neoliberal capitalism, surplus populations like the elderly in care homes do not even serve that purpose. They are an excess that consumes resources and as such are the bearers of a negative value. They are ultimately waste. Like the undocumented migrants in the Mediterranean or in refugee camps like Calais, they are not just superfluous but actually a hindrance to the reproduction and needs of capitalism. Their death will contribute to liberate resources (inheritances, for instance) and thus contribute to reduce scarcity.

In the neoliberal citizenship of coronavirus, the notion of the camp acquires renewed relevance, yet not in the sense originally envisioned by Agamben. For the Italian philosopher, the camp is inhabited by those who 'are no longer representable inside [and represent a threat to] the nation-state' (Agamben 2000: 20). In my account, the camp stands as a space of sacrifice and death for those who are no longer useful and relevant to the requirements of neoliberalism; hence, for those who are no longer 'representable' in the regime of neoliberal citizenship and, as such, embody a threat to the market order, irrespective of their citizenship status and alleged guilt. In the bioeconomy of the camp there is no tension between state and market. The state has been economized to the extent that it now demands not just the sacrifice of undocumented migrants and dispossessed citizens of austerity but also of the elderly in care homes. They are an expensive burden whose sacrifice at a time of acute health crisis will make it possible to save the market and, in the long run, make it grow healthier and stronger.

Conclusion

One of the most famous stories of the Book of Genesis (the first book of the Hebrew Bible and the Christian Old Testament) is the Binding of Isaac. God orders Abraham to kill his son Isaac. Although God decrees that it is forbidden to kill an innocent, Abraham obeys and brings Isaac on to mount Moriah to execute him, only to be stopped at the last moment by a messenger from God. According to Thomas Aquinas' scholastic interpretation, Abraham's compliance does not make him a potential murderer. Abraham is obeying a direct order from God and while this order may seemingly contradict God's immutable will, this is not the case as God 'has foreknown and pre-ordained [what] He would do' (Aquinas, cited in Ojakangas 2012: 511). Hence, even if Abraham cannot understand the reason for God's order, even if this order apparently undermines the very notion of God as love and goodness, and even if God's command requires him to sacrifice his son, Abraham regards God as the ultimate source of truth and revelation and follows his lead unconditionally. Abraham's faith is ultimately rewarded. He proves his ultimate allegiance to God who eventually intervenes to save the innocent Isaac.

Earlier in the book, I discussed how Hayek's understanding of the market crucially resembles the scholastic idea of God. For Hayek, the market is a transcendent and superior intellect that vastly transcends our capacity to grasp it in its totality. It is also the ultimate expression of goodness, even if we may not be able to understand its mysterious workings. Hence, the suffering caused by the market in the form of crises, shocks, and recessions is not random, meaningless, or the product of an inner violence. It is a necessary and inescapable sacrifice that holds the promise of a future reward of freedom and economic abundance. For Hayek, the market is a source of truth and revelation even—and possibly even more—when its love and goodness are apparently denied by the tragic outcomes of its sacred workings.

The killing and letting die of the elderly in care homes resembles the biblical narrative of Abraham and Isaac. Much like Abraham with Isaac, we have reached such an unconditional belief in the market-God that we are now willing to sacrifice the innocent on its altar without interrogating ourselves on our actions. Unlike the biblical narrative though, the market-God is not asking us to sacrifice our children but our parents and grandparents; nor is it intervening at the last moment to halt the slaughter. Does this mean that the market-God disavows the scholastic injunction that it is forbidden to kill an innocent? It does not, because while not guilty as are the undocumented migrants who directly threaten our material and ideological survival, the elderly in care homes are not completely innocent either. They represent an economic burden that we cannot afford at a time of acute crisis. They represent a hindrance to the sacred workings of the market. Hence, the regime of neoliberal citizenship requires their sacrifice.

More explicitly in the USA—where Texas Lieutenant Governor Dan Patrick declared that he and 'lots of grandparents' would rather die than see the economy destroyed by lockdown measures aimed at preventing him and his age peers from dying (Beckett 2020)—and slightly more understatedly in Europe, this view has been voiced by pundits, commentators, and politicians. The idea that the elderly should accept the possibility of dying for the sake of the economy because the latter is essential for the well-being of the country highlights the entanglement and affective compenetration of the economy and life in the neoliberal era. It also indicates the hegemonic power of the idea that a country that sacrifices its elderly to preserve its consumption of commodities is stronger and better than one that would rather do the opposite. As discussed in this chapter, this sacrificial rationality cannot be reduced to the contingent outcome of an unexpected crisis. It is the product of the carefully cultivated politics of scarcity at the heart of the neoliberal citizenship regime. This sacrifice does not invalidate the inherent goodness of the Hayekian market-God. If anything, it restates the principle that those who deserve to live are only the economically productive who do not stand in the way of the proper functioning of the market. Everything else needs to be removed and disposed of as per the dictates of the 'calculus of life'.

The COVID-19 pandemic has thus inaugurated a new and even more radical phase of the neoliberal citizenship regime. In this new phase the 'squalor, hardship and indignity' (Davies, Isakjee, and Dhesi 2017: 1274) once reserved for undocumented migrants is now thrust upon our elderly and being regarded as not guilty does not necessarily make you innocent and spare you from sacrifice if the termination of your life is regarded as beneficial for the economy. Neoliberal citizenship has completely rewritten the grammar of affects in economic terms to the effect that the best the elderly can do is to accept their sacrifice as the necessary and inescapable condition to reactivate the cycle of production and consumption disrupted by the virus.

9

Conclusion: Neoliberal citizenship in a post-COVID-19 world

In an obscure and largely forgotten book published in the mid-1990s, *The Sovereign Individual*, James Dale Davidson (an American conservative propagandist) and William Rees-Mogg (a British Lord, former editor of *The Times*, and father of arch-Brexiteer Jacob Rees-Mogg) argue that, by the year 2020, the institution of citizenship will have disappeared to be replaced by the 'Sovereign Individual'. In the new world created by the 'technological revolution' of the 'Information Age', the most talented and entrepreneurial subjects will take advantage of the limitless opportunities of the capitalist 'cybereconomy' and free themselves from the shackles of tax-greedy states. The latter, in turn, bent under the weight of an unsustainable debt caused by out-of-control welfare provisions, will struggle to provide their citizens with 'low-cost or free schooling, ... medical care, [and] unemployment insurance' (Davidson and Rees-Mogg 1997). The world will end up being split into two camps: the 'cognitive elite' and the 'losers' of the new market order.

The 'cognitive-elite', 'already equally home' in the world's capitals, will become further 'denationalized' and its members 'will operate like the gods of myth in the same physical environment as the ordinary, subject citizen, but in a separate realm politically' (Davidson and Rees-Mogg 1997: 6). In unimaginable ways, this 'elite group of rich'—'a more coherent and effective body than a large mass of citizens'—will 'redesign governments and reconfigure economies in the new millennium' (Davidson and Rees-Mogg 1997: 6). The 'dramatic extension of markets' will enable the wealthy upper class to no longer be dependent on one single country for their security, health provisions, investment opportunities, and the like. Its members will cease to be citizens to become 'customers' of countries in competition with each other to attract them. This new world 'will prove wildly unpopular with the losers in the new information economy' (Davidson and Rees-Mogg 1997: 201). Hence, 'the information poor, the remainder of the population who are largely monoglot

Neoliberal Citizenship. Luca Mavelli, Oxford University Press.
 DOI: 10.1093/oso/9780192857583.003.0009

and do not excel in problem-solving or possess some globally marketable skill' will 'continue to identify their well-being with the political life of existing nation-states' (Davidson and Rees-Mogg 1997: 201). These 'left-behinds', 'the primary beneficiaries of government spending, will be at the forefront of a nostalgic reaction seeking to reassert the claims of nationalism' (Davidson and Rees-Mogg 1997: 201).

Some of the prophecies of this neoliberal dystopia ominously resonate with aspects of the neoliberal transformation of citizenship explored in this book. As we saw, the progressive blurring of the divide between citizens and residents (with wealthy foreigners granted more rights than dispossessed citizens), the transformation of citizenship into a commodity, the exponential growth of citizenship-by-investment schemes, the emergence of a new 'denationalized' class of wealthy transnational citizens, and the growing competition among states for foreign high net-worth individuals through privileged settlement schemes and fiscal red carpets have all become realities. Revealingly, billionaire Peter Thiel (discussed in Chapter 3) recently stated that *The Sovereign Individual* is the book that has influenced him the most (Beckett 2018). Predictive merits aside, Davidson and Rees-Mogg's neoliberal eschatology is a primer of deeply entrenched beliefs in the sacredness of the market and an ideal-type expression of the neoliberal rationality that I have investigated and challenged. As such, it illustrates in an almost archetypal fashion a dimension of neoliberal citizenship that I have implicitly referred to but not explicitly addressed: the creative destruction of meaning. In these concluding pages, I wish to elaborate on this concept and advance some final reflections on the future of neoliberal citizenship in a post-COVID-19 world.

The notion of perverse incentives is a prime example of the neoliberal creative destruction of meaning. It reverses the order of causation and the grammar of solidarity to the effect that it turns helping the poor into a way of perpetuating their debasement, rescuing migrants into a 'pull factor' that will cause more deaths, and saving the elderly into the destruction of the economy and society. In a similar fashion, the very notion that the welfare state is unsustainable, as Davidson and Rees-Mogg claim, because scarce resources are distributed to unproductive members of society unable to adjust to the requirements of the new market-friendly world, is also an instance of creative destruction that completely obliterates the politics of instituted scarcity. On the whole, the creative destruction of meaning performed by neoliberal citizenship rests on the ontological separation of the winners and losers of the market order, and the scapegoating of the losers, who are blamed for the consequences of the extractive, dispossessive, upwardly redistributionist, and biopolitically racist neoliberal rationalities they endure.

As discussed, the construction of the Eurozone crisis as a sovereign debt crisis, rather than a banking debt crisis, was part of a process of scapegoating which made it possible to blame the governments and citizens of the PIIGS for their profligacy, rather than the European banking system for its irresponsible moral hazard. The notion of scapegoating does not aim to conceal the responsibilities of these countries and particularly of Greece, which became the primary scapegoat, but to reveal how responsibilities for the decade of austerity in Europe were shifted: from overleveraged banks which had recklessly lent money to Greece and a political system which has failed its most vulnerable and marginalized to the irresponsible overspending of Greece and its 'lazy' citizens who live in a 'culture of dependency'. Through the same scapegoating process, migrant deaths in the Mediterranean have been blamed on irresponsible migrants undertaking the dangerous sea journey, rather than on European fears of undocumented migrants and the unwillingness to carry out search-and-rescue missions.

Although the scapegoating process is underpinned by biopolitical racism, biopolitical racism is itself scapegoated onto the 'losers' and 'left-behinds' who fail to comply with the requirements of the neoliberal order. As Davidson and Rees-Mogg (1997: 201) explain, only those who lack human capital and resilience will embrace miserable feelings of envy, anger, and resentment towards immigrants. They will cling to out-of-date ideologies, such as nationalism and 'seek to thwart the movement of capital and people across borders' (Davidson and Rees-Mogg 1997: 201). Conversely, the members of the 'cognitive elite', blessed by the market-God with the human capital required to prosper and thrive under its rule, will deservingly become Gods themselves and advance mankind on the path of prosperity and growth by shaking off racism and discrimination. In the neoliberal order, Davidson and Rees-Mogg claim, '[i]t will not matter what most of the people on earth might think of your race, your looks, your age, your sexual proclivities, or the way you wear your hair… The ugly, the fat, the old, the disabled will vie with the young and beautiful on equal terms in utterly color-blind anonymity on the new frontiers of cyberspace' (Davidson and Rees-Mogg 1997: 4).

This market-based utopia, reminiscent of Friedman's fantasies, projects racism onto its very victims. By turning 'losers' and 'left-behinds' into Malthusian mean-spirited 'savages' unable to rise to the ranks of 'sovereign individuals', the neoliberal citizenship regime decrees that they can be sacrificed and, in a typical scapegoating move, turns their sacrifice into an act that purges neoliberalism of its very biopolitically racist fundamentals. Contrary to Davidson and Rees-Mogg's (1997: 201) predictions, however, neoliberal sacrifice requires 'out-of-date' ideologies like nationalism in order to 'thwart the movement of … people across borders'. Yet, in a regime of economized nationalism, what is thwarted is not the mobility of those 'that are visibly different from the former national group' (Davidson and Rees-Mogg 1997: 197). Quite the opposite, to be excluded or differentially included in a condition of subjugation are those undocumented migrants who are mimetic doubles of dispossessed and debased citizens. The fear governing this process is that of sameness, not difference, as part of a race-to-the-bottom egalitarianism that has instituted a new equality of the poor, the debased, and the unwanted, irrespective of their citizenship status. Likewise, in a regime of economized nationalism, those regarded as deserving of inclusion and protection are not primarily the culturally similar, but the economically valuable.

Hence, in the theodicy of suffering and good fortune of neoliberal citizenship, individuals merely deserve their due—be it full membership, some degree of protection, differential inclusion, subjugation, or the altogether denial of 'the right to have rights'—which is ultimately a product of neoliberal rationalities of value. These rationalities transcend mere economic determinations and invest emotions, affects, identities, moral frameworks, and self-understandings. In the homogenizing commodification of the sacralized market, the state's decision to include groups as diverse as wealthy foreigners and refugees who can clearly be recognized as victims is governed by the same neoliberal metric of valuation: their inclusion will boost the value of the country, whether in economic or emotional terms. Neoliberal citizenship thus blurs the divide between economic and human rights considerations—the emergence of neoliberal humanitarianism is a case in point—as well as that between members and strangers, and between insiders and outsiders. Neoliberal citizenship rearranges, organizes, and ranks the 'right to have rights' of individuals and groups according to their value in a perspective than transcends traditional conceptual and physical boundaries. In Europe's multiple crises, albeit in different degrees, undocumented migrants, debased citizens of austerity, and Greek workers have all been blamed and sacrificed as surplus/waste populations for the threat posed to the neoliberal market order.

The ongoing coronavirus pandemic has further radicalized these rationalities of value by partially severing the link between blame and sacrifice. Whereas the sacrifice of the above groups required them to be identified and publicly declared a threat, this has not been the case with the slaughter of the elderly in care homes during the first months of the coronavirus pandemic.

And yet, while not framed as a threat, they have nonetheless been regarded as a hindrance to the need of preserving the functionality of the sacred market, and thus as disposable surplus/waste populations. As this and the other cases explored in this book indicate, in the neoliberal order and specifically in the neoliberal citizenship regime, the relational connection between those who thrive, expand, and prosper and those who struggle, fail, and die is a biopolitical one. The death of the latter is essential for the former to 'grow, proliferate, and expand'. The 'losers' of neoliberalism are seen as the bearers of a negative economic value which is regarded as a product of their inner deficiencies. They are a liability, whose elimination will generate a capital gain for the 'winners'.

Neoliberalism is thus a rationality of government that constantly produces a deceptive image of itself. First, it claims that winners and losers of the market order are ontologically independent from each other and ascribes their successes and failures to inner qualities. In fact, not only do 'winners' and 'losers' transcend binary classifications and exist as a multitude of groups ranked according to their value, but most of all they interact in a biopolitical-type relationship in which the death of those at the bottom of the scale will benefit those immediately on top. Second, neoliberalism claims to have transcended racism as it is exclusively concerned with value, irrespective of the race, gender, and religion of those who embody it. In fact, neoliberalism actively relies on biopolitical racism for the elimination of surplus populations and, to the effect that it invests all domains of human existence and its rationalities of value transcend mere economic determinations, it can reinforce traditional manifestations of racism (as in the case of the undocumented migrants, where the poor, the black, and the Muslim coalesce in the same 'threatening other'). Third, neoliberalism presents itself as the ultimate enabler of individual freedom, while in fact it enthrones a transcendent structure—the market as a sacred entity beyond human comprehension and criticism—with the power to govern all spheres of human existence and rule who must live and who must be sacrificed for its sake.

As we saw, the biopolitics of sacrifice of the neoliberal citizenship regime is crucially mediated by the principle of scarcity. Scarcity is not natural but a socially instituted governmental rationality. It is both a threat to the neoliberal order—people fight for scarce resources—and one of its fundamental conditions of possibility—an alleged positive incentive that encourages individuals to work, produce, invest, and create value. In the neoliberal citizenship regime, scarcity also performs the biopolitical task of making live by letting die. Austerity, the suspension of search-and-rescue missions, and the lack of medical equipment during the coronavirus pandemic are all illustrations of an instituted bioeconomy of scarcity aimed at eliminating less valuable or 'worthless' individuals.

Scarcity is also a crucial parameter for establishing the value of a commodity, including life. The value of wealthy foreigners is due to their scarcity compared to the oversupply of surplus populations produced by neoliberal capitalism. Likewise, the value of a refugee will increase if suffering is packaged and marketed as a scarce commodity—as in the case of Alan Kurdi—or decrease and turn negative if overabundant as in the case of the overcrowded vessels crossing the Mediterranean. This system of valuation has also been at play in one of the latest (at the time of writing) attempts by undocumented migrants to reach European shores. The 8000 that crossed the border from Morocco to the Spanish enclave of Ceuta in May 2021, either by swimming or by walking at low tide, once again confront us with the overabundance of an intimidating mass that threatens the life and well-being of Europe and the packaging and marketing of suffering humanity as a scarce commodity, in this case in the tiny shape of a migrant baby rescued by a Spanish Guardia Civil officer.

The photo of an officer lifting the seemingly unconscious newborn from the water quickly went viral, bringing back memories of the picture of Alan Kurdi's lifeless body on the shore, and prompting feelings of compassion, humanity, sympathy, and solidarity. As in the case of Alan, this compassion is confined to the innocent child, not to the mass of desperate adults. Unlike the case of Alan, which became an indictment of Europe's callousness and lack of humanity, the picture of the newborn rescued off the coast of Ceuta is a celebration of the emotional value of Europe, capable of rescuing an endangered child, and is an indictment of irresponsible migrants, doubly irresponsible for putting their life and that of their own children at risk (see Chapter 4, Section 4). The overabundance of this threatening mass must therefore be neutralized, and indeed Spain was quick to deploy the army to patrol the border and send back to Morocco those who had succeeded in their attempt to cross, thus restoring a valuable scarcity of undocumented migrants. The neoliberal citizenship regime creates scarcity and requires us to accept, comply with, and thrive under its rule. Those who fail because they either display an excess of resilience—like the undocumented migrants crossing borders—or because they lack the necessary resilience—like the debased citizens of austerity or the elderly in care homes—must be sacrificed.

These considerations raise a final question: How much sacrifice can the regime of neoliberal citizenship allow and withstand before the excess of sacrifice begins to undermine the regime itself? Differently said, to the extent that neoliberal citizenship rests on a theology of sacred market and sacrificial lives, is there a limit to the lives that can be sacrificed before belief in the sacredness of the market begins to crumble? This question acquires even more relevance in light of the ongoing debate on the possible 'end of neoliberalism' prompted by the COVID-19 pandemic. Do the failures of neoliberalism as materialized in thousands of excess deaths that could have been avoided raise reasonable doubts on the long-term chances of its survival?

Marxist economist Alfredo Saad-Filho (2020: 482) argues that the current crisis has exposed the 'inhumanity and criminality' of neoliberalism, thus paving the way for its 'end' and the emergence of a 'progressive alternative'. Slavoj Žižek (2020: 39) has also raised the possibility of 'an alternate society' capable of pursuing 'global solidarity and cooperation' beyond the market. For economist Bill Mitchell (2020), the pandemic has revealed 'how [neoliberal] capitalism is now on life support'. This is an opportunity to '"reclaim the state" for progressive ends and build in the essential redundancy that allows us to minimise the damage that arises when unpredictable events confront us' (Mitchell 2020). Shortly after the beginning of the coronavirus pandemic, claims that this crisis 'spells the end of the neoliberal era' have multiplied (Lent 2020). A recurrent argument in support of this thesis—which, it should be noted, unwittingly employs the same neoliberal idea of 'creative destruction' it would want to challenge—is that the response to the pandemic crisis has been significantly different from the response to the 2008 financial crisis. Whereas the latter focused on 'quantitative easing and the bank bailouts' which 'directly supported those whose income derived from capital', in the COVID crisis state intervention has materialized in 'jobs creation schemes and support for workers' wages' (Cooper 2020). These measures 'which once would have been condemned as socialism show how far neoliberalism proper is out of fashion' (Cooper 2020).

This view may well be too swift and optimistic a reading. A central idea that I have advanced in this book is that to understand neoliberal citizenship, we need to look at its underlying rationalities of value, irrespective of whether they have ultra-high net worth individuals or desperate refugees as referent objects. Accordingly, under the veneer of the different types of interventions (supporting income from capital or income from labour), which are contingent upon the differences between the two crises, lies un underlying problem of scarcity and the same neoliberal rationality aimed at preserving the status quo. The Eurozone crisis was one of scarcity of liquidity that, by threatening to devastate the European financial system, also threatened the neoliberal financialized life of Europe. Hence, the bailout was instrumental not just to save the banks, but European citizens whose lives are now inextricably tied to the neoliberal financial order. This, in turn, required redrawing the line between who should be regarded as a deserving citizen of Europe and who should not and, therefore, between those who should live and prosper and those who should bear the burden of the crisis. The repackaging and marketing of the crisis as one of public finances followed by the socialization of losses has decreed that, in different degrees, the Greeks and the lower classes affected by the adoption of austerity measures (particularly the citizens of the 'PIIGS') should become sacrificial citizens.

The COVID-19 pandemic has engendered a different crisis of scarcity: that of income. This is due to the pandemic lockdown—'workers who stay home are prevented from producing goods and services'—which has generated both an aggregate supply and demand shock (Guerrieri et al. 2020), namely, a condition of supply and demand scarcity which threatens the existence of the neoliberal order. This threat, particularly on the demand side, has been warded off by directly supporting those whose incomes depend on wages. As in the case of the Eurozone crisis, this has required redrawing the biopolitical boundary between who should be granted protection and who should be sacrificed for 'saving the market'. As documented in Chapter 8, the emergence of elderly residents in care homes as sacrificial victims during the first months of the pandemic represents a new and more radical iteration of neoliberal citizenship as it overcomes the need of apportioning blame to exact sacrifice. Beyond this new iteration, however, the 2009 intervention to support income from capital and the 2020 intervention to support income from labour share the same neoliberal rationality.

To use an organic metaphor, both interventions can be considered an immune response of the neoliberal market order to preserve its existence by smoothing the potentially devastating effects of an excess of scarcity. This entails sacrificing those 'less valuable lives' which are regarded as a burden, as consumers of resources, or as responsible for the crisis and overall as superfluous if not altogether damaging to the existence of the market order. This, to be sure, is not an auto-immune reaction as philosopher Roberto Esposito might suggest. Esposito famously argues that a distinctive feature of modern biopolitics is that of 'immunizing life through the production of death' (Campbell 2008: xxiv), that is, it 'tries to protect life through the death of a part of the population' (Esposito 2020b). As he explains, 'every community does have an immune system, without which it would explode' (Esposito 2020a). Biopolitics is increasingly turning immune responses into autoimmune ones to the extent that 'the immune system [of existing political communities] ends up discharging against the same body it wants to defend, as it happens in so-called autoimmune diseases' (Esposito 2020a).

The underlying assumption of this 'autoimmune' argument is that, as I discussed in relation to the humanitarian government of refugees, 'the very lives that are identified as in need of protecting and saving can also become targeted by lethal apparatuses of security' (Little and Vaughan-Williams 2017: 19), hence they are mistakenly identified as a threat. In my 'immune' reading no mistake is made. Those targeted by the neoliberal-biopolitical apparatus are, to continue with the organic metaphor, cancerous cells: not just superfluous but threatening the very existence of the healthy neoliberal body of society. To better appreciate this argument, let me bring Karl Polanyi's (2001 [1944]) renowned thesis of the 'double movement' into the discussion. For Polanyi (2001 [1944]), capitalism has produced an increasing economic disembeddedness whereby markets are no longer at the service of the social, but exist as autonomous entities that increasingly shape social relations. This has prompted a series of countermovements, primarily engineered by governments and other institutions such as trade unions, focused on the care of the population and thus aimed at the (partial) social re-embedding of markets. These countermovements include the introduction of social protections (such as welfare provisions, labour standards, public education, health programmes) which are essential to govern the market economy.

The reason for these countermovements is that, Polanyi explains, 'if left to evolve according to its own laws,' the market economy 'would create great and permanent evils' to the point of causing its own demise (Polanyi, 2001 [1944]: 136). Leaving 'the faith of soil and people to the market would be tantamount to annihilating them' (Polanyi 2001 [1944]: 137), as this would result, for instance, in the brutal exploitation of the labour force (Guizzo and Vigo de Lima, 2017: 105). Caring for the population and its well-being is essential for the preservation of the market economy, which would otherwise collapse under the weight of its successes and contradictions. The dialectical process of social disembedding and re-embedding of the market is for Polanyi a defining feature of the modern capitalist economy. Foucault's notion of biopolitics as a set of technologies of power aimed at governing populations by installing security mechanisms fostering life resonates with Polanyi's idea of countermovements as mechanisms of social re-embedding of the market. Some scholars have even suggested that 'the social disembeddedness of markets claimed by Polanyi had the birth of biopolitical practices as one of its effects' (Guizzo and Iara Vigo de Lima 2017: 103).

There is, however, an important difference between Foucault's and Polanyi's arguments. Polanyi describes the laissez-faire movement aimed at expanding the market and the protective countermovement aimed at engendering its social re-embedding as opposing forces. In particular, for him countermovements express 'the principle of social protection aiming at the conservation of man and nature' and, as such, they are 'incompatible with the self-regulation of the market, and thus with the market system itself' (Polanyi 2001 [1944]: 138, 136). Ultimately, they epitomize an underlying tension between market and life. For Foucault, neoliberalism and biopolitics mark an overcoming of this tension: the former through a process of economization of the political and the social domain; the latter through the production of a life that is already imbued with market values (such as competition, productivity, and entrepreneurship). Accordingly, a joint Foucauldian-Polanyian reading suggests that the goal of biopolitical countermovements is not the protection of life as opposed to the market, but the protection of *neoliberal life*, namely, a life that is already inscribed in and draws its meaning from the neoliberal market.

With the process of sacralization of the market as a further extremization of the principle of economization—the extension of the logic of the market to all spheres and domains of existence—valuable life cannot be disentangled from the neoliberal order from which it takes meaning. It follows that biopolitical countermovements are immune reactions aimed at preserving the neoliberal order by preserving the life that makes it possible. Life is only sacred insofar as it sustains the sacred market order. This life, to be sure, is not just that of, to use Davidson and Rees-Mogg's expression, the 'winners' of the market order but also that of the 'losers'. The subjugated, the exploited, the debased, and the dispossessed are an essential component of the mechanics of extraction of the neoliberal order. Some 'losers', however, become superfluous, redundant, or threatening. They become the embodiment of a negative value that requires their disposal. The neoliberal citizenship regime performs the fundamental task of screening, assessing, evaluating, ranking, and ultimately establishing the degree of protection, differential inclusion, or altogether exclusion that individuals deserve. It decrees which lives have to be sacrificed on the altar of the market to ensure its preservation and unhampered might.

From this perspective, the support of income from wages is not a sign of the demise of neoliberalism. It is a countermovement aimed at preserving the existence of the neoliberal market order by partially compensating the effects of scarcity (of income and aggregate supply/demand) caused by the pandemic lockdown in the same way that the 2009 bailout of financial institutions (supporting income from capital) was a countermovement aimed the addressing a different crisis of scarcity (of financial liquidity). These compensatory measures do not aim to eliminate scarcity, which remains a fundamental tenet of neoliberal governance, but to modulate its effects, including through the sacrifice of those lives which are regarded as no longer valuable and compliant with the neoliberal citizenship regime. The fact that several governments across Europe quickly began reducing or suspending wage-support schemes towards the end of the first pandemic wave (summer 2020), save for partially backtracking when the second wave hit (autumn 2020), indicates that neoliberal rationalities are alive and well. They are once again deliberately instituting an artificial condition of scarcity that places growing sections of the lower classes at risk of debasement and destitution, thus framing them as potential sacrificial citizens.

In the sacralized neoliberal order, even apparent attempts to reduce scarcity are ultimately a restatement of its centrality and a manifestation of the creative destruction and perversion of meaning performed by neoliberalism. Consider the exhortation 'solidarity is self-interest' uttered in May 2020 by the head of the International Monetary Fund, Christine Lagarde, to advocate greater international cooperation, and in September 2020 by the United Nations Secretary-General Antonio Guterres, to make a plea for universal access to COVID-19 vaccines, as only a vaccine truly available to all, and not just to the wealthiest people and countries, will effectively eradicate the pandemic. These calls appeal to the self-interested, calculative, and cost/benefit rationalities of neoliberalism. In doing so, they rewrite solidarity in neoliberal terms. Neoliberal solidarity does not mean eradicating scarcity—of international cooperation or COVID-19 vaccines—but only reducing their scarcity as long as it is in 'our' interest, namely, in the interest of the wealthiest countries and people.[1]

Hence, these calls are not dissimilar from the decision to rescue some migrants (possibly women and children), to bail out banks, and to provide some degree of wage support for those hit hardest by the pandemic. In all these cases, solidarity is not beyond neoliberalism, but fully inscribed in a neoliberal rationality of value and self-preservation. Some migrants have to be saved to retain some sense of moral righteousness, banks have to be saved to preserve

[1] In fact, the development of vaccines has created new scarcities. Access to COVID vaccines has been governed by extreme competition between the wealthy countries of the Global North and has rewarded those countries, such has the UK, Israel, and the USA, which have been early bidders, have outbid the competition, and have been willing to take risks by shortening the approval process. The neoliberal 'vaccine nationalism' at the heart of the COVID-19 vaccine governance has resulted in a condition of extreme scarcity for the Global South and perceived scarcity for regions of the Global North, such as the European Union. The EU centralized approach to vaccine procurement and distribution, its precautionary approach to vaccine approval, and a not insignificant level of strategic ineptitude and bureaucratic incompetence, have ultimately proved defeating in the cutthroat race to secure vaccine supplies during the second wave of the pandemic (autumn 2020 - spring 2021).

neoliberal financialized life, and wage workers need to retain some degree of purchasing power, without which the market order would collapse. Likewise, some citizens must be actively dispossessed and deprived of their dignity because their debasement will not only boost the economic value of the healthy part of the country, but also its sense of moral worth. As Jacob Rees-Mogg (son of William) recently observed with reference to the dramatic growth in the use of foodbanks across the UK: '[T]o have charitable support given by people voluntarily to support their fellow citizens, I think is rather uplifting and shows what a good, compassionate country we are' (cited in Walker and Butler 2017). In a remarkable perversion, reducing citizens to poverty becomes something that contributes to boost the moral worth and self-esteem of the country.

In these discursive and practical interventions (between 2012–16, Jacob Rees-Mogg voted 52 times to reduce spending on welfare benefits; Bloomer 2017), neoliberal citizenship is a crucial tool of government in the mechanism of reproduction of the neoliberal order. Neoliberal citizenship evaluates, ranks, and allocates citizens and non-citizens alike on a biopolitical continuum. It redraws boundaries and differential regimes of inclusion. It performs the biopolitical 'calculus of lives' and decrees who must live and how, and who must be sacrificed for the sake of the sacred market. In an ultimate act of creative destruction and perversion of meaning, neoliberal citizenship presents this sacrifice as an act of care not only for those in whose name the sacrifice is committed, but also for those who are being sacrificed. This is the 'self-interested solidarity' praised by Lagarde and Guterres. In the refugee crises, self-interested solidarity meant that the suspension of search-and-rescue missions was presented as being in 'our' interest, but also in the best interests of undocumented migrants as this would prevent them from undertaking the dangerous sea journey. In the Eurozone crisis, self-interested solidarity meant that it was in 'our' interest to rescue the banks by imposing harsh austerity measures, but also in the interest of Greece, which would learn fiscal discipline, and in the interest of the debased citizens of austerity, who would be prompted to emancipate themselves from a culture of dependency.

In the COVID-19 pandemic self-interested solidarity meant that it was in 'our' interest to discharge elderly patients from hospital to care homes without proper COVID-19 testing in order to free hospital beds and not waste scarce testing kits. For the same reason—not wasting scarce resources—it was also in 'our' interest to facilitate their death by denying them 'access to hospitals and other medical services' and make them the target of 'blanket Do Not Attempt Resuscitation (DNAR) orders' even without their consent, as a recent report by Amnesty International (2020) extensively documents in relation to the UK. Yet, it was also in the interest of elderly patients to be in care homes, rather than hospitals, where they would allegedly receive better care for their needs and, if their conditions worsened, they would not to be resuscitated as this would spare them unnecessary suffering.

It must be stressed that the neoliberal creative destruction and perversion of meaning is different from the use of false, distorted, inaccurate, and deceptive information. This is the so-called phenomenon of 'post-truth politics', that is, 'circumstances in which objective facts are less influential in shaping public opinion than appeals to emotion and personal belief' (Oxford Languages 2016). Whether concerning the real numbers of migrant arrivals on European shores, which are far from those of an invasion, or the percentage of welfare expenses on the state's budget, which is a fraction of what is generally believed, the production and consumption of fake news that amplifies fears and disinformation has been on the rise over the last few years. Recently, the barrage of misinformation surrounding the COVID-19 health crisis has prompted some scholars to describe it as the first 'post-truth pandemic' (Shelton 2020; Parmet and Paul 2020). Several 'technical' factors are considered responsible for these developments, including the algorithmic personalization of information vehiculated by social media and the exponential demand for 'echo chambers, filter bubbles, and confirmation bias' (Glaser 2016; see also Harsin 2015) in a context of commodification of information. What has received less attention, though, are the conditions of possibility that make us receptive to false, contradictory, and distorted claims.

The neoliberal creative destruction of meaning plays a key role in this dynamic. The extensive use of the discourse of crisis as a governmental tool; the shifting of responsibility from private to public, and from the structural to the individual; the glorification of resilient suffering; the blaming of the victims; the deceptive idea that 'we are all in the same boat'; the race-to-the-bottom egalitarianism; the simultaneous construction of scarcity as a threat and condition of possibility of the social order; the economic rendering of affects and solidarity; the subjection of humanitarianism to rationalities of value; the morphing of freedom into a disciplined entrepreneurial regime of consumption; the logical inversion whereby market-based inaction replaces political intervention; the moral inversion whereby caring for undocumented migrants, debased citizens of austerity, or the elderly in a pandemic becomes political correctness, weakness, do-goodism, lack of identity, wokeness, naivety, left-wing elitism, Marxism, and betrayal of one's own people—these are all instances of a neoliberal epistemic perversion that originates from the master inversion of sacred markets and sacrificial lives.

In this system of transfigurations, the very exercise of biopolitical violence is concealed, disguised, dissimulated, and calibrated to achieve a homeostatic immunity without precipitating in a condition of autoimmunity. Once again, it is helpful to see how my argument differs from Esposito's. For the Italian philosopher, the distinctive feature of biopolitics is the constant production of death as a mechanism of immunization. Death 'is necessary to preserve life', but a life 'nourished by the deaths of others' will eventually feed itself with 'its own death' as in the case of Nazism, which for Esposito (2008: 39) represents the ultimate manifestation of the biopolitical apparatus. A vivid illustration of the Nazi autoimmune biopolitics can arguably be found in 'First they came . . .', the famous poetic version of a speech given by Martin Niemöller (2020 [1946]: 738), a German Lutheran pastor and outspoken critic of Nazism, in 1946:

> First they came for the Socialists, and I did not speak out—
> Because I was not a Socialist.
> Then they came for the Trade Unionists, and I did not speak out—
> Because I was not a Trade Unionist.
> Then they came for the Jews, and I did not speak out—
> Because I was not a Jew.
> Then they came for me—and there was no one left to speak for me.

In this account, biopolitical violence takes place through the active infliction of death that ultimately becomes an autoimmune reaction in which the body politic attacks and destroys itself. For Esposito (2020b), the idea of herd immunity without vaccine floated during the early stages of the pandemic is another iteration of this dynamic: it represents 'a form of autoimmune disease' in which the protection of the population becomes simultaneously the death of some of its parts. This argument relies on three assumptions: a static understanding of population; the idea that biopolitics aims to protect the population 'as a whole'; and the axiom that because biopolitics is locked in a paradox whereby its task of 'insuring, protecting, and augmenting life' is possible 'only through the progressive enlargement of the circle of death' (Esposito 2008: 39, 110), its attempt to protect life can only materialize in autoimmune reactions. The notion of neoliberal citizenship that I have advanced in this book challenges these assumptions.

First, neoliberal citizenship's internal reduplication of external borders through regimes of differential inclusion governed by rationalities of value points to an evolving and mobile understanding of population, not a static one.

In particular, the task of biopolitics in the neoliberal citizenship regime is not that of protecting the population 'as a whole' but only those economically and emotionally valuable. The related sacrifice of the less valuable and of the bearers of a negative value is not an autoimmune crisis. It does not destroy healthy organs of the social body but cancerous cells, which threaten the existence of the healthy parts of the population. This is an immune, rather than autoimmune, reaction that constantly rewrites the boundaries of the population—as I have discussed at length, by including new wealthy foreigners, the latest migrant hero, and the trendiest 'womenandchildren' refugees, while excluding unfashionable and emotionally valueless 'fake' child refugees, such as those of the Dubs scheme, and unproductive citizens, such as the elderly in care homes.

In the neoliberal citizenship regime, this biopolitical exclusion—which encompasses multiple regimes of differential inclusion, subjugation, debasement, dispossession, and ultimately deprivation of life—materializes primarily not through the active infliction of death, but through a process of withdrawal of care: of search-and-rescue missions, of welfare provisions, of elderly and refugee care. Biopolitical violence manifests itself primarily through inaction, neglect, withdrawal, and abandonment. The violence of neoliberal citizenship endured by surplus populations is not caused by those who 'first came for' as in Niemöller's poem, but by those who are not coming, who are not helping, who are not rescuing, who are not listening. This is the violence endured by migrants who are left to drown, by dispossessed citizens who are left struggling with the consequences of austerity, by children who are left hungry because denied free school meals, by Greek workers who are left with collapsed living standards, by refugees who are left in undignified conditions in refugee camps, and by elderly citizens who are left soiled and humiliated in care homes.

Undoubtedly, this violence is in the first instance the active outcome of neoliberalism's extractive, dispossessive, upward-redistributionist, and biopolitically racist rationalities. The neoliberal active infliction of death thus continues to exist and perform its deadly practices. Yet, these practices are almost indistinguishable from those that enable, govern, and regulate life and ultimately represent its conditions of possibility. As we saw, saving the banks in the Eurozone crisis was not just for the sake of the banks, but for the sake of the preservation of neoliberal financialized life. The related sacrifice of sectors of the Greek population and debased citizens of austerity, like the sacrifice of undocumented migrants and elderly citizens, was and continues to be required not to disrupt the reproduction of neoliberal life. Life can no longer be conceived independently from its neoliberal conditions of possibility and yet neoliberalism is not just what makes life possible, but also what threatens its very existence. The withdrawal, suspension, and interruption of care authorizes the unleashing of these deadly rationalities for certain 'low' or 'negative value' populations. This has resulted in the creation of physical zones of abandonment, such as the Mediterranean, refugee camps, and care homes, and in immaterial spaces of debasement, like those encircling hopeless and dispossessed citizens of austerity.

The year 2020 has arrived and passed, but contrary to Davidson and Rees-Mogg predictions, we have not witnessed the end of citizenship and the rise of the 'sovereign individual', but the morphing of citizenship into neoliberal citizenship. Likewise, racism has not disappeared among the 'winners' of the market order and turned into a prerogative of the 'losers', but has retained its systemic hold and evolved into biopolitical racism; solidarity has become self-interested and humanitarianism is now neoliberal in its logics and practices. We are not even more secular ('godless'), as we now worship the neoliberal market-God. In its name, in the deserted spaces of abandonment, we perform human sacrifices, in the hope that the market-God may reward us with economic growth, prosperity, and the possibility to continue the unabated consumption of commodities. We accept these sacrifices because the neoliberal citizenship regime has normalized the idea that those with little or negative economic value do not deserve the 'right to have rights', and ultimately do not deserve to live, particularly at a time of crisis when resources are scarce and the socio-economic order is threatened.

Ultimately, the neoliberal 'sovereign individual' imagined by Davidson and Rees-Mogg does not even resemble 'the gods of ancient and primitive myths', not even the demigods. Consider the mythical founder of Rome, the demigod Aeneas, son of Greek goddess Aphrodite (Venus, in Roman mythology) and mortal Trojan prince Anchises. As the poet Virgil narrates in the *Aeneid*, Aeneas fled from a burning Troy ransacked by the Greeks with his infirm father Anchises on his back and holding his son Ascanius by the hand. Aeneas—a man 'made a refugee by fate' (*Aeneid*, Book 1) who will long wander the Mediterranean before eventually reaching Italy—knew that Anchises had little time left to live and that carrying him would considerably slow down the escape and increase the risk of being captured and killed. Nonetheless, Aeneas is a devoted father and son and chooses not to abandon his father behind in the name of a bond, a love, a *pietas* which are the expression of a not-yet-economized rationality of value.

We neoliberal citizens have obliterated this *pietas* and behave like Abraham on Mount Moriah. We have sacrificed our innocent elderly to please the market-God (which did not intervene at the last moment to halt the slaughter) and the 'guilty' undocumented migrants—guilty in our eyes of stealing our wealth, resources, culture, and identity. We are blind to the possibility that the latter may be present-day Aeneas who have endured incredible hurdles and performed remarkable acts of generosity—unless, of course, these acts are captured in an image or a video for our valuable enjoyment and consumption. After all, why should we care about distant strangers if we no longer care about our own fellow dispossessed citizens? Why should we care about those who lack in—or have a negative—economic and emotional value? We may still read Aeneas' story nowadays and, individually, feel moved and inspired by his bravery and love, but collectively we have accepted the idea that the sacrifice of the 'less valuable', including ourselves (should our value decline), is the inescapable requirement for a life that can no longer be disentangled from and imagined outside its neoliberal conditions of possibility.

This bleak diagnosis is not an invitation to acquiesce to the regime of neoliberal citizenship. The argument advanced in this book has been an effort to identify the extent and depth of the neoliberalization of citizenship by showing how neoliberalism is a totalizing rationality that, through the creative destruction and perversion of meaning, infiltrates every dimension of human existence, including those domains that seemingly challenge its logics. As such, this book is also an implicit call to imagine, strive for, and practise forms of humanitarianism, solidarity, compassion, and ultimately citizenship beyond neoliberalism in the awareness that every attempt runs the risk of being absorbed and reinscribed into neoliberal logics.

This should not lead 'to apathy but to a hyper- and pessimistic activism' (Foucault 1983: 256). As Foucault (1983: 256) once wrote: 'My point is not that everything is bad, but that everything is dangerous, which is not exactly the same as bad. If everything is dangerous, then we always have something to do.' This view encapsulates the spirit of critique, contestation, and resistance at the heart of my argument, with an important addition: to be able and most of all willing 'to do' and 'to act', we must desire it. In focusing on the most marginalized and dispossessed, in denouncing the hypocrisy, violence, and oppression of neoliberal citizenship, in denaturalizing the category of citizenship and of the myriad subject positions that substantiate it, this was ultimately my goal: not to outline the contours of a vision of citizenship beyond neoliberalism and even less to offer a roadmap on how to get there, but rather to instil the *desire* for a post-neoliberal idea of citizenship.

Bibliography

Addley, Esther. 2017. 'Why has the UK ended its "Dubs" child refugee scheme?' *The Guardian*. 10 February, https://www.theguardian.com/uk-news/2017/feb/10/why-has-the-uk-ended-its-dubs-child-refugee-scheme, last accessed 23 May 2021.

Agamben, Giorgio. 1998. *Homo Sacer: Sovereign Power and Bare Life*. Stanford, CA: Stanford University Press.

Agamben, Giorgio. 2000. *Means Without End: Notes on Politics*. Minneapolis: University of Minnesota Press.

Agamben, Giorgio. 2005. *State of Exception*. Chicago: University of Chicago Press.

Agamben, Giorgio. 2007. *Profanations*. New York: Zone Books.

Agamben, Giorgio. 2009. *The Signature of All Things, On Method*. New York: Zone Books.

Agamben, Giorgio. 2011. *The Kingdom and the Glory: For a Theological Genealogy of Economy and Government*. Stanford, CA: Stanford University Press.

Agamben, Giorgio. 2020a. 'Una Voce'. *Quodlibet*. https://www.quodlibet.it/una-voce-giorgio-agamben, last accessed 23 May 2021.

Agamben, Giorgio. 2020b. 'The State of Exception Provoked by an Unmotivated Emergency'. *Positions Politics*. http://positionspolitics.org/giorgio-agamben-the-state-of-exception-provoked-by-an-unmotivated-emergency/, last accessed 23 May 2021.

Agamben, Giorgio. 2020c. 'Una Domanda'. *Quodlibet*. 14 April, https://www.quodlibet.it/giorgio-agamben-una-domanda, last accessed 23 May 2021.

Agamben, Giorgio. 2020d. 'Chiarimenti'. *Quodlibet*. 17 March, https://www.quodlibet.it/giorgio-agamben-chiarimenti, last accessed 23 May 2021.

Aghilar, Antonio. 2020. Il Coronavirus e l'Emergenza Sanitaria Mondiale: Storia del Fallimento Totale di 30 anni di Neoliberalismo. *Neifatti.it*. 16 March, https://www.neifatti.it/2020/03/16/il-coronavirus-e-lemergenza-sanitaria-mondiale-storia-del-fallimento-totale-di-30-anni-di-neoliberismo/, last accessed 23 May 2021.

Agier, Michel. 2011. *Managing the Undesirables: Refugee Camps and Humanitarian Government*. Cambridge: Polity Press.

Ahmed, Sara. 2003. *The Cultural Politics of Emotion*. Edinburgh: Edinburgh University Press.

Ainge Roy, Eleanor. 2016. 'Prestigious Academic to Quit New Zealand After Autistic Son Refused Residency'. *The Guardian*. 16 February, http://www.theguardian.com/world/2016/feb/16/prestigious-academic-to-quit-new-zealand-after-autistic-son-refused-residency, last accessed 23 May 2021.

Ainge Roy, Eleanor. 2017. 'Documents Reveal How Peter Thiel Was Granted New Zealand Citizenship'. *The Guardian*. 1 February, https://www.theguardian.com/technology/2017/feb/01/documents-reveal-how-peter-thiel-was-granted-new-zealand-citizenship, last accessed 23 May 2021.

Alston, Philip. 2018. 'Statement on Visit to the United Kingdom, by Professor Philip Alston, United Nations Special Rapporteur on extreme poverty and human rights', https://www.ohchr.org/documents/issues/poverty/eom_gb_16nov2018.pdf, last accessed 23 May 2021.

Amnesty International. 2020. 'As If Expendable: The UK Government's Failure to Protect Older People in Care Homes During the COVID-19 Pandemic'. 4 October, https://www.amnesty.org/en/documents/eur45/3152/2020/en/, last accessed 23 May 2021.

Amoore, Louise. 2006. 'Biometric Borders: Governing Mobilities in the War on Terror'. *Political Geography* 25(3): 336–51.

Anderson, Ben. 2012. 'Affect and Biopower: Towards a Politics of Life'. *Transactions of the Institute of British Geographers* 37(1): 28–43.

Andersson, Ruben. 2014. *Illegality, Inc.: Clandestine Migration and the Business of Bordering Europe*. Oakland, CA: University of California Press.

ANSA. 2019a. 'Un Parente Di Ramy Ha Precedenti, Per Ora Niente Cittadinanza'. ANSA.it. 25 March, https://www.ansa.it/sito/notizie/cronaca/2019/03/25/un-parente-di-ramy-ha-precedenti-per-ora-niente-cittadinanza_3dfa5243-ff88-4866-a7a9-7d9dee7ccf4a.html, last accessed 23 May 2021.

ANSA. 2019b. 'Salvini: 'Sì Cittadinanza a Ramy, E' Come Mio Figlio', ANSA.it. 26 March, https://www.ansa.it/sito/notizie/politica/2019/03/26/salvini-si-cittadinanza-a-ramy-e-come-mio-figlio-_dddf1f7d-353a-40f4-8a55-c87fe8a70948.html, last accessed 23 May 2021.

Aradau, Claudia and Rens Van Munster. 2011. *Politics of Catastrophe: Genealogies of the Unknown*. Abingdon: Routledge.

Arendt, Hannah. 1973. *The Origins of Totalitarianism*, 2nd edition. New York: Harcourt Brace.

Asad, Talal. 2006. 'Trying to Understand French Secularism'. In *Political Theologies: Public Religions in a Post-Secular World*, edited by Hent de Vries and Lawrence E. Sullivan, pp. 494–526. New York: Fordham University Press.

Bagus, Philipp. 2016. 'Why Austrians Are Not Neoliberals'. *Mises Institute*. https://mises.org/library/why-austrians-are-not-neoliberals, last accessed 23 May 2021.

Balibar, Étienne. 2004. *We, The People of Europe? Reflections on Transnational Citizenship*. Princeton, NJ: Princeton University Press.

Balibar, Étienne. 2015. 'The Relations Greece and Europe Need: Part II'. *Verso*. 2 July, https://www.versobooks.com/blogs/2086-etienne-balibar-the-relations-greece-and-europe-need-part-ii, last accessed 23 May 2021.

Barbulescu, Roxana. 2014. 'Global Mobility Corridors for the Ultra-Rich. The Neoliberal Transformation of Citizenship'. In *Should Citizenship Be for Sale?*, edited by Ayelet Shachar and Rainer Baubock, pp. 15–16. EUI Working Papers 2014/01.

Barnett, Michael. 2020. 'COVID-19 and the Sacrificial International Order'. *International Organization* 74(S1): E128-E147.

Barr, Nicholas. 2020. *Economics of the Welfare State*, 6th edition. Oxford: Oxford University Press.

Basaran, Tugba. 2015. 'The Saved and the Drowned: Governing Indifference in the Name of Security'. *Security Dialogue* 46(3): 205–20.

Bauböck, Rainer. 2009. 'The Rights and Duties of External Citizenship.' *Citizenship Studies* 13(5): 475–99.

Bauböck, Rainer. 2014a. 'Global, European and National Questions about the Price of Citizenship'. In *Should Citizenship Be for Sale?*, edited by Ayelet Shachar and Rainer Baubock, pp. 1–2. EUI Working Papers 2014/01.

Bauböck, Rainer. 2014b. 'What is Wrong With Selling Citizenship? It Corrupts Democracy!' In *Should Citizenship Be for Sale?*, edited by Ayelet Shachar and Rainer Baubock, pp. 19–22. EUI Working Papers 2014/01.

Bauder, Harald. 2014. 'Citizenship as Capital: The Distinction of Migrant Labor'. *Alternatives* 33(3): 315–33.

Bauman, Zygmunt. 2004. *Wasted Lives: Modernity and Its Outcasts*. Cambridge: Polity Press.

BBC News. 2015a. 'David Cameron Urges EU Countries to Follow UK's Lead on Refugees'. 14 September, http://www.bbc.co.uk/news/uk-34242346, last accessed 23 May 2021.

BBC News. 2015b. 'David Cameron: "Swarm" of Migrants Crossing Mediterranean'. 30 July, http://www.bbc.co.uk/news/uk-politics-33714282, last accessed 23 May 2021.

BBC News. 2015c. 'David Cameron: Taking More and More Refugees Not Answer'. 2 September, https://www.bbc.co.uk/news/uk-politics-34130067, last accessed 23 May 2021.

BBC News. 2020. 'Legal Threat over HC-One Care Home Covid Deaths'. 10 September, https://www.bbc.co.uk/news/uk-scotland-highlands-islands-54100665, last accessed 23 May 2021.

BBC News. 2021. '"Greed" and "Capitalism" Helped UK's Vaccines Success, says PM'. 24 March, https://www.bbc.co.uk/news/uk-politics-56504546, last accessed 29 May 2021.

BBC World at One. 2020. 9 March, https://www.bbc.co.uk/programmes/m000g4zh, last accessed 23 April 2020.

Beaglehole, Ann. 2009. 'Looking Back and Glancing Sideways: Refugee Policy and Multicultural Nation-building in New Zealand'. In *Does History Matter? Making and Debating Citizenship, Immigration and Refugee Policy in Australia and New Zealand*, edited by Klaus Neumann and Gwenda Tavan, pp. 105–23. Canberra, AU: ANU Press.

Beck, Ulrich and Edgar Grande. 2007. *Cosmopolitan Europe*. Cambridge: Polity.

Becker, Gary S. 1965. 'A Theory of the Allocation of Time'. *The Economic Journal* 75(299): 493–517.

Becker, Gary S. 1968. 'Crime and Punishment: An Economic Approach'. *Journal of Political Economy* 76(2): 169–217.

Becker, Gary S. 1973. 'A Theory of Marriage: Part I'. *Journal of Political Economy* 81(4): 813–846.

Becker, Gary S. 1974. 'A Theory of Marriage: Part II'. *Journal of Political Economy* 82(2): S11–S26.

Becker, Gary S. 1976. *The Economic Approach to Human Behavior*. Chicago: Chicago University Press.

Becker, Gary S. 1993. 'Illegal Immigration: How to Turn the Tide'. *Bloomberg*. 22 February, https://www.bloomberg.com/news/articles/1993-02-21/illegal-immigration-how-to-turn-the-tide, last accessed 23 May 2021.

Becker, Gary S. 1993 [1964]. *Human Capital: A Theoretical and Empirical Analysis with Special Reference to Education*, 3rd edition. Chicago: Chicago University Press.

Becker, Gary S. 1993 [1981]. *A Treatise on the Family. Enlarged Edition*. Cambridge, MA: Harvard University Press.

Becker, Gary S. 2011. *The Challenge of Immigration: A Radical Solution*. London: The Institute of Economic Affairs.

Becker, Gary S. and Julio Jorge Elias. 2007. 'Introducing Incentives in the Market for Live and Cadaveric Organ Donations'. *Journal of Economic Perspectives* 21(3): 3–24.

Becker, Gary S. and Julio Jorge Elias. 2014. 'Cash for Kidneys: The Case for a Market for Organs'. *The Wall Street Journal*. 18 January, https://www.wsj.com/articles/cash-for-kidneys-the-case-for-a-market-for-organs-1389992925, last accessed 23 May 2021.

Becker, Gary S. and Edward P. Lazear 2013. 'A Market Solution to Immigration Reform'. *The Wall Street Journal*. 1 March, http://www.wsj.com/articles/SB10001424127887323375204578271531542362850, last accessed 23 May 2021.

Beckett, Andy. 2018. 'How to Explain Jacob Rees-Mogg? Start with His Father's Books'. *The Guardian*. 9 November, https://www.theguardian.com/books/2018/nov/09/mystic-mogg-jacob-rees-mogg-willam-predicts-brexit-plans, last accessed 23 May 2021.

Beckett, Lois. 2020. 'Older People Would Rather Die Than Let Covid-19 Harm US Economy—Texas Official'. *The Guardian*. 24 March, https://www.theguardian.com/world/2020/mar/24/older-people-would-rather-die-than-let-covid-19-lockdown-harm-us-economy-texas-official-dan-patrick, last accessed 3 May 2021.

Bellamy, Richard. 2008. *Citizenship: A Very Short Introduction*. Oxford: Oxford University Press.

Bellon, Tina and Caroline Copley. 2015. 'In Aging Germany, Refugees Seen as Tomorrow's Skilled Workers'. *Reuters*. 10 September, https://www.reuters.com/article/us-europe-migrants-germany-training-anal-idUSKCN0RA1E920150910, last accessed 23 May 2021.

Bennhold, Katrin (2008) 'German Stimulus Plan Includes Tax Breaks on Cars'. *The New York Times*, 5 November, http://www.nytimes.com/2008/11/06/business/worldbusiness/06stimulus.html, last accessed 15 September 2021.

Benjamin, Walter. 2004 [1921]. 'Capitalism as Religion'. In *Walter Benjamin: Selected Writings 1: 1913-1926*, edited by Marcus Bullock and Michael W. Jennings, pp. 288–91. Cambridge, MA: Harvard University Press.

Berg, Anastasia. 2020. 'Giorgio Agamben's Coronavirus Cluelessness'. *The Chronicle of Higher Education*. 23 March, https://www.chronicle.com/article/Giorgio-Agamben-s/248306, last accessed 23 May 2021.

Betts, Alexander. 2016. 'The Elephant in the Room: Islam and the Crisis of Liberal Values in Europe'. *Foreign Affairs* 2, https://www.foreignaffairs.com/articles/europe/2016-02-02/elephant-room, last accessed 23 May 2021.

Biskamp, Floris. 2018. 'Populism, Religion, And Distorted Communication'. *Zeitschrift für Religion, Gesellschaft und Politik* 2(2): 247–76.

Blaming the Rescuers. 2017. 'Blaming the Rescuers: Criminalising Solidarity, Re-Enforcing Deterrence'. https://blamingtherescuers.org/, last accessed 23 May 2021.

Bleiker, Roland and Emma Hutchison. 2008. 'Fear No More: Emotions and World Politics'. *Review of International Studies* 34(1): 115–35.

Block, Fred and Margaret R. Somers. 2014. *The Power of Market Fundamentalism: Karl Polanyi's Critique*. Cambridge, MA: Harvard University Press.

Bloomer, Natalie. 2017. 'Week in Review: The Likes of Jacob Rees-Mogg Pick and Choose Their Religious Beliefs to Suit Them'. *Politics.co.uk*, 8 September, https://www.politics.co.uk/blog/2017/09/08/week-in-review-the-likes-of-jacob-rees-mogg-pick-and-choose-their-religious-beliefs-to-suit-them/, last accessed 23 May 2021.

Blyth, Mark. 2013. *Austerity: The History of a Dangerous Idea*. Oxford: Oxford University Press.

Booth, Robert. 2020. '"Unacceptable" Drop in Care at Kettering Home with 12 Covid-19 Deaths'. *The Guardian*. 26 June, https://www.theguardian.com/world/2020/jun/26/unacceptable-drop-in-care-at-kettering-home-with-12-covid-19-deaths, last accessed 23 May 2021.

Booth, Robert and Pamela Duncan. 2020. 'More Than 16,000 People in UK Care Homes Have Died from Coronavirus'. *The Guardian*, 16 June, https://www.theguardian.com/world/2020/jun/16/more-than-16000-people-in-uk-care-homes-have-died-from-coronavirus, last accessed 23 May 2021.

Born, Benjamin, Alexander M. Dietrich, and Gernot J. Müller. 2021. 'The Lockdown Effect: A Counterfactual for Sweden'. *Plos One* 16(4): e0249732, https://doi.org/10.1371/journal.pone.0249732.

Bosworth, Mary. 2014. *Inside Immigration Detention*. Oxford: Oxford University Press.

Brassett, James and Christopher Holmes. 2016. 'Building Resilient Finance? Uncertainty, Complexity, and Resistance'. *The British Journal of Politics and International Relations* 18(2): 370–88.

Brasset, James and Nick Vaughan-Williams. 2012. 'Crisis is Governance: Sub-Prime, The Traumatic Event, and Bare Life'. *Global Society* 26(1): 19–42.

Bristow, Gabriel. 2018. 'This Migrant Crackdown Has Exposed the Brutal Limits of Macron's Liberalism'. *The Guardian*, 22 February, https://www.theguardian.com/commentisfree/2018/feb/22/immigration-macron-liberalism-migrants-refugees, last accessed 23 May 2021.

Brock, Timothy. 1968. 'Implications of Commodity Theory for Value Change'. In *Psychological Foundations of Attitudes*, edited by Anthony G. Greenwald, Timothy C. Brock, and Thomas M. Ostrom, pp. 243–75, Academic Press.

Bröckling, Ulrich. 2011. 'Human Economy, Human Capital: A Critique of Biopolitical Economy'. In *Governmentality: Current Issues and Future Challenges*, edited by Ulrich Bröckling, Susanne Krasmann, and Thomas Lemke, pp. 247–68. London: Routledge.

Bröckling, Ulrich. 2015. *The Entrepreneurial Self: Fabricating a New Type of Subject*. London: Sage.

Brown, Wendy. 2010. *Walled States, Waning Sovereignty*. Boston, MA: MIT Press.

Brown, Wendy. 2015. *Undoing the Demos: Neoliberalism's Stealth Revolution*. New York: Zone Books.

Brown, Wendy. 2016. 'Sacrificial Citizenship: Neoliberalism, Human Capital, and Austerity Politics'. *Constellations* 23(1): 3–14.

Burnett, Jon. 2017. 'Austerity and The Production of Hate.' In *The Violence of Austerity*, edited by Vickie Cooper and David Whyte, pp. 217–24, London: Pluto Press.

Butler, Judith. 2004. *Precarious Life: The Powers of Mourning and Violence*. London: Verso.

Butler, Judith and Athena Athanasiou. 2013. *Dispossession: The Performative in the Political*. Cambridge: Polity.

Byrne, John A. 2011. *World Changers: 25 Entrepreneurs Who Changed Business as We Knew It*. New York: Penguin.

Cameron, David. 2009. 'The Age of Austerity'. *Conservative Party Speeches*. 26 April, https://conservative-speeches.sayit.mysociety.org/speech/601367, last accessed 23 May 2021.

Campbell, Timothy. 2008. 'Bios, Immunity, Life: The Thought of Roberto Esposito'. In Roberto Esposito, *Bios: Biopolitics and Philosophy*, vii-xlii, Minneapolis, University of Minnesota Press.

Campbell, Zach. 2017. 'Abandoned at Sea'. *The Intercept*, 1 April, https://theintercept.com/2017/04/01/europe-keeps-its-rescue-ships-far-from-the-coast-of-libya-where-thousands-of-refugees-have-drowned/, last accessed 23 May 2021.

Caporaso, James A. 2018. 'Europe's Triple Crisis and the Uneven Role of Institutions: The Euro, Refugees and Brexit'. *JCMS: Journal of Common Market Studies* 56(6): 1345–61.

Caputo, John D. 2000. 'Adieu–sans Dieu: Derrida and Levinas on Hospitality'. In *The Face of the Other and the Trace of God: Essays on the Philosophy of Emmanuel Levinas*, edited by Jeffrey Bloechl, 276–312. Fordham: Fordham University Press.

Carling, Jørgen. 2015. 'Refugees are Also Migrants. And All Migrants Matter'. *Border Criminologies*. 3 September, http://bordercriminologies.law.ox.ac.uk/refugees-are-also-migrants, last accessed 23 May 2021.

Carr, Matt. 2015. 'In the Kingdom Of TINA'. *Infernal Machine*. 26 January, http://infernalmachine.co.uk/in-the-kingdom-of-tina, last accessed 23 May 2021.

Carrera, Sergio. 2014. 'How Much Does EU Citizenship Cost? The Maltese Citizenship-for-Sale Affair.' *CEPS Papers in Liberty and Security in Europe* 64: 1–52.

Cartwright, Alistair. 2020. 'Supply Chains: A Neoliberal Crisis'. *Counterfire*. 26 March. https://www.counterfire.org/articles/opinion/21018-supply-chains-a-neoliberal-crisis, last accessed 23 May 2021.

Casanova, José. 1994. *Public Religions in the Modern World*. Chicago: University of Chicago Press.

Casanova, José. 2006a. 'Religion, European Secular Identities, and European Integration'. In *Religion in an Expanding Europe*, edited by Timothy A. Byrnes and Peter J. Katzenstein, pp. 65–92. Cambridge: Cambridge University Press.

Casanova, José. 2006b. 'Secularization Revisited: A Reply to Talal Asad'. In *Powers of the Secular Modern: Talal Asad and His Interlocutors*, edited by David Scott and Charles Hirschkind, pp. 12–30. Stanford: Stanford University Press.

Castles, Stephen and Alastair Davidson. 2000. *Citizenship and Migration: Globalization and the Politics of Belonging*. New York: Routledge.

Cavero, Teresa and Krisnah Poinasamy. 2013. 'A Cautionary Tale: The True Cost of Austerity and Inequality In Europe'. *Oxfam International*. https://oxfamilibrary.openrepository.com/bitstream/handle/10546/301384/bp174-cautionary-tale-austerity-inequality-europe-120913-en.pdf?sequence=25&isAllowed=y, last accessed 23 May 2021.

CBC. 2020. 'In Brief: Global Scramble for PPE Is "Utter, Cutthroat Chaos"'. 14 April, https://www.cbc.ca/radio/frontburner/in-brief-global-scramble-for-ppe-is-utter-cutthroat-chaos-1.5532086, last accessed 23 May 2021.

Cerny, Philip G. 1997. 'Paradoxes of the Competition State: The Dynamics of Political Globalization'. *Government and Opposition* 32(2): 251–74.

Cerny, Philip G. 2000. 'Structuring the Political Arena: Public Goods, States and Governance in a Globalizing World'. In *Global Political Economy: Contemporary Theories*, edited by Ronen Palan, pp. 21–35. New York, Routledge.

Cerny, Philip G. 2010. 'The Competition State Today: From Raison d'État to Raison du Monde'. *Policy Studies* 31(1): 5–21.

Cerny, Philip G. 2016. 'In the Shadow of Ordoliberalism: The Paradox of Neoliberalism in the 21st Century'. *ERIS–European Review of International Studies* 3(1): 78–92.

Chadwick, Vince. 2015. 'The Top 10 Wackiest Anti-Refugee Remarks.' *Politico*. 23 October, https://www.politico.eu/article/toxic-news-refugees-migrants-eu/, last accessed 23 May 2021.

Chandler, David. 2014a. 'Beyond Neoliberalism: Resilience, The New Art of Governing Complexity'. *Resilience: International Policies, Practices and Discourses* 2(1): 47–63.

Chandler, David. 2014b. *Resilience: The Governance of Complexity*. Abingdon and New York: Routledge.

Chandler, David and Julian Reid. 2016. *The Neoliberal Subject: Resilience, Adaptation and Vulnerability*. London: Rowman and Littlefield International.

Channel 4 News. 2015. 'Aylan Kurdi: Images That Changed UK Views on Refugees?'. 3 September, https://www.channel4.com/news/aylan-kurdi-refugee-crisis-dead-beach-uk-crisis-syrian, last accessed 24 May 2021.

Christiaens, Tim. 2020. 'Must Society be Defended from Agamben?' *Critical Legal Thinking*. 26 March, https://criticallegalthinking.com/2020/03/26/must-society-be-defended-from-agamben/, last accessed 23 May 2021.

Christophers, Brett. 2009. 'Complexity, Finance, and Progress in Human Geography'. *Progress in Human Geography* 33(6): 807–24.

CIS: Centre for Immigration Studies. 2015. 'Sen. Feinstein Announces She Is Opposed to the EB-5 Program'. 4 November, http://cis.org/north/sen-feinstein-announces-she-opposed-eb-5-program, last accessed 23 May 2021.

Clark, Simon. 2019. 'Give Us Your Rich, Europe Tells the U.K.' The Wall Street Journal. 14 October, https://www.wsj.com/articles/give-us-your-rich-europe-tells-the-u-k-11571050397, last accessed 8 July 2020.

Clarke, John and Janet Newman. 2012. 'The Alchemy of Austerity'. *Critical Social Policy* 32(3): 299–319.

Clarke, Tom. 2020. 'Coronavirus: "'Delays in Action on Care Home Crisis Cost Thousands of Lives", Documents Reveal'. *ITV News*, 6 May, https://www.itv.com/news/2020-05-06/coronavirus-delays-in-action-on-care-home-crisis-cost-thousands-of-lives-documents-reveal, last accessed 23 May 2021.

Clough, Patricia T. 2008. 'The Affective Turn: Political Economy, Biomedia and Bodies'. *Theory, Culture and Society* 25(1): 1–22.

CNBC. 2020. 'UK Prime Minister Boris Johnson Orders Britons to Stay at Home to Halt Spread of Coronavirus'. 23 March, https://www.cnbc.com/2020/03/23/uk-prime-minister-boris-johnson-orders-britons-to-stay-at-home-to-halt-spread-of-coronavirus.html, last accessed 23 May 2021.

Cohen, Joshua. 2020. 'Sweden's Gamble on Coronavirus: Has It Paid Off?'. *Forbes*. 23 May, https://www.forbes.com/sites/joshuacohen/2020/05/23/swedens-gamble-on-coronavirus-has-it-paid-off/#6d9eb0842dcd, last accessed 23 May 2021.

Comas-Herrera, Adelina, Joseba Zalakaín, Elizabeth Lemmon, David Henderson, Charles Litwin, Amy T. Hsu, Andrea E. Schmidt, Greg Arling, and Jose-Luis Fernández. 2020. 'Mortality Associated with COVID-19 in Care Homes: International Evidence'. *International Long Term Care Policy Network*. 14 October, https://ltccovid.org/wp-content/uploads/2020/10/Mortality-associated-with-COVID-among-people-living-in-care-homes-14-October-2020-3.pdf, last accessed 3 May 2021.

Conservative Party. 2008. 'Responsibility Agenda, Work for Welfare'. *Policy Green Paper* 9.

Cooper, Anderson. 2017. 'France's Marine Le Pen Says She's Not Waging A Religious War'. *60 Minutes*. 5 March, https://www.cbsnews.com/news/frances-marine-le-pen-says-shes-not-waging-a-religious-war/, last accessed 23 May 2021.

Cooper, Charlie and Ashleigh Furlong. 2020. 'Going Viral: Boris Johnson Grapples To Control Coronavirus Message'. *Politico*. 16 March, https://www.politico.eu/article/going-viral-british-prime-minister-boris-johnson-grapples-to-control-coronavirus-covid19-message/, last accessed 3 March 2021.

Cooper, Luke. 2020. 'The End of Neoliberalism? Why the Current Crisis Is Different To 1989, 2001 and 2008'. *LSE Blogs*. 24 June, https://blogs.lse.ac.uk/covid19/2020/06/24/the-end-of-neoliberalism-why-the-current-crisis-is-different-to-1989-2001-and-2008/, last accessed 23 May 2021.

Cooper, Melinda. 2011a. *Life as Surplus: Biotechnology and Capitalism in the Neoliberal Era*. Washington: University of Washington Press.

Cooper, Melinda. 2011b. 'Complexity Theory after the Financial Crisis: The Death of Neoliberalism or the Triumph of Hayek?' *Journal of Cultural Economy* 4(4): 371–85.

Cooper, Vickie and David Whyte. 2017. *The Violence of Austerity*. London: Pluto Press.

Costabile, Michele. 2020. 'Salute e Ripresa, Dicotomia Ingannevole', *Il Sole 24 Ore*. 8 April, https://www.ilsole24ore.com/art/salute-e-ripresa-dicotomia-ingannevole-ADWDpkI, last accessed 23 May 2021.

Croft, Stuart and Nick Vaughan-Williams. 2017. 'Fit for Purpose? Fitting Ontological Security Studies "Into" the Discipline of International Relations: Towards a Vernacular Turn'. *Cooperation and Conflict* 52(1): 12–30.
Crouch, Colin. 2011. *The Strange Non-Death of Neo-Liberalism*. Cambridge: Polity.
Cusumano, Eugenio. 2017. 'Emptying the Sea with a Spoon? Non-Governmental Providers of Migrants Search and Rescue in the Mediterranean.' *Marine Policy* 75: 91–8.
Cuttitta, Paolo. 2018. 'Repoliticization through Search and Rescue? Humanitarian NGOs and Migration Management in the Central Mediterranean.' *Geopolitics* 23(3): 632–60.
D'Emilio, Frances. 2021. 'Salvini: "In Graying Italy, The Old Defy Biases Laid Bare by Pandemic"'. AP News. 2 January, https://apnews.com/article/international-news-pandemics-italy-coronavirus-pandemic-rome-fefe4c3814aafd09da55cf7ac02f932f, last accessed 3 May 2021.
Dalmia Shikha. 2016. 'The Dystopian, Anti-Immigration Book *The Camp of the Saints* Is Really Racist'. *The Week*. 17 March, http://theweek.com/articles/611274/dystopian-antiimmigration-book-camp-saints-really-racist-why-are-bunch-smart-conservatives-praising, last accessed 23 May 2021.
Dardot, Pierre, and Christian Laval. 2013. *The New Way of the World: On Neoliberal Society*. London: Verso.
Darling, Jonathan. 2009. 'Becoming Bare Life: Asylum, Hospitality, and the Politics of Encampment'. *Environment and Planning D: Society and Space* 27(4): 649–65.
Datz, Giselle. 2013. 'The Narrative of Complexity in the Crisis of Finance: Epistemological Challenge and Macroprudential Policy Response'. *New Political Economy* 18(4): 459–79.
Davidson, James Dale and Lord William Rees-Mogg. 1997. *The Sovereign Individual: Mastering the Transition to The Information Age*. London: Simon and Schuster.
Davies, Thom and Abel Polese. 2015. 'Informality and Survival in Ukraine's Nuclear Landscape: Living with the Risks of Chernobyl'. *Journal of Eurasian Studies* 6(1): 34–45.
Davies, Thom, Arshad Isakjee, and Surindar Dhesi. 2017. 'Violent Inaction: The Necropolitical Experience of Refugees in Europe'. *Antipode* 49(5): 1263–84.
De Genova, Nicholas and Nathalie Peutz (eds). 2010. *The Deportation Regime: Sovereignty, Space, and the Freedom of Movement*. Durham, NC: Duke University Press.
De Genova, Nicholas and Martina Tazzioli (eds). 2016. 'Europe/Crisis: New Keywords of "The Crisis" in and of "Europe"'. *Zone Books: Near Futures Online* 1: 1–45, http://nearfuturesonline.org/europecrisis-new-keywords-of-crisis-in-and-of-europe/, last accessed 23 May 2021.
Dean, Mitchell. 1991. *The Constitution of Poverty: Toward a Genealogy of Liberal Governance*. London: Routledge.
Dean, Mitchell. 2014. *Rethinking Neoliberalism. Journal of Sociology* 50(2): 150–163.
Dean, Mitchell. 2015. 'The Malthus Effect: Population and the Liberal Government of Life'. *Economy and Society* 44(1): 18–39.
Death by Rescue. 2015. 'Death by Rescue: The Lethal Effects of the EU's Policies of Non-Assistance'. https://deathbyrescue.org/report/narrative/, last accessed 23 May 2021.
Debrix, François. 2015. 'Katechontic Sovereignty: Security Politics and the Overcoming of Time'. *International Political Sociology* 9(2): 143–57.
Delanty, Gerard. 2005. 'The Idea of a Cosmopolitan Europe: On the Cultural Significance of Europeanization'. *International Review of Sociology—Revue Internationale de Sociologie* 15(3): 405–21.
Derrida, Jacques. 1998. 'Plato's Pharmacy'. In *Literary Theory: An Anthology*, edited by Julie Rivkin and Michael Ryan. Malden, 429–450, MA: Blackwell.
Derrida, Jacques. 2000. *Of Hospitality*. Stanford: Stanford University Press.
Derrida, Jacques. 2002. *Acts of Religion*. New York: Routledge.

Di Feo, Gianluca, Floriana Bulfon, Michele Bocci, Zita Dazzi, Rosario Di Raimondo, Alessia Gallione, and Laura Pertici. 2020. 'La Strage Silenziosa Delle Rsa', *La Repubblica*. 27 May. https://rep.repubblica.it/pwa/longform/2020/05/27/news/rsa_morti_coronavirus_trivulzio-257664697/, last accessed 23 May 2021.

Dillon, Michael and Luis Lobo-Guerrero. 2008. 'Biopolitics of Security in the 21st Century: An Introduction'. *Review of International Studies* 34(2): 265–92.

Dillon, Michael and Luis Lobo-Guerrero. 2009. 'The Biopolitical Imaginary of Species-Being'. *Theory, Culture & Society* 26(1): 1–23.

Dillon, Michael and Julian Reid. 2009. *The Liberal Way of War: Killing to Make Life Live*. London: Routledge.

Dinan, Desmond, Neill Nugent, and William E. Paterson (eds). 2017. *The European Union in Crisis*. London: Palgrave.

Doty, Roxanne L. 2011. 'Bare Life: Border-crossing Deaths and Spaces of Moral Alibi'. *Environment and Planning D: Society and Space* 29(4): 599–612.

Dreyfus, Hubert L. and Paul Rabinow. 1982. *Michel Foucault: Beyond Structuralism and Hermeneutics*. Chicago, IL: University of Chicago Press.

Dumouchel, Paul. 2014. *The Ambivalence of Scarcity and Other Essays*. East Lansing, MI: Michigan State University Press.

Dupuy, Jean-Pierre. 2002. 'Detour and Sacrifice: Ivan Illich and René Girard'. In *The Challenges of Ivan Illich: A Collective Reflection*, edited by Lee Hoinacki and Carl Mitcham, pp. 189–204. New York, SUNY Press.

Durkheim, Émile. 1995 [1912]. *The Elementary Forms of Religious Life*: New York: Free Press.

Dzankic, Jelena. 2012. 'The Pros and Cons of Ius Pecuniae: Investor Citizenship in Comparative Perspective'. *EUI Working Papers* 2012/14: 1–18.

Dzankic, Jelena. 2014. 'The Maltese Falcon, or: My Porsche for a Passport!' In *Should Citizenship Be for Sale?*, edited by Ayelet Shachar and Rainer Baubock, pp. 17–18. EUI Working Papers 2014/01.

Dzankic, Jelena. 2015. 'Investment-based Citizenship and Residence Programmes in the EU'. *EUI Working Papers* 2015/08: 1–25.

Ebenstein, Alan. 2014. *Friedrich Hayek: A Biography*. London: St. Martin's Press.

The Economist. 2020a. 'Covid-19 Presents Stark Choices Between Life, Death and the Economy'. 2 April, https://www.economist.com/leaders/2020/04/02/covid-19-presents-stark-choices-between-life-death-and-the-economy, last accessed 23 May 2021.

The Economist. 2020b. 'The Hard Choices Covid Policymakers Face'. 2 April, https://www.economist.com/briefing/2020/04/04/the-hard-choices-covid-policymakers-face, last accessed 23 May 2021.

ECRE (European Council for Refugees and Exiles). 2014. 'UK Slammed for Axing Rescue Missions on the Basis that Saving Migrants Encourages Others'. 31 October, https://www.ecre.org/uk-slammed-for-axing-rescue-missions-on-the-basis-that-saving-migrants-encourages-others/, last accessed 23 May 2021.

Elliott, Larry and Ian Traynor. 2010. 'Greek Debt Crisis: Europe Feels Shockwaves as Bailout Falters'. *The Guardian*. 28 April, https://www.theguardian.com/business/2010/apr/28/greek-debt-crisis-europe-bailout, last accessed 23 May 2021.

Elshtain, Jean Bethke. 2008. *Sovereignty: God, State, And Self*. New York: Basic Books.

Engdahl, William. 2015. 'Greek Guilt and Syriza Perfidy'. *NEO-New Eastern Outlook*. 16 July, http://journal-neo.org/2015/07/16/greek-guilt-and-syriza-perfidy/, page no longer available; Italian translation available at https://www.ariannaeditrice.it/articolo.php?id_articolo=51608, last accessed 23 May 2021.

Epicentro. 2020. 'Caratteristiche dei Pazienti Deceduti Positivi All'infezione Da SARS-Cov-2 In Italia'. *Istituto Superiore di Sanita'*. https://www.epicentro.iss.it/coronavirus/sars-cov-2-decessi-italia, last accessed 23 May 2021.

Esping-Andersen, Gøsta. 1990. *The Three Worlds of Welfare Capitalism*. Princeton, NJ: Princeton University Press.

Esposito, Roberto. 2008. *Bios: Biopolitics and Philosophy*. Minneapolis: University of Minnesota Press.

Esposito, Roberto. 2020a. 'Our Destiny, Attached to Life and Exposed to Death: An Interview with Roberto Esposito'. *Security Praxis*. 20 April, https://securitypraxis.eu/destiny-life-death-roberto-esposito/, last accessed 23 May 2021.

Esposito, Roberto. 2020b. 'The Biopolitics of Immunity in Times of COVID-19: An Interview with Roberto Esposito'. *Antipode Online*. 16 June, https://antipodeonline.org/2020/06/16/interview-with-roberto-esposito/, last accessed 23 May 2021.

European Commission. 2015. 'EC Reply to Civil Society', 26 September. https://www.tni.org/es/node/14461#sept26, last accessed 23 May 2021.

European Commission. 2017. 'Poverty and Social Exclusion'. *Employment, Social Affairs & Inclusion*, https://ec.europa.eu/social/main.jsp?catId=751&langId=en#:~:text=22.4%25%20of%20the%20EU%20population,18.2%25%20of%20those%20over%2065, last accessed 23 May 2021.

Eurostat. 2017. 'Asylum Statistics'. Accessed 24 January 2017. http://ec.europa.eu/eurostat/statistics-explained/index.php/Asylum_statistics, last accessed 23 May 2021.

Evans, Brad and Julian Reid. 2013 'Dangerously Exposed: The Life and Death of the Resilient Subject', *Resilience*, 1(2): 83–98.

Evans, Brad and Julian Reid. 2014. *Resilient Life: The Art of Living Dangerously*. Cambridge: Polity Press.

Fassin, Didier. 2011. 'Policing Borders, Producing Boundaries. The Governmentality of Immigration in Dark Times.' *Annual Review of Anthropology* 40(1): 213–26.

Fassin, Didier. 2012. *Humanitarian Reason: A Moral History of the Present*. Berkeley, CA: University of California Press.

Feher, Michel. 2009. 'Self-Appreciation; or, the Aspirations of Human Capital'. *Public Culture* 21(1): 21–41.

Feher, Michel. 2020. 'Disposing of the Discredited: A European Project'. In *Mutant Neoliberalism: Market Rule and Political Rupture*, edited by William Callison and Zachary Manfredi, pp. 146–76. New York: Fordham University Press.

Feldenkirchen, Marcus and Rene Pfister. 2016. 'The Isolated Chancellor: What Is Driving Angela Merkel?' *Der Spiegel*. 25 January, http://www.spiegel.de/international/germany/why-has-angela-merkel-staked-her-legacy-on-the-refugees-a-1073705.html, last accessed 23 May 2021.

Ferguson, Neil M., Daniel Laydon, Gemma Nedjati-Gilani, Natsuko Imai, Kylie Ainslie, Marc Baguelin, Sangeeta Bhatia, Adhiratha Boonyasiri, Zulma Cucunubá, Gina Cuomo-Dannenburg, Amy Dighe, Ilaria Dorigatti, Han Fu, Katy Gaythorpe, Will Green, Arran Hamlet, Wes Hinsley, Lucy C. Okell, Sabine Van Elsland, Hayley Thompson, Robert Verity, Erik Volz, Haowei Wang, Yuanrong Wang, Patrick G.T. Walker, Caroline Walters, Peter Winskill, Charles Whittaker, Christl A. Donnelly, Steven Riley, and Azra C. Ghani. 2020. 'Report 9: Impact of Non-Pharmaceutical Interventions (NPIS) To Reduce COVID-19 Mortality and Healthcare Demand'. Imperial College COVID-19 Response Team. 16 March, https://www.imperial.ac.uk/media/imperial-college/medicine/sph/ide/gida-fellowships/Imperial-College-COVID19-NPI-modelling-16-03-2020.pdf, last accessed 24 May 2021.

Fetzer, Thiemo. 2019a. 'Did Austerity in the UK Lead to the Brexit Crisis?' *Harvard Business Review*. 23 August, https://hbr.org/2019/08/did-austerity-in-the-uk-lead-to-the-brexit-crisis#, last accessed 23 May 2021.

Fetzer, Thiemo. 2019b. 'Did Austerity Cause Brexit?' *American Economic Review* 109(11): 3849–86.

Fetzer, Thiemo. 2019c. 'Debunking Myths on Links Between Austerity and Brexit'. *LSE Blog*, 17 October, https://blogs.lse.ac.uk/brexit/2019/10/17/long-read-debunking-myths-on-links-between-austerity-and-brexit/, last accessed 3 May 2021.

Fiddian-Qasmiyeh, Elena. 2016. '*Repress*entations of Displacement from the Middle East and North Africa'. *Public Culture* 28(3): 457–73.

Fiddian-Qasmiyeh, Elena. 2017. 'The Faith–Gender–Asylum Nexus: An Intersectionalist Analysis of Representations of the "Refugee Crisis"'. In *The Refugee Crisis and Religion: Secularism, Security and Hospitality in Question*, edited by Luca Mavelli and Erin K. Wilson, pp. 207–22. London: Rowman and Littlefield.

Financial Times. 2015. 'David Cameron Has Misjudged Europe's Refugee Crisis'. 2 September, https://www.ft.com/content/fb41c922-5171-11e5-8642-453585f2cfcd, last accessed 23 May 2021.

Financial Times. 2016. 'EU border force flags concerns over charities' interaction with migrant smugglers', 15 December, https://www.ft.com/content/3e6b6450-c1f7-11e6-9bca-2b93a6856354, last accessed 16 September 2021.

Financial Times. 2020. 'UK's Chief Scientific Adviser Defends "Herd Immunity" Strategy for Coronavirus'. 13 March, https://www.ft.com/content/38a81588-6508-11ea-b3f3-fe4680ea68b5, last accessed 23 May 2021.

Fitoussi, Jean-Paul and Francesco Saraceno. 2013. 'European Economic Governance: The Berlin–Washington Consensus'. *Cambridge Journal of Economics* 37(3): 479–96.

Floris, Francesco and Lorenzo Bagnoli. 2017. 'Accusations against Ngos at Sea: What Is False or Misleading in that Smear Campaign.' *Open Migration*. 19 May, https://openmigration.org/en/analyses/accusations-against-ngos-at-sea-what-is-false-or-misleading-in-that-smear-campaign/, last accessed 23 May 2021.

Foucault, Michel. 1974. 'Prisons et Asiles dans le Mécanisme du Pouvoir' in *Dits et Ecrits, 1954–1988, Volume 2*, pp. 523–524. Paris: Gallimard.

Foucault, Michel. 1978. *The History of Sexuality: Volume 1*. New York: Pantheon Books.

Foucault, Michel. 1983. 'On the Genealogy of Ethics: An Overview of Work in Progress'. *Michel Foucault: Ethics, Subjectivity and Truth (Vol. 1)*, edited by Paul Rabinow, pp. 253–80. New York: The New Press.

Foucault, Michel. 1984. 'Nietzsche, Genealogy, History'. In *The Foucault Reader*, edited by Paul Rabinow, pp. 76–100. New York: Pantheon Books.

Foucault, Michel. 1994. '*Omnes et Singulatim*: Toward a Critique of Political Reason'. In *Power: The Essential Works of Michel Foucault 1954–1984, Volume 3*, edited by James D. Faubion, pp. 298–323. New York: Penguin Books.

Foucault, Michel. 2002 [1970]. *The Order of Things: An Archaeology of the Human Sciences*. London: Routledge.

Foucault, Michel. 2003. *'Society Must be Defended': Lectures at the Collège de France, 1975–76*. Translated by David Macey. New York: Picador.

Foucault, Michel. 2008. *The Birth of Biopolitics: Lectures at the Collège de France, 1978–79*. Translated by Graham Burchell. Basingstoke: Palgrave Macmillan.

Foucault, Michel. 2009. *Security, Territory, Population: Lectures at the Collège de France, 1977–78*. New York: Palgrave.

Fougner, Tore. 2006. 'The State, International Competitiveness and Neoliberal Globalisation: Is There a Future beyond "The Competition State"?' *Review of International Studies* 32(1): 165–85.

Fouskas, Vassilis K. and Bulent Gokay. 2020. 'COVID-19 and the Bankruptcy of Neoliberalism in the Context of Global Shift'. *Open Democracy*. 5 May, https://www.opendemocracy.net/en/can-europe-make-it/covid-19-and-bankruptcy-neoliberalism-context-global-shift/, last accessed 23 May 2021.

French Government (Gouvernement). 2015. 'Lassana Bathily: The Pride of Being French', https://www.gouvernement.fr/en/lassana-bathily-the-pride-of-being-french, last accessed 23 October 2021.

Frey, Isabel. 2020. '"Herd Immunity" is Epidemiological Neoliberalism'. Economic Sociology & Political Economy. 24 April 24, https://economicsociology.org/2020/04/24/herd-immunity-is-epidemiological-neoliberalism/, last accessed 23 May 2021.

Friedman, Jeffrey. 2005. 'Popper, Weber, And Hayek: The Epistemology and Politics of Ignorance'. *Critical Review: A Journal of Politics and Society* 17(1–2): 1–58.

Friedman, Milton. 1953. 'The Methodology of Positive Economics.' In *Essays in Positive Economics*. Chicago: University of Chicago Press.

Friedman, Milton. 1993. *Why Government is the Problem*. Stanford: Hoover Press.

Friedman, Milton. 2002. *Capitalism and Freedom*, Fortieth Anniversary Edition. Chicago: University of Chicago Press.

Frontex. 2017. 'Risk Analysis for 2017'. http://frontex.europa.eu/assets/Publications/Risk_Analysis/Annual_Risk_Analysis_2017.pdf, last accessed 23 May 2021.

Gaffney, Adam. 2017. *To Heal Humankind: The Right to Health in History*. London and New York: Routledge.

Geisser, Vincent. 2018. '«Bon Nègre» Méritant Versus «Mauvais Nègre» Délinquant?' *Migrations Societe* 172(2): 3–11.

Gillespie, Michael Allen. 2008. *The Theological Origins of Modernity*. Chicago: The University of Chicago Press.

Girard, René. 1966. *Deceit, Desire and the Novel: Self and Other in Literary Structure*. Translated by Yvonne Freccero. Baltimore, MD: Johns Hopkins University Press.

Girard, René. 1986. *The Scapegoat*. Baltimore, MD: John Hopkins University Press.

Girard, René. 1987. *Things Hidden since the Foundation of the World: Research Undertaken in Collaboration with J.-M. Oughourlian and G. Lefort*. Translated by Stephen Bann and Michael Metteer. Stanford, CA: Stanford University Press.

Girard, René. 1996. *The Girard Reader*. Edited by James G. Williams. New York: Crossroad.

Girard, René. 2001. *I See Satan Fall Like Lightning*. Translated by James G. Williams. Maryknoll, NY: Orbis Books.

Glaser, Eliane. 2016. 'Is Digital Culture Responsible for Post-Truth Politics?' *Open Transcripts*. 29 October, http://opentranscripts.org/transcript/post-truth-politics/, last accessed 23 May 2021.

Global Burden of Disease 2016 Greece Collaborators. 2018. 'The Burden of Disease in Greece, Health Loss, Risk Factors, and Health Financing, 2000–16: An Analysis of The Global Burden of Disease Study 2016.' *The Lancet Public Health* 3(8): e395–e406, https://doi.org/10.1016/S2468-2667(18)30130-0.

Göle, Nilüfer. 2010. 'Manifestations of the Religious-Secular Divide: Self, State, and the Public Sphere'. In *Comparative Secularisms in a Global Age*, edited by Linnell E. Cady and Elizabeth Shakman Hurd, pp. 41–53. New York: Palgrave.

Goodwin, Matthew and Caitlin Milazzo. 2017. 'Taking Back Control? Investigating the Role of Immigration in the 2016 Vote for Brexit'. *The British Journal of Politics and International Relations* 19(3): 450–64.

Gordon, Colin. 1991. 'Governmental Rationality: An Introduction', in *The Foucault Effect: Studies in Governmentality*, edited by Graham Burchell, Colin Gordon, and Peter Miller, pp. 1–52. Chicago: University of Chicago Press.

GOV.UK. nd. 'Investor visa (TIER 1)', https://www.gov.uk/tier-1-investor, last accessed 23 May 2021

Graeber, David and Thomas Piketty. 2014. 'Soak the Rich.' *The Baffler*. 25, July, https://thebaffler.com/odds-and-ends/soak-the-rich, last accessed 23 May 2021.

Grierson, Jamie. 2019. 'Have the Tories Cut 17,000 Hospital Beds in The Past 10 Years?' *The Guardian*. 10 December, https://www.theguardian.com/politics/2019/dec/10/have-the-tories-cut-17000-hospital-beds-over-the-past-10-years-labour-jonathan-ashworth, last accessed 23 May 2021.

Griffith, Phoebe. 2016. 'Theresa May Must End This Obsession with Net Migration.' *The Telegraph*. 20 July, http://www.telegraph.co.uk/news/2016/07/20/theresa-may-must-end-this-obsession-with-net-migration-all-migra/, last accessed 23 May 2021.

The Guardian. 2014. 'David Cameron Defends "Moral Mission" on Welfare'. 19 February, https://www.theguardian.com/society/2014/feb/19/david-cameron-moral-mission-welfare-archbishop-westminster, last accessed 23 May 2021.

The Guardian. 2015a. 'Merkel Urges Germans to see Refugee Arrivals as "An Opportunity" in New Year Address'. 31 December, https://www.theguardian.com/world/2015/dec/31/merkel-urges-germans-to-see-refugee-arrivals-as-an-opportunity-in-new-year-address, last accessed 23 May 2021.

The Guardian. 2015b. 'Cameron Says Migrants Trying to "Break in" to UK Illegally'. 15 August, https://www.theguardian.com/uk-news/2015/aug/15/david-cameron-says-migrants-trying-to-break-in-to-uk-illegally, last accessed 23 May 2021.

The Guardian. 2016. '"Like Dunkirk": Brexit Donor Trumpets "Fantastic Insecurity" of Leaving EU'. 12 May, https://www.theguardian.com/politics/2016/may/12/billionaire-brexit-donor-leaving-eu-like-dunkirk, last accessed 23 May 2021.

The Guardian. 2017. 'NGO Rescues Off Libya Encourage Traffickers, Says EU Borders Chief'. 27 February, https://www.theguardian.com/world/2017/feb/27/ngo-rescues-off-libya-encourage-traffickers-eu-borders-chief, last accessed 23 May 2021.

The Guardian. 2020a. 'Johnson: Many More People Will Lose Loved Ones to Coronavirus'. 12 March. https://www.theguardian.com/world/2020/mar/12/uk-moves-to-delay-phase-of-coronavirus-plan, last accessed 23 May 2021.

The Guardian. 2020b. 'No 10 Denies Claim Dominic Cummings Argued to "Let Old People Die"'. 22 March, https://www.theguardian.com/politics/2020/mar/22/no-10-denies-claim-dominic-cummings-argued-to-let-old-people-die, last accessed 23 May 2021.

The Guardian. 2021. 'Pressure Mounts on Johnson over Alleged "Let the Bodies Pile High" remarks'. 26 April, https://www.theguardian.com/politics/2021/apr/26/pressure-mounts-on-boris-johnson-over-alleged-let-the-bodies-pile-high-remarks, last accessed 29 May 2021.

Guerrieri, Veronica, Guido Lorenzoni, Ludwig Straub, and Iván Werning. 2020. 'Viral Recessions: Lack of Demand During the Coronavirus Crisis'. *VoxEU*. 6 May, https://voxeu.org/article/lack-demand-during-coronavirus-crisis, last accessed 23 May 2021.

Guild, Elspeth. 2009. *Security and Migration in the 21st Century*. Cambridge: Polity Press.

Guizzo, Danielle and Iara Vigo De Lima. 2017. 'Polanyi and Foucault on the Issue of Market in Classical Political Economy: Complementary Approaches to the Radical Theory of Social Control'. *Review of Radical Political Economics* 49(1): 100–13.

Gunter, Joel. 2015. 'Alan Kurdi: Why One Picture Cut Through', *BBC News*, 4 September, http://www.bbc.co.uk/news/world-europe-34150419, last accessed 23 May 2021.

Habermas, Jürgen. 1996. 'Three Normative Models of Democracy'. In *Democracy and Difference: Contesting the Boundaries of the Political*, edited by Seyla Benhabib, pp. 21–30. Princeton, NJ: Princeton University Press.

Habermas, Jürgen. 2003. 'Making sense of the EU: Toward a Cosmopolitan Europe'. *Journal of Democracy* 14(4): 86–100.

Habermas, Jürgen. 2008. *Between Naturalism and Religion: Philosophical Essays*. Cambridge: Polity Press.

Habermas, Jürgen et al. 2011. *An Awareness of What is Missing: Faith and Reason in a Post-Secular Age*. Cambridge: Polity Press.

Hadjimichalis, Costis. 2014. 'Crisis and Land Dispossession in Greece as Part of the Global "Land Fever"'. *City*. 18(4–5): 502–8.

Hague, William. 2015. 'The Migrant Crisis Is a Mere Gust of the Hurricane that Will Soon Engulf Europe'. *The Telegraph*. 11 November, http://www.telegraph.co.uk/news/newstopics/eureferendum/11986994/The-migrant-crisis-is-a-mere-gust-of-the-hurricane-that-will-soon-engulf-Europe.html, last accessed 23 May 2021.

Hall, David, John Lister, Cat Hobbs, Pascale Robinson, Chris Jarvis, and Helen Mercer. 2020. 'Privatised and Unprepared: The NHS Supply Chain'. *University of Greenwich and We Own It*, https://gala.gre.ac.uk/id/eprint/28230/, last accessed 23 May 2021.

Halliday, Fred. 1999. '"Islamophobia" Reconsidered'. *Ethnic and Racial Studies* 22(5): 892–902.

Hamilton, Scott. 2018. 'The Measure of All Things? The Anthropocene as a Global Biopolitics of Carbon.' *European Journal of International Relations* 24(1): 33–57.

Hardin, Garret. 1974. 'Living on a Lifeboat'. *Bioscience* 24(10): 561–8.

Hardin, Garret. 1980. 'Lifeboat Ethics: A Malthusian View'. In *Dialectics of Third World Development*, edited by Ingolf Vogeler and Anthony de Souza, pp. 171–85. New Jersey: Allanheld.

Hardin, Garret. 1988. 'The Feast of Malthus'. *The Social Contract* 8: 181–7.

Harrington, Austin. 2007. 'Habermas and the "Post-Secular Society"'. *European Journal of Social Theory* 10(4): 543–60.

Harris, Chris. 2021. 'COVID Vaccine: Who in Europe Is Leading the Race to Herd Immunity?', *Euronews*. 19 May, https://www.euronews.com/2021/05/19/covid-19-vaccinations-in-europe-which-countries-are-leading-the-way, last accessed 19 May 2021.

Harsin, Jayson. 2015. 'Regimes of Posttruth, Postpolitics, and Attention Economies'. *Communication, Culture & Critique* 8(2): 327–33.

Harvey, David. 2005. *A Brief History of Neoliberalism*. Oxford: Oxford University Press.

Harvey, David. 2006. 'Neo-Liberalism as Creative Destruction'. *Geografiska Annaler: Series B, Human Geography* 88(2): 145–58.

Harvey, David. 2010. *The Enigma of Capital and the Crises of Capitalism*. Oxford: Oxford University.

Harvey, David. 2014a. *Seventeen Contradictions and The End of Capitalism*. Oxford: Oxford University Press.

Harvey, David. 2014b. 'The Crises of Capitalism'. In *The Globalization and Development Reader: Perspectives on Development and Global Change*, edited by Roberts J. Timmons, Amy Bellone Hite, and Nitsan Chorev, pp. 333–6. Oxford: John Wiley & Sons.

Hayek, Friedrich A. 1945. 'The Use of Knowledge in Society'. *American Economic Review* 25(4): 519–30.

Hayek, Friedrich A. 1952. *The Sensory Order, An Inquiry into the Foundations of Theoretical Psychology*. London: Routledge and Kegan Paul.

Hayek, Friedrich A. 1967. 'The Theory of Complex Phenomena'. In *Studies in Philosophy, Politics and Economics*, pp. 22–42. London: Routledge and Kegan Paul.

Hayek, Friedrich A. 1988. *The Fatal Conceit: The Errors of Socialism*. Edited by W.W. Bartley, III. London: Routledge.

Hayek, Friedrich A. 1989. 'The Pretence of Knowledge'. *The American Economic Review* 79(6): 3–7.

Hayek, Friedrich A. 1998. *Law, Legislation and Liberty: A New Statement of the Liberal Principles of Justice and Political Economy*. London: Routledge.

Hayek, Friedrich A. 2005 [1944]. *The Road to Serfdom*. London: Routledge.

Hayek, Friedrich A. 2011 [1960]. *The Constitution of Liberty*. Chicago: University of Chicago Press.

Helm, Toby. 2019. 'Austerity to Blame for 130,000 "Preventable" UK Deaths—Report'. *The Guardian*. 1 June, https://www.theguardian.com/politics/2019/jun/01/perfect-storm-austerity-behind-130000-deaths-uk-ippr-report, last accessed 23 May 2021.

Henley & Partners. 2015a. 'Over EUR 1 billion Committed through the World's Highest Ranked Citizenship-by-Investment Program'. *Henley & Partners*, https://www.henleyglobal.com/latest-news-details/one-billion-committed-to-malta-program/, last accessed 6 November 2020.

Henley & Partners. 2015b. 'Citizenship-by-Investment in Cyprus'. https://www.henleyglobal.com/citizenship-cyprus-citizenship/, last accessed 21 February 2016, page no longer available.

Hewitt, Marsha Aileen. 2014. *Freud on Religion*. London: Routledge.

Hinnant, Lori and Bram Janssen. 2018. '56,800 Dead and Missing: The Hidden Toll of Migration'. *Associated Press*. 1 November, https://apnews.com/article/6481dbc005d647af9be52b7106d59c8f, last accessed 23 May 2021.

Hobolt, Sara B. 2016. 'The Brexit Vote: A Divided Nation, A Divided Continent'. *Journal of European Public Policy* 23(9): 1259–77.

Holmes, Seth M. and Heide Castaneda. 2016. 'Representing the "European Refugee Crisis" in Germany and Beyond: Deservingness and Difference, Life and Death'. *American Ethnologist* 43(1): 12–24.

Home Office. 2016. Immigration Act 2016. http://www.legislation.gov.uk/ukpga/2016/19/pdfs/ukpga_20160019_en.pdf, last accessed 6 May 2021.

Huerta De Soto, Jesus. 2010. *Socialism, Economic Calculation and Entrepreneurship*. London: Edward Elgar.

Huntington, Samuel P. 1996. *The Clash of Civilizations and the Remaking of the World Order*. New York: Simon & Schuster.

Hurd, Elizabeth Shakman. 2004. 'The Political Authority of Secularism in International Relations'. *European Journal of International Relations* 10(2): 235–62.

Hurd, Elizabeth Shakman. 2017. *Beyond Religious Freedom: The New Global Politics of Religion*. Princeton, NJ: Princeton University Press.

Huysmans, Jef. 2008. 'The Jargon of Exception – On Schmitt, Agamben and the Absence of Political Society', *International Political Sociology* 2(2): 165–83.

The Independent. 2016a. 'David Cameron Sparks Outrage Referring to Calais Refugees as "Bunch of Migrants"'. 27 January, http://www.independent.co.uk/news/uk/politics/pmqs-david-cameron-calais-refugees-bunch-of-migrants-jeremy-corbyn-a6836566.html, last accessed 23 May 2021.

The Independent. 2016b. 'What Theresa May Said about Immigration in her Infamous Speech to Tory conference'. August 25, http://www.independent.co.uk/news/

uk/politics/theresa-may-immigration-policies-speech-conference-2015-tory-conservative-party-views-a7209931.html, last accessed 23 May 2021.

Independent Panel for Pandemic Preparedness and Response. 2021. 'COVID-19: Make it the Last Pandemic', https://theindependentpanel.org/wp-content/uploads/2021/05/Summary_COVID-19-Make-it-the-Last-Pandemic_final.pdf, last accessed 20 May 2021.

InfoMigrants. 2020a. 'Spain Grants Residency to Migrant Who Saved Disabled Man'. 6 January, https://www.infomigrants.net/en/post/21906/spain-grants-residency-to-migrant-who-saved-disabled-man, last accessed 23 October 2021.

InfoMigrants. 2020b. 'Over 20,000 Migrant Deaths in Mediterranean Since 2014'. 9 March, https://www.infomigrants.net/en/post/23295/over-20-000-migrant-deaths-in-mediterranean-since-2014-iom, last accessed 23 May 2021.

IOM (International Organization for Migration). 2017. 'Mediterranean Migrant Arrivals Top 363,348 in 2016; Deaths at Sea: 5,079'. https://www.iom.int/news/mediterranean-migrant-arrivals-top-363348-2016-deaths-sea-5079, last accessed 19 September 2021.

IOM (International Organization for Migration). 2020. 'Missing Migrants: Tracking Deaths Along Migratory Routes'. https://missingmigrants.iom.int/region/mediterranean, last accessed 7 July 2020.

Isin, Engin F. 2002. *Being Political: Genealogies of Citizenship*. Minneapolis: University of Minnesota Press.

Isin, Engin F. and Peter Nyers. 2014. 'Introduction: Globalizing Citizenship Studies'. In *Routledge Handbook of Global Citizenship Studies*, edited by Engin F. Isin and Peter Nyers, pp. 23–33. London: Routledge.

Jabri, Vivienne. 2007. 'Michel Foucault's Analytics of War: The Social, The International, and the Racial'. *International Political Sociology* 1(1): 67–81.

Jarvis, Lee. 2019. 'Toward a Vernacular Security Studies: Origins, Interlocutors, Contributions, and Challenges'. *International Studies Review* 21(1): 107–26.

Jarvis, Lee, and Michael Lister. 2013. 'Vernacular securities and their study: A qualitative analysis and research agenda'. *International Relations* 27(2): 158–179.

Jessop, Bob. 2017. 'The Organic Crisis of the British State: Putting Brexit in its Place'. *Globalizations* 14(1): 133–41.

Joseph, Jonathan. 2013. 'Resilience as Embedded Neoliberalism: A Governmentality Approach'. *Resilience: International Policies, Practices and Discourses*. 1(1): 38–52.

Joseph, Jonathan. 2016. 'Governing through Failure and Denial: The New Resilience Agenda'. *Millennium: Journal of International Studies* 44(3): 370–90.

Judt, Tony. 1992. 'The Past Is Another Country: Myth and Memory in Postwar Europe'. *Daedalus* 121(4): 83–118.

Judt, Tony. 2005. *Postwar: A History of Europe Since 1945*. New York: Penguin.

Karakayali, Serhat. 2016. 'Rights or Philanthropy: Emotions of Solidarity with Refugees'. *Compas*. 1 March, https://www.compas.ox.ac.uk/2016/rights-or-philanthropy-emotions-of-solidarity-with-refugees/, last accessed 23 May 2021.

Kassam, Ashifa. 2020. 'Legal Remedies'. *Tortoise Media*. 19 May, https://members.tortoisemedia.com/2020/05/19/care-homes-spain-coronavirus-ashifa-kassam/content.html, last accessed 23 May 2021.

Katzenstein, Peter J. 2006. 'Multiple Modernities as Limits to Secular Europeanization?' in *Religion in an Expanding Europe*, edited by Timothy A. Byrnes and Peter J. Katzenstein, pp. 1–32. Cambridge: Cambridge University Press.

Kellam, Amy. 2020. 'Domestic Abuse during the UK's Covid-19 Lockdown: From Normal to New Normal and What Survivors' Experiences Might Teach Us'. *Amicus Curiae* 1(3): 361–78.

Kelly, M.G.E. 2015. *Biopolitical Imperialism*. Winchester: Zero Books.

Kirby, Tony. 2020. 'Evidence Mounts on the Disproportionate Effect of COVID-19 on Ethnic Minorities.' *The Lancet Respiratory Medicine* 8(6): 547–8.

Klein, Naomi. 2007. *The Shock Doctrine: The Rise of Disaster Capitalism*. London: Penguin.

Knight Frank. 2019. 'Care Homes Trading Performance Review—2019'. https://content.knightfrank.com/research/548/documents/en/care-homes-trading-performance-review-2019-6698.pdf, last accessed 23 May 2021.

Knight Frank Wealth Report. 2017. https://content.knightfrank.com/research/83/documents/en/the-wealth-report-2017-4482.pdf, last accessed 23 May 2021.

Kochenov, Dimitry. 2014. 'Citizenship for Real: Its Hypocrisy, Its Randomness, Its Price'. In *Should Citizenship Be for Sale?*, edited by Ayelet Shachar and Rainer Baubock, pp. 27–30. EUI Working Papers 2014/01.

Kofman, Eleonore and Helena Wray. 2013. 'The Fiscal Implications of New Family Migration Rules: What does the Evidence Tell Us?' *Middlesex University Briefing*, http://sprc.info/wp-content/uploads/2013/07/MRN-Mdx-briefing.pdf, last accessed 23 May 2021.

Konings, Martijn. 2014. 'Hoodwinked by Hayek'. *Journal of Cultural Economy* 7(4): 527–31.

Konings, Martijn. 2016. 'Governing the System: Risk, Finance, and Neoliberal Reason'. *European Journal of International Relations* 22(2): 268–88.

Lakoff, George and Mark Johnson. 2003 [1980]. *Metaphors We Live By*. Chicago: University of Chicago Press.

The Lancet: Diabetes & Endocrinology. 2020. 'COVID-19: Underlying Metabolic Health in the Spotlight'. *The Lancet. Diabetes & Endocrinology* 8(6): 457.

Langley, Paul. 2014. *Liquidity Lost: The Governance of the Global Financial Crisis*. Oxford: Oxford University Press.

Laporte, Vincent. 2012. 'The European Union - An Expanding Security Community?' *EU Diplomacy Paper 06/2012*. Bruges: College of Europe.

Laterza, Vito and Louis Philippe Romer. 2020. 'Coronavirus, Herd Immunity and the Eugenics of the Market', *Al Jazeera*. 14 April, https://www.aljazeera.com/indepth/opinion/coronavirus-herd-immunity-eugenics-market-200414104531234.html, last accessed 23 May 2021.

Latour, Bruno. 2020. 'Is This a Dress Rehearsal?' *Critical Inquiry*. 26 March, https://critinq.wordpress.com/2020/03/26/is-this-a-dress-rehearsal/, last accessed 23 May 2021.

Lawrence, Jessica. 2018. *Governmentality in EU External Trade and Environment Policy: Between Rights and Market*. Abingdon: Routledge.

Leisinger, Klaus M. and Karin Schmitt. 1994. *All Our People. Population Policy with a Human Face*. Washington DC: Island Press.

Lemke, Thomas. 2002. 'Foucault, Governmentality, and Critique'. *Rethinking Marxism: A Journal of Economics, Culture & Society* 14(3): 49–64.

Lemke, Thomas. 2003. 'Comment on Nancy Fraser: Rereading Foucault in the Shadow of Globalization'. *Constellations* 10(2): 172–9.

Lemke, Thomas. 2011. *Biopolitics: An Advanced Introduction*. New York: New York University Press.

Lemm, Vanessa and Miguel Vatter (eds). 2014. *The Government of Life: Foucault, Biopolitics, and Neoliberalism*. New York: Fordham University Press.

Lent, Jeremy. 2020. 'Coronavirus Spells the End of the Neoliberal Era. What's Next?' *Open Democracy*. https://www.opendemocracy.net/en/transformation/coronavirus-spells-the-end-of-the-neoliberal-era-whats-next/, last accessed 23 May 2021.

Leys, Colin. 2012. 'Commodification: The Essence of Our Time'. *Open Democracy*. https://www.opendemocracy.net/en/opendemocracyuk/commodification-essence-of-our-time/, last accessed 23 May 2021.

Linklater, Andrew. 1998. *The Transformation of Political Community: Ethical Foundations of the Post-Westphalian Era*. Cambridge: Polity Press.

Lintern, Shaun. 2020. 'Coronavirus: More than 25,000 Patients Discharged to Care Homes in Crucial 30 Days before Routine Testing', *The Independent*. 2 June, https://www.independent.co.uk/news/health/coronavirus-care-homes-nhs-hospital-discharges-deaths-a9544671.html, last accessed 23 May 2021.

Little, Adrian and Nick Vaughan-Williams. 2017. 'Stopping Boats, Saving Lives, Securing Subjects: Humanitarian Borders in Europe and Australia'. *European Journal of International Relations* 23(3): 533–56.

Löfflmann, Georg and Nick Vaughan-Williams. 2018. 'Vernacular Imaginaries of European Border Security among Citizens: From Walls to Information Management'. *European Journal of International Security* 3(3): 382–400.

Lundborg, Tom and Nick Vaughan-Williams. 2011. 'Resilience, Critical Infrastructure, and Molecular Security: The Excess of "Life" in Biopolitics'. *International Political Sociology* 5(4): 367–83.

Lynch, Cecelia. 2011. 'Religious Humanitarianism and the Global Politics of Secularism'. In *Rethinking Secularism*, edited by in Craig Calhoun, Mark Juergensmeyer, and Jonathan VanAntwerpen, pp. 204–24. Oxford: Oxford University Press.

Magni Berton, Raul. 2014. 'Citizenship for Those Who Invest into the Future of the State Is Not Wrong, the Price Is the Problem.' In *Should Citizenship Be for Sale?*, edited by Ayelet Shachar and Rainer Baubock, pp. 11–12. EUI Working Papers 2014/01.

Maley, William. 2003. 'Asylum-Seekers in Australia's International Relations'. *Australian Journal of International Affairs* 57(1): 187–202.

Malone, Barry. 2015. 'Why Al Jazeera will not say Mediterranean "migrants"'. *Al Jazeera*. 20 August, http://www.aljazeera.com/blogs/editors-blog/2015/08/al-jazeera-mediterranean-migrants-150820082226309.html, last accessed 23 May 2021.

Malta Independent. 2016. 'Government will consider whether to launch second round of passport sale scheme – Bonnici', http://www.independent.com.mt/articles/2016-11-16/local-news/Government-will-consider-whether-to-launch-second-round-of-passport-sale-scheme-Bonnici-6736166707, last accessed 15 September 2021.

Malthus, Thomas R. 1820. *Principles of Political Economy Considered with a View to Their Practical Application*. London: William Pickering.

Malthus, Thomas R. 1992 [1803]. *An Essay on the Principle of Population*, edited by Donald Winch. Cambridge: Cambridge University Press.

Marcetic, Branko. 2017. 'New Zealand's Neoliberal Drift'. *Jacobin Magazine*. 15 March, https://www.jacobinmag.com/2017/03/new-zealand-neoliberalism-inequality-welfare-state-tax-haven/, last accessed 23 May 2021.

Marsh, David. 2015. 'We Deride Them As "Migrants". Why Not Call Them People?' *The Guardian*. 28 August, http://www.theguardian.com/commentisfree/2015/aug/28/migrants-people-refugees-humanity, last accessed 23 May 2021.

Marx, Karl. 1976. *Capital: A Critique of Political Economy, Volume1*. Translated by Ben Fowkes. New York: Penguin.

Marx, Karl and Friedrich Engels. 2008 [1848]. *The Manifesto of the Communist Party*, translated by Samuel Moore. London: Pluto Press.

Marzouki, Nadia, Duncan McDonnell, and Olivier Roy (eds). 2016. *Saving the People: How Populists Hijack Religion*. Oxford: Oxford University Press.

Mathiesen, Karl. 2015. 'Germany's Hypocrisy over Greece Water Privatisation'. *The Guardian*. 14 August, http://www.theguardian.com/sustainable-business/2015/aug/14/germanys-hypocrisy-over-greece-water-privatisation, last accessed 23 May 2021.

Mavelli, Luca. 2012a. *Europe's Encounter with Islam: The Secular and The Postsecular*. Abingdon and New York: Routledge.

Mavelli, Luca. 2012b. 'Security and Secularization in International Relations'. *European Journal of International Relations* 18(1): 177–99.

Mavelli, Luca. 2014. 'Widening Participation, the Instrumentalization of Knowledge and the Reproduction of Inequality.' *Teaching in Higher Education* 19(8): 860–9.

Mavelli, Luca. 2016. 'Governing Uncertainty in a Secular Age: Rationalities of Violence, Theodicy and Torture'. *Security Dialogue* 47(2): 117–32.

Mavelli, Luca. 2017. 'Governing Populations through the Humanitarian Government of Refugees: Biopolitical Care and Racism in the European Refugee Crisis.' *Review of International Studies* 43(5): 809–832.

Mavelli, Luca. 2017. 'Governing the Resilience of Neoliberalism through Biopolitics', *European Journal of International Relations* 23(3): 489–512.

Mavelli, Luca. 2018. 'Citizenship for Sale and the Neoliberal Political Economy of Belonging.' *International Studies Quarterly* 62(3): 482–493.

Mavelli, Luca. 2019. 'Resilience beyond Neoliberalism? Mystique of Complexity, Financial Crises, and the Reproduction of Neoliberal Life.' *Resilience: International Policies, Practices and Discourses* 7(3): 224–39.

Mavelli, Luca. 2020. 'Neoliberalism as Religion: Sacralization of the Market and Post-truth Politics.' *International Political Sociology* 14(1): 57–76.

Mavelli, Luca and Erin K Wilson (eds). 2017. *The Refugee Crisis and Religion: Secularism, Security and Hospitality in Question*. London: Rowman and Littlefield.

May, Theresa. 2010. 'Home Secretary's Speech of 5 November 2010.' https://www.gov.uk/government/speeches/immigration-home-secretarys-speech-of-5-november-2010, last accessed 23 May 2021.

Mazlish, Bruce. 1989. *A New Science: The Breakdown of Connections and the Birth of Sociology*, New York: Oxford University Press.

Mazzucato, Mariana. 2015. 'Grecia, Quando l'Errore è Nella Diagnosi'. *La Repubblica*. 1 July. https://www.repubblica.it/esteri/2015/07/01/news/grecia_quando_l_errore_e_nella_diagnosi-118048518/, last accessed 23 May 2021.

Mazzucato, Mariana. 2016. 'Austerity Is the Cause of Our Economic Woes. It's Nothing to Do with the EU', *The Guardian*. 27 June, https://www.theguardian.com/commentisfree/2016/jun/27/austerity-economic-woes-eu-referendum-brexit, last accessed 23 May 2021.

McClintock, Brent. 1998. 'Whatever Happened to New Zealand? The Great Capitalist Restoration Reconsidered'. *Journal of Economic Issues* 32(2): 497–503.

McCutcheon, Russell T. 2007. '"They Licked the Platter Clean", On the Co-Dependency of The Religious and The Secular'. *Method and Theory in The Study of Religion* 19(3): 173–99.

McGowan, Todd. 2016. *Capitalism and Desire: The Psychic Cost of Free Markets*. New York: Columbia University Press.

McGregor, Jena. 2015. 'What Business Leaders Are Doing about the Refugee Crisis'. *The Washington Post*. 8 September, https://www.washingtonpost.com/news/on-leadership/wp/2015/09/08/what-business-leaders-are-doing-about-the-refugee-crisis, last accessed 23 May 2021.

McIntyre, Michael. 2011. 'Race, Surplus Population and the Marxist Theory of Imperialism'. *Antipode* 43 (5): 1489–515.

McKenna, Helen, Beccy Baird, and Jonathon Holmes. 2019. 'Brexit: The Implications for Health and Social Care'. *The King's Fund.* https://www.kingsfund.org.uk/publications/articles/brexit-implications-health-social-care, last accessed 23 May 2021.

McLaughlin, Carly. 2018. '"They Don't Look Like Children": Child Asylum-Seekers, The Dubs Amendment and the Politics of Childhood'. *Journal of Ethnic and Migration Studies* 44(11): 1757–73.

Meotti, Giulio. 2017. 'A Replacement of Population is Taking Place in Europe'. *Gatestone Institute.* June 14, https://www.gatestoneinstitute.org/10525/europepopulationreplacement, last accessed 23 May 2021.

Metcalf, David. 2016. 'A Shortage of Nurses?' *CentrePiece—The Magazine for Economic Performance* 476, Centre for Economic Performance, LSE. http://cep.lse.ac.uk/pubs/download/cp476.pdf, last accessed 23 May 2021.

Mezzadra, Sandro and Brett Neilson. 2012. 'Between Inclusion and Exclusion: On the Topology of Global Space and Borders'. *Theory, Culture & Society* 29(4–5): 58–75.

Mezzadra, Sandro and Brett Neilson. 2013. *Border as Method, Or, The Multiplication of Labor*. Durham and London: Duke University Press.

Micallef, Keith. 2017. 'Documents Reveal how Peter Thiel Was Granted New Zealand Citizenship'. *The Guardian.* February 1, https://www.theguardian.com/technology/2017/feb/01/documents-reveal-how-peter-thiel-was-granted-new-zealand-citizenship, last accessed 23 May 2021.

Migration Watch UK. 2016. 'Public Services and Infrastructure'. https://www.migrationwatchuk.org/key-topics/public-services-infrastructure#, last accessed 23 May 2021.

Míguez, Néstor, Joerge Rieger, and Jung Mo Sung. 2009. *Beyond the Spirit of Empire: Theology and Politics in a New Key*. London: SCM Press.

Mirowski, Philip. 2013. *Never Let a Serious Crisis Go to Waste: How Neoliberalism Survived the Financial Meltdown*. London: Verso Books.

Missing Migrants. 2017. 'Tracking Deaths along Migratory Routes'. https://missingmigrants.iom.int/mediterranean, last accessed 23 May 2021.

Mitchell, Bill. 2020. 'The Coronavirus Crisis Is just Exposing the Failure of Neoliberalism'. *Modern Monetary Theory: Macroeconomic Research, Teaching and Advocacy.* http://bilbo.economicoutlook.net/blog/?p=44914&cpage=1, last accessed 23 May 2021.

Moreton, Bethany. 2009. *To Serve God and Wal-Mart*. Cambridge, MA: Harvard University Press.

Mountz, Alison. 2011. 'The Enforcement Archipelago: Detention, Haunting, and Asylum on Islands'. *Political Geography* 30(3): 118–28.

Moura, Jean-Marc. 1988. 'Littérature et Idéologie de la Migration: «Le Camp des Saints» de Jean Raspail'. *Revue Européenne des Migrations Internationales* 4(3): 115–24.

Nadesan, Majia Holmer. 2010. *Governmentality, Biopower, and Everyday Life*. Abingdon: Routledge.

Nail, Thomas. 2016. 'A Tale of Two Crises: Migration and Terrorism after the Paris Attacks'. *Studies in Ethnicity and Nationalism* 16(1): 158–67.

Nardelli, Alberto and Silvia Merler. 2015. *The Greek Debt: What Creditors May Stand to Lose. The Guardian.* http://www.theguardian.com/world/datablog/2015/jun/19/the-greek-debt-what-creditors-may-stand-to-lose, last accessed 23 May 2021.

Nethery, Amy, and Rosa Holman. 2016. 'Secrecy and Human Rights Abuse in Australia's Offshore Immigration Detention Centres'. *The International Journal of Human Rights* 20(7): 1018–38.

New Scientist. 2020. 'Covid-19 Death Rates Twice as High in England's Most Deprived Areas'. *News Break.It*. June 11, https://www.newsbreak.com/news/0PK1a8q3/covid-19-death-rates-twice-as-high-in-englands-most-deprived-areas, last accessed 23 May 2021.

New Zealand Citizenship Act. 1977. http://www.legislation.govt.nz/act/public/1977/0061/latest/whole.html#DLM443855, last accessed 21 March 2017.

New Zealand Herald. 2015. 'Syrian Crisis: NZ to Take in Hundreds More Refugees'. 7 September, http://www.nzherald.co.nz/nz/news/article.cfm?c_id=1&objectid=11508899, last accessed 23 May 2021.

Newham Recorder. 2015. 'Migrant Crisis: Newham MPs Call for Britain To Do More'. 2 September, https://www.newhamrecorder.co.uk/news/migrant-crisis-newham-mps-call-for-britain-to-do-more-1-4219797, last accessed 23 May 2021.

Newheiser, David. 2016. 'Foucault, Gary Becker and the Critique of Neoliberalism'. *Theory, Culture & Society* 33(5): 3–21.

NHS. 2020a. 'Important and Urgent—Next Steps on NHS Response To COVID-19'. 17 March, https://www.england.nhs.uk/coronavirus/wp-content/uploads/sites/52/2020/03/urgent-next-steps-on-nhs-response-to-covid-19-letter-simon-stevens.pdf, last accessed 23 May 2021.

NHS. 2020b. 'COVID-19 Hospital Discharge Service Requirements'. 19 March, https://assets.publishing.service.gov.uk/government/uploads/system/uploads/attachment_data/file/880288/COVID-19_hospital_discharge_service_requirements.pdf#page=10, last accessed 23 May 2021.

Niemöller, Martin. 2020 [1946]. 'First They Came', *Academic Medicine* 95(5): 738.

Norwegian Refugee Council. 2020. '10 Things You Should Know about Coronavirus and Refugees'. 16 March, https://www.nrc.no/news/2020/march/10-things-you-should-know-about-coronavirus-and-refugees/, last accessed 23 May 2021.

O'Carroll, Lisa. 2017. 'Assuring EU Citizens of Right to Stay "Would Lose UK Negotiating Capital"'. *The Guardian*. January 9. https://www.theguardian.com/uk-news/2017/jan/09/uk-eu-citizens-right-remain-brexit-negotiating-capital-home-office-letter, last accessed 23 May 2021.

Oakley, Francis. 1998. 'The Absolute and Ordained Power of God in Sixteenth and Seventeenth-Century Theology'. *Journal of the History of Ideas* 59(3): 437–61.

Ochoa, Paulina. 2014. 'What Money Can't Buy: Face-to-Face Cooperation and Local Democratic Life'. In *Should Citizenship Be for Sale?*, edited by Ayelet Shachar and Rainer Baubock, pp. 23–24. EUI Working Papers 2014/01.

OECD. 2019. 'State of Health in the EU—United Kingdom'. https://www.oecd-ilibrary.org/docserver/744df2e3-en.pdf?expires=1621850042&id=id&accname=guest&checksum=B2438E35A589B76991A1A46E56BC0C0A, last accessed 23 May 2021.

Ojakangas, Mika. 2005. 'Impossible Dialogue on Bio-Power: Agamben and Foucault'. *Foucault Studies* 2(4): 5–28.

Ojakangas, Mika. 2012.'Potentia Absoluta Et Potentia Ordinata Dei: On the Theological Origins of Carl Schmitt's Theory of Constitution'. *Continental Philosophy Review* 45(4): 505–17.

Ojakangas, Mika. 2016. *On the Greek Origins of Biopolitics: A Reinterpretation of the History of Biopower*. London: Routledge.

Ong, Aihwa. 1999. *Flexible Citizenship: The Cultural Logics of Transnationality*. Durham, NC and London: Duke University Press.

Ong, Aihwa. 2006a. 'Mutations in Citizenship'. *Theory, Culture & Society* 23(2–3): 499–505.

Ong, Aihwa. 2006b. *Neoliberalism as Exception: Mutations in Citizenship and Sovereignty*. Durham, NC and London: Duke University Press.

Owen, David. 2014. 'Trading Citizenship, Human Capital and the European Union'. In *Should Citizenship Be for Sale?*, edited by Ayelet Shachar and Rainer Baubock, pp. 31–32. EUI Working Papers 2014/01.

Owens, Patricia. 2009. 'Reclaiming "Bare Life"? Against Agamben on Refugees'. *International Relations* 23(4): 567–82.

Oxford Languages. 2016. 'Word of the Year 2016', https://languages.oup.com/word-of-the-year/2016/, last accessed 23 May 2021.

Palaver, Wolfgang. 2013. *René Girard's Mimetic Theory*. East Lansing, MI: Michigan State University Press.

Pallister-Wilkins, Polly. 2015. 'The Humanitarian Politics of European Border Policing: Frontex and Border Police in Evros'. *International Political Sociology* 9(1): 53–69.

Parker, Owen. 2017. 'Commercializing Citizenship in Crisis EU: The Case of Immigrant Investor Programmes'. *Journal of Common Market Studies* 55(2): 332–48.

Parmet, Wendy E. and Jeremy Paul. 2020. 'COVID-19: The First Posttruth Pandemic'. *American Journal of Public Health* 110(7): 945–6.

Payne, Adam. 2020. 'Boris Johnson Told Italy's Prime Minister the UK Had Been Aiming for Coronavirus Herd Immunity, New Documentary Reveals'. *Business Insider*, https://www.businessinsider.com/boris-johnson-told-italian-pm-conte-corona virus-herd-immunity-plan-2020-6?r=US&IR=T, last accessed 23 May 2021.

Peck, Jamie, Nik Theodore, and Neil Brenner. 2009. 'Postneoliberalism and its Malcontents'. *Antipode* 41(s1): 94–116.

Peoples, Columba and Nick Vaughan-Williams. 2020. *Critical Security Studies: An Introduction*. 3rd edition. Abingdon and New York: Routledge.

Peron, James. 2018. 'What Milton Friedman actually Said about Illegal Immigration'. *Medium*. https://medium.com/the-radical-center/what-milton-friedman-actually-said-about-illegal-immigration-6b19efaf7a5, last accessed 23 May 2021.

Perruchoud, Richard and Jillyanne Redpath-Cross (eds). 2011. *Glossary on Migration*. 2nd edition. Geneva: International Organization for Migration.

Pertek, Sandra, Jenny Phillimore, and Pip McKnight. 2020. 'Forced Migration, SGBV and COVID-19'. *Refugee Women Connect/University of Birmingham*, https://www.birmingham.ac.uk/Documents/college-social-sciences/social-policy/iris/2020/sgbv-covid-19.pdf, last accessed 23 May 2021.

Peston, Robert. 2015. 'Why Germany Needs Migrants More than UK'. *BBC News*. 7 September, http://www.bbc.co.uk/news/business-34172729, last accessed 23 May 2021.

Petrella, Ivan. 2008. *Beyond Liberation Theology: A Polemic*. London: SCM Press.

Piketty, Thomas. 2014. *Capital in the Twenty-First Century*. Translated by Arthur Goldhammer. Cambridge, MA and London: The Belknap Press of Harvard University Press.

Plehwe, Dieter. 2009. 'Introduction'. In *The Road From Mont Pèlerin: The Making of the Neoliberal Thought Collective*, edited by Philip Mirowski and Dieter Plehwe, pp. 1–42. Cambridge: Harvard University Press.

Polanyi, Karl. 2001 [1944]. *The Great Transformation*. Boston, MA: Beacon Press.

Polanyi-Levitt, Kari and Marguerite Mendell. 1989. 'The Origins of Market Fetishism—Critique of Friedrich Hayek's Economic Theory'. *Monthly Review* 41: 11–32.

Poole, Steven. 2018. 'You Want to Be a Citizen of France? Only Superheroes Need Apply'. *The Guardian*. 28 May, https://www.theguardian.com/commentisfree/2018/may/28/citizenship-france-mamoudou-gassam-emmanuel-macron-france-immigrants, last accessed 23 May 2021.

Pope Francis. 2013. 'Apostolic Exhortation Evangelii Gaudium of the Holy Father Francis to the Bishops, Clergy, Consecrated Persons and the Lay Faithful on the Proclamation of the Gospel in Today's World'. *Vatican*, http://www.vatican.va/evangelii-gaudium/en/files/assets/basic-html/page1.html, last accessed 23 May 2021.

Pushkar, Piyush. 2020. 'What Are Matt Hancock and Boris Johnson Talking about when They Talk about Protecting the NHS? And Why Does It Matter?' *Journal of Medical Ethics Blog*, 20 May, https://blogs.bmj.com/medical-ethics/2020/05/20/what-are-matt-hancock-and-boris-johnson-talking-about-when-they-talk-about-protecting-the-nhs-and-why-does-it-matter/, last accessed 23 May 2021.

Racy, Gustavo. 2016. 'Walter Benjamin's Capitalism as Religion, Is there any Chance for Freedom?' *Heathwood Journal of Critical Theory* 1(3): 84–97.

Rajaram, Prem Kumar. 2018. 'Refugees as Surplus Population: Race, Migration and Capitalist Value Regimes'. *New Political Economy* 23(5): 627–39.

Rankin, Jennifer. 2020. 'Migration: EU Praises Greece as "Shield" after Turkey Opens Border'. *The Guardian*. 3 March, https://www.theguardian.com/world/2020/mar/03/migration-eu-praises-greece-as-shield-after-turkey-opens-border, last accessed 23 May 2021.

Rankin, Jennifer and Helena Smith. 2015. 'The Great Greece Fire Sale'. *The Guardian*. 24 July. https://www.theguardian.com/business/2015/jul/24/greek-debt-crisis-great-greece-fire-sale, last accessed 23 May 2021.

Rasmussen, Kim Su. 2011. 'Foucault's Genealogy of Racism'. *Theory, Culture & Society* 28(5): 34–51.

Raspail, Jean. 1994 [1973]. *The Camp of the Saints*. Translated by Norman R. Shapiro. Petoskey, MI: The Social Contract Press.

Rathje, William and Cullen Murphy. 2001. *Rubbish! The Archaeology of Garbage*. Tucson: The University of Arizona Press.

Reding, Viviane. 2014. 'Citizenship Must Not Be up for Sale.' *Plenary Session Debate of the European Parliament on 'EU citizenship for sale'*. Strasbourg, 15 January, http://europa.eu/rapid/press-release_SPEECH-14-18_en.htm, last accessed 23 May 2021.

Rhodes, A., P. Ferdinande, H. Flaatten, B Guidet, P. G. Metnitz, and R. P. Moreno, 2012. 'The Variability of Critical Care Bed Numbers in Europe'. *Intensive Care Medicine* 38(10): 1647–53.

Rizzuti, Stefano. 2019. 'Migranti, Matteo Salvini: "Hanno Il Record Di Malattie Come Tubercolosi E Scabbia"'. *Fanpage.it*, 1 June, https://www.fanpage.it/politica/migranti-matteo-salvini-hanno-il-record-di-malattie-come-tubercolosi-e-scabbia/, last accessed 23 May 2021.

Robbins, Lionel. 1932. *The Nature and Significance of Economic Science*. London: Macmillan.

Rocholl, Jörg and Axel Stahmer. 2016. 'Where Did the Greek Bailout Money Go?' *ESMT White Paper* WP–16–02, http://static.esmt.org/publications/whitepapers/WP-16-02.pdf, last accessed 23 May 2021.

Roitman, Janet. 2013, *Anti-crisis*. Durham, NC: Duke University Press.

Rumford, Chris. 2007. 'Does Europe Have Cosmopolitan Borders?' *Globalizations* 4(3): 327–39.

Rutland, Ted. 2015. 'Enjoyable Life: Planning, Amenity and the Contested Terrain of Urban Biopolitics'. *Environment and Planning D: Society and Space*, 33(5): 850–68.

Ruz, Camila. 2015. 'The Battle over the Words Used to Describe Migrants'. *BBC News*. 28 August, http://www.bbc.co.uk/news/magazine-34061097, last accessed 23 May 2021.
Rygiel, Kim. 2011. *Globalizing Citizenship*. Vancouver: UBC Press.
Rygiel, Kim. 2016. 'Dying to Live: Migrant Deaths and Citizenship Politics along European Borders: Transgressions, Disruptions, and Mobilizations.' *Citizenship Studies* 20(5): 545–60.
Saad-Filho, Alfredo. 2020. 'From COVID-19 to the End of Neoliberalism'. *Critical Sociology* 46(4–5): 477–85.
Sabater, Jordi. 2005. 'The Social Welfare Regimes in Europe (with Special Attention to the Spanish Case)'. In *De- and Reconstruction in European Social Work*, edited by Brian Littlechild, Peter Erath and Jan Keller, pp. 113–130. Stassfurt: BK-Verlag.
Safe Passage. 2018. 'Hundreds More Child Refugees Now Eligible for Dubs Scheme'. https://www.safepassage.org.uk/news/hundreds-more-children-now-eligible-for-dubs-scheme-following-home-office-decision-to-scrap-the-cut-off-date, last accessed 23 May 2021.
Saker, Rowan. 2010. 'New Zealand: Beyond the Quota'. *Forced Migration Review* 35: 25–26. http://www.fmreview.org/sites/fmr/files/FMRdownloads/en/disability/FMR35/25-26.pdf, last accessed 23 May 2021.
Salerno, Daniele. 2015. 'Stragi del Mare e Politiche del Lutto sul Confine Mediterraneo'. In *Il Colore della Nazione*, edited by Gaia Giuliani, pp. 125–41. Firenze: Le Monnier.
Sammond, Nicholas. 2007. 'Commodities, Commodity Fetishism, and Commodification'. In *The Blackwell Encyclopedia of Sociology*, edited By George Ritzer, pp. 607–12. Oxford: Blackwell Publishing.
Scavo, Nello. 2020. 'Migranti: Strage Di Pasquetta, La Nostra Ricerca Della Verità Per 12 Morti'. *Avvenire*. 22 April, https://www.avvenire.it/attualita/pagine/controinchiesta-strage-di-pasquetta-libia-malta-scavo, last accessed 23 May 2021.
Schäuble, Wolfgang. 2016. 'Afrika Wird Unser Problem Sein'. *Zeit Online*. 8 June, http://www.zeit.de/politik/deutschland/2016-06/wolfgang-schaeuble-aussenpolitik-wandel-afrika-arabische-welt, last accessed 28 June 2016.
Scherer, Matthew. 2013. *Beyond Church and State: Democracy, Secularism, and Conversion*. Cambridge: Cambridge University Press.
Schmidt, Vivien A. and Mark Thatcher (eds). 2013. *Resilient Liberalism in Europe's Political Economy*. Cambridge: Cambridge University Press.
Schmidtke, Oliver. 2015 'Why Germany Is Taking in So Many Refugees—The Benefits and Risks?' *CBC News*, 14 September, http://www.cbc.ca/news/world/why-germany-is-taking-in-so-many-refugees-the-benefits-and-risks-1.3226962, last accessed 23 May 2021.
Schumpeter, Joseph A. 2003. *Capitalism, Socialism and Democracy*. London and New York: Routledge.
Schwarz, Christoph H. 2016. 'German Refugee Policy in the Wake of the Syrian Refugee Crisis'. In *'Guests and Aliens': Re-Configuring New Mobilities in the Eastern Mediterranean After 2011—With a Special Focus on Syrian Refugees*. Edited by Elif Aksaz and Jean-François Pérouse, pp. 63–8. Istanbul: Institut Français d'Études Anatoliennes.
Scott, Geraldine. 2019. 'Residents Were Frightened, Dirty, and at Risk of Harm in Care Home which Was Shut Down, Report Reveals'. *Eastern Daily Press*, https://www.edp24.co.uk/news/health/cqc-report-released-into-holmwood-care-home-norwich-1-5869602, last accessed 23 May 2021.
Seale, Alexander. 2019. 'Migrants in France Are only Treated like Humans if They Can Perform Superhuman Feats or Save Lives'. *The Independent*. 6 February, https://www.

independent.co.uk/voices/migrants-in-france-are-only-treated-like-humans-if-they-can-perform-superhuman-feats-or-save-lives-a8765536.html, last accessed 23 May 2021.

Selgin, George. A. 1988. 'Praxeology and Understanding: An Analysis of the Controversy in Austrian Economics'. *The Review of Austrian Economics* 2(1): 19–58.

Semmelroggen, Jan. 2016. 'Britain's Obsession with Net Migration Makes It a Global Anomaly'. *The Conversation*. 15 November, http://theconversation.com/britains-obsession-with-net-migration-makes-it-a-global-anomaly-67093, last accessed 23 May 2021.

Sengupta, Somini. 2015 'Migrant or Refugee? There Is a Difference, With Legal Implications. *The New York Times*, 27 August, http://www.nytimes.com/2015/08/28/world/migrants-refugees-europe-syria.html?_r=0, last accessed 23 May 2021.

Shachar, Ayelet. 2014. 'Dangerous Liaisons: Money and Citizenship'. In *Should Citizenship Be for Sale?* edited by Ayelet Shachar and Rainer Baubock, pp. 3–8. *EUI Working Papers* 2014/01.

Shachar, Ayelet and Rainer Baubock (eds). 2014. *Should Citizenship Be for Sale?, EUI Working Papers* 2014/01.

Shachar, Ayelet and Ran Hirschl. 2014. 'On Citizenship, States, and Markets'. *Journal of Political Philosophy* 22(2): 231–57.

Shapiro, Michael J. 2016. *Deforming American Political Thought: Challenging the Jeffersonian Legacy*. Abingdon: Routledge.

Sharpe, Matthew. 2009. 'Is Neoliberalism a Liberalism, or a Stranger Kind of Bird? On Hayek and Our Discontents'. *Critical Horizons*, 10(1): 76–98.

Shelton, Taylor. 2020. 'A Post-Truth Pandemic?' *Big Data & Society* 7(2): 1–6.

Siddique, Haroon. 2020. 'Despite PM's Praise Of Nurses, It's Tory Policies that Made Them Suffer'. *The Guardian*. 13 April, https://www.theguardian.com/society/2020/apr/13/despite-pms-praise-of-nurses-its-tory-policies-that-made-them-suffer, last accessed 23 May 2021.

Skopeliti, Clea. 2019. 'UK's Number of Doctors Per Capita Is One of Lowest in Europe'. *The Guardian*, 23 December, https://www.theguardian.com/society/2019/dec/23/uk-has-second-lowest-number-of-doctors-per-capita-in-europe, last accessed 23 May 2021.

Sky News. 2015. 'UK May Accept "Several Thousand" More Refugees'. 3 September, https://news.sky.com/story/uk-may-accept-several-thousand-more-refugees-10347601, last accessed 23 May 2021.

Smith, Adam. 1957 [1776]. *An Inquiry into the Nature and Causes of the Wealth of Nations, Vol.1*. London: J.M. Dent & Sons LTD.

Smith, Adam. 1979 [1776]. *The Wealth of Nations*. Baltimore: Penguin.

Smith, Adam. 2010. *The Theory of Moral Sentiments*. London and New York: Penguin.

Smith, Evan. 2010. '"Managing Migration": Discourses on Immigration and "Race Relations" from Thatcherism to New Labour'. In *Domestic Policy Discourse in the US and the UK in the New World Order*, edited by Lori Maguire, pp. 256–62. Newcastle: Cambridge Scholars Publishing.

Sobolewska, Maria, and Robert Ford. 2020. *Brexitland: Identity, Diversity and the Reshaping of British Politics*. Cambridge: Cambridge University Press.

Solty, Ingar. 2020. 'The Bio-Economic Pandemic and The Western Working Classes'. *SP: The Bullet*. March 24, https://socialistproject.ca/2020/03/bioeconomic-pandemic-and-western-working-classes/, last accessed 23 May 2021.

Somers, Margaret R. 2008. *Genealogies of Citizenship: Markets, Statelessness, and the Right to Have Rights*. Cambridge: Cambridge University Press.

Somers, Margaret R. 2011. 'Reply to the Critics.' *Trajectories* 22(2): 25–34.

Somers, Margaret R. and Fred Block. 2005. 'From Poverty to Perversity: Ideas, Markets, and Institutions over 200 Years of Welfare Debate'. *American Sociological Review* 70(2): 260–87.

Sommerlad, Nick. 2020. 'Brit Teacher Says Kids "Physically Shake in Class" Because They're So Hungry'. *Mirror*. 8 March, https://www.mirror.co.uk/news/uk-news/heartbreaking-reality-poverty-stricken-children-21656083, last accessed 23 May 2021.

Sorman, Guy. 2014. 'Markets Everywhere: How Economist Gary Becker Changed Our Lives'. *City Journal*. Autumn, https://www.city-journal.org/html/markets-everywhere-13683.html, last accessed 23 May 2021.

Sparke, Matthew B. 2006. 'A Neoliberal Nexus: Economy, Security and the Biopolitics of Citizenship on the Border'. *Political Geography* 25(2): 151–80.

Spiegel. 2010. 'Germany's New Economic Miracle', 19 July, http://www.spiegel.de/international/business/a-keynesian-success-story-germany-s-new-economic-miracle-a-707231.html, last accessed 23 May 2021.

Spiro, Peter. 2014. 'Cash-for-passports and the End of Citizenship.' In *Should Citizenship Be for Sale?*, edited by Ayelet Shachar and Rainer Baubock, pp. 9–10. EUI Working Papers 2014/01.

Squire, Vicki. 2017. 'Governing Migration through Death in Europe and the US: Identification, Burial and the Crisis of Modern Humanism'. *European Journal of International Relations* 23(3): 513–32.

Squire, Vicki. 2020. *Europe's Migration Crisis: Border Deaths and Human Dignity*. Cambridge: Cambridge University Press.

Squire, Vicki and Jonathan Darling, 2013. 'The 'Minor' Politics of Rightful Presence: Justice and Relationality in City of Sanctuary'. *International Political Sociology* 7(1): 59–74.

Statewatch. 2017. 'EU: New Evidence Shows Frontex "Quibbled with Definitions of Distress" to Avoid Search and Rescue'. 11 April, https://www.statewatch.org/news/2017/april/eu-new-evidence-shows-frontex-quibbled-with-definitions-of-distress-to-avoid-search-and-rescue/, last accessed 23 May 2021.

Statista. 2020a. 'Number of Recorded Deaths of Migrants in the Mediterranean Sea from 2014 to 2020'. https://www.statista.com/statistics/1082077/deaths-of-migrants-in-the-mediterranean-sea/, last accessed 23 May 2021.

Statista. 2020b. 'Number of Immigrants Who Arrived by Sea in Italy from 2014 to 2020'. https://www.statista.com/statistics/623514/migrant-arrivals-to-italy/, last accessed 23 May 2021.

Statista. 2021a. 'Cumulative Number of Coronavirus (COVID-19) Deaths in France, Germany, Italy, Spain and the United Kingdom'. https://www.statista.com/statistics/1115043/coronavirus-deaths-timeline-in-the-eu-5/, last accessed 13 May 2021.

Statista. 2021b. 'Incidence of Coronavirus (COVID-19) Deaths in the European Economic Area and the United Kingdom as of May 16, 2021, by Country (Per 100,000 Population)'. https://www.statista.com/statistics/1111779/coronavirus-death-rate-europe-by-country/, last accessed 22 May 2021.

Stiglitz, D. Joseph. 2009. 'Moving Beyond Market Fundamentalism to a More Balanced Economy'. *Annals of Public and Cooperative Economics* 80(3): 345–60.

Stone, Jon. 2016. 'Immigrants Who "Consume" Britain's Wealth Are Not Welcome, Liam Fox Says'. *The Independent*. October 4, http://www.independent.co.uk/news/uk/politics/liam-fox-immigration-brexit-conservative-party-conference-live-2016-speech-a7345006.html, last accessed 23 May 2021.

Strange, Susan. 1996. *The Retreat of the State: The Diffusion of Power in the World Economy*. Cambridge: Cambridge University Press.

Stuff. 2016. '$17.2m Funding Boost to Support Syrian Refugees' Health.' 8 August. http://www.stuff.co.nz/national/politics/82918544/17-2m-funding-boost-to-support-Syrian-refugees-health, last accessed 23 May 2021.

Swinford, Steven. 2013. 'Immigrants Create Overcrowding and Fuel Tensions, Report Finds'. *The Telegraph*. 3 July, http://www.telegraph.co.uk/news/politics/10158678/Immigrants-create-overcrowding-and-fuel-tensions-report-finds.html, last accessed 23 May 2021.

Tanasoca, Ana. 2016. 'Citizenship for Sale: Neomedieval, not Just Neoliberal?' *European Journal of Sociology* 57(1): 169–95.

Taylor, Adam. 2015. 'Is it Time to Ditch the Word "Migrant"?' *The Washington Post*. 24 August, https://www.washingtonpost.com/news/worldviews/wp/2015/08/24/is-it-time-to-ditch-the-word-migrant, last accessed 23 May 2021.

Tazzioli, Martina. 2016. 'Border Displacements: Challenging the Politics of Rescue between Mare Nostrum and Triton'. *Migration Studies* 4(1): 1–19.

Tellmann, Ute. 2013. 'Catastrophic Populations and the Fear of the Future: Malthus and the Genealogy of Liberal Economy'. *Theory, Culture & Society* 30(2): 135–55.

Tellmann, Ute. 2015. 'Austerity and Scarcity: About the Limits and Meanings of Liberal Economy'. *Ephemera* 15(1): 21–40.

Tellmann, Ute. 2017. *Life and Money: The Genealogy of the Liberal Economy and the Displacement of Politics*. New York: Columbia University Press.

Ticktin, Miriam. 2006. 'Where Ethics and Politics Meet: The Violence of Humanitarianism in France'. *American Ethnologist* 33(1): 33–49.

Ticktin, Miriam. 2011. *Casualties of Care: Immigration and the Politics of Humanitarianism in France*. Berkeley, CA: University of California Press.

The Times. 2020. 'Economic Crash Could Cost more Life than Coronavirus, Says Expert'. 24 March, https://www.thetimes.co.uk/article/economic-crash-could-cost-more-lives-than-coronavirus-study-warns-nxrn3bzbs, last accessed 23 May 2021.

Tolhurst, Alain. 2020. 'Lack of PPE for Health and Social Care Staff A "Crisis Within a Crisis", Unions Warn', *PoliticsHome*, 1 April, https://www.politicshome.com/news/article/lack-of-ppe-for-healthand-social-carestaffacrisiswithin-a-crisisunions-warn, last accessed 23 May 2021.

Tondo, Lorenzo. 2020. 'Italy Declares Own Ports "Unsafe" to Stop Migrants Arriving'. *The Guardian*, 8 April, https://www.theguardian.com/world/2020/apr/08/italy-declares-own-ports-unsafe-to-stop-migrants-disembarking, last accessed 23 May 2021.

Tooze, Adam. *Crashed: How a Decade of Financial Crises Changed the World*. New York: Penguin, 2018.

Townsend, Mark. 2020. 'Patel Refuses to Take Children from Greek Camps Threatened by Covid-19'. *The Guardian*. 13 April, https://www.theguardian.com/world/2020/apr/12/patel-refuses-to-take-children-from-greek-camps-threatened-by-covid-19, last accessed 23 May 2021.

Tracy, James F. 2012. 'Covering "Financial Terrorism": The Greek Debt Crisis in US News Media'. *Journalism Practice* 6(4): 513–29.

Trautvetter, Christoph and Eric Winkler. 2019. 'Competing for the Rich, the Greens/EFA Group in the European Parliament'. http://extranet.greens-efa-service.eu/public/media/file/1/5920, last accessed 23 May 2021.

Travis, Alan. 2015. 'UK Axes Support for Mediterranean Migrant Rescue Operation'. *The Guardian*. 28 October, http://www.theguardian.com/politics/2014/oct/27/uk-mediterranean-migrant-rescue-plan, last accessed 23 May 2021.

Travis, Alan. 2017. 'Supreme Court Backs Minimum Income Rule for Non-European Spouses'. *The Guardian*. 22 February, https://www.theguardian.com/law/2017/feb/22/supreme-court-backs-minimum-income-rule-for-non-european-spouses, last accessed 23 May 2021.

Troya, María Sosa. 2020. 'Data Shows over 17,500 Confirmed or Probable Covid-19 Deaths at Spain's Care Homes'. *El País*. 7 May, https://english.elpais.com/society/2020-05-07/data-shows-over-17500-confirmed-or-probable-covid-19-deaths-at-spains-care-homes.html, last accessed 23 May 2021.

Trumbo, Sol and Nick Buxton. 2016. 'Making a Killing from "Austerity": The EU's Great Privatisation Fire Sale'. *The Ecologist*. 24 February, http://www.theecologist.org/News/news_analysis/2987270/making_a_killing_from_austerity_the_eus_great_privatisation_fire_sale.html, last accessed 23 May 2021.

Tyner, James A. 2013. 'Population Geography I: Surplus Populations'. *Progress in Human Geography* 37(5): 701–11.

UN (United Nations). 2015. 'Replacement Migration: Is it a Solution to Declining and Ageing Populations?' https://www.un.org/en/development/desa/population/publications/ageing/replacement-migration.asp, last accessed 23 May 2021.

UNHCR (United Nations High Commissioner for Refugees). 2014. 'UNHCR Concerned Over Ending of Rescue Operation in the Mediterranean'. http://www.unhcr.org/cgi-bin/texis/vtx/search?page=search&docid=5440ffa16&query=UNHCR, last accessed 23 May 2021.

UNHCR (United Nations High Commissioner for Refugees). 2016. 'Rifugiati E Salute. Dalla Tbc Alla Scabbia, I Dati Che Smentiscono Gli Allarmi Infondati'. https://www.unhcr.org/it/risorse/carta-di-roma/fact-checking/rifugiati-salute-dalla-tbc-alla-scabbia-dati-smentiscono-gli-allarmi-infondati/, last accessed 23 May 2021.

UNHCR (United Nations High Commissioner for Refugees). 2017. 'Malta: Figures at Glance'. https://www.unhcr.org/mt/figures-at-a-glance, last accessed 23 May 2021.

UNHCR (United Nations High Commissioner for Refugees). 2020. 'Mediterranean Situation', https://data2.unhcr.org/en/situations/mediterranean, last accessed 22 December 2020.

UNICEF (United Nations Children's Fund). 2021. 'Malnutrition'. 20 March, https://data.unicef.org/topic/nutrition/malnutrition/, last accessed 23 May 2021.

Valenta, Marko, Jo Jakobsen, Drago Župarić-Iljić, and Hariz Halilovich. (2020). 'Syrian Refugee Migration, Transitions in Migrant Statuses and Future Scenarios of Syrian Mobility'. *Refugee Survey Quarterly* 39(2): 153–76.

Vance, Andrea. 2015. "Prime Minister Bows to Pressure to Accept More Refugees." *Stuff*, September 7, http://www.stuff.co.nz/national/politics/71789199/prime-minister-bows-topressure-to-accept-more-refugees, last accessed 15 September 2021.

Vasilaki, Rosa. 2020. 'How Greece Became Europe's 'Shield' against Refugees' *Jacobin Magazine*, 10 March 2020, https://www.jacobinmag.com/2020/03/greece-refugees-european-union-migrants-turkey-border, last accessed 23 May 2021.

Vatter, Miguel. 2009. 'Biopolitics: From Surplus Value to Surplus Life'. *Theory & Event* 12(2): 1–12.

Vaughan-Williams, Nick. 2015. *Europe's Border Crisis: Biopolitical Security and Beyond*. Oxford: Oxford University Press.

Vaughan-Williams, Nick. 2021. *Vernacular Border Security: Citizens' Narratives of Europe's' Migration Crisis*. Oxford: Oxford University Press.

Vaughan-Williams, Nick and Maria Pisani. 2020. 'Migrating Borders, Bordering Lives: Everyday Geographies of Ontological Security and Insecurity in Malta'. *Social & Cultural Geography* 21(5): 651–73.

Vaughan-Williams, Nick and Daniel Stevens. 2016. 'Vernacular Theories of Everyday (In) Security: The Disruptive Potential of Non-Elite Knowledge'. *Security Dialogue* 47(1): 40–58.

Von Der Leyen, Ursula. 2019. 'Mission Letter'. *European Commission*. 10 September, https://ec.europa.eu/info/sites/default/files/mission-letter-margaritis-schinas-2019_en.pdf, last accessed 23 May 2021.

Vynz Research. 2020. 'Global Personal Protective Equipment Market was Valued at USD 52.7 billion in 2019 and is Expected to Reach USD 92.5 billion by 2025'. 14 April, https://www.vynzresearch.com/press-release/global-personal-protective-equipment-ppe-market, last accessed 23 May 2021.

Wagenvoorde, Renée. 2017. 'How Religion and Secularism Don't Matter in the Refugee Crisis'. In *The Refugee Crisis and Religion: Secularism, Security and Hospitality in Question*, edited by Luca Mavelli and Erin K Wilson, pp. 61–74. London: Rowman and Littlefield.

Walker, Jeremy and Melinda Cooper. 2011. 'Genealogies of Resilience from Systems Ecology to the Political Economy of Crisis Adaptation'. *Security Dialogue* 42(2): 143–60.

Walker, Peter and Patrick Butler. 2017. 'Jacob Rees-Mogg View on Food Banks Is Unchristian, Say Charities'. *The Guardian*, 14 September, https://www.theguardian.com/politics/2017/sep/14/jacob-rees-mogg-increased-use-food-banks-rather-uplifting, last accessed 23 May 2021.

Walters, William. 2002. 'Deportation, Expulsion and the International Policing of Aliens'. *Citizenship Studies* 6(3): 265–92.

Walters, William. 2011. 'Foucault and Frontiers: Notes on the Birth of the Humanitarian Border'. In *Governmentality: Current Issues and Future Challenges*, edited by Ulrich Bröckling, Susanne Krasmann, and Thomas Lemke, pp. 138–64. London: Routledge.

Warner, Jeremy. 2020. 'Does the Fed Know Something the Rest of Us Do not with Its Panicked Interest Rate Cut?' *The Telegraph*, 3 March, https://www.telegraph.co.uk/business/2020/03/03/does-fed-know-something-rest-us-do-not-panicked-interest-rate/, last accessed 3 May 2021.

Weber Max. 1946 [1915]. 'Religious Rejections of the World and Their Directions'. In *From Max Weber: Essays in Sociology*, edited by Hans H. Gerth and C. Wright Mills, pp. 323–62. Oxford: Oxford University Press.

Weber, Max. 1946 [1919a] 'Politics as Vocation'. In *From Max Weber: Essays in Sociology*, edited by Hans H. Gerth and C. Wright Mills, pp. 77–128. Oxford: Oxford University Press.

Weber, Max. 1946 [1919b]. 'Science as a Vocation'. In *From Max Weber: Essays in Sociology*, edited by Hans H. Gerth and C. Wright Mills, pp. 129–157. Oxford: Oxford University Press.

Weber, Max. 1946 [1922] 'The Social Psychology of the World Religions'. In *From Max Weber: Essays in Sociology*, edited by Hans H. Gerth and C. Wright Mills, pp. 267–301. Oxford: Oxford University Press.

Weber, Max. 2003 [1905]. *The Protestant Ethic and the Spirit of Capitalism*. Translated by Talcott Parsons. New York: Courier Dover Publications.

Welch, Ellen. 2018. *The NHS at 70: A Living History*. Philadelphia, PA: Pen and Sword.

Welsh, Tom. 2016. 'The Uber Ruling Is Bad for Drivers and Customers—Self-Employment Is the Way Forward'. *The Telegraph*. 20 October. https://www.telegraph.co.uk/news/

2016/10/29/the-uber-ruling-is-bad-for-drivers-and-customers—self-employme/, last accessed 23 May 2021.

White, Michael. 2010. 'Immigration Should Be Talked About More Than It Is'. *The Guardian*. 6 January, https://www.theguardian.com/politics/blog/2010/jan/06/michael-white-immigration-talked-about, last accessed 23 May 2021.

WHO (World Health Organization). 2015. 'Together We Can Close the Immunization Gap'. 22 April, https://www.who.int/mediacentre/commentaries/vaccine-preventable-diseases/en/, last accessed 23 May 2021.

WHO (World Health Organization). 2019. 'Drinking Water'. 14 June, https://www.who.int/news-room/fact-sheets/detail/drinking-water, last accessed 23 May 2021.

Wike, Richard, Bruce Stokes, and Katie Simmons. 2016. 'Europeans Fear Wave of Refugees Will Mean More Terrorism, Fewer Jobs.' *Pew Research Center*. https://www.pewresearch.org/global/2016/07/11/europeans-fear-wave-of-refugees-will-mean-more-terrorism-fewer-jobs/, last accessed 23 May 2021.

Williams, Jill M. 2015. 'From Humanitarian Exceptionalism to Contingent Care: Care and Enforcement at the Humanitarian Border.' *Political Geography* 47: 11–20.

Williams, Mark. 2020. 'Coronavirus Class Divide—The Jobs Most at Risk of Contracting and Dying From COVID-19'. *The Conversation*. 19 May, https://theconversation.com/coronavirus-class-divide-the-jobs-most-at-risk-of-contracting-and-dying-from-covid-19-138857, last accessed 23 May 2021.

Williams, Owain. 2020a. 'Neoliberalism, Aged-Care and COVID: Market Failure 1/2'. *Global Public Health, COVID-19 Diaries*. 5 May, https://covid19healthdiaries.com/diary?did=183, last accessed 23 May 2021.

Williams, Owain. 2020b. 'Neoliberalism, Aged-Care and COVID 2/2, Global Public Health', *Global Public Health, COVID-19 Diaries*. 8 May, https://covid19healthdiaries.com/diary?did=194, last accessed 23 May 2021.

Wilson, Erin K. and Luca Mavelli. 2016. 'Taking Responsibility: Sociodicy, Solidarity, and Religious-Sensitive Policymaking in the Global Politics of Migration'. In *Intersections of Religion and Migration. Religion and Global Migrations*, edited by Jennifer Beth Saunders, Elena Fiddian-Qasmiyeh, and Susanna Snyder, pp. 261–84. New York: Palgrave Macmillan.

Wilson, Erin K. and Luca Mavelli. 2017. 'The Refugee Crisis and Religion: Beyond Conceptual and Physical Boundaries'. In *The Refugee Crisis and Religion: Secularism, Security and Hospitality in Question*, edited by Luca Mavelli and Erin K Wilson, pp. 1–22. London: Rowman and Littlefield.

WREDA (Wellington Regional Economic Development Agency). 2017. 'LookSee Wellington'. https://www.wellingtonnz.com/work/looksee-wellington/, last accessed 23 May 2021.

Xenos, Nicholas. 1989. *Scarcity and Modernity*. New York: Routledge.

Yates, Michelle. 2011. 'The Human-as-Waste, The Labor Theory of Value and Disposability in Contemporary Capitalism.' *Antipode* 43(5): 1679–95.

Young, Toby, 2020. 'Has the Government Overreacted to the Coronavirus Crisis?' *The Critic*. 17 March, https://thecritic.co.uk/has-the-government-over-reacted-to-the-coronavirus-crisis/, last accessed 23 May 2021.

Zeballos-Roig, Joseph. 2020. 'The Coronavirus Pandemic Has Exposed how Profit-Driven Decisions Undercut the US' Ability to Fight an Outbreak'. *Business Insider*. 12 April, https://www.businessinsider.com/coronavirus-profit-decisions-healthcare-us-weak-response-ability-fight-outbreak-2020-4?r=US&IR=T, last accessed 23 May 2021.

Zenturo Ltd. nd. 'Malta Citizenship for International Investors', https://malta-citizenship.info/index.html#:~:text=Malta%20citizenship%20offers%20full%20European, North%2C%20Central%20and%20South%20America, last accessed 6 November 2020.
ZEW. 2014. 'The Fiscal Effects of Foreigners and Immigration in Germany'. 27 November, https://www.zew.de/en/zew/news/the-fiscal-effects-of-foreigners-and-immigration-in-germany, last accessed 6 November 2020
Žižek, Slavoj. 2020. *PANDEMIC!: Covid-19 Shakes the World*. New York: OR Books.

Index